REVOLUTI(
YUCATÁN, MEXIC(
1880−1924

MW01075167

REVOLUTION FROM WITHOUT

YUCATÁN, MEXICO, AND THE UNITED STATES
1880–1924

G. M. JOSEPH

2000 victory priced

1500

7747-7999

DUKE UNIVERSITY PRESS   DURHAM 1988

Second printing, 1995
Published by Duke University Press by arrangement
with Cambridge University Press.
Foreword and preface to the 1988 edition © Duke University Press
Text © Cambridge University Press 1982.
First published 1982; paperback edition published 1988.
Printed in the United States of America
Library of Congress Cataloging in Publication Data
Joseph, Gilbert M., 1947–
Revolution from without.
Bibliography: p. 373
Includes index.
1. Yucatan (Mexico) – Rural conditions.
2. Henequen – Mexico – Yucatan – History.
3. Land Reform – Mexico – Yucatan – History
I. Title.
HD795.Y8J67   330.972'65081   81-9958
ISBN 0-8223-0822-3 (pbk.)

To my father and mother

There is no truth in the words of strangers.

—Maya prophecy of Chilám Balám

Las cosas de Yucatán,
Dejarlas como están.
(What is Yucatán's own,
Is best left alone.)

—Spanish colonial aphorism

Contents

Tables and figures

Tables

Figures

Foreword

It is a sign of the growing sophistication of Mexican historiography in the last twenty or so years that, like the historiography of several other major countries, it has received its greatest impulse from regional and local studies. Previously, revolutionary participants – caudillos and políticos – penned their memoirs and apologia (some, like Yucatán's proconsul Salvador Alvarado, with great force and at great length). Previously, too, generations of eyewitness observers sought to capture for posterity the fleeting reality of the Revolution they confronted: Frank Tannenbaum, who applauded a noble but anonymous popular struggle; Jorge Vera Estañol, who saw a sordid struggle for power; Ernest Gruening, who soberly weighed the balance of the Sonoran-led revolution of the 1920s.[1] And a previous generation of historians, pioneering a reflective, researched style of academic history, focused on the national leaders and the national events: José Valadés, Charles Cumberland, Stanley Ross.[2]

By the 1960s, however, a change – and an advance – were apparent. Historians, no longer content to praise famous men or to conceive of a monolithic national Revolution, began to dissect the local roots of revolutionary movements, stressing the diversity, complexity, even the chaos of the "Mexican Revolution." Mexico was, in fact, "many Mexicos," productive of "many revolutions."[3] John Womack's masterly study of Zapata, later complemented by Arturo Warman's analysis of the Morelos peasantry, set a high standard for others to follow; and Luis González, researching – with no less skill, insight, and commitment – a very different rural microcosm, inspired a generation of historians both by his individual example and his persuasive "invitation to micro-history."[4] Since then, local and regional histories have proliferated, with Mexican, U.S., and European historians all making valuable and original contributions – so many, indeed, that it would be a major task to list them all, and invidious to single out but a few. In addition, microhistorical research has acquired new institutional backing, with the growth of regional centers which, appropriately and very effectively, have ensured that the study of provincial history does not become a Mexico City monopoly: in Michoacán, Jalisco, Veracruz, Nuevo León, Sonora, and, of course, Yucatán. No other genre of history has so deepened and enriched our knowledge of the Revolution, its origins, course, and outcome. And there are few examples of this genre that, in terms of breadth and illumination, can equal Gilbert Joseph's *Revolution from Without*.

It is readily apparent that *Revolution from Without* is based on wide, meticulous research, clearly and cogently presented. But accurate, ample research is a necessary, not a sufficient, condition for writing good history. The latter also demands imagination and insight. Professor Joseph's book, in meeting these further desiderata, displays two particular yet contrasting merits. We (historians) are raised on the notion that – potentially, at least – history straddles the disputed frontier of art and science; that it combines an idiographic concern for the individual and the particular with a nomothetic quest for valid, broader generalizations ("laws," tendencies, higher-range hypotheses). There is no inherent superiority attached to either of these historical rhetorics; Clio speaks as well in both. In practice, however, many historians are temperamentally inclined one way or the other, and it is natural, though not inevitable, that local/regional historians, steeped in their subject and sometimes passionate for the *patria chica*, often prefer the idiographic – the unique event, the distinctive experience, the individual protagonist.

Professor Joseph deftly combines both rhetorics. His portrait of Yucatán is finely etched, sympathetic, and evocative. But the pull of empathy is stoutly resisted. Perhaps Felipe Carrillo Puerto's failings are a little indulged (other critics have been much sharper), but the sociopolitical environment in which Felipe acted – and against which he labored – is fully and dispassionately analyzed, just as the obfuscating myths, of right and left, are dispelled. We know where the author's sympathies lie, but this knowledge enhances, and does not obstruct, our understanding of the historical reality he depicts.

So, too, with Yucatán in toto. It is well known that peninsular society, since its remote Mesoamerican origins, has been distinct from, separate from, the highland society around which independent Mexico crystallized. When Manuel Gamio ordered a beer in Mérida, and was asked whether he preferred "foreign or national," his request for "foreign" was met with a foaming glass of Orizaba Dos Equis.[5] In *Revolution from Without* the author does justice to Yucatán's distinctive character and separatist leanings, but he does not retreat into idiographic obscurity; the exoticism of the *patria chica* does not blind him to what is also general or even global in the peninsula's history. Thus, he weaves Yucatán's story into the greater fabric of the Revolution, in its Maderista, Constitutionalist, and Sonoran phases, and he gives due attention, as the title suggests, to relations with the United States. But, even more important, Joseph is alive to those theories, models, comparisons that can inform the Yucateco case and, in turn, can be informed by it. Themes of general significance for Latin Americanists and others are introduced, but without their introduction traducing the Yucateco reality or spoiling the story.

The author presents, for example, a lucid résumé of the old "Latin America, feudal or capitalist?" debate, which shows, once again, that neither formulation can fully comprehend the ambivalent nature of dependent Latin American economies. He investigates "dependency" in concrete, empirical terms without resorting to abstract assertion, and he further shows that, even in an extreme case like Yucatán, dependency was a two-way process – not a crude, unilateral, "imperialist" imposition – and that its historical effects were mediated through domestic sociopolitical structures. Dependency thus figures as a valid explanatory device and not a bland analytical one. Finally, in one of the most original sections of the book, Joseph discusses that most ubiquitous but still poorly understood Latin American phenomenon, *caciquismo*. Indeed, the crux of the story is formed by the dual determinism foisted upon Yucatán – and its successive revolutionary reformers – by external economic dependency on the one hand and domestic *caciquismo* on the other. The first, the product of henequen monoculture, placed reformist projects at the mercy of the international market (and a market dominated by a monopsonistic buyer); and the second similarly constrained such projects by obliging reformers – who sought to mobilize a quiescent peasantry, in thrall to a powerful plantocracy – to rely on a risky *caciquista* system.

Reformers battled manfully against both constraints. Alvarado achieved most practical success, since times were economically propitious, and for all his classic, Sonoran-style moralism Alvarado was prepared to temper proconsular policy to suit Yucateco circumstances. His assault on peninsular mores could be tolerated because he hiked henequen prices and co-opted members of the Yucateco elite into his economic project; like other Sonoran leaders, he favored superstructural radicalism – temperance and feminism, for example – and infrastructural pragmatism. Such "bourgeois" reformism suited the Yucateco context. It accelerated a transition to agrarian capitalism that Yucateco elites – planters and emergent caciques alike – were ready to accept, if not always enthusiastically. In contrast, Carrillo Puerto and, later, Cárdenas, both confronted an economy in recession; they also sought to go further in their domestic reforms, to restructure the henequen economy, to probe, perhaps, the "limits of state autonomy" within the existing capitalist system.[6]

In doing so, they mounted a more serious challenge to the status quo. Carrillo Puerto was ousted and killed after a brief, radical tenure of power in 1924; Cárdenas, descending on the peninsula in characteristic style thirteen years later, sponsored a rushed agrarian reform that was soon subverted by a combination of planter opposition and unfavorable global trends. This final reformist thrust figures as a postscript to Joseph's study, and the author – a good deal more severe with Cárdenas than with Carrillo Puerto – conceives of it as a botched alien imposition, to be contrasted with Carrillo Puerto's homegrown radical project. Yet the parallels between the two are striking, too (not least at the individual level: both Carrillo Puerto and Cárdenas were autodidacts rather than learned *licenciados*; both drew upon the old popular liberal-patriotic tradition; both were also sons of petty bourgeois provincial shopkeepers, raised next-door to the town pool hall). More important, however, both sought to create vigorous popular coalitions, embracing the peasantry, which would provide the backing for radical projects. True, their projects did not imply instant social revolution or runaway political mobilization. They sought a controlled mobilization, serving ends they, the leaders, approved. But the ends went beyond "bourgeois" reformism and incurred strong conservative opposition. And the means adopted in their pursuit included a degree of political violence. For both Carrillo Puerto and Cárdenas were young men in a hurry; they realized that time was pressing, that it was vital to create some sort of popular political momentum before their brief tenures of power concluded.

Ultimately, both failed. Carrillo Puerto was violently and prematurely ousted; Cárdenas was forced first to retrench, then to witness, after 1940, the progressive dismantling of his reformist coalition/project. They failed not only because their ends were radical and optimistic, their opponents powerful and numerous, but because they faced the eternal dilemma of the official radical reformer in Mexico, the reformer who seeks to utilize the system and finds, at the end of the day, that the system had utilized him. Popular mobilization, whether in Yucatán in 1915–24 or Mexico as a whole in 1934–40, was compromised by opportunism and timeserving; radical movements fell under the sway of political bosses – *caciques*, ejidal bureaucrats, *charro* labor leaders – who appropriated the rhetoric of radicalism, while spurning its real content. In the early 1920s Carrillo Puerto, "a socialist committed to profound structural change," proved "adept at working through the maze of formal and informal networks that, in organizing peasants and enlisting the support of *caciques* at the local level, had previously started him on the road to political power."[7] But Yucatán's *caciques* – like any machine politicians – were committed more to political survival and self-aggrandizement than to profound structural change. When the De la Huerta rebellion shook the state, they deserted Carrillo Puerto en masse, conniving at his ouster and death. Cárdenas, of course, witnessed no such bloody apostasy. But his regime, too, was based on a congeries of political machines, great and small: state bosses like Cedillo, Alemán, the Avila Camachos; the emergent Mexico City labor machine of Fidel Velázquez and the *cinco lobitos*; rural *caciques* – such as Flavio Ramírez of Arandas or Porfirio Rubio of Pisaflores – who, at best, espoused a spurious agrarismo; ruthless ejidal bosses, like Friedrich's "Princes of Naranja"; pseudoindigenistas who "laid in wait for Federal initiatives . . . in order to give an apparent display of support and then subsequently to prostitute them and convert them into simple instruments of personal gain."[8] Their betrayal of their political mentor was discreet, peaceful, and cumulative. During the 1930s they emulated their colonial predecessors, seeking refuge in formal compliance (*obedezco pero no cumplo*); then, during the 1940s, they rapidly – even enthusiastically – came to terms with the new conservative order. And more recently, too, recurrent promises of top-down political reform have been dashed on the flinty rocks of *caciquismo*.

This does not, of course, mean that all reform from the top, mediated through traditional political machines, has been futile. Alvarado, Carrillo Puerto, and Cárdenas did not labor wholly in vain. And, it should be said, the likely historical alternative to this flawed reform from above was not flawless revolution from below. Probably – and in Yucatán almost certainly – it was no reform at all. But, as Joseph clearly shows, reforms were fragile, vulnerable to external buffeting and internal betrayal. Alvarado's Reguladora collapsed; Carrillo Puerto's *ligas de resistencia* put up little resistance in 1924; Cárdenas's collective ejido did not live up to radical hopes, least of all in Yucatán, the site of its most sweeping implementation. Despite – or perhaps because of – their ultimate failures, these three great exponents of reform-from-above were readily accommodated in the spacious revolutionary pantheon where, Joseph ironically notes, they encountered none other than the old Yucateco *científico* (who would have considered himself, too, a reformer-from-above): Olegario Molina. Thus, a sequence of self-styled reformers, *científico*, Constitutionalist, socialist, Cardenista, all took their posthumous place within the mythic procession of the Revolution; but the anonymous *cacique* – "the flesh of the Revolution"[9] – survived, and was still to be found alive and well and living in Yucatán.

Alan Knight
Austin, Texas

Notes

1. F. Tannenbaum, *The Mexican Agrarian Revolution* (Washington, D.C., 1929); Jorge Vera Estañol, *La revolución mexicana: orígines y resultados* (Mexico City, 1957); Ernest Gruening, *Mexico and Its Heritage* (New York, 1928).

2. José C. Valadés, *Imaginación y realidad de Francisco I. Madero* (Mexico City, 2 vols., 1960); Charles C. Cumberland, *The Mexican Revolution Genesis Under Madero* (Austin, 1952), and *The Mexican Revolution: The Constitutionalist Years* (Austin, 1972); Stanley R. Ross, *Francisco I. Madero, Apostle of Mexican Democracy* (New York, 1955).

3. Leslie B. Simpson, *Many Mexicos* (New York, 1941), coined the phrase, which has been recast to provide the title of an excellent symposium illustrative of recent regional research: Thomas Benjamin and William McNellie, *Other Mexicos: Essays on Regional Mexican History, 1876–1911* (Albuquerque, 1984).

4. John Womack, Jr., *Zapata and the Mexican Revolution* (New York, 1969); Arturo Warman, *Y venimos a contradecir: los campesinos de Morelos y el estado nacional* (Mexico City, 1976); Luis González, *Pueblo en vilo, microhistoria de San José de Gracia* (Mexico City, 1968), and *Invitación a la microhistoria*

(Mexico City, 1973).

5. Manuel Gamio, *Forjando patria* (Mexico City, 1916), p. 12.

6. Nora Hamilton, *The Limits of State Autonomy: Postrevolutionary Mexico* (Princeton, 1982).

7. Below, p. 195.

8. Tomás Martínez Saldana and Leticia Gándara, *Política y sociedad en México: el caso de los Altos de Jalisco* (Mexico City, 1976), p. 69; Frans J. Schryer, *The Rancheros of Pisaflores: The History of a Peasant Bourgeoisie in Twentieth-Century Mexico* (Toronto, 1982), p. 92; Paul Friedrich, *The Princes of Naranja: An Essay in Anthrohistorical Method* (Austin, 1987), pp. 125–29, 146–63; "La actidud de los estados en el problema de la educación indígena" (anexo al proyecto de organización del Departamento de Asuntos Indígenas), Mexico City, 31 December 1935, in Archivo General de la Nación, Presidentes, Lázaro Cárdenas, 533.4/12.

9. Carleton Beals, *Mexican Maze* (Philadelphia, 1931), chap. 13.

Preface to the Paperback Edition

The central questions which fifteen years ago inspired the doctoral dissertation that became the core of *Revolution from Without* are no less relevant today. Why have there been so few "social revolutions" in Latin America and the Third World? Why is effective structural change at once so urgently needed yet so difficult to achieve? How do we sort out the obstacles to revolutionary change: that is, how do we conceptualize the complex interaction of internal and external forces that has historically constrained revolutionary movements? Might a more adequate analysis of the problem yield practical consequences, informing the agendas and strategies of those attempting future transformations?

Back in 1973, when I began my investigation of the rise and fall of what was arguably the Americas' first attempted transition to socialism, my doctoral research on the Carrillo Puerto regime proceeded against a backdrop provided by the tragic denouement of Chilean President Salvador Allende's more recent Marxist experiment. As the dissertation (completed in 1978) metamorphosed by degrees into the present book (first published in 1982), revolutionary movements were challenging old-style, U.S.-backed oligarchical regimes on the Central American isthmus. In Nicaragua, after ousting the Somozas in 1979, the Sandinista Front of National Liberation embarked upon what appeared to be a rather unorthodox, ideologically pragmatic road to socialism. Nevertheless, predictably and almost immediately, the Nicaraguan Revolution was forced to contend with a formidable array of domestic and international obstacles and opponents which, as of this writing, have already altered its trajectory and render its future course uncertain.

In addition to the relevance provided by contemporary events, the republication of *Revolution from Without* comes at a particularly effervescent moment in Latin American revolutionary studies. An ongoing discourse among political sociologists, anthropologists, and historians has greatly enriched our understanding of the political economy and social history of revolutions and popular insurgencies. At a macro level, theorists seeking to explain social revolutions and the pivotal role of subaltern classes in them (e.g., Barrington Moore, Eric Wolf, James Scott, Theda Skocpol, and Charles Tilly) have increasingly emphasized the importance of developing a holistic frame of reference, one that would examine internal class structure – focusing particularly on the conditions that produce popular grievances and the capacity to redress them – the rise and fall of national states, and international economic and political relations. Such political-sociological theory has informed, and in turn built upon, monographs by social historians and anthropologists which have analytically reconstructed and often narratively evoked the experiences of local participants involved in larger revolutionary transformations. As the field has undergone fundamental change in the last decade, the prevailing paradigms of the 1970s and early 1980s, "dependency" and "world systems analysis," have inevitably been refined, modified, even transcended.

Following its appearance in 1982, *Revolution from Without* has generally been received as an important contribution in this process of literary evolution. With Charles Bergquist's *Coffee and Conflict in Colombia, 1886–1910* (Durham, 1978; Duke Paperback edition, 1986), it remains one of only a handful of monographs on Latin America to subject the "dependency" model to empirical scrutiny and the canons of historical scholarship. Based on extensive primary research in Mexico and the United States, my study supported certain fundamental assumptions of the "dependency" approach, historically documenting important connections between the expanding international economy and the social formation of regional Mexico. Nevertheless, the book leveled a pointed critique at much of the theoretically abstract "dependency" and "world systems" literature.

Among other things, I argued that the radical *dependentistas'* ahistorical assertion of "capitalist" relations at the periphery of the world system, based only on the nexus of the external market, provided little guidance for understanding developments within the dependent society. Borrowing conceptual tools from economic anthropology (the literature on "articulation of modes of production"), comparative imperial history ("the collaborator model"), and the burgeoning interdisciplinary literature on "clientelism," I attempted a more nuanced analysis of the social relations of dependency at the periphery, one that would more precisely establish the dialectical relationship between internal social forces and external linkages. *Revolution from Without*'s greatest contribution may well lie in its power to explain how the formidable institutional and cultural legacies of dependent capitalist development, particularly in monocultural settings, can impede popular participation, narrow ideological options, and effectively undercut the potential for local revolutionary change.

It is no longer surprising that such larger issues come within the purview of a regional study. When my book first appeared, regional studies were still something of a novelty in professional scholarship. Interestingly, some critics labored to categorize the book and rarely agreed on its central contribution. Was this primarily a case example of the Mexican Revolution, providing a corrective view from the nation's far periphery? Was it, more broadly, an essay on the limitations of state-managed mobilization and agrarian reform? Didn't the book also address concerns in the more external realms of U.S. diplomatic and business history and the comparative history of imperialism? Of course, it was my intention to employ the regional approach to address a variety of larger problems at several levels of analysis. Now, as the 1980s draw to a close, such a multilayered strategy is increasingly finding its way onto the research agenda. The appearance of *Revolution from Without* in paperback testifies to the tremendous vitality and breadth which regional analysis now brings to the writing of Mexican and Latin American history.

In effect, regional historians are attempting a new conceptualization of the physical boundaries of historical space. Armed with ever more sophisticated analytical models of political economy and, increasingly, with methodological tools borrowed from what has been called the "new social (or labor) history," scholars such as Steve Stern and Florencia Mallon (Peru), Barbara Weinstein (Brazil), and a variety of Mexicanists have sought to incorporate locality and region into larger national and supranational structures. In the process conventional periodizations have been reformulated, the experiences of both elites and everyday people have been re-created, the complex role of the State has been fleshed out and debated, and our comparative understanding of the global expansion of capitalism has been further refined. Although regionalists have occasionally failed rigorously to define or delimit their regions – a critical problem that must be remedied – they are increasingly less vulnerable to the charge of "localism." The concerns of the new regional history now greatly transcend restrictive notions of geography or place.

Probably nowhere has the new regional approach made more of an historiographical impact than in the field of Mexican Revolutionary studies. A recent harvest of regional studies has done more than redress the worst abuses of a traditional *historiografía capitalina*; it has recast the prevailing "populist" interpretation of the Revolution as a whole. Prior to the 1970s, most professional historians essentially concurred with the "official" view of the PRI, portraying the upheaval as a spontaneous, genuinely popular, essentially agrarian revolt against a backward and abusive hacienda regime. They argued that while the Revolution was initially brutal and chaotic, it ultimately forged a modern nation – more stable, prosperous, and socially just than the Porfiriato.

The new regional historiography has captured the Revolution's significance in decidedly darker hues. The study of regional society in times of crisis – that is, during moments of revolt and regime response to them – has provided scholars with a valuable opportunity to probe power relationships and divisions within campesino and worker society and within the dominant class, as well as to examine certain tactical alliances forged between working-class groups and factions of the dominant class (and the new Revolutionary State) through the agency of brokers and *caciques*. If a "revisionist" consensus has emerged from these regional studies, it is that although the Mexican Revolution may have begun as mass mayhem with the active participation of truly popular groups, it rapidly witnessed the ascendancy of aspiring bourgeois and petit bourgeois elements. These chiefs often employed traditional patterns of authority, based on patron-client exchanges, to co-opt and manipulate the masses of peasants and workers. Ultimately, in the 1930s, the more independent of these regional and local power-holders were themselves subordinated (or eliminated) by the emerging Revolutionary State. A modern Leviathan, the new State swallowed up regional political configurations, eventually perfecting, in Toquevillian fashion, the formula of political centralization and dependent capitalist development that had begun to emerge under the ancien régime.

Clearly, the revisionists have succeeded in focusing attention on important continuities between the Porfirian regime and the new Revolutionary State. Yet, as Alan Knight persuasively argues in his recent prize-winning synthesis of the first decade, *The Mexican Revolution* (2 vols., Cambridge, England, 1986), frequently the revisionists overstate the case. Often they reduce the Revolution to "a series of chaotic, careerist episodes, in which popular forces were, at best, the instruments of manipulative caciques."[1] Stressing continuity rather than rupture, they posit the rise of a Machiavellian central government as the key element of the epic Revolution. Knight argues insightfully that this lends much revisionist scholarship "a teleological colour which is essentially the mirror image" of the traditional "populist" interpretation: "the benign progress of the Revolution towards social justice is replaced by the malign – or neutral – advance of the state towards national integration and centralized bureaucracy." Such "Statolotry," Knight contends, provides a false homogeneity to the complex history of the 1910 Revolution – a complexity which, ironically, the revisionists skillfully document in their well-crafted regional monographs. Moreover, such uncompromising "revisionism" ignores the pressures, particularly those emanating from below, which acted upon the State; it mistakenly stresses the inertia of the peasants and workers and the unbroken political hegemony of elites and middle strata.[2]

Like Knight, I have argued elsewhere that what is needed is an eventual synthesis of the populist and revisionist interpretations. This would require a more sophisticated reconstruction of peasant and worker mobilizations as well as a greater appreciation of the impacts that these popular movements registered locally, regionally, nationally – occasionally even internationally. While the revisionists have made important advances in reinterpreting the larger events and the political-economic context of the Mexican Revolution from the regional – as opposed to the national – level, they have been rather less successful in understanding the experiences and mentalities of the popular classes – particularly their ideology and culture. Indeed, perhaps the principal challenge for Revolutionary specialists today is to incorporate the perspectives of the participants themselves – to put everyday Mexicans back into the Mexican Revolution.

If the Mexican Revolution's "low politics," its regionally diverse popular movement, must be seen as the necessary precursor of the "Statist" revolution that followed in the 1920s and 1930s, at the same time the nature of that State bears out the revisionists' contention that the crises and changes unleashed by the popular classes were never profound enough to break capitalist domination of production. In fact, recent studies provide compelling evidence that Mexico's dependence upon international capitalism only deepened during the Revolution.

Revolution from Without, which focuses upon a particularly unusual one of the "many Mexicos," fundamentally supports the "revisionist" interpretation of the Revolution as a whole. Indeed, in the remote peninsula, both *initially as well as ultimately*, the Revolution was made from above and imposed from without upon the region and its popular classes. Yet much of the book, particularly the treatment of Felipe Carrillo Puerto's idiosyncratic "socialist" revolution, examines the relationship that resonated between progressive revolutionary movements organized from the top and local forces at the grass roots of society. In the process I take issue with both traditional "populist" interpretations and the more recent Marxist thesis advanced by Mexican sociologists Francisco Paoli and Enrique Montalvo in their stimulating essay, *El socialismo olvidado de Yucatán* (Mexico City, 1977).

Paoli and Montalvo argue that Carrillo Puerto's revolutionary party was a truly popular one and might have engineered a transition to socialism had it been given a fighting chance. As the title of their work suggests, their purpose is to recover and reformulate the history of the Mexican Revolution: they seek to rescue Carrillo Puerto and the Socialist Party of the Southeast (PSS) from the official mythmakers and give them back to the pueblo. At the same time they hope to extract from Yucatán's revolutionary past lessons that might provide a coherent basis for political action to challenge the PRI and reform the nation's schlerotic institutions – laudable goals to be sure.

But does Carrillo's PSS provide modern-day activists with an inspirational episode of popular mobilization? It is not my intention to minimize the positive, "subjective" factors of revolutionary struggle that can be found in the history of Yucatán's "forgotten socialism," but they must be read against the formidable "objective" constraints of the global economy, the national state, and the region's social formation. Ultimately, my judgment of the viability of Yucatán's socialist experiment is a more pessimistic one than that provided by Paoli and Montalvo.

In large part our conflicting interpretations derive from different presuppositions and sources. In my view the strength or weakness of social movements and revolutionary regimes cannot be assessed primarily on the basis of their programmatic statements and formal political organizations. In addition to examining these and the external constraints that act upon them, we must also consider the political culture in which they operate. Here, the role which informal networks of power play in the revolutionary process is particularly critical. These networks were (and still are) ordered vertically rather than horizontally through traditional patron-client arrangements. In such a political culture, which in the 1920s was managed largely by ambitious local *caciques* and recalcitrant *hacendados*, could socialist ideology and the PSS's new iconography really transform traditional attitudes in the countryside, particularly given the regime's short duration?

These are important questions, and truly definitive answers will emerge only when historians succeed in penetrating the *mentalité* of Yucatán's Maya campesinos and fully reclaim the past of the region's articulate yet illiterate rural working class. It is this last problem, particularly as it bears on forms of popular resistance and social control during the late Porfiriato and early Revolutionary period, which presently occupies me.

Gilbert M. Joseph
Chapel Hill, North Carolina

Notes

1. I, xi.
2. Knight, book review in *Journal of Latin American Studies* 16:2 (1984): 525–26.

Acknowledgments

To express personal gratitude to everyone who helped make this work possible might require the preparation of a second volume. Some special thanks are due, however. My research and writing in Mexico and the United States, 1974–1976, were facilitated by a Foreign Area Fellowship provided by the Social Science Research Council. The eighteen months of actual research were made more efficient by the efforts of a number of skilled and patient archivists. In Chicago, J. H. Henn and Greg Lennes guided me through the recently indexed archives of the International Harvester Company. In Cambridge, Massachusetts, Robert Lovett, director of the Harvard School of Business Administration's Baker Library, introduced me to several important collections that highlighted the cordage interests of lesser North American corporations. In Washington, D.C., and Suitland, Maryland, the staffs of the Library of Congress and the National Archives were largely responsible for making my foray into the dense thicket of diplomatic, military, commercial, and personal papers a manageable adventure. In Mexico City, the (then) director of the Archivo General de la Nación, Lic. Jorge Ignacio Rubio Mañé, a *Yucateco*, steered me to important collections and counseled me on a number of sensitive points regarding the people of his region. Berta Ulloa and her staff at the Archivo de la Secretaría de Relaciones Exteriores and the archivists at the Centro de Estudios de Historia de Mexico, Condumex, were especially helpful in locating documentary collections illuminating the early years of the Revolution in Mexico and Yucatán.

In Mérida, *Yucatecos* Lic. Luis López Rivas (Archivo General del Estado), Lic. Rodolfo Ruz Menéndez (Universidad de Yucatán), Lic. Clemente López Trujillo, and Don Pedro Castro Aguilar (Hemeroteca "Pino Suárez"), through their encyclopedic knowledge, courtesy, and good sense of humor, did much to keep my research project and spirits afloat. Their camaraderie was refreshing and, indeed, often vital in order to endure a succession of work days when it was 95 degrees in the shade! The recent surge of interest in Yucatecan history by Mexicans and foreigners owes more to these modest, energetic men than can be acknowledged here. Thanks also go to North American businessman Richard Hedlund, Sr., who opened his private library to me. It contains perhaps the world's most extensive collection of materials on henequen and cordage. The hours I spent drawing upon his broad knowledge of the fiber business, gained from years in the trade, have proved invaluable for telling the story that follows.

There are many intellectual debts as well. Richard Morse, Emilia Viotti da Costa, and Robin Winks, the professors who advised me at Yale, each emphasized a different thematic and methodological approach to my project while encouraging me to explore other approaches. North Carolina colleagues Joseph Tulchin, Leon Fink, and Carl Pletsch and Mexicanists John Womack, Friedrich Katz, David Brading, Juan Felipe Leal, and Barry Carr each provided helpful insights in the research or writing phases of the project. My fellow participants at the University of Cambridge's international conference on "Peasant and Caudillo in Modern Mexico" – including Raymond Buve, Hans Werner Tobler, Alan Knight, and Héctor Aguilar Camín – made constructive suggestions regarding my material on *caciquismo* and the Carrillo Puerto regime. Fellow *yucatólogos* Philip Thompson, Robert Patch, A. J. G. Knox, Michael Fallon, Diane Roazen, Allen Wells, and Ramón Chacón listened, discussed, and shared data. The warm and generous support of the last three, in particular, demands extra thanks. I must also express my special gratitude to writer Julia Preston, a dear friend and a demanding critic, whose knowledge of Latin American issues and command of the English language rescued me time and again from both conceptual and literary mishaps. The insight and rigor of her critique of the manuscript at several stages were instrumental in shaping a dissertation into a book. All of these friends and colleagues helped make this a better volume. I alone, however, bear responsibility for its shortcomings.

For their care and cheer in typing the manuscript at various stages, I wish to thank Mary Cash, Patricia Reefe, and Jean Holke.

Finally, I would surely be remiss if I failed to acknowledge the guidance of the numerous *Yucatecos* with whom I spoke. Veteran *revolucionarios* and latter-day Party officials, henequen workers and

Meridano intellectuals, former *hacendados* and current *caciques*, local businessmen and student leaders – each took time to tell his story and, in the process, to explain why the promise of the Revolution has not yet been fulfilled in Yucatán. I only hope I have been equal to the task of retelling their story here.

PROLOGUE

Yucatán receives a revolution

The Revolution appeared in Yucatán as something strange and
exotic.

—Antonio Mediz Bolio

As the March morning broke full upon the white walls and dusty
streets of their city, the people of Mérida braced themselves behind
locked doors to receive their conquerors. Once again, Mexico was
invading Yucatán.

The *huaches*, soldiers from the interior of Mexico,[1] had come
earlier under Santa Anna in 1843 to "persuade" the secessionist
sister republic to incorporate itself into a central Mexican nation.
They returned on behalf of Júarez in 1867 to subdue the last
remnants of Maximilian's fading empire, which, appropriately,
had found a final resting place in the Yucatecan capital. Now, in
March 1915, as the city attempted to collect itself after a troubled
night of seige, a Mexican army was about to confer the blessings
of the Revolution upon the state of Yucatán.

That the Revolution had taken its time getting there – five
years, to be exact – was not an accident. The Yucatán peninsula's
offside position, which permitted regular access only by sea, had
traditionally isolated the state and its immediate neighbors, Campeche and the Territory of Quintana Roo, from the Mexican political mainstream. Beginning in 1910, this geographical isolation had made it difficult for home-grown revolutionaries to
obtain news of the movement's progress in the rest of the
Republic.

A more compelling factor in the region's isolation was the deep-
seated reluctance of Yucatán's rulers to join the revolutionary tide.
The system of oligarchical rule, exploitation, and repression of the
Indian masses that had flourished throughout Mexico under the
Old Regime had gained an extended lease on life in Yucatán. Prior
to the outbreak of rebellion in 1910, Yucatán's entrepreneurial
hacendados had constructed a multitiered coercive system that
commanded the respect and envy of their counterparts elsewhere

in the Republic. The toppling of Porfirio Díaz's thirty-four-year dictatorship at the national level had little effect on Yucatán, where local landowners could still count on the support of state and municipal constabularies, as well as their own private forces.[2] From 1910 to 1915, Yucatán's planter–merchant bourgeoisie, adapting skillfully to changing political circumstances, maintained a firm hold on the levers of political and economic power.[3]

Rarely did the tumultuous events at the national level find a resonance within the region. The local plantocracy dutifully celebrated Don Porfirio's eightieth birthday in September 1910, but few Yucatecans answered Francisco Madero's call to revolt against the despotic regime in late November. Throughout the Republic, Mexicans had watched Madero, a veritable David, stand up to the Porfirian Goliath, and thousands were encouraged or shamed into revolt. In Yucatán, several pathetic episodes of isolated rural protest flared up and expired in 1910 and 1911, but none was directly inspired by Madero's crusade to bring clean politics – "a real vote and no boss rule" – to Mexico. Madero's subsequent regime, fourteen troubled months (November 1911–February 1913) during which Mexico experimented with multiparty democracy for the only time in its history, brought only cosmetic changes to the Yucatecan political landscape, where Porfirian oligarchs conveniently transformed themselves into leading *Maderistas*.

The terrible spectacle of General Victoriano Huerta's betrayal of his president and Madero's murder in February 1913, which shook Mexico to its foundations and unleashed popular passions throughout the Republic, found no echo in Yucatán. Not only was there scarcely a ripple of protest, but the local rulers saw to it that their state won the dubious distinction of being the first to recognize Madero's assassin. The planters now called for peace at any cost and advised President Huerta to deal firmly with the rebels who had immediately opposed him, notably Emiliano Zapata's peasant Army of the South and the Constitutionalist forces in the north, led by Governor Venustiano Carranza of Coahuila. Like their counterparts elsewhere in Mexico, Yucatán's oligarchs had disapproved of Madero's gentle manner and meddlesome efforts to transform Mexico into a bourgeois democracy with freedom of speech and press and the rule of law. Moreover, they resented even the vague, modest promises of social reform that he had made to workers and peasants, perceiving that any tampering with the Porfirian Peace would ultimately give rise to anarchy.

But a restoration of Mexico's old social order was not possible in 1913–1914; the revolutionary tide was already too strong. More numerous and more militant than they had been in 1910, the nation's revolutionaries had also come to appreciate the shortcomings of Madero's political revolution. Almost instinctively, they regrouped under Carranza and Zapata. They intended to restore the constitutional order shattered by Huerta's coup, then implement urgent reforms in Mexico's factories and fields. Clean government was no longer a broad enough change; the revolutionary process would now go beyond the channels of regular politics. Revolutionary chiefs unwilling to entertain at least some formula for social renovation would lose out.

For the moment, Carranza's designation as First Chief seemed correct. A shrewd politician with roots in the old order, Don Venus had observed Madero's demise and learned the lessons of the immediate past. He was determined to dissolve the Porfirian bureaucracy and army while consolidating a strong central state, one that would *eventually* by capable of implementing change. Meanwhile, only revolutionary unity could defeat the usurper Huerta and also withstand the inevitable pressures on national sovereignty that the "Colossus to the North" would apply.

After eighteen months of struggling against the revolutionaries as well as U.S. President Woodrow Wilson's hostile administration, Huerta yielded to the rebels in July 1914. Yet even as they stood momentarily united in triumph – *Carrancistas* and *Obregonistas*, *Villistas* and *Zapatistas* – their internal divisions were painfully obvious. Almost four years after the declaration of Madero's rebellion, the configuration of revolutionary forces revealed Mexico to be a human mosaic with needs so different and often so contradictory that they virtually defied any immediate form of national organization.

Following the triumph over Huerta, two major parties – or better, two large, amorphous constellations of rival armies and bands – vied for control, each determined to manage and guarantee the future of the Revolution. On one side were the supporters of Carranza, a former Porfirian senator and *hacendado* and the founding father of the Constitutionalist movement. The *Carrancistas'* military strength lay in the Divisions of the Northwest and Northeast, led by General Álvaro Obregón of Sonora and General Pablo González of Coahuila, respectively. On the other side was the opposition to Carranza, grouped around Francisco ("Pancho") Villa, the onetime social bandit who had now become Mexico's most famous revolutionary. Villa, the "Centaur of the North," commanded the Republic's largest, most successful fighting force, the Chihuahua-based Division of the North. Thus, like the *Carrancistas*, the *Villistas* were predominantly a northern movement, however late in 1914 they entered into a tenuous alliance with the *Zapatista* agrarians of south-central Mexico. The rivals also resembled each other in including within their ranks a variety of former *Maderistas*, ex-federal soldiers, and opportunists who changed sides with each shift in the Revolution's fortunes.

War between the two sides became inevitable in October 1914 when a convention at Aguascalientes of revolutionary leaders and their delegates to settle the conflict between Villa and Carranza only sharpened the animosity on both sides. There were personal tensions involved, most notably the First Chief's jealousy of Villa as a rival caudillo, but probably more important was Carranza's failure to define his position on fundamental issues, such as the agrarian question, the rights of labor, and the shape of the new political order. Northern cowboys, drifters, mule skinners, miners, bandits, itinerant laborers and peddlers, refugee *peones* and plot holders, the *Villistas* were highly mobile, perhaps "more a force of nature than of politics."[4] Yet as underdogs and outcasts of the great Chihuahuan expanses, they espoused a freewheeling brand of populism that clashed with Carranza's more gradualist, aristocratic notions of reform. When Villa attempted in July 1914 to obtain Carranza's approval of an agreement defining the Revolution as "a struggle of the poor against the abuses of the powerful" and committing the Constitutionalists "to implement a democratic regime . . . to secure the well-being of the workers; to emancipate the peasants economically, making an equitable distribution of lands or whatever else is needed to solve the agrarian problem," Carranza flatly declined.[5]

Like their *Villista* allies, the *Zapatistas* were also a popular movement. However, unlike the inchoate conglomeration of uprooted northern types that was *Villismo*, the *Zapatista* peasants were distinguished by their extraordinary political solidarity and local attachments. Isolated and impoverished, their traditional way of life imperiled, Zapata's agrarians stubbornly dug in, defining their purpose as the defense of their Morelos farms and villages.

The world view of the *Carrancista* leadership was alien to *Zapatistas* and *Villistas* alike and threatened them both. If the "popular" revolutionaries of *Villismo* and *Zapatismo* pursued the modest goals of the common man, *Carrancismo* aspired to greater things.

The movement's generals, ideologues, and local chiefs were budding entrepreneurs who thought in national terms and carried out a deliberate, unequivocal strategy. Unlike the *Villistas*, who did a bit of plundering when the need or opportunity arose, or the *Zapatistas*, who fought to protect what was theirs, *Carrancista* generals sought the huge, socially acceptable fortunes that would fall to them as the legitimate future leaders of a new, modernized Revolutionary state. Having defeated the Old Regime, they would purge its bureaucratic vestiges completely, then organize their own political system, predicated upon sound principles of bourgeois reform and nationalism. Obsessed as they were with legitimacy and the forms of the modern nation–state, these "official revolutionaries" could not tolerate the anarchic style and regional orientation of their rivals.

Thus, when the *Villista–Zapatista* majority at the Convention of Aguascalientes decided to depose him as First Chief, Carranza disputed the authority of the decision, retreating with his depleted forces to Veracruz in November 1914. Although his enemies now controlled Mexico City and much of the Republic, Carranza refused to relinquish his claim to formal legitimacy. Immediately he set up his Constitutionalist government in Veracruz and, aided by a talented staff of intellectuals and politicians, promulgated a series of social reform decrees designed to win the support of nonaligned peasants and workers.

Although they held a military and political advantage late in 1914, the Conventionists – as the *Villista–Zapatista* alliance came to be called – quickly squandered it. The regionally based *Villistas* and *Zapatistas* communicated poorly with each other and found it difficult to coordinate movements of troops and supplies. Their lack of a national vision, of a plan to gain and hold state power, cost them dearly. Ironically, although their movement's origins and concerns were genuinely closer to Mexico's peasants and workers, the Conventionist leaders' failure to forge a clear national program that could unite the interests of rural and urban workers left the door open for Carranza's middle-class politicians, through skillful, opportunistic appeals, to separate the Convention from its natural allies. Among the troops that Constitutionalist General Álvaro Obregón used to launch an offensive against Villa early in 1915 were six "red battalions" of urban workers who had allied themselves with Carranza's government.

As a result of these domestic developments and President Wilson's decision to throw North American support behind Carranza

– Villa and Zapata were obviously unacceptable to U.S. investors and policy makers – the balance of forces had abruptly shifted in favor of the Constitutionalists by mid-1915. By year's end, they would nullify the Convention as a military and political threat, reducing Villa and Zapata to defensive guerrilla campaigns in their Chihuahua and Morelos homelands. However, 1915 would be the bloodiest, most chaotic year of the revolutionary struggle, a "fiesta of bullets" according to a young journalist-participant.[6] At Celaya in May, for example, Obregón employed trench warfare and withering machine gun fire to turn back a desperate charge by Villa's crack gold-shirted cavalrymen. Thousands died or were maimed in the carnage. Intervals of peace were rare; cease-fires became events for local balladeers to sing about.[7]

Yet as *Obregonista* killed *Villista* and worker fought peasant, peace continued to rage in Yucatán. In fact, early in 1915 the southeastern portion of Mexico revealed itself to be a virtual vacuum of revolutionary activity.[8] Riding the crest of an export boom, the planters increased their acreage in henequen fiber, and *campesinos* continued to labor like slaves on the plantations. While the rest of the Republic made war, Yucatán made money.

The local rulers had not forgotten how to accommodate new national bosses. Shortly after Huerta fell in July 1914, they provided a warm welcome to Carranza's military governor, Major Eleuterio Ávila, who was, in fact, a native son. Ávila sent a momentary shock through the peninsular bourgeoisie by reading a proclamation abolishing forced labor on Yucatán's henequen plantations, but after a series of anguished meetings among themselves and consultations with the agents of International Harvester, the monopolistic buyer of Yucatán's single crop, the planters found ways to bring their *paisano* (countryman) to his senses, and the decree was never enforced.[9]

By late 1914, then, Yucatán's rulers had managed to keep the Revolution at arm's length. Occasional flare-ups erupted and subsided in the countryside – as they had since 1910 – and discontented intellectuals continued to conjure up visions of the apocalypse in the cafés and salons of Mérida. But supportive conditions for a local revolutionary movement plainly did not exist. Only a military stroke administered from the outside could curb the political and repressive power of the *hacendados*, a fact they appreciated only too well. However, with Ávila safely under control, life in the peninsula returned to its normal rhythm, and the ruling elite began to believe it had weathered the revolutionary storm.

As 1914 became 1915, the shifting configuration of national revolutionary politics created new possibilities in Yucatán. As Carranza and his finance minister, Luis Cabrera, became increasingly desperate for money to wage the Constitutionalist struggle against the *Villistas* and *Zapatistas*, a tighter control over Yucatán's rich henequen receipts became more desirable. When Ávila, now little more than the planters' errand boy,[10] balked at Cabrera's stepped-up tax schedule, Carranza replaced him in late January 1915 with General Toribio de los Santos, a Mexican. The new governor made it clear immediately that he would not be bought and underscored the point by pressing a sizable forced loan upon the wealthiest planters and merchants. Then, playing upon traditional regional fears, he threatened to send Yucatecan soldiers out of the peninsula and announced his intention to activate Ávila's decree abolishing forced labor. De los Santos boasted to the First Chief that he had begun a campaign against "reactionaries," then taunted the *Yucatecos* that although their region "had not participated in the revolutionary movement . . . nor felt its effects," the Revolution would *now* come to Yucatán.[11]

Stung by this first serious threat to its dominance, the oligarchy found its champion in ex-*Huertista* Colonel Abel Ortiz Argumedo, whom Ávila had appointed Mérida's military commander. Capitalizing on the discontent that de los Santos had created at virtually every level of regional society, Ortiz Argumedo united Yucatán's militia battalions behind him and ousted de los Santos and his *Carrancista* federals from the state in mid-February.[12] As de los Santos fled, he cut the telegraph wires linking Yucatán and Mexico City, a standard logistical tactic but this time infused with a special symbolic importance. For once again Yucatán was turned in upon itself, detached from Mexico and, as in the past, determined to remain so. In order to buy time, Ortiz Argumedo – now the governor and military commander of Yucatán – immediately pledged his loyalty to Carranza, then actively set about consolidating a separatist movement in the state. Moving decisively, Ortiz Argumedo declared the sovereignty of Yucatán and sent a commission to the United States to negotiate a fiber-backed loan, purchase arms, and explore the possibility of a North American protectorate – much as the Yucatecan state government had done in 1848.[13] The big planters and merchants played an active role in encouraging the break with Mexico, contributing money to Ortiz Argumedo's war chest, and enlisting their sons in his state battalion.[14]

However, roughly a month later, it was readily apparent to Yucatán's rulers that this latest separatist gambit – to be Yucatán's last – had failed. Infuriated by what he immediately regarded as a regional insurrection, Carranza quickly moved to bring Yucatán to heel. With much of Mexico still in the hands of the Conventionists, the First Chief could not afford to lose control of Yucatán's henequen riches, which, along with the customs duties of the port of Veracruz, produced the bulk of his government's income and financed the war effort. This time, as his agent of retribution Carranza chose Salvador Alvarado, one of his senior generals of division rank and the man who, next to Álvaro Obregón, was considered to be his foremost strategist and administrator. As Ortiz Argumedo rounded up what remained in the state treasury and sailed for Cuba, Alvarado's 7,000-man Army of the Southeast made short work of the *Yucatecos* – essentially an amateur band of students, merchants, and servants one-tenth the federals' size – in what amounted to skirmishes, with limited casualties at the town of Halachó and the hacienda Blanca Flor.[15]

So, with the Constitutionalists bearing down on the state capital that morning in March 1915, panic and terror gripped the *Meridanos*. Thousands fled, fearing destruction and pillage at the hands of the *huaches*. Revolutionary atrocities elsewhere in Mexico had been common knowledge in Yucatán, but now the stories abounded. Familiar images of miles of railroad track where each telegraph pole doubled as a gallows suddenly became horribly immediate. One eyewitness recalls:

> The confusion heightened to such a degree that in those final moments one could say that there existed a "classless society": there was no aristocracy or plutocracy . . . only families who whispered prayers or made fervent supplications, imploring the saints to save their wives and daughters from the bestial instincts of the soldiers who would soon enter the city . . .[16]

Most fearful were the planters, who fidgeted in their town houses as they awaited Alvarado's entry into Mérida, believing that a reckoning was imminent. Many of them had already evacuated the city for the relative safety of their estates in the countryside. Several of the wealthiest members of Yucatán's oligarchy, known as the *Casta Divina* (Divine Caste), had left with Ortiz Argumedo on the steamer for Havana. Others had sailed for New Orleans or New York.[17]

However, as he waited with his forces outside the city, the invader did not seem anxious to play upon the fears that gripped

General Salvador Alvarado. (From Gustavo Casasola, *Historia gráfica de la Revolución Mexicana, 1910–1970*, 2d ed., Mexico, 1973, vol. 5, p. 1675. Casasola, INAH.)

the Yucatecan capital. To be sure, Carranza had given him a free hand. Tetchy, his patience exhausted, the First Chief had demanded the *Yucatecos*' immediate "unconditional submission," instructing Alvarado to "take whatever action against them you believe convenient" – provided henequen revenues were not jeopardized.[18] Yet, Alvarado had already decided upon a strategy of leniency. Some days before, he had startled the residents of Mérida by deploying a string of airplanes – still very much a novelty in the peninsula – to leaflet the city, calling upon the *Yucatecos* to submit peacefully and explaining that he was coming to further the goals of the Revolution but would not infringe upon the rights of life or property.[19] Moreover, he had already made good on his promise by personally intervening to save the lives of hundreds of middle- and upper-class youths who had been captured at Blanca Flor and Halachó and were awaiting a firing squad by order of the general's more impulsive subordinates.[20] Finally, Alvarado had chosen to camp on the outskirts of Mérida on the eve of 19 March and to take the city in broad daylight the following day, thereby avoiding any violence and looting that might result from a nighttime occupation of an enemy town.[21]

A monumental task awaited Yucatán's conqueror. The regional poet Antonio Mediz Bolio, who would become Alvarado's friend and intellectual advisor, recalls the general's dilemma at the time he took control of Yucatán:

He found himself confronted by a land of tradition, whose internal life, sculptured drop by drop like a stalactite by the accumulation of centuries, was far removed and sheltered from the energetic reach of a revolution which had only just touched its borders . . .

The Revolution appeared in Yucatán as something exotic and strange . . . yet in spite of this, or perhaps because of it, Yucatán was one of the regions of Mexico where the Revolution was most urgently needed and would be felt most deeply . . . But first Alvarado would have to make the Revolution with his government, from above, for it could not issue from below. He would have to remake this society which, in many ways, still lived in the colonial period, and he would have to remake it down to its roots . . . He would have to be not only Yucatán's revolutionary governor but also its revolutionary mentor . . .[22]

We now examine the formation of this regional society that had so stubbornly resisted the encroachment of Mexico's revolution.

PART I

The parameters of revolution

1

Plant and plantation: the development of a monocrop economy

All the state is for henequen and outside of it there is nothing.
                                                    –Serapio Baqueiro, 1881

The whites have made this land alien to the Indian.
                                    –Ermilo Abreu Gómez, *Canek:*
                                    History and Legend of a Maya Hero

Yucatán's revolutionary experience and at least the last hundred years of the region's historical development have been shaped by the erratic fortunes of a single species of cactus plant, indigenous to the peninsula. One of Mexico's poorest states in the mid-nineteenth century, Yucatán rode the crest of a late-century fiber export boom to become, arguably, the Republic's richest state by 1915.[1] Six decades later, the region's fortunes are still tied to – or, as many *Yucatecos* perceive it, impaled upon – the fibrous spines of the hardy cactus that the ancient Maya revered as "Ki," modern botanists have classified as *agave fourcroydes*, North American fiber traders have labeled "sisal hemp," and Yucatecans call *henequén*. Here, too, the cactus and its fiber will be referred to as "henequen," to distinguish it from "sisal" (*agave sisalena*), the closely related species that, unlike henequen, will grow in most other tropical regions (e.g., the Caribbean, South America, Africa, and the East Indies) and has, since the First World War, become henequen's bitter rival for the North American hard fiber market. Although henequen has a significantly longer productive life than sisal (twenty-five to thirty against eight to ten years), it will not yield fiber for seven years, whereas sisal begins producing after about three years. Moreover, sisal and Filipino manila fiber, a much earlier competitor, produce substantially more twine per hundred kilograms of fiber and may be spun into a longer, stronger, cleaner, softer, and more uniform twine.[2]

Why, then, was Yucatecan henequen able virtually to monopolize the world market prior to 1915? Put simply, Yucatecan henequen was far cheaper and far more accessible than any of its rivals. The peninsula's close proximity to its North American buyers kept transportation costs low and facilitated a regular commerce. More importantly, at an opportune historical moment, Yucatán had already made its transition to large-scale commercial henequen production. At a time when the invention of a mechanical knotting device for the McCormick grain binder (1878) was creating a nearly limitless demand for hard fibers needed in the manufacture of binder twine, among the fiber-producing regions only Yucatán had achieved the necessary economic base to produce an adequate supply to meet it. During the decades of peak demand – the 1880s to the 1900s – New Zealand hemp and Indian jute were too costly to produce and ship; political conditions were hampering the cultivation and delivery of manila fiber from the Philippines; and the English, German, and Dutch colonies in East Africa and Java were still years away from establishing the stable conditions under which viable sisal plantations might flourish. Yucatán's *hacendados*, on the other hand, were the masters of a technically advanced, highly capitalized plantation economy predicated upon a labor system that reduced production costs to a bare minimum.

The thirty-four-year reign of President Porfirio Díaz (1876–1910) witnessed Mexico's great economic transformation. In reality, Yucatán, like Mexico, was unable to avoid the accelerated process of transformation that overtook it during the Porfiriato. Proliferating patterns of trade that accompanied the burgeoning industrial development of the United States and Western Europe bound Mexico and Yucatán ever more closely to the global economy. An international economic division of labor was negotiated between foreign industrialists and entrepreneurs, who urgently needed primary products, markets for goods, and opportunities for investment, and national and regional elites, who welcomed infrastructural improvements, modern machinery, an array of consumer goods, and the increasing availability of foreign capital.

The signs of Yucatán's accommodation to this age of industrial capitalism were everywhere apparent by 1915, the time of Alvarado's arrival. In the countryside, the green cornfields and idly grazing cows of the peninsula's colonial-style haciendas had been replaced by endless rectilinear rows of bluish-gray spines and the brisk factorylike pace of the modern henequen plantation. Recently laid railroad tracks extended from Mérida in every direction, and over them passed convoy after convoy of boxcars stuffed with bales of fiber. Processed daily on the plantations, this *oro verde* (green gold) made its way via mule-drawn trams to the nearest railhead, where it continued its journey through Mérida to the port of Progreso. The final destination of this hemp would be New Orleans or New York, where stateside cordage manufacturers would convert the raw fiber into binder twine for the grain farmers of North America.

Mérida itself had undergone a radical facelift. No longer the dingy, overgrown village of 1850 with horses meandering down muddy streets, it was now the Republic's "White City": clean, well-lit, increasingly motorized, and paved with asphalt. The seat of Yucatán's recently created henequen millionaires and universally recognized as the world's most active fiber market, Mérida boasted urban services and amenities at the turn of the century that the national capital was hard pressed to match.[3] However, if the well-to-do *Meridano's* life had been brightened and modernized, this had occurred largely at the expense of the indebted Maya *campesino*, who was now subjected to a labor system on the expanding plantation that condemned him to a second serfdom many times worse than the one that had provoked the traumatic Caste War of recent memory.

Natural constraints on Yucatecan development

The rise of the henequen plantation was conditioned, above all, by the peculiarities of Yucatecan geography and ecology: the region's peripheral location, its lack of cultivable soil, and its acute scarcity of water. Jutting out into the Gulf of Mexico, washed by the Caribbean on its eastern shore, and separated from Mexico proper by an almost unbroken succession of swamps and rain forests, Yucatán has always been more naturally oriented toward the United States, Central America, and the Caribbean islands than toward the remainder of the Mexican Republic. Yucatán's communication by sea with the Mexican port of Veracruz was inefficient, and neither rail nor adequate road communications with central Mexico were established until the middle of this century. Indeed, the entire course of Yucatecan history suggests that rather early the federal government resigned itself to the inevitability of Yucatán's geographical isolation and then formulated political and economic policies that further marginalized the region within the national political structure. For much of the early nineteenth century, Yucatán was regarded as a foreign country for tax purposes and forced to pay discriminatory duties on its exports. Under the national regimes of generals Santa Anna and Bustamante, for example, Yucatecan sugar, hides, and tobacco required higher duties than rival foreign imports. In the 1840s, in the face of intense regional separatism that had been provoked largely by his earlier fiscal policies, Santa Anna banned all Yucatecan products from Mexican ports and declared Yucatecan ships to be pirates.[4]

The recurrence of such conflicts throughout the nineteenth century accentuated Yucatán's pronounced geographical affinity for the United States and Cuba that, over time, would translate into a tradition of close commercial relationships. Already during the colonial period, Yucatecan *hacendados* had marketed their meat and hides in Cuba. When independence from Spain cut off Yucatán from its Havana market and deprived the peninsula of its traditional source of sugar and rum, *Yucatecos* responded by diverting their capital into sugar production within the region. Later, when these plantations were devastated during the Caste War of the late 1840s and Yucatán's economic elite turned its full attention to cultivating henequen, they again found themselves shipping their primary product abroad to meet foreign rather than domestic demand. In return, they purchased necessary provisions and luxury goods that Mexican merchants either could not deliver or were not prepared to provide on such good terms as their counterparts in the United States and Europe.[5]

However, at least as influential in their effects upon the region's economic development in general and the henequen plantation in particular were the ecological constraints of soil and water scarcity. One early European visitor wrote of Yucatán as "the country with the least earth that I have ever seen, since all of it is one living rock."[6] Centuries later, a well-traveled U.S. consul judged Yucatán to be "one of the harshest regions in the world: a great limestone ledge covered over with rocky fragments and sparse deposits of soil, and honeycombed with pot-holes and caves."[7] Geologists have estimated that the soil cover overlying the limestone rock is, at best, no more than 2.5 centimeters thick throughout the northwestern henequen zone and not markedly deeper elsewhere in the state, except for a narrow strip along the southeastern frontier with Campeche and Quintana Roo. Moreover, agriculturalists have found, after painful trial and error, that the porous limestone will not retain commercial fertilizers to enrich what little topsoil exists; the fertilizer passes through the rock with the first rains. The plant cover is, at best, dry scrub.[8] In addition to the little henequen that they cultivated in small back-yard plots to provide rope and articles of clothing for their families, the Yucatecan Maya employed a particularly rigorous form of slash-and-burn agriculture to wrest forth what corn the poor soil would yield. *Milpa* (cornfields) were sown for two years, after which the exhausted soil was left fallow for the next twelve to fifteen. In recent times, *Yucatecos* have resorted to the use of dynamite to blow away rock and increase the soil cover in preparation for crop cultivation.[9]

Perhaps to a greater extent than in most other regions in Mexico, water has been, and remains, a strategic resource in Yucatán. Surface water is almost entirely lacking. In fact, the name of Yucatán's indigenous people, the Maya, means "land without water."[10] This contrasts to the image that outsiders, including many Mexicans, have of the region as a vast, humid, tropical rain forest in which jaguars prowl and monkeys swing from lush over-hanging foliage. Parts of the neighboring states of Quintana Roo, Campeche, and the Guatemalan Petén do, in fact, approximate this romanticized description; Yucatán itself, however, has always had an arid, dusty environment, the type of biota in which agave cacti grow best.[11]

Essentially, there are three main sources of water that *Yucatecos* have historically tapped: (1) rainfall, which is most abundant during the so-called monsoon season (June to September) and is collected on the roofs of houses and stored in reservoirs known as *aguadas*; (2) natural wells (*cenotes*), which are created when the limestone surface rock gives way and collapses into subterranean caves; and (3) artificial wells. During the late Porfiriato and into the twentieth century, Mérida was known as the "city of wind-mills." Each mill – there were 3,500 in Mérida and over 10,000 throughout the state on the eve of the Revolution – was used to raise water from wells into galvanized iron storage tanks. Today many of the region's wells are of the costly artesian variety and, in the southern part of the state, must be drilled over 20 meters before they reach the water table.[12] The original Spanish conquerors used the limited number and localized sources of water as a major device in defeating and controlling the Maya, and their Yucatecan descendants have followed their lead in using access to water as a means of consolidating larger estates and reducing *campesinos* to a dependent labor force.[13]

Rainfall in the Yucatán peninsula follows two gradients, one running north to south, the other west to east. Along the north–

south gradient, precipitation increases from 75 to 100 centimeters per year along the northern Gulf Coast to a high of almost 162.5 centimeters along the southern border of the Petén region. The west–east gradient has a low of 85.82 centimeters annually at Mérida and increases to 118.75 centimeters at Valladolid.[14] (See Figure 1.) These rainfall gradients and the varying soils and vegetation that they have produced have played a critical role in the historical development of the region. In effect, they defined zones that would foster one cash crop or economic cycle but remain marginal for another. These economic cycles highlighting major cash crops usually followed each other serially.

The peninsula's first economic cycle, that of logwood, took place in the seventeenth and eighteenth centuries and affected Yucatán only marginally. The dye-producing wood was gathered mostly along the coast of what is today Campeche, Quintana Roo, and Belize, although Mérida ultimately became one of the collecting points from which the wood was marketed abroad.[15] More or less simultaneously, the dry areas of northern and western Yucatán were developing into a center for the kind of cattle- and maize-producing family haciendas that would become common throughout Latin America. Beef, hides, and tallow were exported to Cuba as cash crops, whereas maize was grown as the chief source of food for all segments of the population, white, mestizo, and Indian alike.[16] Sugar, replacing livestock as Yucatán's major cash crop beginning in the 1830s, required the somewhat more abundant rainfall and deeper soils of the southeastern portion of the state. Finally, with the onset of the henequen cycle in the 1850s following the destruction of the sugar industry, the agricultural center of gravity was again shifted to the drier, thin-soiled northwest.

From hacienda to plantation

This succession of economic cycles, accompanied by a constant shifting of the large estate among a variety of subregional ecological niches, would exercise a profound effect upon Yucatán's communities of Maya *campesinos*. Indeed, the ever-intensifying demands of production that these economic cycles made upon the Maya labor force would be a crucial determinant of the region's transition from a hacienda to a plantation system, which, in turn, was one of the important foundations of henequen monoculture in Yucatán.[17]

The colonial cattle and maize hacienda did not place a great strain on the Maya *campesinado*.[18] After the initial traumas accom-

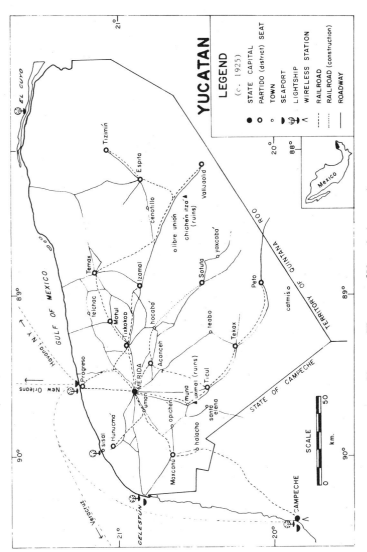

Figure 1. The state of Yucatán (c. 1925).

panying the conquest (1517–1547) had subsided, the Yucatecan Maya were asked to adapt themselves to conditions of labor far simpler than those experienced by the conquered highland peoples of Peru and central Mexico. The basic subsistence crop continued to be corn. The Spanish found, to their chagrin, that none of their traditional European foods would grow in Yucatán's harsh environment. Consequently, they could not demand that their Indian tributaries grow wheat and tend vines and other crops, as they did in central Mexico and the Andean highlands. And unlike these latter areas, there were no mines in Yucatán and, hence, no labor obligations as onerous as the *mita* (forced mine draft). In fact, the Maya were not called upon to make any major shift in their traditional agricultural cycle. To be sure, by 1800, many if not most of the Indian pueblos in the peninsula's northwest quadrant had been despoiled of their communal lands, converting free villagers (*comuneros*) into resident hacienda laborers (*peones acasillados*). Some of these *campesinos* had been drawn onto the estates by recurrent famine and drought, to gain access to the water and grain that, increasingly, the *hacendados* came to control. Yet even when they moved onto the hacienda, most *acasillados* preserved their access to the land, cultivating plots provided by the *patrón*.

Elsewhere, beyond a radius of roughly 80 kilometers from Mérida, the predominant agrarian unit was the indigenous peasant village. Almost completely in 1800 but less and less thereafter, these pueblos remained free of hacienda dominance and maintained their communal lands. The great majority of *comuneros* were accustomed to paying civil and ecclesiastical tribute and participating in a market economy, yet they remained beyond the direct control of the seignorial regime. Thus, although Yucatán possessed a dichotomous agrarian structure at the beginning of the nineteenth century, setting off a northwestern zone of haciendas from a predominantly *comunero* hinterland of small plots (*minifundia*), the rather meager production demands of the traditional hacienda ensured a mild labor system. Because the Spanish depended upon beef and hides for their cash exports – production that was labor-extensive – no serious labor burden was placed on the subject population. This left the Maya *campesino* more or less free to cultivate his *milpa* which, in addition to providing physical sustenance exerted a powerful cultural force, serving as the locale for a major religious rite: the planting of corn.

However, the Maya's relatively enviable situation rapidly came to an end during the first half of the nineteenth century. The cattle and maize hacienda, predicated upon a system of production that was labor-, land-, and capital-extensive, was replaced by the sugar plantation, which, relatively speaking, made intensive use of these factors of production. "The European attack on the basic subsistence patterns of the Maya, which had not occurred in 1547, was finally to occur three hundred years later." [19] The commercial sugar plantation represented the initial phase in the transformation of Yucatecan agriculture, a process that would culminate during the final decades of the nineteenth century in the henequen boom.

The transition from hacienda to plantation did not occur uniformly throughout Yucatán. The northwest, soon the seat of the henequen cycle, was too arid and thin-soiled to nurture sugar cane. Rather, the sugar plantations expanded rapidly throughout the deeper-soiled, more humid regions along the southeastern frontier, first south into the *partido* (district) of Tekax and then east to Peto, Valladolid, and beyond. (See Figure 1.) Where the transition did occur, it wreaked havoc with the Maya *campesino's* traditional *milpa* agriculture. Unlike the northern corn and cattle hacienda, which facilitated a virtually identical labor cycle on both hacienda and Maya maize plots, the sugar plantation demanded a work cycle that brought the large estate and the *milpero* directly into conflict. First, it expanded onto land that had previously been ignored by the creole economy and cultivated by the independent Maya of the frontier. The *hacendados* in the north had stripped the Maya of his property without denying him access to his *milpa*. Such access now became more and more difficult under the new system of production that sugar required. The cane demanded immediate processing after cutting; consequently, the harvest period was circumscribed. Large amounts of labor were needed at harvest time, and each laborer was obliged to be available on a full-time basis. The high cost of processing cane with modern machinery made it essential that field and mill operations be synchronized. The semisedentary slash-and-burn subsistence agriculture of the Maya was no longer complementary with the highly integrated and controlled work regime of the sugar plantation.

For the first time, Yucatán's landed creole elite attacked *milpa* agriculture as an inefficient and primitive means of production. They also remonstrated against those Maya who sought to evade their labor obligations on the plantation by fleeing into the dense bush on the far side of the sugar frontier. In order to stanch the flow of escapees, laws were passed requiring that all independent

Maya be brought under effective municipal jurisdiction. The text
of these laws recalls the *reducciones* of the early colonial period.[20]

Those Maya who refused to capitulate to the plantation's demand for increasingly larger amounts of labor found themselves
pushed even further into the Quintana Roo bush. Meanwhile, the
plantation continued to advance, incorporating the best Indian
lands into sugar production. Ultimately, these free Maya, subsequently joined by dissident hacienda and plantation Maya, initiated the Caste War of 1847, the most sustained and bloody Indian
rebellion in the history of Mexico and perhaps of all Latin
America.[21] This would be the last and most far-reaching Maya
revolt in Yucatecan history. Led by mestizos, the *campesino* rebels
actually succeeded in laying siege to Mérida in 1848, at which
time they held 80 percent of the peninsula. In all, 300,000 people
were killed, one-half of the population of Yucatán.[22] From this
point on, the fortunes of the Maya would decrease steadily.

The "sugar episode" transformed the relationship between the
Yucatecan *hacendado* and his Maya laborer:

> The direction that changes took was less towards direct
> suppression of habitual native ways than the extension of new
> enterprises which were predicated on somewhat different re-
> lationships between Maya and creole than was usual in the
> early days. Colonial economy rested on Maya labor and effort,
> but more or less accepted the fact that Indians were permitted
> to go their own way, so long as tribute goods appeared at the
> designated time. The newer doctrines, however, began a con-
> scious or unconscious drift toward the native as a human
> tool, as part of a disciplined and fixed labor force necessary
> for operation of large scale commercial enterprises.[23]

These "newer doctrines" would become further refined and fully
ascendant on Yucatán's henequen plantations before the century
was out.

The rise of commercial henequen production

Although henequen replaced sugar as the most important cash
crop in the peninsula in the 1850s, the production of henequen
for commercial purposes had begun several decades before the
Caste War. The cactus was cultivated throughout the colonial
period, in Maya pueblos and on haciendas, chiefly to fulfill immediate local needs for rope, hammocks, and sacks. The traditional technology of the Maya was uniformly employed: Plants

were grown in small garden plots rather than in special fields, and the leaves (*hojas* or *pencas*) were cleaned (stripped of their fiber) by hand.[24] However, in 1830, the first henequen corporation, a prototype of the commercial henequen plantation, was established a few kilometers outside of Mérida by a group of *Meridano* entrepreneurs. The investors created the cooperative for the purpose of raising, processing, and manufacturing henequen – a significant departure from the form of agricultural management and investment then prevailing not only in Yucatán and Mexico but throughout Latin America. Initially, 32 hectares were put under cultivation. But the venture was short-lived. Still, from this time forth, the concept of the henequen plantation – a rationalized, large-scale operation predicated upon an intensive use of capital, land, and labor, motivated more by profit than considerations of status and security – became a reality.[25] Moreover, early economic statistics show that, by this time, small quantities of henequen goods as well as raw fiber were being exported to Cuba and Europe.[26]

Then, in 1839, an especially notable milestone was reached: For the first time, a significant quantity of raw fiber was shipped to the United States. Henequen generated a ready demand in New York and New England, where Yankee shipbuilders judged it to be the best available material for the manufacture of cables and riggings for their clipper ships.[27] Yet, although Yucatán's *hacendados* were steadily increasing the amount of their land under fiber cultivation and, in the process, moving from small garden plots to demarcated fields (*henequenales*), they were handicapped in their efforts to meet the new demand by their outmoded preconquest technology of processing the leaves. Decortication[28] by hand with wooden raspers was a ponderous and doubly wasteful process: It used up an unnecessary number of field workers and significantly raised production costs.[29] As demand in the United States increased, the Yucatecan planters and their government actively sought the new technology that would rescue them from their predicament. As early as 1833, a patent had been granted to Henry Perrine, the U.S. consul at Campeche, who claimed to be able to invent a mechanical rasping device. Perrine failed and was followed in the 1840s by a succession of European and North American engineers, none of whom could design a viable machine. In 1852, increasingly desperate, the state government threw open the competition, offering a reward of 2,000 pesos to the man who could produce a functional, economically feasible

Table 1. *The commercial growth of Yucatecan henequen, 1845–1890*

Year	Estimated *mecates*[a] (thousands)	Remarks
1845	16?	Exploitation of henequen planted in 1838
1847	60?	Maximum exploitation during the Caste War
1855	65	Use of mechanical reaper begins; availability of North American credit
1865	400	Introduction of steam-driven raspers
1878	780	Invention of McCormick knotter–binder
1879	1,130	Immediate effects of binder's demand for fiber
1890	2,478	Rapid exploitation

[a]A *mecate* is a Yucatecan unit of land measuring 20 by 20 meters.
Source: Howard Cline, "The Henequen Episode in Yucatán," *Inter-American Economic Affairs*, 2:2 (Autumn 1948), 41.

desfibradora (rasper). Finally, in 1854 and 1856, much to the *hacendados'* surprise, two *Yucatecos* succeeded in perfecting machines (and then battled each other for well over a decade in the courts to claim the government's reward and the future patents, profits, and honor that went with it).[30]

With this technological hurdle overcome, the production and export of henequen would increase rapidly in the years ahead. (See Table 1.) It has been said, with good reason, that "the [rasping] machine . . . did for Yucatán what the cotton gin had done for the American South."[31] Human arms were replaced by oxen and, in succeeding decades, the *desfibradora* was harnessed to steam (1861) and, ultimately, to diesel engines (1913). Each successive improvement enabled the *hacendado* to strip the leaves more rapidly and at less cost.[32]

However, although henequen had long since overtaken cattle as the chief cash product in the northwestern region, and more and more *hacendados* – sensing the sizable profits to be made (see Table 2) – were now embarked upon the gradual process of transforming their mixed corn and cattle haciendas into bona fide plantations, this process still had not progressed far enough by the end of the Caste War in the mid-1850s to generate more than minimal spatial conflict between the expanding *henequenales* and the traditional Maya *milpa*. The agave would grow best on land that would not

Table 2. *The early profitability of henequen cultivation, 1848–1868 (returns received on 500 mecates of henequen)*

Year	Cycle of cultivation	Annual balance (pesos/*mecate*)		Cumulative balance (pesos/*mecate*)	
		Profit	Loss	Profit	Loss
1	Original planting		3.17		3.17
2			.46		3.63
3			.48		4.11
4	First commercial leaves		.31		4.42
5		.43			3.99
6		.70			3.29
7		1.04			2.25
8	Optimum maturity	1.10			1.15
9	Amortization complete	1.17		.02	
10		1.35		1.37	
11		1.35		2.72	
12		1.35		4.07	
13		1.35		5.42	
14		1.35		6.77	
15		1.35		8.12	
16	Declining yield	1.10		9.22	
17		.85		10.07	
18		.80		10.87	
19		.65		11.52	
20	Abandoned	.50		12.02	

Notes: Average annual profit per *mecate* over 20 years = .60 peso. Average annual profit for 500 *mecates* = 300 pesos. Total profit for 20-year period = 6,000 pesos.

Source: Cline, "The Henequen Episode," pp. 45–46.

nourish other crops. Consequently, at this early stage in the development the regional fiber industry, Yucatán's northwest was still capable of feeding itself.

Nevertheless, the potential for serious future conflict between the two systems of production was quite real. Although different from sugar in many respects, henequen also demanded a work schedule that would not complement the seasonal planting and harvest cycle of maize. Grown commercially, henequen requires almost constant weeding (*chapeo*) – especially during its first seven years before entering production – and almost constant harvesting. Once the leaves are cut, they must be processed quickly or the fiber embedded in the outer husk will begin to deteriorate. The need for a year-round harvest is reinforced by the high cost of the rasping machinery, which, for economic reasons, the planter prefers to keep in almost constant operation.[33]

Held by many to be the central event in Yucatecan history, the Caste War had important consequences for the henequen industry.[34] In the terrible violence of the late 1840s and early 1850s, the henequen handicraft industry in the southeastern pueblos was destroyed. More importantly, the war virtually paralyzed henequen production in its early stages, depriving the northern estates of their labor force because the *peones* had either fled to join the rebels or been press-ganged to fight them.

However, the Caste War also provided some of the conditions that hastened the rise of henequen monoculture in later years. Though southeastern agriculture and industry were obliterated in the fighting, the estates in the northwest around Mérida suffered only temporarily and ultimately benefited by a dramatic alteration in the peninsula's demographic balance. For once the north had been cleared of rebels, the *hacendados* lobbied successfully for the use of their former *peones*, who were discharged from military service. More importantly, these former workers were joined by great numbers of refugees from the war-torn zones of the southeast. As the tides of war turned against the rebel Indians, many opted for the food and relative security of the plantations in the northwest rather than a renegade life in the bush on the Quintana Roo frontier. Thus, the Caste War firmly established the center of gravity of the henequen plantation in the northwest, as well as shaping the base of a dependent labor force that would power the ever-expanding henequen estates in the subsequent decades.

The triumph of monoculture

It was not until the 1870s, however, that the modern henequen plantation began to complete its metamorphosis from the old mixed hacienda of corn, cattle, and small-scale fiber production. Not until the improved McCormick knotter–binder appeared on the plains of North America in 1878 was the demand for fiber sufficiently great to compel planters to complete the regional transformation to monoculture. In fact, the expansion of the Yucatecan fiber industry that had taken place prior to this event was negligible compared to what was to come. Whereas the *hacendados* of the northwest had been in an advantageous position to combine the factors of production required gradually to transform their estates to supply the fiber needs of the 1830s and 1840s, their capacity for expansion would now be severely tested by the galloping demands of the North American market. Although a dependable technology (the mechanical rasper) had been developed during the earlier commercial period, a campaign was now launched for ever greater amounts of land, labor, and capital.

The plantation owners were given a free hand to expand their land base at the expense of the neighboring Indian villages. Throughout the nineteenth century and up to 1915, the percentage of free villagers living in northwestern pueblos constantly diminished as their communal lands (*ejidos*) were appropriated by *henequeneros* aided by a concerted legislative and judicial offensive mounted by the state government. By 1900, Yucatán's dichotomous agrarian structure had largely broken down. Frank Tannenbaum has estimated that by 1910, at least 75 percent of all rural dwellers in Yucatán were residents of large estates.[35] According to another study, 96.4 percent of all family heads had no land of their own by 1910.[36] Sooner or later, these landless *campesinos* found their way to the northwestern henequen plantations as dependent laborers. Indeed, a comparison of late-nineteenth-century censuses reveals that the number of *peones acasillados* increased from 20,767 in 1880 to 80,216 in 1900.[37] Some sources place the number of *peones* as high as 120,000 to 125,000 by 1910.[38] The expansion of the large estate brought "an almost total dissolution of the primitive communal sector . . . and an almost complete concentration of property in the hands of a small group of planters."[39]

In fact, there are those who maintain that the advance of the large estate and the influence of henequen monoculture were so pervasive in Yucatán during the late nineteenth and early twentieth centuries as to discount the applicability of the traditional notion of a peasantry throughout the region.[40] For even after the plantation ceased its territorial expansion and became entrenched in the northwestern quadrant of the peninsula (about 1900), its influence extended well beyond this henequen zone (see Figure 2), drawing *comuneros* into the zone to work as day laborers or as a temporary labor force.[41] Even outside the henequen zone, the Yucatecan hacienda approached the archetype of the tropical southern Mexican hacienda during the Porfiriato: an extremely powerful, land-controlling institution that subordinated and pro-

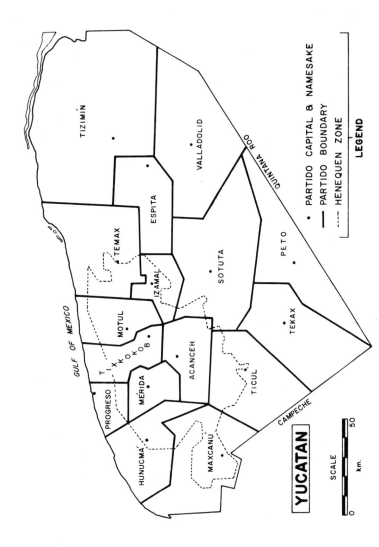

Figure 2. Yucatecan political divisions and the modern henequen zone. (Roland E. P. Chardon, *Geographic Aspects of Plantation Agriculture in Yucatán*, Washington, D.C., 1961, p. 11.)

letarianized the local Indian villages to a much greater extent than its central Mexican counterpart.[42]

Labor shortage would prove to be a chronic problem for the planters as they sought to meet the increased henequen demand after 1880. In large part, a scarcity of field hands was responsible for the henequen plantation's failure greatly to transcend the old colonial zone of haciendas in the northwest.[43] Expansion of the large estate was often motivated as much by a desire to control the Maya villagers' labor as it was to despoil them of their communal lands. Throughout the Porfiriato, *henequeneros* sought new sources of labor, importing a diverse mixture of thousands of Yaqui slaves, Mexican contract workers and political dissidents, and Korean, Puerto Rican, and small numbers of European immigrants. Even the influx of these new recruits was not enough. The inexorable market demand would force an intensification of plantation labor that, over the course of a generation, involuted the relations of production, transforming Yucatán into a de facto slave society.

The final obstacle to the transformation and expansion of the henequen estate was capital. It took about $130,000 to finance an average-size henequen plantation and maintain it for seven years until a return could be realized. However, there was a dearth of investment capital in the region following the Caste War, owing to the destruction of Yucatán's most profitable industry, sugar. Accordingly, prior to 1870, most planters preferred to shift piecemeal from old to new production techniques and crops, using existing *henequenales* to finance the capital investment of new fields.[44]

However, as the demand for fiber and twine began to expand geometrically in the 1870s, the pattern of gradual transition typical of the 1840s, 1850s, and 1860s was no longer a viable option. Increasingly, large estates were purchased expressly for immediate and exclusive henequen production. In addition to representatives of Yucatán's oldest landed families, who had skillfully adapted to the new export economy, a new type of proprietor arrived on the scene: the urban entrepreneur who had no previous experience as an *hacendado* and invested in a henequen plantation primarily to make a profit. Of course, although profitable fiber speculation was uppermost in the minds of these parvenu planters, it was not their sole motivation. Social position was also important; successful urban merchants purchased the choicest plantations to validate their arrival in regional society.[45]

Reacting to the sharp rise in North American demand, Yucatecan *henequeneros* took more active steps to overcome their capital shortage. Local banking institutions did not yet exist to service their needs, and private usurers commanded exorbitant rates of interest. In 1878, the state government lamented to the new Díaz administration in Mexico City: "We lack capital and there is no alternative but to borrow it at the usual rates of 18 to 24%."[46] Increasingly, the Yucatecan *henequeneros* found themselves financially dependent upon capital provided at 9 percent, first by bankers from the North American market area they were supplying and subsequently by cordage brokers and manufacturers from the same area. In return for giving these credits, the North Americans, working through local exporting houses, demanded to be paid back in fiber rather than cash, and at the market price prevailing at the moment of repayment. The *Yucatecos* would realize in the decades ahead how onerous this arrangement could be. Gradually, the North American creditors would come to control a majority of the region's henequen production.[47]

Furthermore, in order to satisfy North America's appetite for raw fiber, the Yucatecan henequen industry found itself compelled to adjust its basic orientation. Henequen fiber had formerly been used to a considerable extent in the local manufacture of ropes, cables, and other crafted articles; now the raw material would be channeled almost exclusively to North American cordage factories, which would manufacture it into binder twine. Local cordage industries found themselves no longer able to obtain fiber to keep up with their North American competitors and were forced to close down by the early 1880s.[48]

Thus, with more than a half-century's experience in the gradual development of methods of cultivation, processing, and marketing their native product, the *Yucatecos* found themselves uniquely able to supply the market on a scale previously unimagined. During the Porfiriato, the region would be thoroughly transformed by the requirements of North American mechanized agriculture and governed by its fluctuating rhythms. The production of Yucatán's incipient monocrop increased furiously, as exports rose from slightly less than 40,000 bales in 1875 to more than 600,000 bales at the close of the Porfirian era. (See Figure 3.)

By 1880, virtually no other crop could compete with henequen in land use, especially in the northwestern part of the state. The rapid growth of the fiber can best be appreciated statistically in its proportional increase in acreage vis-à-vis other crops. In 1845,

Year	Bales (in thousands)
1873	30
1874	35
1875	40
1876	na
1877	na
1878	na
1879	90
1880	113
1881	155
1882	151
1883	203
1884	261
1885	267
1886	243
1887	225
1888	218
1889	252
1890	280
1891	324
1892	364
1893	361
1894	374
1895	383
1896	397
1897	420
1898	419
1899	446
1900	500
1901	518
1902	528
1903	590
1904	606
1905	597
1906	600
1907	612
1908	652
1909	607
1910	619
1911	621
1912	775
1913	837
1914	965
1915	950

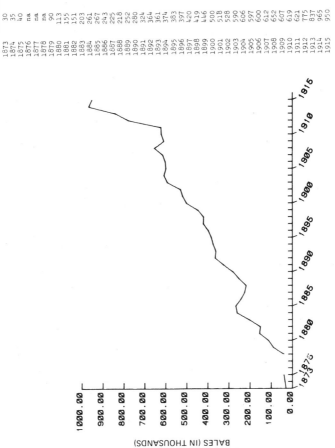

Figure 3. Henequen production, 1873–1915. One bale equals 157.5 kilograms; I have rounded off to the nearest thousand. (Figures derived from annual publications of the Cámara Agrícola de Yucatán.)

henequen and tobacco together covered 7,400 hectares, or 8.6 percent of the state's total cultivated acreage. In 1881, henequen alone claimed 46,000 hectares, 72.6 percent of the total. (By 1930, the figure would be close to 80 percent.)[49] Writing in 1881, regional historian Serapio Baqueiro observed: "All the state is for henequen, and outside of it there is nothing."[50] Baqueiro's observation was not meant to be rhetorical, for "outside" essentially meant the southeastern frontier, where, despite the constant threat of Indian raids, some food – the state's 27 percent acreage of corn, beans, and a little sugar – was still grown by the 18 percent remnant of the population that still lived there. Little wonder that Yucatán, once self-sufficient in maize, now was forced to import most of its corn, and that the cost of a hotel dinner in Mérida would now be worth ten to twenty days' salary for the average rural worker.[51] A decade later, in the 1890s, it was estimated that seven-eighths of the state's population was engaged in some aspect of cultivating, processing, or marketing henequen. Lured by the planters' promise of corn in the face of decades of famine and war, more and more *campesinos* abandoned their *milpas* in the southeast to live and work in the northwest. By the turn of the century, the southeast was little more than a colonial appendage of the dominant henequen zone. With the henequen interests refusing to divert investment capital to build infrastructure on the frontier, that region continued to lose its traditional markets to cheaper and more efficient foreign and central Mexican food suppliers, to exist only as a conduit of Indian labor to the burgeoning northwestern plantations.[52]

For those would-be entrepreneurs unable to deduce that "all the efforts of the inhabitants and government were devoted to supporting the cultivation of hemp, because it is the life of the state,"[53] there were a variety of object lessons calculated to show that few economic opportunities existed outside the henequen export sector. He who would buck the tide of henequen monoculture not only found loan capital and cheap labor denied to him but came up against a tax structure that was unfavorable to almost everyone except the large producer.[54] In short, although tangible signs of prosperity were not lacking, there was no denying that Yucatán's livelihood had become almost completely dependent upon a single export crop, tied to a fluctuating market over which *Yucatecos* had little control.

2

The henequen boom: oligarchy and informal empire, 1880–1915

Poor Mexico, so far from heaven and so near to the United States.

-Attributed to Porfirio Díaz (and others)

Of Yucatecan society at the end of the nineteenth century, Nelson Reed observed, tongue in cheek: "If a happy country is one without history, then Yucatán was happy." [1] And certainly, for the *gente decente* (the "decent people," as the region's planter elite was called) the last quarter of the century was comfortably uneventful. In unbroken and peaceful succession, Yucatán's most prominent planter–politicians followed one another to the governor's palace. One of their more arduous duties proved to be an annual recounting of the state's rapidly accumulating wealth. Over 73 million pesos' worth of fiber was exported from 1895 to 1900, over 22.5 million in the latter year alone. Yucatán, the politicans never tired of repeating, had become the richest state in Mexico. A generation before, in 1878, local officials had reported to the federal government: "There are no great riches in these parts; only three individuals possess more than 200,000 pesos." [2] Now, at the turn of the century, million-dollar fortunes were no longer exceptional, and new lavish stone mansions competed with one another for the attention of the passer-by strolling down Mérida's elegant Paseo de Montejo.

Nor were the *nouveaux riches* merely content to showcase their wealth within the peninsula. "The *gente decente* who had timidly gone to Havana in the 1850's could now elbow their way confidently past bowing waiters to the roulette tables of San Remo with the silver-Peruvians, the cattle-Argentines, and the steel-Americans." [3] French lessons became the rage in the best circles of local society and, once a year, a team of Parisian milliners and modistes visited Mérida to take orders from the city's grandest dames. At least once a year, *Yucatecos* made sure to polish their newly acquired linguistic skills and exhibit their sartorial splendor abroad, and local social columnists faithfully reported their European triumphs.[4]

The region's harsh climate and obvious physical limitations did little to blunt this growing tendency toward hyperconsumption. No matter that Yucatán had no lakes, rivers, or even a protected harbor, and no paved roads outside of Mérida; hundreds of automobiles, sailboats, and several luxury yachts had been sold in the state by 1910. Nor was there much concern that fine woods would warp and ivory discolor in the stifling climate; a run on Steinways and Baby Grands – all eminently replaceable – was on during the first decade of the new century. No sooner did heavy corsets make their appearance in the salons and boutiques of London and Paris than they were being worn, despite the sweltering heat, by the stylish matrons of Mérida, determined to appear wasp-waisted at any cost. And, so what if their emaciated livestock barely scrounged enough to eat and drink in the moister eastern parts of the peninsula? Yucatán's *hacendados* were determined to become cattle barons as well as planters. They imported specimens of the finest English blooded stock, only to watch them slowly waste away in the bone-dry northwest. One frustrated cattle breeder went so far as to invest over $100,000 in a sophisticated steam-driven sprinkler system needed to maintain two large paddocks of clover for his prize bulls.[5]

More significant as indicators of the planters' progress and more eloquent testimony to Yucatán's arrival at economic prominence were the improvements that had taken place in the region's communications and transportation network. Although the internal road system remained rudimentary, by 1890 Yucatán had the most extensive rail lines of any state in the Republic. Over 800 kilometers of standard-gauge track constituted Yucatán's main lines, and these were augmented by another 600 kilometers of privately owned, intermediate-gauge track that connected the major rail-heads with the planters' *desfibradoras*. These private railroads, in turn, were fed by over 1,000 additional kilometers of movable Decauville tram tracks that penetrated the individual *henequenales*. All in all, Yucatán's integrated rail system assured any shipper of fiber within 72 kilometers of Mérida of ready rail access to the wharves at the port of Progreso. Complementing this remarkable rail hookup was a systematic network of telegraph and telephone lines that, like the railways, connected Yucatán's henequen plantations with their principal market (Mérida) and port (Progreso).[6] What these infrastructure developments did *not* facilitate was a comprehensive system of internal communication among the various pueblos and haciendas. The pueblos of rural Yucatán remained isolated from the economic centers and from each other. As we shall see, this internal isolation would have important negative consequences for revolutionary mobilization within the region during the 1910s and early 1920s.[7]

However, no better advertisements existed for the Yucatecan elite's brand of "Order and Progress," paid for with the receipts from its "green gold," than the transformed physical presence of its capital city and major port. British writers Channing Arnold and Frederick Frost, although bitingly critical of the parvenu mentality that pervaded Yucatecan high society during the late Porfiriato and the social injustice on which it sustained itself, were deeply impressed with the physical appearance of Mérida. Though given to didactic moralizing, these liberal Englishmen recorded keen travelers' observations of the "White City," which to them was

magically perfect; as unlike any other Spanish-American town as is possible . . . Mérida is in no sense a noble city . . . But she is what perhaps is better – a clean city. Cleanliness is next to godliness. Yet [*Meridanos*] think it comes first . . . The millionaire henequen growers are so rich that they really do not know what to do with their money; and so it came about that the ex-Governor Señor Molina conceived the idea of re-upholstering Mérida till its founders would never recognize their handiwork . . . It took between two and three years [actually four years: 1902–1906] and the result is perfection. From north to south, from east to west, side streets and main streets, for the full three miles' width of the city, the surface is as smooth as glass, as clean as marble.

. . . As we moved easily and without a vibration down street after street of well-matched and well-built houses, we rubbed our eyes and wondered whether we were in a land where it was always washing day, for the people in the passing carriages, the police at the corners in their trim holland uniforms . . . the tradesmen at their shop doors . . . were so spotless as to begger all description . . . The brightness of the city had such a lulling effect that we were almost persuaded that we had reached Utopia.[8]

If Mérida had blossomed, its streets scientifically numbered, paved with macadam, illuminated at night with electric lamps and traversed by day with modern streetcars, the port of Progreso had flourished comparably. It had been founded at the onset of the henequen boom (1870) to replace the insalubrious, more distant, and shallower port of Sisal. Originally a swamp, Progreso had survived a mosquito-infested, disease-ridden infancy to become thoroughly modernized and redecorated by a newer, more affluent generation. By the turn of the century, the port had begun to fulfill the optimistic promise of its name. The incidence of yellow fever and malaria had subsided to the point where the best *Meridanos* were building luxurious resort homes along the port's beach wall, and the U.S. consulate had transferred its offices from Mérida to Progreso to be closer to the pulse of daily commercial transactions. Meanwhile, huge henequen warehouses had been constructed on or near several recently completed wharves, a new custom house had gone up, and a variety of commission, brokerage, and trading houses had either moved their entire operations to the port or opened branch offices there. By 1900, among Mexico's ports, only Veracruz shipped and received a greater volume of goods.[9]

All of these material transformations, and the Yucatecan elite that carried them out, owed their existence to henequen. And by the turn of the century, the henequen plantation and the henequen zone had more or less assumed their final form (see Figure 2), the condition in which General Alvarado would find them upon his arrival in 1915. By Mexican and Latin American standards, the Yucatecan henequen estate (often referred to as an "hacienda," though it was more properly a plantation) was small. Although a few prerevolutionary plantations extended over 5,000 hectares, the vast majority of the large haciendas in Yucatán were approximately 2,000 to 3,000 hectares in size, and the majority of estates were between 1,000 and 2,000 hectares. Even the greatest of Yucatán's plantations, Augusto L. Peón's Yaxche (6,000 hectares), was a veritable *pequeña propiedad* (small property) when compared to the latifundia of Mexico's north and was considerably smaller than many of the haciendas of the near north, the Bajío, and even those of the central plateau.[10] Luis Terrazas's Chihuahuan properties, for example, totaled well over 2.5 million hectares. The extended Terrazas clan controlled almost 5 million hectares, whereas Yucatán's largest landowning family, the Molina–Montes clan, could not have controlled more than one hundred thousand hectares of henequen and *monte* (woodland) combined.[11]

However, although these henequen estates may have been small by national standards, they were remarkably lucrative. The estimated average return per investment during the decade 1900–1910 was no less than 50 percent and rose as high as 400 to 600 percent.[12] Indeed, one conservative estimate holds that, during the entire 1880–1915 period, only four years elapsed (1893–1897) during which the Yucatecan planters did not realize *at least* an 18 percent annual profit and maintains that, during most of those years, the rate of profit was many times that figure.[13] Even when prices fell rapidly, during the recession of 1893–1894 and the panic of 1907–1908, many planters still realized profits.[14]

Elite and oligarchy during the *Olegariato*

One of the most striking aspects of the henequen plantation's evolution and the consolidation of the regional fiber industry during the 1880–1915 period is the progressive concentration of land, productive capacity, and political power in the hands of fewer and fewer families. By the time of Alvarado's arrival, as Yucatecan henequen production approached its highest annual yield, there were slightly more than 1,000 haciendas devoted exclusively to henequen cultivation, of which about 850 had *desfibradoras* and packing plants. Yet regional historians estimate that in 1915, these agro-industrial units were distributed among no more than 300 to 400 families, the majority of whom were also interested in urban commerce and real estate and what little small industry the region had managed to generate, given the tight grip of monoculture.[15] Yucatán's comfortable agro-commercial bourgeoisie was itself dominated by a much smaller, more cohesive group of twenty to thirty families, who at any given time produced about 50 percent and ultimately controlled close to 80 to 90 percent of all the fiber cultivated in the state. This group, a bona fide regional oligarchy, would be referred to sardonically by Alvarado as the *Casta Divina*, a name the oligarchy would proudly appropriate for itself.[16] This caste constituted a ruling group with homogeneous interests, a relatively closed membership, and such absolute control over the economic and political levers of power in the region that it was able to block the opportunities of other groups in Yucatecan society during the Porfiriato.

Within the ruling oligarchy itself, power was generated outward from one powerful political family, or *parentesco*, led by Yucatán's "great modernizer," Governor Olegario Molina (1902–1906), and his son-in-law, Avelino Montes.[17] In a society almost totally dependent upon henequen – by 1915, almost 98 percent of Yucatán's economic production was tied up in the export of raw fiber – Molina's oligarchy had risen to power by virtue of its control of the henequen industry. However, rather than concentrating on fiber production, Molina had focused his attention on building a base of political power and extending his control over the infrastructure of the region's export sector. Neither he nor any other Molinas made substantial investments in henequen before the 1890s, though his financial prospects constantly brightened. Moreover, unlike many of his landed peers in Yucatán – but very much like the modernizing oligarchs (*científicos*) who surrounded President Díaz in Mexico City – Molina quickly grasped the importance of science and technology for his own ambitions as well as for the future economic development of the region and nation.

Molina entered regional politics in his early twenties, simultaneously establishing a reputation as a liberal intellectual, educator, engineer, and builder. In the early 1880s, still one of only a handful of engineers in the peninsula, Molina placed his technological skills at the service of the fledgling Mérida–Progreso railway company. Under his guidance, the export economy took a great step forward, consolidating an adequate transport network that linked its major commercial center and principal port, thereby facilitating a dramatic reduction in shipping costs to distant markets. In 1886, Molina cashed in on the connections and goodwill he had been building in public life by organizing a small company and receiving a succession of government contracts to construct roads, extend Yucatán's railroad system, make improvements in the port, and carry out a variety of other public works with an ever-increasing torrent of henequen income. Ultimately, in 1902 as governor, Don Olegario would commission the same O. Molina y Cía. to pave and drain the streets of Mérida in collaboration with a French firm. Among the list of original investors in Molina's modest company, and in the construction and railroad enterprises that grew out of it, one finds representatives of several of the families related to or closely associated with the Molinas, families that would later be recognized as members of the *Casta Divina*: Regil, Ancona, Cervera, Peón, Evia, Hübbe, Suárez, Rendón, Solís, and Vales.

The other major figure in the Molina *parentesco* was Avelino Montes. A skillful merchant who had come to Yucatán from Spain shortly before the turn of the century, he had married Molina's daughter and subsequently was tapped by Molina as heir to his commercial empire. As the cases of Montes and two other of Molina's sons-in-law, Spaniard Rogelio Suárez and Cuban Luis Carranza, illustrate, Don Olegario successfully used marriage as one means of coopting talented members of the larger elite into his extended family network, which by 1900 had already become acknowledged as the epicenter of Yucatán's ruling oligarchy.

By the late 1890s Molina and Montes were investing heavily in their own henequen plantations, lending money at usurious rates of interest to lesser planters, consolidating their control over an expanded railroad network, and establishing their own Yucatecan import–export house and shipping firm to send fiber directly to the North American buyers. "Unlike the other 99 percent of Yucatecan planters who merely grew henequen and were ignorant of the problems of foreign trade and finance," [18] Molina and Montes realized that more valuable than the henequen itself were the means to market and move the fiber. During the 1890s and 1900s, Montes and Molina not only came to control an increasingly greater share of the local production through liens on the fiber of other *hacendados* indebted to them but also consolidated their control over the means of transporting fiber by land and sea. [19] The partnership was a fortuitous one: Molina's skill as an engineer and infrastructural planner and his political connections, which brought him the governorship in 1902, were well complemented by Montes's entrepreneurial talents and capacity for hard work. By the end of the Porfiriato, Olegario Molina was not only the largest landowner in the state but also its greatest producer of henequen. [20]

By 1910, Don Olegario had done well not only for himself but for most of the members of his extended family as well, who served as Yucatán's district prefects (*jefes políticos*: e.g., Luis Demetrio Molina), received concessions of government monopolies (Rogelio Suárez), headed the railroads and commercial and shipping houses controlled by Molina (Montes, José Trinidad Molina), and fronted for foreign interests in Yucatán and elsewhere in Mexico (Montes). British correspondent Henry Baerlein was impressed enough to write: "A man who has not only made himself, but all his family, down to the nephews, and the sons-in-law of cousins, is a stranger to fatigue." [21]

Meanwhile, however, the Molina *parentesco* had advanced at the expense of the rest of Yucatecan society, including the several hundred other members of the peninsular bourgeoisie. These lesser *hacendados* were powerful rulers of land and men in their own right. Many owned hundreds of parcels of urban real estate in addition to their *fincas* (agricultural holdings), where they kept staffs of Indian servants dressed in white livery. Yet the future prospects of most Yucatecan planters remained fragile. Although given to prodigious displays of consumption, the Yucatecan *henequenero* was hardly representative of a traditional landed gentry. In most cases, he was an entrepreneur who continually sought ways to master the problematical fluctuations of the export economy. Seeking to maximize his profit, he not only speculated in fiber and rural property but invested in urban real estate and commerce, as well as joint-stock shares of regional banks and industry. To survive the inevitable dislocations of a boom–bust economy and ultimately to strike it very rich, the speculating planter needed good business skills, a shrewd sense of timing and, perhaps most importantly, strong family ties to help him avoid (or bail him out of) bankruptcy when he overextended himself. For every successful individual who exercised some measure of economic control over his own destiny, many more fell by the wayside, existing in a perpetual state of indebtedness, fiscal instability, and periodic bankruptcy. Thus an essential paradox characterized the fortunes of all but a small minority of Yucatán's landed bourgeoisie: Although these planters constituted one of the wealthiest classes in Porfirian Mexico, in many respects their economic condition was one of the most unstable and least secure.

Over this plantocracy, proud of its wealth and privileges, Don Olegario was acknowledged as *capitán y amo* – lord and master. Each Saturday, these *henequeneros*, the majority of them in debt to Molina and forced to pay in fiber, were humiliated when they brought their henequen to his company and were compelled to accept his price, often one-fourth to one-half cent lower than the going market price. Typically, they were greeted by Montes, who told them: "Sorry, boys. We've already got more henequen than we can use. But if you want to sell now, we might be able to use the fiber for our next shipment, provided you're willing to come down a little. That's the best price we can give you."[22] Desperate for money to pay off accumulating debts and unable to ship their fiber without the agency of the Molina family, the *hacendados* were forced to sell on the spot.

However, neither Molina's impeccable regional political connections nor his or Montes's refined business acumen could have earned for him the almost absolute political and economic power that he came to wield at the regional level. Nor do they explain the great national recognition and prestige that President Díaz lavished upon Molina and his allies.[23] To account for this concentration of regional power and wealth, rare even by the standards of Porfirian Mexico,[24] we must look elsewhere – to Don Olegario's North American connection, the long-standing relationship between Yucatán's oligarchy and the North American cordage manufacturers that ultimately facilitated indirect foreign control of the Yucatecan economy.

Collaboration and informal imperialism

Even today some *Yucatecos* are reluctant to admit the extent to which North American corporations controlled Yucatán's economic development in the late Porfiriato. It is a venerable regional myth that, unlike the rest of Mexico, where foreigners increasingly dominated most lines of economic activity during the Porfiriato, *Yucatecos* maintained their economic autonomy and were solely responsible for the remarkable growth that the region enjoyed during the 1880–1915 period. This myth, articulated here in its most extreme form by regional historian Manuel Irabién with regard to the growth of Yucatán's railroads, has been uniformly applied by both Mexican and foreign writers to the evolution of the henequen industry as well:

> If there is one thing on which we can pride ourselves, it is that all the work here was done by the sons of Yucatán and all the glory must go to our beloved country, rather than to foreign enterpreneurs. *Yucatecos* were the capitalists, *Yucatecos* were the concessionaires, the engineers, and the laborers. Glory to Yucatán![25]

In part, the regionalists are correct: The henequen estate differed from the classical pattern of late-nineteenth-century plantation agriculture in several important respects. Land tenure and ownership of the means of production were almost exclusively in Yucatecan hands. There was no major influx of technology from abroad; indeed, during the first half of the nineteenth century, Europeans and North Americans had failed miserably in inventing the machinery required to make henequen processing economical on a commercial scale. Nor was management imported from abroad; it, too, was almost completely Yucatecan. And finally, although capital was ultimately imported from the United States, it was made available and distributed, as far as the producers were concerned, on a local basis. A leading student of the henequen plantation has concluded: "The situation in Yucatán was virtually unique in the annals of plantation agriculture, in that the area had, by its own efforts, provided the necessary economic base to produce an adequate, reliable supply of its own product and fulfill a near-inexhaustible demand."[26] Yucatán was the only area of Mexican plantation agriculture that had given rise to commercial export production prior to the development of monopolistic concentration, that is, prior to the ascendancy of the great North American trusts.[27]

However, foreign penetration involves more than mere ownership of the means of production. How significant is a distinction between actual ownership and indirect control? Let us evaluate the extent of foreign domination of the Yucatecan economy by examining the mechanism of control that U.S. interests employed in collaboration with selected agents recruited from the most powerful members of the regional oligarchy.

As early as the 1890s, Cyrus McCormick's Harvesting Machine Company, which in 1902 would merge with several rivals to form the International Harvester Company, had already realized a crucial fact: There was no need to make the large capital investments needed to establish and sustain henequen plantations or to suffer the potential political insecurity attending the ownership of foreign property, provided the same benefits could be obtained through tight control of the marketing of henequen fiber. Market control, in turn, would be achieved by maintaining the existing dependence of Yucatecan planters upon foreign sources of capital. Such financial dependence, it has been suggested, grew in quantum leaps in relation to the expanding demand for Yucatecan fiber.

A collaborative bargain between foreign business interests and local exporting houses (*casas exportadoras*) had to be carefully negotiated to assure a dependable supply of fiber. Foreign interests recognized that it would not do to name a North American representative to operate in a proud, chauvinistic region like Yucatán. Rather, they would attempt to disguise their involvement by employing one or more local agents, each of whom would publicly project an independent image. From the 1870s on, local business leaders had served as fiber purchasing agents and conduits for foreign loan capital, the real purpose of which had been to control local fiber production by imposing liens on future production in payment of existing debts. The propensity of many planters to channel their earnings into a wide variety of speculative investments or into conspicuous consumption only promoted further indebtedness.[28]

Thus, North American brokers and manufacturers, such as Thebaud Brothers and the National Cordage Company, operating during the first decades of the boom, enlisted the services of the large Yucatecan export houses of Eusebio Escalante, Manuel Dondé, and Arturo Pierce, among others, in their bids to corner the local market. For their own part, these "collaborators," in serving as purchasing agents and financial intermediaries for the North American banks and manufacturers, realized sizable profits, usually in the form of commissions and kickbacks but also from the usury that access to foreign capital enabled them to practice. Ideally, just as the foreign investor sought to carve out a durable monopoly or corner on the trade, so the collaborator wished to enjoy exclusively the benefits that would flow from a monopoly over communication with the foreign interests controlling the market.[29]

However, the North Americans were "well aware that to have no options was to have no future, and that options were eliminated in direct proportion to the degree to which they depended upon a single [collaborator]."[30] From the first of its dealings with Yucatán in 1875, for example, the McCormick Harvesting Machine Company had been careful to identify and recruit a primary collaborator and then to maintain its influence over this incumbent while cultivating potential collaborators as well. Thus, during the late nineteenth century, bargains had been struck at one time or another with a variety of *casas exportadoras*, and although McCormick and the other North American concerns might work to help one *casa* gain a temporary advantage over its rivals, they always made sure to have at least one reliable substitute waiting in the wings.[31] Consequently, prior to 1902, a truly exclusive and powerful collaborative mechanism had never characterized the Yucatecan henequen industry. North American cordage manufacturers had experienced only intermittent success in controlling the hard fiber market, which had fluctuated wildly throughout the quarter-century following the introduction of the McCormick reaper-binder. (See Table 3.)

With the 1902 merger creating the International Harvester Company, the collaborative equation and, consequently, the balance of power within the regional industry were transformed dramatically. The very establishment of the new "International," a

Table 3. *U.S. market prices for Yucatecan henequen, 1875–1914 (quotations in cents per kilogram, U.S. currency)*

Year	Average price	General market trends
1875	12.10	Market dominated by Thebaud Brothers, New York bankers
1876	8.80	
1879	4.84	
1880	4.88	
1881	5.39	
1882	5.68	
1883	5.41	
1884	4.11	
1885	3.87	
1886	5.02	Free market restored
1887	8.10	
1888	9.44	
1889	12.58	
1890	5.79	Manipulations of the National Cordage Company; worldwide economic recession and depression
1891	6.16	
1892	7.15	
1893	7.26	
1894	5.54	
1895	4.95	
1896	5.52	
1897	5.81	
1898	13.71	Spanish-American War: boom
1899	13.55	
1900	13.93	
1901	13.66	
1902	21.65	
1903	17.86	Molina–Harvester "secret contract" and collaboration
1904	16.43	
1905	15.31	
1906	13.97	
1907	12.32	
1908	9.53	
1909	10.54	
1910	9.35	
1911	8.16	
1912	10.41	First *Reguladora* (valorization scheme with minimal state participation)
1913	13.97	
1914	16.15	

Source: Siegfried Askinasy, *El problema agrario de Yucatán*, Mexico, 1936, pp. 100–101.

combination of five of the largest harvesting machine companies – McCormick, Deering, Plano, Wardner, Bushnell and Glessner Company, and Milwaukee Harvester – with an initial capitalization of $120 million, eliminated the bulk of existing competition within the farm implements and twine industries and placed at the manufacturers' disposal organizational and financial resources that hitherto had not existed. In the years that followed, Harvester would more closely approximate a genuine trust than any other fiber manufacturing concern before or after the merger. For their part, Harvester's chosen agents in Mérida, Olegario Molina y Compañía, even prior to their collaboration with Harvester, represented an economic and political force in regional affairs substantially more powerful than any of their nineteenth-century predecessors. Together, and before the first decade of their partnership was over, these parties – most notably the North Americans – had gained such complete control over Yucatán's political economy that it is no exaggeration to regard the 1902–1915 years as a period during which Harvester established an informal empire in Yucatán.

Even the most cautious definitions of imperialism, which do not view it as a fundamental stage in the expansion of capitalism but rather demand proof of "conscious" or "deliberate" political or economic control of the local society, would concur in viewing Harvester's control of the Yucatecan henequen industry between 1902 and 1915 as a clear-cut instance of "informal imperialism." Indeed, it is precisely in situations in which monopolistic control of a commodity by a single market or even a single firm exists that the worst abuses of late-nineteenth- and early-twentieth-century economic imperialism become evident.[32] Thus, Harvester's informal empire in Yucatán (the "Sisal Hemp trust") takes its place alongside those of the American Sugar Refining Company in Cuba and the Dominican Republic (the "Sugar trust") and the United Fruit Company in the Caribbean (the "Banana trust"). Of course, Harvester's henequen trust differed from both its sugar and banana counterparts, for it achieved control over production without actual ownership of the land. Moreover, henequen was one of the few products – bananas were another – that remained in the hands of a single distributor or market over a long period of time. In this respect, the majority of Yucatecan *henequeneros* actually bore little resemblance to the sugar and coffee planters of Brazil, the cattlemen of Argentina, and the major nitrate producers of Chile. These, by virtue of their strong political and economic positions within their own societies and the fact that over the long term their products reached beyond a single distributor or market, were from time to time able to hold sway over their buyers. In contrast, in terms of a lack of bargaining power (if not of wealth), the *henequenero* often more closely resembled smaller international commodities producers – for example, Cuban and Colombian tobacco growers, Belizean and Honduran mahogany cutters and *chicleros*, Brazilian rubber tappers, Paraguayan *yerba mate* growers, and Argentine wheat colonists – who invariably found themselves tied to foreign merchants or their agents by traditional credit facilities. Such small producers became dependent on negotiating further credit and were rendered virtually powerless in determining a fair price for their products.[33]

Nevertheless, in its struggle to preserve its economic autonomy and gain a good price for its henequen, Yucatán possessed certain advantages that most other contemporary primary producing regions lacked. Unlike most late-nineteenth-century single crop exporters, Yucatán enjoyed a virtual monopoly on the production of its commodity for the principal market it supplied, the United States. This made it extremely difficult and costly, at least prior to 1915, for the North American buyers to play off one producing region against the other, as happened elsewhere. Second, Yucatán's sole product was not a luxury item but a primary necessity for the United States. It was consumed regularly in large amounts with each grain harvest. Finally, as we have seen, not only were the actual producers of the fiber almost exclusively natives of Yucatán, but the region was part of an independent nation and not a formal colony of the buyer.[34]

Yet, in spite of these natural advantages, *Yucatecos* would lose effective control over their only industry before the end of the first decade of the new century. Let us examine how these advantages were offset and focus more specifically on the manner in which Harvester consolidated its control over the Yucatecan economy.

Toward monopoly control

Three-quarters of a century after the events, historians finally have at their disposal evidence of the two agreements that were the practical foundations for the consolidation of Harvester's informal empire in Yucatán. Each of the agreements records a business transaction concluded in 1902: The first represents a contract between Harvester and Olegario Molina; the second is an agreement between Harvester President Cyrus McCormick and Henry W. Peabody, president of the exporting firm of the same name, which had traditionally purchased fiber for Harvester's closest rival in the manufacturing of twine, the Plymouth Cordage Company.[35] First, let us examine the nature and consequences of the Harvester pact with Don Olegario.

Now referred to in the peninsula as the "notorious secret contract of 1902," the pact was signed in Havana, Cuba, on 27 October but was not widely publicized until 1921.[36] It specified that Molina y Compañía would use "every effort within their power to depress the price of sisal fiber" and would "pay only those prices which from time to time are dictated by the International Harvester Company." More concretely, Harvester agreed to place 10,000 bales of sisal, which they would buy from Molina, "or as much of it as may be needed at the disposal of Molina and Company for sale . . . for the express purpose of depressing prices, any loss or gain on such sales being for account of the International Harvester Company." As for the other principals operating in the henequen market, it would be left to Molina to determine how he would induce the exporting firm of Don Eusebio Escalante, his traditional rival, to cooperate with the arrangement. Harvester, for its part, would see to it that the other trading firms of Peabody and Urcelay "shall not pay higher prices for sisal than those given by Molina and Company."

Over the next decade, the arrangement worked according to plan. Within the first year, the price fell 4.4 cents, from close to 22 cents per kilogram to 17.6 cents. (See Table 3 and Figure 4.) In the years that followed, the collaborators managed to shave a little more than 2 cents a year until, by 1911, raw fiber was being bought at 6.6 cents per kilogram, beyond which it was generally agreed that all *hacendados* would be operating in the red and the smaller ones would be pushed to the wall.[37]

It is tempting, in the face of this contract, to follow the majority of traditional accounts and dismiss Don Olegario as an *entreguista*, a bought politician who, in the ancient tradition of La Malinche, turned his back upon his native land for the economic advantage of siding with the foreigner. Nelson Reed, after recounting Molina's arrangement with Harvester and cataloguing its harmful effects on the henequen industry in terms of lost export earnings, suggests that it is a mystery "why the *Meridanos* didn't lynch the man."[38] Yet the very fact that *Yucatecos* did not share Reed's indignation – indeed, upon Molina's death in 1925, he was

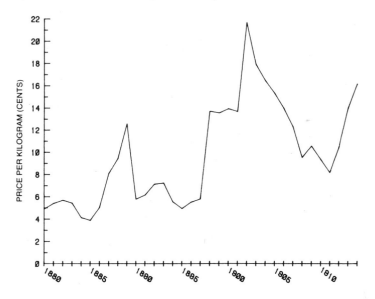

Figure 4. Henequen prices, 1880–1914. (Askinasy, *El problema agrario*, pp. 100–101.)

buried as a hero by the Revolutionary government – hints at the complexity of Molina's role as a collaborator and of his relationship with Harvester. Few collaborators ever choose to cooperate unconditionally; in fact, to do so would endanger their credibility and standing within their own society. More often than not, they seek selectively to channel the privileges of increased trade or technology that the foreign power offers as the price for their cooperation, in order to develop their own societies according to the prevailing notion of progress and to shore up their own positions within them. In many cases, they are or become staunch nationalists (or regionalists), attempting to use the material benefits that the foreigner confers to strengthen their societies against the same foreigner. Unfortunately, too often this latter resolve represents more a reaction than a preemptive move and comes too late, after the local society has been fully penetrated by the foreign power.[39]

In many respects, Don Olegario's career reflects the essential contradictions of the collaborator. First and foremost, he seems to have regarded himself as a builder and modernizer, and it is more for his schools and paved streets than for his secret contract that modern *Yucatecos* remember him. The embodiment of nineteenth-century liberal positivism, Yucatán's own *científico*, Don Olegario saw nothing wrong with making money; indeed, he reasoned that to the extent that he prospered, so would Yucatán. And there can be no question that he intended to profit from his relationship with Harvester. Harvester's own documents reveal that under the terms of the 1902 and subsequent contracts, he and Montes earned a commission of between 0.275 and 0.55 cent (US)[40] on every kilogram of henequen they acquired for Harvester during the decade preceding the Revolution, not to mention the enormous control that the foreign capital placed at their disposal gave them over the local elite.[41] In 1909, Harvester gave Montes a line of credit up to $600,000 for the purpose of controlling fiber production. This enabled the Molina family to acquire mortgages and foreclose on a number of indebted haciendas and to purchase outright a string of others. It also enabled them to consolidate their hold on the region's banks, railroads, warehouses, and shipping lines; initiate new and profitable public works projects; and diversify their interests in new lines of urban commerce and industry. In other words, backed by a continuous supply of foreign capital, Molina and Montes were able to invest even when the economy was depressed and prices were low, precisely when most planters and merchants faced capital shortages. This strategic position enabled them to buy when most investors were compelled to sell out their interests at rock-bottom prices merely to escape financial ruin (e.g., during the panic of 1907–1908). Then, when fiber prices rose and local property values increased, the Molinas had the option of selling their newly acquired assets for a whopping profit or adding them to their expanding empire.[42]

However, in Olegario's mind, this personal enrichment and the relationship with Harvester that underwrote it dovetailed nicely with Yucatán's long-term development. He subscribed to the theory – not without an element of self-justification – that over the long run, a policy of high prices would hurt Yucatán's fiber industry. Only production in volume at a figure low enough to prevent serious foreign competition while simultaneously increasing the market would guarantee Yucatán's future prosperity. This being the case, why not contract with Harvester over the short run to depress fiber prices gradually? The Yucatecan *científico* calculated that such a tactic would provide a needed object lesson to the *hacendados* and would ultimately be for their own good, inculcating in them the habits of thrift and hard work and steering them toward the adoption of new methods to promote increased efficiency and quality control. Molina's apologists suggest that the target figure of Don Olegario's *política bajista* (low pricing policy) was 8.8 to 9.9 cents per kilogram. This was a quotation at which, in the absence of stiff state and federal taxation – which he generally opposed and, as governor, would prevail upon President Díaz to forego – Yucatán's *henequeneros* might produce henequen profitably and forestall the competitive threat of the Philippines and of potential producing regions in the new European colonial possessions of Africa and Asia.[43] Molina's policy was embodied in the phrase: "Producir mucho para poder vender barato" ("Produce more to be able to sell more cheaply"). Should a financially pressed *hacendado* come to him with his problems, Don Olegario invariably counseled the man, "¡Siembre Ud. más henequén!" ("Sow more henequen!").[44]

At the root of Molina's *política bajista*, indeed the basis for his collaboration with Harvester, was his abiding belief in the late-nineteenth-century economic order, predicated upon an international economic division of labor between primary producing regions and the more industrialized nations of Europe and North America.[45] However, Molina's ambiguous dual role of Yucatecan producer and North American buying agent led him periodically to question such a division of labor and pointed up some of the conflicts that inevitably characterize relations between primary producing and manufacturing regions, conflicts that would not find satisfactory resolution in Don Olegario's economic policies.

In 1896–1897, when prices dropped to the point at which fiber export was ceasing to remain profitable, Molina and several other "progressive" Yucatecan *henequeneros* did not hesitate to recruit local and large amounts of foreign (predominantly McCormick) capital, plus the most up-to-date North American machinery, and become involved in the establishment of La Industrial. This factory was to specialize in the manufacture of binder twine and other products from raw fiber, thereby enabling Yucatán to reap the value traditionally added by the North American cordage manufacturers.[46] Initially, Don Olegario had little trouble attracting the planters' capital for the project. Molina and twenty-four Yucatecan entrepreneurs raised 400,000 pesos for the cordage plant early in 1897.[47] A year later, however, when the Spanish-American War caused the demand for raw fiber to skyrocket, additional monies were hard to find and Molina's own interest in the industrialization of henequen began to wane.[48] First, he diverted La Industrial from the manufacture of binder twine into other noncompetitive, experimental manufacturing applications (e.g., the extraction of henequen alcohol, the manufacture of paper) and ultimately, following the signing of his 1902 contract with Harvester, he divested himself of all interests in the manufacture of henequen.[49] Perhaps the most significant aspect of the failed industrialization scheme was that it served to secure a firm working relationship between the Olegario Molina family and Cyrus McCormick. The collaborative mechanism that would alter the political economy of Yucatán with the 1902 contract had been set in 1896.

In evaluating the secret contract and the monopolization of the local industry that ensued, it is important to emphasize the initial interdependence that characterized the relationship between Harvester and Molina. The Yucatecan situation underscores the point that "where informal empires arose, the relationship between the two [collaborating] elements was initially one stemming from conditions of relative equality."[50] As the intermediary or linking group in the local society, the Molinas and their allies (the *Casta Divina*) made sure to interweave their needs and political and economic capabilities with those of Harvester until "a type of equilibrium between those needs was achieved."[51] However, we must be careful not to overvalue the importance of the Yucatecan oligarchs in these imperial relations or the power they were subsequently able to bring to bear against Harvester. The trade statistics of the period suggest a more accurate picture of the power relationship that existed between Molina and Montes and Harvester. (See Figure 5.)

Clearly, it was not until Molina y Compañía (the firm was later entrusted to Montes in 1905)[52] consummated its relationship with Harvester in 1902 that it dramatically pulled away from the Pierce house, its closest competitor in the Mérida buying market. Immediately prior to Molina's commitment to work exclusively for Harvester, the firm had done only half as much business as its rival and prior to that, with the exception of 1896, had consistently trailed Pierce in fiber transactions. Of course, we know that 1902 was also the year in which Molina became governor of Yucatán and that his political clout – and with it, his economic power – were becoming increasingly great. However, Molina had been a powerful force in regional politics for some time prior to

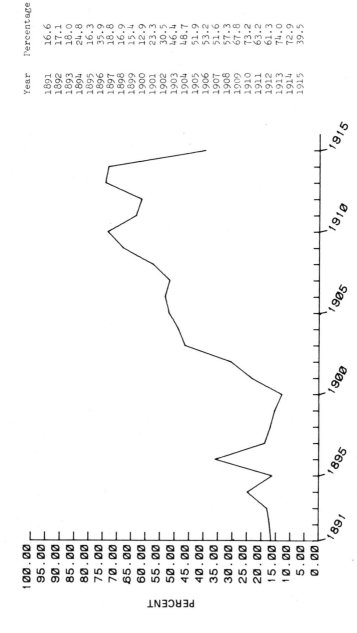

Year	Percentage
1891	16.6
1892	17.1
1893	18.0
1894	24.8
1895	16.3
1896	35.9
1897	18.8
1898	16.9
1899	15.4
1900	12.9
1901	23.3
1902	30.5
1903	46.4
1904	48.7
1905	51.9
1906	53.2
1907	51.6
1908	57.3
1909	67.8
1910	73.2
1911	63.2
1912	61.3
1913	74.0
1914	72.9
1915	39.5

Figure 5. Molina y Compañía's share of the U.S. henequen trade, 1891–1915. (Peabody Papers, vol. L-I, pp. 254–274, and U.S. Congress, Senate, Committee on Agriculture and Forestry, *Importation of Sisal and Manila Hemp*, Washington, D.C., 1916, vol. 2, p. 963.)

1902, and it seems more likely that the huge sums of money placed at Molina's disposal by Harverster had more to do with his meteoric rise after 1902 than the acquisition of the governorship.

More compelling proof of Harvester's position of hegemony over the regional economy and Molina's *Casta* lies in the circumstances surrounding Molina's decision, around 1912–1913, to terminate his collaboration with Harvester. Don Olegario had become increasingly troubled over the extent to which Harvester had succeeded in depressing the market. When he officially turned over the reins of his export firm to Montes in 1905, the price of fiber had been close to 15.4 cents per kilogram; yet, by 1911, it had plummeted to 6.6 cents, less than the 9.9- to 8.8-cent figure that Molina had postulated as healthy for the industry. Early in 1913, Molina was speaking openly about Harvester's harmful monopoly and supporting cooperative efforts by the planters to break the grip of the trust. Then, when Huerta overthrew Madero in February and Carranza inaugurated the Constitutionalist Revolution in March 1913, Molina began to act in support of the First Chief. It seems likely that he now regarded the *Carrancistas*, with their pronounced nationalist ideology, as a means of ridding Yucatán of the informal empire that Harverster had formerly consolidated with his help.[53] In retrospect, Molina "may have been the first and only Porfirian . . . *científico* to have supported a revolutionary faction in the Mexican Revolution."[54] Several of Molina's relatives and close associates – most notably the Rendóns and the Vales – would play important roles in the management of Alvarado's state-regulated economy.[55]

Harvester (and the group of eighteen to twenty smaller North American twine manufacturers that were its economic satellites) were not especially troubled by Molina's defection in the early 1910s; nor were they at a loss to find a replacement. The logical stand-in was Avelino Montes. Montes ostensibly met all of the requirements of a successful collaborator. Years before, he had inherited from Molina near-monopoly control of the region's railroads, shipping lines, and warehouses. In addition, he controlled with other members of the *Casta*, through an intricate network of loans and mortgages, the majority of the fiber produced on Yucatecan henequen plantations.[56] Most importantly, Montes did not share his father-in-law's worries about Harvester domination. Unlike Don Olegario, Montes would continue to support Huerta and, buoyed up by personal profits, to remain comfortable in his role as Harvester's most powerful collaborator. It would be Montes and not Molina who would become the *cabeza de turco*, the hated symbol of the Porfirian "Age of Slavery" for Alvarado's regime.[57] However, as late as 1912–1913, Montes still maintained the kind of credibility within the *hacendado* class and local society that Harvester viewed as an essential prerequisite for striking any collaborative bargain.

Significantly, although Molina and Montes increasingly came to differ on economic strategy and goals, they do not appear to have severed business or personal relations during the 1912–1914 period.[58] However, during these years, Molina, realizing that his room to maneuver economically was limited once he broke with Harvester, began to acquire land and make a series of commercial investments in Cuba, where he would live the final years of his life following the Revolution in 1915.[59] Don Olegario would return to Yucatán for the last time in 1925 – borne in state following his death in Havana. It must be considered one of the ironies of Mexican Revolutionary history that the man who had been most responsible for the consolidation of the worst aspects of the Old Regime, against which the Revolution committed itself in Yucatán, should be brought home by a revolutionary government and accorded a hero's welcome.[60]

Also of importance to Harvester in the creation of its invisible empire in Yucatán was the other agreement referred to above, and also consummated in 1902, between Harvester and Henry W. Peabody.[61] In fact, it is no coincidence that this personal agreement between the presidents of the two companies occurred about the same time that Harvester signed its secret pact with Molina: The two agreements appear to have been crucially linked in Harvester's strategy to control the Yucatecan henequen industry. By the terms of an earlier, more formal contract reached in 1898, Harvester's predecessor, the McCormick Harvesting Machine Company, had lent Peabody and Company more than half the capital it needed to maintain its involvement in the sisal trade. In consideration of this sizable loan – estimated at $200,000 – McCormick exacted the right to determine the nature of Peabody's purchases and transactions in the Yucatecan fiber market.[62] Students of the cordage trade regard this concesssion as tantamount to Henry Peabody's turning over the henequen side of his trading business lock, stock, and barrel to Cyrus McCormick. The records of the McCormick Harvesting Machine Company reveal that this formal contract was terminated shortly after the turn of the century. However, what was not known until recently was that both

Cyrus McCormick and Henry Peabody secretly reaffirmed the general terms of their former agreement – McCormick providing capital to Peabody in exchange for market control – via a series of personal letters in 1902.[63]

The new informal agreement would last out the decade of the 1900s and seems to have terminated around the time of Peabody's death, shortly after 1910. However, by the time it ended, Harvester's hegemony in Yucatán had been indisputably established. Peabody's successor as president, Edward Bayley, would repeatedly deny Peabody's temporary merger with Harvester, both before the U.S. Senate subcommittee in 1916 and on a variety of other occasions.[64] In fact, it is possible that the agreement remained confidential between Peabody and McCormick and that Bayley himself was never briefed on its contents.[65] On the other hand, opponents of Harvester's control of the Yucatecan economy and critics of the cordage trust in the United States never doubted the reality of such an arrangement,[66] and the recent discovery of documentary proof corroborating their judgment has put the matter beyond speculation.

In light of this secret McCormick–Peabody agreement, the language of the subsequent Harverster–Molina contract makes more sense, especially in regard to the third parties mentioned. It will be recalled that the "notorious" pact expressly provided that Molina and Harvester arrange for the cooperation of rival import-export houses.[67] How could Harvester, for example, "agree that Peabody [among others] shall not pay higher prices for sisal than those given by Molina" unless Harvester had at least some control over Peabody, if not the determining voice in the latter's transactions? We know that by 1902, Harvester already had brought local buyers such as Molina and Urcelay into line and would later use Molina's burgeoning political and economic power to eliminate more stubborn rivals such as Don Eusebio Escalante, who would not collaborate. As we have seen above, it was Peabody and Company that, through its local agent, Arturo Pierce, had traditionally controlled a greater share of the henequen market prior to 1902 than Molina and, therefore, constituted the only serious threat to the complete dominance of the industry that Harvester now sought.

Table 4 reveals the extent to which Harvester increasingly controlled the local fiber trade following its 1902 agreements with Peabody and Molina. Nor do these figures reflect possible Harvester control over a sizable portion of the "remainder" column by

Table 4. *Percentage of bales imported to the United States by the leading henequen exporting houses, 1896–1914*

Year	Molina(%)	Peabody(%)	Harvester controlled[a]	Remainder(%)
1896	35.9	27.7		36.4
1897	18.8	38.4		42.8
1898	16.9	35.4		47.7
1899	15.4	36.9		47.7
1900	12.9	42.3		44.8
1901	23.3	37.7		39.0
1902	30.5	39.0		30.5
1903	46.4	34.4	80.8	19.2
1904	48.7	36.8	85.5	14.5
1905	51.9	31.2	83.1	16.9
1906	53.2	36.8	90.0	10.0
1907	51.6	42.1	93.7	6.3
1908	57.3	36.1	93.4	6.6
1909	67.8	28.3	96.1	3.9
1910	73.2	26.6	99.8	0.2
1911	63.2	24.1	87.3	12.7[b]
1912	61.3	24.1	85.4	14.6[b]
1913	74.0	20.9	94.9	5.1[b]
1914	72.2	20.3	92.5	7.5[b]

[a]The percentage of hemp Harvester controlled due to the separate agreements with Molina and Peabody in 1902. Harvester was formed in 1902.
[b]From 1911 to 1914, a large group of Yucatecan henequen planters formed the Compañía de Hacendados y Yucatecos to fight the monopolistic market situation.
Source: Peabody Papers, vol. L-1, pp. 254–274, and U.S. Senate, *Importation of Sisal*, vol. 2, p. 963.

means of more informal arrangements and debt obligations between the Molina family and these smaller, nominally independent buyers.

Thus, even by conservative estimates, it appears that Harvester was controlling more than 90 percent of Yucatán's sole export commodity by the time the Revolution arrived in the region in 1915. In one extraordinary year – 1910 – the corporation exercised its leverage over 99.8 percent of the trade. With good reason, then, General Alvarado would charge in 1915 that the henequen trust ruling Yucatán through Avelino Montes and the *Casta* encompassed not only Harvester but also Peabody and the other so-called independent buyers, who were its satellites in fact if not in name. Accurately, the general perceived that the North American cordage interests in collaboration with Montes were in a position to *fix the price* paid for Yucatán's henequen – essentially the definition of a trust. They did this by channeling loan capital through Montes and the *Casta* to the planters, securing liens on future fiber production and often mortgages on the plantations themselves, enabling the trust to dictate the future price at which the producers would be forced to sell to them. Alvarado's agents would later produce testimony from smaller *hacendados* that Montes and the *Casta* had made loans to them at high interest rates and obliged them to sell their fiber at substantially less per pound than the prevailing market price.[68]

Thus, Molina's and Harvester's campaign to depress prices and control local fiber production appears to have been eminently successful. Questions of price, however, particularly concerning an unstable commodity such as henequen, make short-term analysis a risky proposition. The years immediately preceding Harvester's merger were characterized by bonanza henequen prices induced by the Spanish-American War's curtailment of supplies of manila, henequen's chief competitor. With the outbreak of the war in 1898, average henequen prices climbed from 5.5 cents per kilogram to an astronomical 22 cents per kilogram in 1902. Prices that had effectively quadrupled in four years would inevitably drop when the competitive market between manila and henequen was restored.

Sisal hemp's pricing equation is further complicated when we consider that alternative surges of boom-and-bust fiber prices were the norm rather than the exception throughout the period. The 1898–1902 boom and the subsequent drop in prices after 1903 were symptomatic of the tenuous fiber trade. If we take a close look at the quotations for henequen from 1880 to 1915, we note volatile fluctuations in its world market price.[69] (See Table 3.) Prices rose and fell with startling frequency.[70] Reasons for the unstable fluctuations varied with each cycle of the henequen market. Attempted corners by exporters and buyers, a surge or a decline in manufacturers' demand, freak occurrences such as the 1898 war affecting the Philippines, binder twine competition, and the saturation of the fiber market by overzealous producers – all these combined to play havoc with the manufactuers' and producers' ability to predict future prices. In such an unstable market atmosphere, the decline of henequen prices after the 1898–1902 boom might be interpreted as inevitable given the extraordinary prices paid for the fiber during that period. Generalizations centered on only a single variable offer an incomplete explanation for short-term price changes. Following this same line of reasoning, one might even be tempted to excuse Harvester from blame for its role in depressing prices in the years immediately following the consummation of the agreements with Molina and Peabody.[71]

Yet Harvester's monopolistic control of Yucatecan fiber supply, its ever-tightening grip on the North American binder twine market, and the extent and duration of the drop in fiber prices from 1903 to 1912 demand that the trust be held responsible for the price decline. Further, Harvester's motivation indicts the giant. Its avowed purpose, penciled into the Molina contract, was to depress the market. In addition, the contract led to the destruction of the competitive situation that had existed among *casas exportadoras* prior to 1902. No *casa* could or would challenge Montes and/or Peabody until 1915, when the revolutionary government of General Salvador Alvarado dealt a blow to the monopoly by ordering planters to sell their hemp to a state-controlled *Comisión Reguladora* (henequen Regulating Commission).

By 1911, the net proceeds of IHC's binder twine business exceeded $7 million. The actual profit that Harvester and the manufacturers made on the finished product fluctuated from year to year depending on the price of the raw material and the level of competition among the manufacturers themselves. Twine profits were always small in comparison with Harvester's receipts from its major lines of harvesting machines (binders, mowers, etc.). Nevertheless, twine constituted an important secondary line and, as competition began to intensify in the harvesting machine field after 1910, Harvester would pay increasing attention to its Fiber and Twine Department.[72] Although the manufacturers continually claimed that competition was keen and profits were small, there is evidence to suggest that, as the 1902–1915 period wore on, Harvester's profits in twine generally increased and the corporation was able to turn a very handsome profit on its twine in certain years.

For example, both Yucatecan and North American sources reveal that late in 1914, just before the Revolution came to Yucatán, Harvester's twine profits were exceptionally high. A favorable exchange rate coupled with the depressed price reduced the cost of raw fiber to manufacturers to about 8.8 cents per kilogram, whereas Harvester's quotation for twine was fixed at 17.6 cents, affording fabulous profits once conversion costs and other nominal expenses, estimated at 3.3 cents per kilogram, had been subtracted. During most years, binder twine profits were declared to fluctuate between 1.1 and 2.2 cents per kilogram, which a 1916 U.S. Senate subcommittee did not deem excessive.[73] However, many contemporary observers doubted that the corporation's declaration of profits was valid. Among these was the U.S. consul in Progreso, who voiced the commonly held suspicion that the trust was regularly commanding prices that, "though depressed for sisal purchase, are nominally increased to justify an increase of price in twine."[74] In other words, although the trust (through Montes) was actually paying indebted planters an average of 0.55 to 2.2 cents per kilogram less than prevailing market prices, it represented itself as purchasing its fiber from the independent house of Montes at the nominal market price. Montes would then receive a commission or kickback that, when added to the actual price at which henequen was secured from the planters, still did not approach the nominal market figure.[75]

By 1910, competition in the twine industry had been substantially reduced. Harvester had succeeded in controlling Yucatecan fiber production and thereby gained such a powerful advantage in the manufacturing of twine that numerous smaller North American competitors had either been forced out of business or were compelled to become Harvester's satellites.[76] By 1911, Harvester manufactured almost two-thirds of the binder twine sold on the North American market. Yet it still had to contend with several determined rivals, most notably Plymouth Cordage and the binderies maintained by the state prisons of Minnesota, Michigan, Wisconsin, Indiana, the Dakotas, and Missouri.

In 1914, Harvester was consuming roughly twice as much sisal as all the other significant manufacturers combined:[77]

International Harvester Company	584,000 tons
Plymouth Cordage Company	139,000 tons
Minnesota State Prison	43,400 tons
Michigan State Prison	25,000 tons
Peoria Cordage Company	24,000 tons
Hooven and Allison	18,000 tons
South Dakota State Prison	11,300 tons
Wisconsin State Prison	8,650 tons
Indiana State Prison	7,500 tons
North Dakota State Prison	5,700 tons
Kelly Cordage Company	4,200 tons

Rauschenberger Cordage Company	2,200 tons
Rugg and Company	2,000 tons
Missouri State Prison	2,000 tons

However, whereas a dozen or so of the smaller binderies seem now to have been supplied by Harvester and were strictly governed by its pricing policies, Plymouth and the state prison systems represented more serious competitors. The prisons were able to offer fiber to dealers at lower prices than either Harvester or Plymouth because, although their plants were not as modern, the costs of production using convict labor were exceedingly low. Plymouth estimated that the prisons' advantage in production cost was 1.65 cents per kilogram. "We are, so far as I know, the only industry in the country subject to prison competition," lamented Plymouth's president in 1915, "and the competition has been severe for years."[78]

Yet the venerable and independent-minded Plymouth Cordage Company held on tenaciously, the only remaining competitor in the binder twine field. Plymouth had watched a number of other small, established twine mills fold before Harvester's expansion drive in the early 1900s, surviving primarily because of its healthy business in rope and other cordage products. On at least two separate occasions, in 1910 and 1921, Plymouth resisted bold attempts by Harvester to buy up its stock and secure control of its board of directors.[79] Then, after Harvester had succeeded in monopolizing the import of Yucatecan henequen into the United States, a series of bitter price wars broke out between the two corporations, the explosive rhetoric of which found its way into the trade journals. Recognizing that its traditional agents, Peabody and Pierce, were now collaborating with Montes and Harvester, Plymouth all but conceded defeat in the Mérida market and moved to diversify the sources of its raw fiber, turning increasingly to Filipino manila and experimenting with new sisals from Africa and New Zealand. In 1910, Plymouth sent a "personal letter" entitled "What Every Farmer Should Know about Binder Twine" to all concerned parties in the twine industry. The gist of the message was a warning that "there is a movement on foot to create a monopoly of Sisal fiber . . . If the attempt is successful, the manipulators will try to control all the world's supply of different fibers used for making twine." Plymouth recommended that the American farmer press for the use of manila fiber rather than henequen in order to break up the monopoly of the Harvester "sisal trust."[80]

Indeed, Harvester had not been above extensive market manipulation when opportunities arose. An example from 1906 will serve to illustrate the macro-economic power that Harvester could bring to bear on the international and local fiber markets, invariably to the detriment of Yucatán's henequen industry. Harvester's own records indicate that, by this time, the corporation had invested heavily in Filipino fiber in a bid to blunt Plymouth's advantage in manila and become somewhat less dependent on Yucatán as its only source of supply. (Simultaneously, Harvester also began experimenting with the cultivation of sisal in a variety of Caribbean, Central, and South American countries[81] and was sinking over a million dollars into a disastrous scheme to grow flax twine domestically.)[82] More importantly, however, Harvester used its Filipino fiber operation as a lever to increase the company's control over Yucatecan henequen while further depressing its price. Thus, H. L. Daniels, director of Harvester's Fiber Department, informed President Cyrus McCormick in September 1906 that news of the U.S. government's imminent removal of an export tax on manila would provide Harvester with just the kind of opportunity it had been seeking. Daniels explained that as soon as Harvester's agents in the Philippines had received word of the removal of the tax, they held their stocks off the market. Exulting in the details of Harvester's recent coup, Daniels continued:

> Through our efforts, but without permitting our personality to appear, we have published in the trade journals in New York the facts in connection with the removal of the tax . . . and stocks [of manila] are being held back, which has had a very depressing effect on the market and has permitted us to secure fairly full supplies of [Yucatecan] Sisal which would otherwise have been very difficult . . .
>
> It is probable that never in the history of the trade have [Yucatecan] stocks owned by manufacturers been worked up more closely, and a hand-to-mouth policy of buying seems to be followed by a great majority of the cordage manufacturers.[83]

Yet despite these conditions, Daniels reported that Harvester had already bought up 14,000 bales of henequen at a reduced price and was in the process of transacting for 50,000 more "or as much Sisal as can be secured at the present or at lower prices."[84] To hear Daniels discuss the depressed prices on the Mérida fiber market, one would never have realized that demand for Yucatecan fiber was soaring.

With good reason, then, Harvester was content to maintain its invisible empire in Yucatán, predicated upon indirect control through the collaboration of the regional oligarchy. There was little incentive to press for a more traditional penetration of the local economy based upon actual ownership of the means of production as long as the North American sisal trust possessed the predictive capability to gauge future benefits (i.e., control over local fiber production and a guarantee of low prices) and the power capability to deliver them.[85] Nevertheless, on various occasions during the early twentieth century, Cyrus McCormick and Harvester received a series of offers to purchase or invest in several of Yucatán's largest and most profitable henequen plantations. During 1901 and 1902, McCormick was offered a string of plantations by members of the *Casta* including Blanca Flor, Yaxché, Yaxcopoil, Tabí, and Chichén. Among the inducements to buy was an appeal to McCormick's vanity, for the Yucatecan real estate entrepreneur handling the transactions assured Harvester's president that one day these plantations might be consolidated into an impressive area of settlement to be known as McCormick City (Ciudad McCormick).[86] In each case McCormick demurred, although on at least one occasion, in 1901, his friend and closest advisor, H. L. Daniels, stated that in principle there was nothing wrong with buying plantations, and each offer should be considered on its financial merits.[87] Interestingly, by 1905, after the amazing success of Harvester's contractual arrangements with Molina and Peabody had become fully appreciated, Daniels altered his open-ended approach. When McCormick was offered a purchase option on two of Yucatán's largest henequen haciendas, Daniels reminded him that "two or three years ago you didn't think it wise and there is no reason to change your mind now."[88] The entire process whereby Yucatán's ruling oligarchs offered plantations for sale to North American fiber magnates is in itself an underpublicized and revealing episode of the region's history. It suggests that the extent of the oligarchy's collaboration with the cordage trust was even more widespread than is commonly believed, and it qualifies the rather exaggerated regional assertion that Yucatecans jealously guarded their plantations from foreign ownership to the extent of categorically eschewing all forms of direct foreign investment.

On at least two other occasions, Harvester went a step further and flirted with the prospect of exercising a more direct control over the regional economy. From 1903 until about 1907, Harvester made a concerted attempt to purchase the Yucatecan-owned, *Casta*-controlled railroad system.[89] Friedrich Katz speculates that although Harvester's collaborators controlled virtually all aspects of the region's commercial, financial, and communications infrastructure, "International Harvester wanted to institute the classic means of control already used with such great success by the Standard Oil Company in the United States and introduced around the same time in Central America by the United Fruit Company: direct control of the transportation system as a means of dominating a market."[90] Ultimately, however, the scheme failed for a variety of reasons: the high price demanded for the railroad by Molina and the *Casta*; the opposition of the federal government, which since 1905 had adopted a more nationalistic posture regarding the ownership of railroads; and finally, because Harvester chose to revert to a policy of indirect control. After all, by 1907 Harvester was well satisfied with Molina's and Montes's performance in managing other key sectors of the regional economy (port works, banks, internal fiber production, etc.) and saw no pressing reason to remove the railroads from their control.

A similar pattern characterized Cyrus McCormick's and Harvester's participation in La Industrial and the local campaign to manufacture raw henequen fiber. McCormick became interested in La Industrial shortly after Molina called for a subscription of shares in the new joint-stock company in 1896. In fact, McCormick may have invested a substantial portion of its initial $600,000 capitalization, as well as providing modern machinery and technological supervision and guaranteeing North American markets.[91] McCormick's Harvesting Machine Company actually dominated the plant's operation by dictating production and shipment schedules and standards of quality. Such participation suggests the lengths to which McCormick would go to seek an alternative means of supply of binder twine following a threatening attempt by the National Cordage Company to monopolize the industry during the early 1890s. Of course, McCormick's motivation dovetailed nicely with the desire of Molina and other Yucatecan entrepreneurs to industrialize in the wake of several years of low prices for raw fiber exports. (See Table 3.)

The earliest descriptions of the plant in the principal trade journals reassured McCormick that his efforts would pay off: "It [La Industrial] is in the opinion of the experts, as completely equipped as any similar enterprise in the United States."[92] Yet the vagaries of the world market, a force beyond the control of the plant's sponsors, would soon shatter the early optimism. The outbreak of the Spanish-American War in 1898 and the suspension of manila shipments from the Philippines suddenly restored a favorable market for fiber exports. The new plant found itself unable to compete with the boom prices for raw hemp, and Yucatecan planters were loath to continue investing in La Industrial when such prices assured them healthy, risk-free profits. As interest waned and efficiency deteriorated, executives of the McCormick Harvesting Machine Company quickly concluded that despite their direct involvement in the manufacturing venture, La Industrial would never become their sole source of binder twine. By 1899 McCormick was already constructing his own stateside twine mill (which opened in Chicago in 1900) and, by the time of International Harvester's creation in 1902, La Industrial's primary function as Harvester's supplier was terminated, for McCormick had by now picked up a variety of new cordage plants, including the large-capacity Deering and Osborne mills. Once again, McCormick and Harvester had reiterated their strategic decision to preserve an indirect, informal brand of penetration and control. All future investments in the peninsula would be limited to the area of raw fiber and would be channeled through Molina and Montes.

The retrenchment and ultimate failure of La Industrial and henequen manufacturing in Yucatán represented one of several ill-fated local attempts during the Porfiriato to wrench free from the ever-tightening grip of monocrop dependency and foreign monopoly control. Another potential solution that was frustrated was Yucatán's attempt to find new markets and sell as much fiber as possible to Europe. Although the invention of the binder had increased the demand for fiber on a worldwide scale, the European nations seemed determined to cultivate sisal in their own colonial possessions rather than buy henequen from Yucatán.[93] Moreover, earlier attempts by the Yucatecan government to grant a subsidy to fiber shipped to Europe had drawn an angry protest from the U.S. State Department, acting on behalf of the cordage trust. Without the subsidy, transportation costs made export to Europe unfeasible. For a variety of reasons, then, no more than 5 percent of Yucatán's henequen was ever shipped to Europe in the years prior to 1915.[94]

A third attempted solution was "valorization," the establishment of producers' cooperatives to hold fiber off the market until Yucatán's planters were guaranteed a fair price. A contentious lot even under completely favorable market conditions, the planters were hampered from the start in their cooperative strategy by a lack of solidarity and agreement. In fact, virtually all they could agree upon was their resentment and envy of the *Casta*. A variety of false starts aimed at valorizing the price of fiber resulted. Typically, an important segment of the producers' cooperative would cave in before Montes's pressure, removing its fiber from the organization and thereby defeating the scheme. As a rule, planters made little conscious effort to correlate their production with world market trends. Given the choice of selling at a low price or withholding production to starve demand and raise the price, planters invariably chose the former option. The fact was that even when the price dropped close to 6.6 cents per kilogram, a small return was realized.[95] Finally, in 1908, when the price of fiber had fallen all the way down to 7.7 cents per kilogram – perilously close to the danger point – the planters seemed determined to hold fast. They obtained a loan from the *Banco Nacional de México*, putting up a sizable quantity of fiber as collateral, and collectively resolved to resist the *Casta's* pressure. Yet, scarcely had the price risen a cent when the bank, under the orders of Díaz's minister of development, Don Olegario Molina – still allied with Harvester – dropped the liened fiber onto the market, glutting it and wiping out the price gains the planters had achieved. This scenario, with only slight alterations, would be repeated several times prior to 1915 and the consolidation of General Alvarado's revolutionary regime in Yucatán.[96]

The role of the federal government: marginalization and neglect

This raises the important issue of the federal government's role in the consolidation of Yucatán's monocrop economy and the penetration of the henequen industry by the North American cordage trust. There is no evidence that central Mexicans invested heavily in henequen, or that Harvester and the cordage trust ever felt compelled to lobby or negotiate directly with Mexico City regarding its business in Yucatán. As we have seen, Yucatán's traditional economic orientation away from Mexico and toward the United States obviated this problem. However, the obliging attitude of the Díaz government to foreign business, its commitment to liberal economic postulates, and its reinforcing belief in an international economic division of labor precluded its taking any action that might have mitigated Harvester's control over Yucatán's export economy. Had the Díaz government provided credit to the planters during critical dips in the fiber market, it seems certain that the industry might have resisted, at least to some extent, the economic and political pressure of Harvester and Molina's oligarchy.

Unfortunately for the continued existence of an autonomous regional fiber industry, the federal government chose to support the planters only against the workers, by making almost 16,000 deported Yaquis available to the expanding henequen plantations during the 1907–1910 period and by employing federal *rurales* (rural police) to round up runaway "slaves" or prevent potential or actual disturbances on the haciendas.[97] Against Harvester, the Díaz regime would have been fully capable of aiding the planters in their valorization effort. As we shall see, Alvarado's future state monopoly over the marketing of fiber would prove quite successful, bringing a dramatic increase in price to the planters and breaking, at least temporarily, the monopoly of the henequen trust. Yet, the Díaz government – as well as its revolutionary successors prior to 1915 – did precisely the opposite, permitting Molina, one of its leading executive officials, to break the back of the planters by manipulating the national banking system.[98] In 1915, a number of *hacendados* testified before a U.S. Senate subcommittee investigating the conditions of fiber cultivation and marketing in Yucatán that "the Díaz Government always maintained a hostile position towards the henequen planters of Yucatán."[99]

Actually, this assessment requires some clarification, for the Díaz regime clearly favored Olegario Molina and the thirty or so super-planters of the *Casta Divina*. At the local level, these regional oligarchs were given a free hand to monopolize the fiber sold to the North American trust and to man the state's economic and political infrastructure. Recent research is beginning to reveal too that as early as 1901, Molina, Montes, and members of the *Casta* actually invested in a series of business ventures in Yucatán and other parts of Mexico with foreign (European) entrepreneurs, national *científicos*, and members of the Díaz family.[100] Then, in 1906, following an invitation by Molina, they were honored by a personal visit from Don Porfirio and his wife, the first time a viceroy, monarch, or president of Mexico had ever visited Yucatán. Don Porfirio was so impressed by the lavish reception he and Doña Carmen received, and by the efficiency and modernity of the model plantations he was taken to see, that he brought Molina into his cabinet in 1908, appropriately to head up the Ministry of *Fomento* (Development).[101] Molina would be Yucatán's last bona fide *científico*; in fact, history has also confirmed that he was the last Yucatecan leader to play an important role in national politics, following in the footsteps of earlier nineteenth-century leaders Lorenzo de Zavala and Justo Sierra.[102] However, throughout his tenure in Mexico City, Molina never lost interest in the *patria chica*. In a variety of ways and very much in the manner of the Terrazas–Creel family of Chihuahua and other powerful Porfirian families, he would use his national influence further to enrich himself and the network of relatives and friends that made up Yucatán's oligarchy.[103] As minister of *Fomento*, Molina used his power to arrange for Yaqui deportees, overriding the objections of Sonoran oligarchs competing for this valuable source of labor.[104] Along with another powerful member of the *Casta*, Rafael Peón Losa, and a select group of Mexican *científicos*, he received the most extensive and most lucrative land and forest concessions in the new territory of Quintana Roo. The new territory had been carved out of the state of Yucatán in 1902 and the separation angered the majority of Yucatán's elite, who thereby lost potentially rich investment possibilities.[105] Don Olegario also acquired for himself and his supporters thousands of hectares of *terrenos baldíos* (vacant public lands) in Yucatán, multiplying the number of haciendas he controlled often at the expense of Indian pueblos outside the henequen zone.[106] Through his puppet, Enrique Muñoz Arístegui, who succeeded him as governor, he continued to impose an ever-increasing number of relatives and friends as *jefes políticos* in Yucatán. Finally, he modified Yucatán's tax structure, further removing responsibility from the very wealthy *hacendados* and merchants and placing an increasing burden on the small urban and rural middle class.[107]

After generations of neglect and repression, the nature of Yucatán's relationship with Mexico City and the Republic changed relatively little during the Porfiriato. Rather than being incorporated on more equitable terms into the Mexican nation, Yucatán remained on the periphery. The loss of Quintana Roo in 1902 represented a political defeat for the region as well as a severe economic loss; it demonstrated the complete subjugation of potential regional growth to national interests and priorities. More accurately, we might say that Governor Molina and a small circle of regional oligarchs were incorporated into the national superstructure, as was largely the case throughout Porfirian Mexico.

The process of Yucatán's national integration would develop slowly; indeed, it is doubtful that even after more than a half century of the Mexican Revolution, it has been brought to fruition.

The twilight years of the Porfiriato and the first years of the revolutionary period bore witness to familiar regional discontents and provided further evidence of Yucatán's marginal position within the national power structure. Benign neglect still characterized the federal government's response to regional demands for improved land and sea communications. The Díaz government, for example, refused to lend Yucatecan promoters the money they needed in 1901 to build an important southeastern railroad, linking the henequen zone with its impoverished hinterlands on the Quintana Roo frontier. [108] Despite differences in ideological orientation and political style, Díaz, Huerta, Madero, and Carranza all remained deaf to repeated Yucatecan demands that the peninsula be connected by rail with central Mexico and that shipping routes be rationalized and extended to encompass peninsular traffic. Mexico City – though now in league with a few members of the *Casta* – still imposed the majority of Yucatán's political leaders above the municipal level and, with the notable exceptions of Justo Sierra and Olegario Molina, rarely invited Yucatecans to participate in the national government. Moreover, the federal government continued Santa Anna's hated tradition of the *leva* (military draft), compelling local youths – usually *campesinos* or sons of the urban poor – to fight in distant military campaigns in which the *Yucatecos* had no interest. Mexico City was taking increasingly large chunks of Yucatán's wealth as well, stepping up its tax schedules in proportion to the rise in regional henequen revenues. [109]

By 1915, Yucatán had become, in turn, the milch cow of presidents Díaz, Madero, Huerta, and Carranza. With each successive round of taxes, local resentment grew, for no corresponding federal benefits had been reaped by Yucatán. Bitterly, *Yucatecos* recognized that Father Diego de Landa's old colonial aphorism – "Las cosas de Yucatán, dejarlas como están" ("What is Yucatán's own, is best left alone") – had come to justify Mexican bureaucratic neglect in the area of public works and infrastructural development. [110] Finally, as we have seen, the increased fiscal demands of Mexico's revolutionary governments upon Yucatán rekindled the flames of separatism among the members of the region's dominant agro-commercial bourgeoisie, prompting the ill-fated Ortiz Argumedo revolt in 1915. In a dramatic reversal, *Argumedista* insurgents appropriated Father Landa's slogan to justify their regional rebellion. And although the regional revolt was short-lived, these sentiments, stemming from Yucatán's traditionally marginal position within the national political structure, would continue to plague federal–state relations throughout the revolutionary period. More important for this study, however, Yucatán's isolation and weak bargaining position vis-à-vis Mexico City would play a major role in shaping revolutionary movements within the region, hampering the effectiveness of the revolutionary process.

3

The revolutionary equation within Yucatán: the problem of mobilization

The Indians only hear with their backsides.
—Yucatecan hacendados' proverb
c. 1905

The Indian pays with his blood for the air that he breathes. This is why the Indian travels endless roads sure that the only way which will enable him to find his lost path, is the way which goes toward death.
—Abreu Gómez, Canek

We have examined Yucatán's export economy, dependent upon a single crop tied to a fluctuating market that was controlled by North Americans, and have suggested that the vagaries governing this fragile economy would present serious difficulties, not only for General Alvarado's Constitutionalists in 1915 but for the successive "generations" of revolutionaries that followed. We have noted Yucatán's traditionally peripheral and subordinate position within the national political configuration, which, despite the gains made by Yucatán's oligarchy during the Porfiriato, remained structurally unchanged by 1915. It, too, would limit the options open to future revolutionary regimes. However, there were even more immediate constraints upon the revolutionary process that emanated from within the region itself. Although closely related to the international economy and the national power structure, these internal constraints merit analysis in their own right. It is important to know what effect Yucatán's characteristic agrarian structure, dominated by a plantation system renowned for its onerous labor conditions, would have on revolutionary mobilization once the Revolution arrived in 1915. Specifically, we might ask why Mediz Bolio, the regional poet, and others have so consistently stressed the overriding necessity of making a revolution "from above" in Yucatán, due to the lack of mobilization from below. Is it plausible that, in the region where labor conditions were reputed to be perhaps the most oppressive in all of Porfirian Mexico, unrest and revolutionary activity were among the least developed? And what consequences would this have, in the decades ahead, for mounting a successful revolutionary drive engaging the various social groups and classes?

Labor conditions on haciendas: the mechanism of social control

When Yucatán entered its first revolutionary decade (1915–1924), no authentic revolutionary tradition dwelt in the minds of the Yucatecan people. This should not imply, as some have suggested, that Yucatán's Maya *campesinado*, the victim of centuries of oppression, was a passive, inert mass. Indeed, the region's colonial history is punctuated by frequent Maya revolts against their Spanish and creole overlords. And, of course, mention has already been made of the apocalyptic Caste War of 1847.[1] Clearly, by 1850, the Maya had evolved a strong tradition of protest. It is remarkable, therefore, that by the turn of the twentieth century, only fifty years after the bloodiest battles of the Caste War, Yucatán's plantocracy had effectively buried most of the memories and traces of the event. To a large extent, the logistics of the Caste War assisted the landed bourgeoisie in its goal. The *indios rebeldes* (rebel Indians) had retreated deeper and deeper into the bush across the Quintana Roo frontier, and those Maya who had joined *ladino* (creole) society as *peones* on the plantations in effect gave up their ethnic birthright, coming to be known euphemistically as "mestizos." As a matter of official policy, the ethnic classification *indio* – synonymous with *rebelde* – ceased to exist in Yucatán.[2]

More important than mere semantics, however, Yucatán's emerging plantocracy had, in the aftermath of war, instituted a system of defense that, when coupled with the harsh labor conditions on the haciendas, would guarantee no repetition of the great rebellion.[3] The federal government provided regular army battalions and special detachments of *rurales* that complemented the state militia and constabulary, and private detective and police forces were hired by the large *hacendados* themselves. No other regional elite had such a sophisticated mechanism of repression at its disposal.

The arduous labor regime itself reduced the need for police activity to a minimum throughout the late Porfiriato. As demand for raw fiber rose dramatically in the last two decades of the nineteenth century, Yucatecan *hacendados* generally employed four methods to increase output: (1) the use of new machinery; (2) the employment of workers from outside the region; (3) the increased employment of workers from nearby villages; and (4) an intensification of the utilization of plantation labor.

As we have seen, the mechanization of commercial henequen agriculture was restricted entirely to steam and, later, diesel decortication of the fiber. There was no pressing need to bring machines into the *henequenales* for planting and harvesting because labor was much cheaper than machines. Ironically, although Yucatecan plantation agriculture would gain a reputation for being among the most technologically advanced in Porfirian Mexico, the basic techniques of cultivation and harvesting were thousands of years old and were harnessed to an essentially slave mode of production.

Workers were imported to Yucatán primarily from central Mexico, where labor was in surplus. Attempts to attract European workers were unsuccessful, though several thousand Chinese and Korean indentured laborers were brought in at the turn of the century. Although these laborers were divided between deportees and voluntary contract workers, in practice scarcely any differences existed between them. Deportees included thousands of Sonoran Yaquis; Maya rebels from Quintana Roo and members of other frontier tribes who had resisted encroachment upon their lands by expanding haciendas; political dissidents from the north and center who had opposed the Díaz regime; and criminals and vagrants, often too poor to buy their way out of prison or avoid deportation. The contract workers, commonly known as *enganchados* (literally, "hooked ones"), were typically expropriated *campesinos* from central Mexico and *lumpenproletariat* from Mexico City who were lured to Yucatán by fast-talking *contratistas* (labor contractors) promising well-paying jobs. The reality was much more unsavory. Wallace Thompson, a contemporary observer generally sympathetic to Díaz, paints a picture of the *enganchado's* plight that is virtually identicial to that appearing in John K. Turner's ringing indictment of the Díaz regime, *Barbarous Mexico*. The *enganchado*

> was generally a man who was practically shanghaied from the cities . . . Often disease-ridden, almost inevitably soaked with pulque, captured and signed up for labor when they were intoxicated, these men were brought down practically in chain gangs by the contractors and delivered at so many hundred pesos per head. They were kept in barbed wire enclosures, often under ghastly sanitary conditions, . . . and were easy victims of tropical insects, dirt and infection.[4]

Once arrived in Yucatán, these "hooked ones," as well as the deportees, were kept as virtual prisoners on the estates, and there is little record that many found their way back to central Mexico before 1915.

Moreover, throughout the late Porfiriato the living and laboring conditions of the great majority of workers, the native Maya *acasillados* and dispossessed villagers, were becoming more and more similar to those of the contract workers and deportees. We have already seen how the expansion of the henequen plantation despoiled the autarkic peasant village of its land and transformed the great majority of the region's *campesinos* – including many outside the henequen zone – into a proto-proletariat. Over the course of the Porfiriato, the material plight of these dispossessed villagers became especially grim. Traveling to the nearest plantations from their villages, they were hired as temporary laborers but locked up on the hacienda for the duration of their work stint. In terms of food, medical care, and pay, they never fared as well as the "full-timers," the resident workers or *acasillados*, who represented a larger investment to the *hacendado*. This contrast in treatment is pointed up by Turner in a conversation he had with a temporary worker or "half-timer":

"Which would you rather be," I asked him, "a half-timer or a full-timer?"

"A full-timer," he replied promptly, and then in a lower tone: "They work us until we are ready to fall, then they throw us away to get strong again. If they worked the full-timers like they work us, they would die."[5]

However, by the turn of the century, the lot of the Yucatecan *acasillado* could not have been much better than that of the landless villager. Because of massive increases in the production of fiber to meet the ever-expanding demand, the area of maize production had been cut back from 15,000 hectares in 1845 to 4,500 hectares in 1907.[6] This reduction in maize land was most keenly felt by the *acasillados*, who – a few privileged retainers aside – had lost their traditional right of access to land, which was primarily what distinguished a debt *peón* from a slave.

The traditional system of debt peonage, although inherently a coercive form of labor in an area as prone to labor shortage as Yucatán, had originally enabled the resident *peones* to fare better than deportees, contract workers, and part-time villagers. The *hacendados* exacted a variety of work obligations from their *acasillados* but displayed a certain paternalism toward them that mitigated the worst evils of the system. As late as 1901, a visiting German agricultural expert observed:

> The legal means to bind *criados* [servants] to a hacienda consists in an advance payment which in this State means that a worker who leaves can be returned by force by the police to the hacienda. These advance payments are generally made when a young man born on the hacienda reaches the age of 18 or 20 and marries. His master then gives him a hundred to a hundred and fifty, sometimes two hundred pesos, to set up a household and both parties silently agree that this sum, as well as other sums which might be advanced at a later date in case of accident or illnesses, would never be repaid. They are the price for which the young *Yucateco* sells his freedom.[7]

However, by 1915, the conditions of the *acasillado* on the henequen plantations had become progressively worse. Market pressures forced an intensification of the *peón's* work, and paternalism ceased to buffer the harshness of the new relations of production, which came to approximate slavelike conditions. This "involution" or regression in the labor regime to an essentially slave mode of production manifested itself in a variety of ways.[8] To begin with, *hacendados* no longer had to lure their workers into debt with juicy advance payments. As the price of raw fiber deteriorated and the henequen trust's pressure on the Yucatecan producers increased, wage advances to field hands constantly decreased. The planter continued to pay his workers a nominal salary that theoretically enabled them, through hard work, to pay off the debts they had accumulated. Yet, once lured into debt, the worker found it practically impossible to regain his freedom.

To be sure, the Yucatecan *peón's* salary was reasonable by Porfirian standards. However, throughout Mexico, and especially in Yucatán, an absolute decline in real wages made existence difficult and savings impossible. The advent of monoculture necessitated the importation of most foodstuffs and drove prices for corn, beans, and meat well above the national average, especially after 1898. Wage levels not only failed to keep pace in good times but were rolled back when fiber prices dipped, as during the 1907 panic.[9]

Ultimately, however, the real debt was irrelevant if the *hacendado* was determined to keep the worker. Backed by the Porfirian political and legal establishment, the planter had the option of falsifying records, making debts hereditary, or merely declaring the indebtedness of the *peón* under oath. Indeed, by the turn of the century, the worker had become a commodity whose market value was unrelated to the debt but determined by the fluctuations in the henequen market. Thus, the going price for a man was 200 to 300 pesos in 1895; 1,500 to 3,000 pesos after the sharp rise in price during and after the Spanish-American War; and 400 pesos after the world economic crisis of 1907.[10]

This de facto slave system – blatantly unconstitutional though no less real for being so – existed for the sole purpose of enriching the highly capitalized henequen plantations of the 400 or so entrepreneurial *hacendados* who formed the heart of Yucatán's ruling bourgeoisie. The intensification of work meant that the easygoing days of the past were gone. Whatever charm there had been to hacienda life faded.

The henequen plantation was a huge agricultural factory-in-the-field, operated year-round on scientific lines and geared for total output for the world market. Although it performed most of the functions of a small rural village and averaged a population of about 100 to 150 persons (larger plantations had over 600 and some numbered well over 1,000), unlike the traditional hacienda, there was no longer an attempt at self-sufficiency. Food, clothing, and other necessities were now brought in from the outside. Virtually all of the labor used, from field to *desfibradora* to warehouse, was unskilled. Although conditions akin to slavery existed, workers were theoretically paid on a piecework basis: so much per 1,000 leaves cut, so much per *mecate* weeded, so much per 1,000 leaves decorticated. Furthermore, almost all of the jobs except those in the decorticating plant could be carried out by individual men working alone. At the same time, it became increasingly rare for workers to have any personal contact with their *hacendado* or *patrón*; the modern planter was an entrepreneur who lived in Mérida and made only occasional visits to the *campo* to inspect his investment. Day-to-day operation of the plantation was left in the hands of an administrator or *encargado*. Beneath him was a hierarchy of overseers and foremen (*mayordomos, mayacoles*) who were entrusted with the control and discipline of the predominantly Maya *peones*.[11]

A good foreman was one who extracted the greatest production from his *peones* at the least expense. The failure to fulfill the assignment of individual tasks – for example, so many leaves cut, so many *mecates* weeded or sown – resulted in monetary fines and corporal punishment in the form of flogging. One of the wealthiest members of the *Casta*, Felipe G. Cantón, "justified" the planters' recourse to the whip when, with a smile on his face, he informed North American journalist John Turner: "It is necessary to whip them . . . for there is no other way to make them do what you wish. What other way is there of enforcing the discipline of the farm? If we did not whip them, they would do nothing." [12] Cantón's fellow *henequeneros* echoed these statements in the form of a crude, turn-of-the-century proverb: "Los indios no oyen sino por las nalgas" ("The Indians only hear with their backsides"). [13]

By any account, the Maya *jornalero* was far from lazy. Even before the export boom greatly intensified plantation work, the field hand's chores had been demanding enough. Clearing and sowing the rocky soil, weeding and harvesting the spiny agave were difficult, often dangerous tasks under any conditions, let alone under a broiling tropical sun. Work began early, virtually at dawn, to make the most of the "cooler" morning hours.

> By the second hour of work the sun is fully up and the dew has evaporated into a steam which makes the clothes stick to the body and the flesh prickly. During the rainy season, the mosquitos come out in such swarms that sometimes the workers cannot stop to make their *pozole* [corn gruel]. Almost as bad are the horse flies. In addition to the insects there are varied types of nettles which sting the feet . . . Added to these, there is always the possibility of coming upon a rattlesnake hidden in the undergrowth . . . [14]

The year-round task of harvesting leaves (*pencas*) was especially rigorous. The *jornalero* lopped off the sharp spine at the end of the *penca* prior to severing the leaf from the man-sized plant. This forced him to work among the spines of the other leaves, drawing his *coa* (a curved iron blade mounted on a wooden shaft about 60 centimeters long) directly across the base of the plant while holding the leaf steady with his free hand. Harvested leaves were bound in bundles of fifty, then carried to the foot of a row of the field (*plantel*), where they were transported by a mule-drawn tram to the estate's *desfibradora*. At the onset of the boom, *jornaleros* harvested an average of 1,000 *pencas* per day. By 1915, it was not uncommon for *peones* to cut and bind 1,500 or 2,000 leaves per day, depending upon the production schedule demanded by the plantation administrator. [15]

Writer Fernando Benítez paints a vivid portrait of the Yucatecan *jornalero*. Hunched over in the *plantel*, he worked by himself, "covered with twigs, insects and sweat, his hair matted with dust,

Maya workers tending a *plantel* on a henequen estate.

virtually transformed into a tree . . . I saw his hands: pierced by the prickly spines, bloody yet constantly in motion, almost independent of his body, contorted like an agonizing Christ." [16]

The new work regime reduced the laborers' rights and expectations in other areas as well. The planters now refused to permit their *peones* to marry outside the estate. In a tight labor situation, exogamy might mean losing the benefit of future generations of workers. Nor were the sons and daughters of the plantation exposed to serious educational training. Consequently, illiteracy among Yucatán's estimated 100,000 agricultural workers was almost total. Medical facilities generally suffered the same fate as schools: Doctors and medicines existed only on the larger plantations, and even then they were inadequate to meet existing needs. On the other hand, many planters made sure to reward their workers frequently with a supply of liquor. [17]

Not surprisingly, the longevity of Yucatán's "slaves" was far from great. Two of Olegario Molina's closest associates in the

Casta, Joaquín Peón and Enrique Cámara Zavala – the latter president of the *hacendado*-controlled *Cámara Agrícola* (Chamber of Agriculture) – candidly told John Turner that among the native Maya workers, who constituted the great bulk of the labor force, the mortality rate far outstripped the birthrate. With regard to the Yaqui deportees, who represented the second greatest component of the plantation work force, Peón and Cámara pointed out that two-thirds could be expected to die within their first year in Yucatán.[18] Why, then, did the planters permit such harsh treatment of their workers in a region where labor shortage had become chronic? Better, it would seem, to promote more gentle treatment, thereby preserving their valuable human property, the worth of which would rise steadily with the demand for fiber.

Two economic arguments, however, seem to have dissuaded the planters from implementing a milder labor regime. First, the thinking of most *henequeneros* had been molded by the sharp fluctuations in the price of their commodity that had already occurred during the first two generations of regional fiber cultivation. In a single year, 1897–1898, the price of henequen had risen 300 percent and the planters' increase in profits had been estimated at 600 percent. A boom mentality had taken hold: The planter realized that such dramatic surges in price would characterize the industry's fortunes for only a limited time, and he was prepared to make the most of them when they occurred. This implied a maximum intensification of labor in terms of both hours and tasks. That the worker might die after only a few years was not significant; each *año de auge* (fat year) that he did work at peak capacity would yield a multiple rate of profit that would more than make up for the *años de baja* (lean years) that might soon follow. Moreover, given Molina's political connections in Mexico City and the monopoly of force that they maintained in the region, the planters had every reason to expect that additional Yaqui deportees and *enganchados* could be secured and incorporated into the existing system at a low enough cost to replace immediately "expired laborers."[19]

A second consideration, intimately related to the first, was the question of planter indebtedness to the *Casta* (and, by extension, to the North American henequen trust). Here, especially, the lack of unity that existed among the members of the Yucatecan elite had severe consequences for the region's agricultural workers. Most small and medium *hacendados* (as well as some larger planters addicted to lavish spending) had gone deeply into debt and were consequently burdened by greatly increased production costs. Downward fluctuations in price (e.g., the early 1890s, 1906–1907) frequently carried them to the brink of bankruptcy. Not surprisingly, the most preferred method of skirting or postponing financial collapse was to shift the weight of their crises to their labor force, reducing cash advances, salaries, access to land, and traditional medical care and other services while intensifying work obligations. Molina, as governor, although prodding these planters to pay off their debts, made it clear that labor would continue to be cheap because many more Yaquis would be arriving from the north. In justification, the federal and state governments explained that the payment of low wages might be turned to important advantage: It would help the planters to strike a blow against the North American trusts by digging themselves out from under their accumulated debts.[20]

We should emphasize, however, that uniform labor conditions did not exist throughout Yucatán. Conditions varied from plantation to plantation, as did the composition of the work force. Thus, for example, on some estates, contract workers were used in significant numbers; others relied mainly upon *acasillados* with an admixture of landless villagers and deportees. On certain *fincas*, an older form of paternalism lingered, with *hacendados* spending extended periods of time on their estates and, in some cases, preserving the traditional regime of peonage by providing their retainers with cash advances and access to *milpa* plots.[21] On the whole, however, it seems clear that the relations of production on Yucatán's henequen plantations were among the most oppressive in the tropical southeast, a region that maintained the most onerous labor regime in the Mexican Republic.[22]

A review of the socioeconomic and geographical conditions that shaped the Yucatecan Porfiriato – still referred to by villagers as the "Age of Slavery" – suggests why such conditions began to appear in the region at a time when slaveholding was being legally abolished or declining irreversibly elsewhere in the Americas. The sharp increase in the international demand for fiber; the development of railroads and tramways linking the plantations to their regional market and international port; the existence in central Mexico of a large labor surplus of landless *campesinos* that was not absorbed by domestic industry and constituted a ready pool for *enganchadores*; the lack of significant industry or mining in the southeast to compete with the planters for scarce labor and thereby give the workers greater mobility; a strong government willing to aid in the use and enforcement of this neo-slave system; and, finally, Yucatán's geographical isolation, which facilitated control and made escape difficult — these conditions were exceptionally conducive to a slave mode of production. In addition, because the demand for henequen was constant, it was grown on a year-round basis and required a stable, sedentary work force. With the exception of a few skilled jobs in the decorticating plant (for which well-paid free laborers were usually imported from Mérida), most of the work required no specific skills or prior training. The tasks were calculated and carried out on an individual basis, making supervision relatively easy.

The anomalous mixture of visible twentieth-century modernity with a decidedly colonial form of bondage drew the attention of contemporary travelers and remains perplexing. Was prerevolutionary Yucatán a society in which a modernized capitalist economy dominated by *hacendados* and foreign interests bred off a backward rural social structure, as the prevailing view suggests?[23] The strength of such an interpretation is that it emphasizes the de facto system of slavery as the motor force behind Yucatán's monoculture. However, in ignoring the essential nature of these relations of production and characterizing the society as a modernized capitalist one, this view glosses over the most important contradiction in Yucatán's social and economic structure on the eve of the Revolution.

The ambivalence of such a position is clear. To characterize the society as anything but "capitalist" might be to suggest that the region's predominant agrarian sector, the henequen industry, was "feudal" (or "slave") and would necessarily involve advancing a "dualist" thesis. Dualism implies that no extensive connections exist between the "modern" or progressive sector of a society and the closed or "traditional" sector. Yet we need not be forced into the dilemma of having crudely to categorize a society as capitalist even when its predominant labor system is coercive or dependent.[24] This interpretation — articulated more theoretically in the works of André Gunder Frank[25] — has been too willing to overlook the issue of free versus dependent labor, judging a society capitalist merely on the basis of its participation in the world capitalist economic system. Its exponents have done so in order to avoid the dualist posture that would undercut what they hold to be the essential "dependency" position: that the external structure of capitalist development generates underdevelopment within Latin American societies. Clearly, we should not minimize their contribution in establishing that important connections exist between the expanding international economy and the social formation of Latin American society. However, having brought us to the periphery, these *dependentistas* provide little guidance, for they fail to specify the nuances of social relations within the dependent country. Rather, they prefer to regard all social relations under the rubric of capitalism.

The possibility exists of retaining two interrelated points of analysis – the internal and the external relations of dependency – without falling into a trap of dualist modernization theory. Important connections do exist between a modern and a traditional sector. Thus, servile exploitation of Maya *campesinos* recently alienated from their traditional villages was accentuated and consolidated by Yucatán's planter entrepreneurs, modern in type, in order to maximize profits in an international market. The modernity of one sector was, therefore, a function of the backwardness of the other. Far from being incompatible with production for the world market, the essentially "precapitalist" or "slave" character of the system of labor relations on the henequen plantations in Yucatán was actually intensified by the expansion of the world market. In other words, we need not ignore the precapitalist character of production and the social relations that flow from it within the dependent society. Moreover, we should recognize that such relations are the product of the dynamic interaction of two different sectors of social relations, the external capitalist trade nexus and a precapitalist mode of production within the Latin American society (a de facto slave society in the case of Yucatán). With this in mind, we would be careful to distinguish in Yucatán between the modernization and private profitability of a small planter bourgeoisie and the underdevelopment and stagnation of the great mass of society that has been generated by the advancement of that bourgeoisie.[26]

Rather than assigning labels such as "capitalist," "precapitalist," or "feudal" to Yucatán's predominant economic system on the eve of the Revolution, we might more profitably view it as representative of a "plantation economy."[27] As such, prerevolutionary Yucatán possessed most of the social relations of production that have historically characterized plantation societies – namely, monopolization of the productive assets by a small planter class, often in alliance with foreign interests; production of a staple for external markets; absence of a vital domestic labor market and, consequently, reliance on a dependent or forced labor system; absence of a developed internal market for consumption; and the existence of a truncated social class structure, promoting a highly uneven distribution of income. I dwell upon these problems of definition in the larger context of dependency theory because more than semantics is involved. By concentrating on relations of production and labor systems, and not only on the nexus of the external market, we can better conceptualize and localize the relations of dependency *within* the local society and more precisely examine the connection or dialectical relationship between internal class structure and external linkages. Thus, we are not trapped into asserting, in static fashion, that Yucatán's uneven development was simply imposed upon the region from without by a powerful North American marketing trust. Indeed, there was also a dynamic internal logic to the process, and Yucatán's dependency was simultaneously an element of its internal socioeconomic configuration. As we have seen, exploitation of the Maya *campesinado* by a small landowning class did not begin with Harvester hegemony in Yucatán. Rather, the existing pattern of class relations based upon a traditional system of peonage quickly became transformed into a neo-slave regime as the local economy became ever more engaged by, and ultimately subordinated to, the demands of international capitalism (here represented by the foreign cordage trust). As a result, an alliance was established within Yucatán that, though it embodied essential contradictions, unified external interests with those of the local dominant groups. This collaboration consigned the unfortunate Yucatecan *campesino* to a "double exploitation" [28] that was graphically reflected in the involution of the labor system from traditional peonage to outright slavery.

The problem of mobilization

Upon visiting Yucatán's henequen plantations in 1909, Francisco Madero commented: "If there is a social revolution in Mexico, it will begin in Yucatán." [29] Of course, popular revolutions require many more preconditions than the mere reality of social injustice. But, in certain respects, Madero would be proven correct during the 1920–1923 period. For, as we shall see, during that period middle-class socialist revolutionaries recruiting dispossessed villagers and resident *peones* introduced what was perhaps the most radical social movement in the country. However, this would become possible only after much of the political and repressive power of the Old Regime had been curbed by outside forces during the 1915–1918 period. And even then, a popular ground swell would be slow to emerge, and the lack of it would seriously undercut the local revolutionary drive. In large part, this lack of a popular mobilization may be regarded as a legacy of Yucatán's economic structure, based on the formidable trinity of monoculture, dependent labor, and the large estate.

Economically exploited, isolated, and without allies, Yucatán's Maya *campesinado* was decidedly a nonrevolutionary force in 1915. Despite a history of collective protest in Yucatán, beginning in the 1850s the demographic and geographical dislocation of traditional peasant society, followed by the mobilization of intense forces of repression by the expanding planter class, broke the continuity of this tradition. In some agrarian societies, the actual events and experiences stored in such a tradition have often been exaggerated and mythologized by rural leaders for political and ideological reasons. Thus, the past history of struggle may never have been as vital as the present mythology would imply.[30] Ironically, for prerevolutionary Yucatán the converse seems to have been true. The Maya *campesinos*, heirs to a rich experience of agrarian struggle, had so lost touch with this tradition in the half-century of exploitation and repression following the Caste War that they themselves began to minimize the rebelliousness of their forefathers.

Most destructive of this collective tradition was the expansion of the henequen estate, which systematically alienated the Yucatecan peasant from his land base, disrupting his established community and forcing him onto the factorylike plantation, thereby commencing the process that eventually would transform him into a rural proletarian. Students of Mexican agrarian movements seem united in their agreement that such protests "had their basis in landowning village communities rather than on haciendas."[31] An important further distinction has been drawn between "revolutionary peasants" who become mobilized fighting for the survival of their landholding communities (e.g., the *Zapatistas* of Morelos) and "nonrevolutionary peasants" who, although poor, are allowed to maintain some traditional access to land, endure as a viable community, and prefer to stand pat rather than risk losing the little they have (e.g., the free villagers of Oaxaca).[32] The Yucatecan *campesinado* in 1915 would appear to represent a third possibility. For in Yucatán, the free village was neither poor but viable nor fighting to avoid becoming obsolete. With few exceptions, mostly in the remote southern and eastern sections of the region, the traditional peasantry had *already* become obsolete. Landless or very nearly so, free villagers became helpless to avoid the domination of the large estate.

Once pulled into the large estate's sphere, the *campesino* became subject to the full weight of its political, economic, and social control. The monopoly of force that the planters exercised in the region through federal, state, and private police forces, reinforced by a monopoly of all political and judicial offices, made resistance unlikely and escape difficult. Bounty hunters responding to advertisements in the local press and "security agents" on retainer tracked down runaways. Identification papers became required for *peones* temporarily leaving their estates.[33] In 1902, when the independent Maya state in Quintana Roo, which had given asylum to plantation runaways, was conquered by the Mexican army, the last avenue of escape was closed.[34]

Yet the planters took still other precautions. Whenever possible, they made sure that their work forces were heterogeneous groups, combining, say, Maya *campesinos*, Yaqui deportees, indentured oriental immigrants, and central Mexican *enganchados*. Such diverse conglomerations of human beings represented settlements rather than true communities of *peones acasillados* (rooted workers). The constant influx of outsiders and the extraordinarily high death rate among laborers disrupted collective relationships among immigrants and Maya alike. The old-timers who meant so much to the *Zapatista* rebellion in Morelos were rare on the Yucatecan plantations, which were drained of experience and renewed with ignornace. By intensifying the labor regime, then replenishing his work force with new arrivals, the *hacendado* accomplished a double purpose: He combatted the chronic labor shortage while minimizing the chances of organized resistance. In this regard, the Yucatecan henequen plantation had less in common with the paternalistic slaveholding regimes of the Old South than with the young, expansive cotton plantations on the Alabama and Mississippi frontier or the newer sugar estates of the Caribbean, where exploitation was so severe that it would not foster cohesive communities, only physical settlements where workers stayed temporarily before checking out for good.

Moreover, the Yucatecan *peones* were allowed virtually no contact with the world outside the plantation. *Hacendados* discouraged fraternization or intermarriage among workers of different estates, which Yucatán's rudimentary road system made difficult anyway. The *campesino* was completely sealed off from potential allies in the urban areas. Whenever possible, city visitors and peddlers were kept off the haciendas and *peones* restricted to them. In this respect, Yucatán's *campesinado* differed radically from its counterpart in central Mexico. In the central valley, for example, free Indian villages had from colonial times been situated near the urban centers of political and economic power. Often, in order to survive the economic privation attending the loss of their lands and the other demands that the dominant society made upon them, they were forced to seek work in neighboring mines, workshops, and factories, as well as on nearby haciendas. In addition to obtaining essential income, they learned new cultural skills – some ceased to be peasants – and made important urban contacts, thereby recruiting valuable allies and actual leaders during times of rebellion.[35]

In Yucatán, rural–urban exchanges were much rarer. Beyond the physical isolation promoted by the planters and a poor road system, there existed "an even more pernicious cultural isolation": an almost "absolute disinterest among *Meridanos* for the Indian countryside."[36] The tight bonds between urban workers and *campesinos*, which would be largely responsible for the creation, leadership, and ideology of the agrarian leagues in Veracruz and Michoacán, would never occur in Yucatán. Yucatán's urban proletariat seems to have come from other parts of Mexico or from Mérida, Progreso, and smaller local urban centers; recent recruits from the Yucatecan countryside were rare. The *Veracruzano* proletariat included the same complement of service workers – stevedores, railroad workers, and electricians – that made up the heart of Yucatán's urban labor movement. However, because – unlike the Yucatecan monoculture – Veracruz's economy was much more industrialized and diversified (producing oil, textiles, tobacco, and sugar), there existed not only a much larger urban proletariat in Veracruz but also much greater opportunities for rural–urban exchanges and migrations.[37] If some writers regard the failure of the Mexican Revolution to be due to the scuttling by the bourgeoisie of a highly plausible potential alliance between the rural and urban working classes,[38] Yucatán may constitute a significant exception, for such an alliance never appeared as a realistic possibility. Yucatecan urban and rural workers maintained separate identities and pursued different destinies. Whereas the *campesinado* remained immobilized, railroad and dock workers spearheaded a small but determined urban labor movement that had established itself by 1915. Barbers, bakers, food caterers, mechanics, carriage drivers, carters, and construction workers had all established *sindicatos* prior to General Alvarado's arrival. Fiercely independent, these artisans and workers fought first to establish job security, then to maintain their real wages. Beyond appreciating the fluctuations of the fiber market, upon which their wage schedules depended, they concerned themselves little with the countryside or the plight of the *campesino*.

In addition to the involuted condition of the *campesinado*, for Yucatán as a whole the revolutionary equation was substantially skewed. In its social organization, Yucatecan society during the Porfiriato had much in common with the colonial plantation and slave societies of an earlier period of Latin American history.[39] An enormous chasm separated the two extremes on the social scale: the tiny minority of planters and the great majority of slaves (*peones*). Nor was there much of a social infrastructure between these extremes. The urban working class, though at times well organized politically, was limited in its growth by the insignificant level of industrialization in the region, due to the persistence of monocrop agriculture and the failure of an internal market. With the exception of beer, candy, and cigarette factories, several ice-making plants, and a glass and cement operation – all small by national standards – the little money that had gone for industrial development had been put primarily into the failed attempts to produce binder twine or manufactured goods locally, or into service industries directly related to the production and transport of henequen (e.g., railroads, tramways, decorticating plants, and repair shops).[40]

Prerevolutionary Yucatán also possessed a middle class, very small even by the Latin American standards of the time: 3 to 5 percent of the population. This middle sector consisted mostly of intellectuals, journalists, professionals, small merchants, and small rural producers, most of whom served the agro-commercial elite and appropriated, or at least aspired to, its social outlook.[41] Nevertheless, there was an increasingly vocal minority that felt pinched by a lack of opportunity in the society. For in the stifling atmosphere of large-scale plantation agriculture, there was little room for any other major activity. Anything that was not connected to significant commercial production of henequen for export was relegated to secondary status.

At the same time, in the countryside, the rural petty bourgeoisie, a diverse constellation of small henequen and food producers, found itself without political influence, vulnerable to discrimination by the existing tax structure, powerless to secure reasonable freight rates or regular rail service for its goods, and unable to acquire additional land by denouncing *terrenos baldíos*.[42] In fact, where land was concerned, the probability was that these increasingly impoverished small henequen producers, like the even smaller *parcelarios* (rich *campesinos* who, in addition to growing corn and beans, harvested small plots of henequen), would become indebted to Molina, Montes, and the *Casta* and lose the land they currently had rather than increase their holdings. At any rate, these smaller producers and *rancheros* (plot holders) usually lived in the pockets of the large plantations and often eventually became its tenants and clients or, worse still, lost everything and succumbed as indebted *peones*. As we shall see, it was often from this *déclassé* rural petty bourgeoisie that "social bandits" and rural *caciques* (bosses) came, actors who would greatly affect the course of Yucatán's revolutionary experience in later years.[43]

These rural middle sectors and their urban counterparts were most immediately vulnerable during the times of economic instability and crisis that continued to plague an economy based on short-lived cycles and fluctuations. The 1907–1908 crisis swept away scores of recently established small commercial firms that had attempted to challenge the big *hacendado*-controlled import–export houses that handled the major food, dry goods, and hardware lines.[44] In the countryside, such crises worked to concentrate henequen production in fewer and larger hands. Those small producers of henequen not entirely under the oligarchy's control opposed Molina's call for mass production at low prices, arguing that they could not afford to wait for profits, so indebted were they already. Thus, the so-called *hacendado* class was far from a unified entity: In addition to the select few who had chosen to collaborate with the North American corporations and the several hundred other large planters who envied them their exclusive position, there were a number of smaller producers who increasingly found little common ground with the main body of large planters. Quite often, these smaller producers felt pressures more in common with the *parcelarios* and, beginning in 1915, many would find it in their interest to support Yucatán's revolutionary governments against the larger *henequeneros*, inasmuch as the revolutionaries offered them a more generous source of cash and credit.[45]

Madero, then, in predicting that Mexico's social revolution would begin in Yucatán, had correctly gauged the intense oppression of the Maya *campesinado*, as well as recognizing in Yucatán's middle-sector intellectuals the same discontents he was encountering throughout his tour of the Mexican Republic during 1909. Subsequent history has revealed to us the relative ease with which Madero's modest forces toppled Díaz's gerontocracy at the national level. Following the dictator's fall in 1911, Yucatán's *Maderista* intellectuals began to challenge the political dominance of Molina's oligarchy, expressing in the political arena the bitterness that accompanied a lack of social and economic opportunity.[46] At the same time, however sincere their concern for the condition of the masses (probably it was not overly so), they knew that practically speaking there was no immediate prospect of bringing a social revolution to Yucatán.

Due to the lack of mobilization or even a serious collective expression of unrest among the rural masses, as well as the monopoly of economic power and social control that the agro-commercial bourgeoisie exercised in the region, that was exactly what it would take – a revolution *brought in* from the outside and made from above. Theorists of agrarian movements are agreed that *campesinos* rarely play an initiating and leading role in making important changes in their institutional environment as long as social control over them remains firmly established.[47] In Yucatán, the extent of such social control was extraordinary. Despite their political triumph, the *Maderistas* would leave no lasting mark upon the region; indeed, in a variety of cases they were themselves coopted by Molina's ruling oligarchy.[48] A major power shift in favor of the Yucatecan *campesinos* would be required merely to gain access to them for purposes of mobilization. Even then, the cultural isolation of the *campesino* had been so great and his tradition of collective protest so undermined that from his point of view, any revolution engaging him, whether imported from central Mexico or initiated within the region by Yucatecan revolutionaries, was likely to appear as something essentially foreign to his social microcosm – a revolution from without. Significantly, the isolated episodes of violent *campesino* protest that took place in Yucatán during the late Porfiriato always came in response to specific *local* causes, to air local grievances. They flared up and died without consequence, except perhaps to frighten the local *patrón* into excessive counterforce and a tightening of control mechanisms that only further isolated the *campesinos*.[49]

This caveat should be kept in mind as we examine the two revolutionary moments that overtook the region during the 1915–1924 period. These two episodes, although issuing from a different source, predicated upon a different ideological program, drawing upon a different set of economic and human resources, and operating at a different historical juncture, were alike in attempting to bring a viable social revolution to a society that, although in desperate need of revolutionary change, was at the same time almost completely unprepared to participate in the revolutionary process. Thus, though we will examine the radical social programs implemented from 1920 to 1923 by Felipe Carrillo Puerto and other local revolutionaries, identifying these as an attempt at revolution from within, in a sense *both* of the major revolutionary moments in Yucatán were revolutions from without. First, we turn to General Alvarado's campaign to bring bourgeois revolutionary change to the region during the 1915–1918 period.

PART II

The bourgeois revolution, 1915–1918

4

Salvador Alvarado and bourgeois revolution from without

Peace is raging down here, as usual . . .
                    –The U.S. Consul, Progreso, 1916

It should surprise no one that today we do things that none have done before. The old governments have fallen; their laws have been overthrown; their gods are dead. All the so-called eternal truths have been altered. Such is the law of the Revolution.
                    –Salvador Alvarado, 1915

They came from the north, at dawn. A brave few *Meridanos* opened their windows a crack to catch a glimpse of the strangers. Mounted and on foot, wearing Stetson hats, with rifles in hand and ammunition belts crisscrossing their khaki tunics, Salvador Alvarado's Constitutionalists wound their way through the narrow city streets. "HUACH, HUACH squeaked the soles of their muddy boots on the newly paved stones: HUACH, HUACH, HUACH, as if to identify themselves to us as they marched through our city."[1]

At the head of the column rode the squat, mustachioed ex-pharmacist who was the Constitutionalist leader. Despite the tropical heat, General Alvarado's woolen tunic was buttoned to the neck, and he wore heavy riding pants tucked neatly into knee-high black leather boots. Hatless, his forelock pasted down over his brow, Alvarado surveyed the quiet city, his eyes barricaded behind the wire rims that would become his trademark. From the ranks of soldiers following came strains of the "Adelita." And behind them walked the women, some with infants slung across their backs.[2]

Well over a half-century later, Alvarado's orderly invasion – the day in March 1915 when the Mexican Revolution came to Yucatán – is still recalled by *Meridanos* with awe. How foreign these northern and central Mexican soldiers must have appeared to the Yucatecan civilians, the men decked out in panamas and loose-fitting white *guayaberas* (tropical-style shirts), many of the women wearing the traditional white, embroidered *huipil* (shift).[3]

93

The *huaches* came, as we have seen, because Venustiano Carranza's Constitutionalist Revolution could no longer afford to take Yucatán lightly. Only continued access to the region's henequen wealth would keep the First Chief's armies in the field against their rivals. The national struggle had reached a critical juncture by March 1915. Following Huerta's defeat in July 1914, the Mexican Revolution had become an internecine struggle between two conglomerations of rival bands and factions, designated "Constitutionalists" and "Conventionists." In the midst of this national disintegration, which produced a situation akin to warlordism throughout much of the Republic, only Carranza's Constitutionalists, led predominantly by petty bourgeois caudillos from Sonora and óther northern states, seemed ultimately capable of filling the political vacuum that existed at the center. Better organized, tactically shrewder, empowered by a long-term strategy for integrating Mexico's political and economic future within a centralized Revolutionary state, they had secured North American support. By March 1915 they were mounting a final offensive against the Conventionist forces led by Francisco Villa and Emiliano Zapata.

Immediately, Carranza's northern group began to implement the national strategy of domination and control upon which Mexico's new Revolutionary state would be built. As the Constitutionalists conquered the bulk of the nation's territory from the poorly integrated forces of the Convention, Carranza stationed trusted military caudillos in the occupied regions to consolidate power. These *norteño* "proconsuls" were expected to enact fiscal measures to finance further Constitutionalist military expansion while simultaneously incorporating their domains into an emerging centralized state.[4] In time, a clear-cut victory would bring this preconstitutional period of military rule to an end, and, as Mexico's elected president in 1917, Carranza would inaugurate civilian rule under a new Revolutionary constitution.

By no means were these *Carrancista* chiefs a homogeneous group. Some operated opportunistically on their own account, even forming alliances with members of the old Porfirian oligarchy.[5] Others cast their lot with the people and boldly attempted far-reaching social reforms. The majority of the *Carrancista* caudillos, however, probably fell somewhere in between these extremes and sought to balance the increased demands of the nation's workers and peasants with the interests of the new middle class and the surviving remnant of the traditional elite. Participants in the revolutionary process since 1910, these petty bourgeois chiefs had been sensitized to popular demands and now moved to satisfy them, provided they could be accommodated within the blueprint of the modern capitalist state that would emerge from the Revolution.[6] In Yucatán and the other conquered regions, Constitutionalist caudillos like Salvador Alvarado set about constructing multiclass coalitions to guarantee the emergence of the new Revolutionary state.

Although in large part Yucatecan henequen underwrote the Constitutionalists' political strategy, prior to Alvarado's arrival in March 1915 the movement's record in the region had been dismal. Alvarado's predecessors, military governors Eleuterio Ávila and Toribio de los Santos, had both failed to harness Yucatán's wealth or enlist its political support for the *Carrancista* cause. Ávila, a *Yucateco*, had buckled before the oligarchy; de los Santos, a Coahuilan, had been unnecessarily authoritarian and insensitive to the regional milieu. Both military chiefs had discredited the Constitutionalist Revolution, leaving in their wake a tradition of bribery and forced loans, of personal corruption and cruelty. Salvador Alvarado came to modify the image that the region had of the Mexican Revolution. Rather than tinker with the existing system, imposing new taxes and forced loans on a resentful populace, he was determined to reorganize the economic and social system on more rational, progressive, capitalist lines. In Yucatán's traditional plantation society, in which social and productive relations were often coercive or paternalistic, General Alvarado rightly perceived the revolutionary possibilities of bourgeois reform.

But before he could assemble a populist coalition that would modernize the region's traditional social cast, Alvarado would have to win over the fearful, suspicious *Yucatecos*. The initial care that the general took to ease tensions, safeguard rights, and respect regional pride did much to heal the old wounds so recently inflamed by General de los Santos. Prior to invading Mérida, Alvarado had guarded against inflicting gratuitous violence upon a helpless civilian population. After accepting control of the city, Alvarado further dispelled the *Yucatecos'* doubts by declaring as his first official act that anyone caught looting or assaulting a *vecino* (resident) would be shot. Ironically, the only casualties attending Alvarado's occupation of Mérida were several criminals and four of his own soldiers, who ran afoul of this edict. The general made a special example of two of his men who were convicted of raping two young girls, hanging them publicly in the central plaza and leaving their bodies suspended on the gallows for twelve hours.[7]

In the weeks and months ahead, Alvarado's actions reflected a basic decision that the people of Yucatán should not be punished for their regional sympathies, fanned and exploited by the oligarchs who had instigated the separatist *Argumedista* rebellion only one month before Alvarado's arrival.[8] Perhaps most reassuring to the *Yucatecos*, and symbolic of his respect for their region, was Alvarado's decision to marry a *Yucateca* of modest background, Laura Manzano of Mérida. A widower when he came to the peninsula, Alvarado made sure to conduct a lengthy courtship in the traditional style, complete with dawn *serenatas* and interminable visits with the bride's family.[9]

However, Alvarado left no doubt that the Revolution had come to Yucatán and would brook no further opposition from the region's old rulers. Although the rank-and-file recruits of the Ortiz Argumedo revolt were pardoned and given 10 liters of corn and free railroad passage home,[10] a stern example was made of the high-ranking officers and members of the *Casta Divina* who bankrolled the rebellion. The *Argumedista* brass who had not fled were jailed; those privileged backers of the rebels who had escaped to Cuba or the United States now had their assets expropriated by the Revolution's new *Departamento de Bienes Incautados* (Department of Attached Properties). Within a month of Alvarado's arrival, the new department's register read like a *Who's Who* of the *Casta Divina*, listing the impounded estates and businesses of twenty self-exiled super-planters and merchants, among them Avelino Montes, Ricardo Molina, José Rafael de Regil, Antonio Palomeque, and Julián Aznar. The total value of the attached properties was estimated at 20 million pesos. Alvarado's government retained the administrators and employees of these enterprises, who now ran them for the state's profit. By mid-1916, Alvarado had realized $60,673 in income from their operation, most of which he invested in an expanded program of public education.[11]

To underscore further that the old days were gone, the general systematically dismantled the old repressive mechanism that had supported the oligarchical regime. Municipal policemen were disarmed and placed under the supervision of Alvarado's district military commanders, who now replaced the former local authorities, the hated district prefects (*jefes políticos*).[12] The state's *guar-*

dias territoriales, the militia units that had been the backbone of *Argumedismo*, were declared counterrevolutionary and disbanded.[13] Finally, thirty-seven high-ranking ex-federal officers who had served the Díaz and Huerta regimes were deprived of public employment and placed under strict surveillance.[14]

However, although Yucatán would now be subject to a tight system of military rule until a new Revolutionary constitution could be promulgated for Mexico, Alvarado made it clear that he would not act hastily or prevent *Yucatecos* from playing an important role in the revolution that would transform the region.[15] For six full months following his arrival, the general patiently studied regional conditions, appointing a local committee to provide him with facts and to recommend specific reforms. The committee was made up of Yucatecans from various points on the social spectrum, including several prominent *hacendados* and merchants. Indeed, having already singled out the most powerful elements of the *Casta* for exemplary punishment, Alvarado now adopted a conciliatory posture toward the larger planter elite, going so far as to invite home those who had gone into exile.[16]

Mexican intellectuals and military men served as Alvarado's chief advisors during the early days of the regime, imported along with a *norteño* mariachi band that spent most of its time playing "La Cucaracha" in the courtyard of the governor's palace.[17] In addition to a triumvirate of colonels – the Ramírez Garrido brothers (José and Calixto) and Rafael Aguirre Colorado – who initially directed the Education Department, police, and executive staff, Alvarado brought to Yucatán a number of talented civilian orators and specialists to promote and coordinate his reform program. Modesto Rolland, director of the *Comisión Local Agraria*, Mario Calvino, director of the Agricultural Department, and Gregorio Torres Quintero, subsequently head of the Education Department, would all go on to earn national reputations.[18]

However, increasingly it was *Yucatecos* who assumed the principal responsibility for running Alvarado's sizable revolutionary bureaucracy. By and large, the general drew his government's personnel from the middle ranges of regional society: disaffected members of the intellectual and professional middle sectors and the urban working class. Yet he did not hesitate to enlist the services of some of the highest-ranking members of the agro-commercial bourgeoisie – the Peóns, the Vales, the G. Cantóns, the Escalantes, Manuel Zapata Casares, Fidencio Márquez, and Arcadio Escobedo Guzmán, to name but a few – to manage key agencies and departments in his administration, most notably the state-controlled henequen monopoly (*Comisión Reguladora del Mercado de Henequén*), the state-owned railroads (*Ferrocarriles Unidos de Yucatán*), and the state-managed cordage plant (La Industrial).[19]

By contrast, the middle- and working-class *Yucatecos* generally held less glamorous, lower-paying positions in the bureaucracy. However, they operated at the grass-roots level as political organizers, cadres of the general's agrarian and rural education programs, and key operatives in the urban labor movement. Their contact with the masses enabled them to assume greater power once the preconstitutional period of military rule gave way to an era of partisan politics about the middle of 1917. An entire generation of Yucatecan Socialist Party leaders, including Rafael Gamboa, Rafael Cebada, Felipe Valencia López, Manuel González, and future governors Carlos Castro Morales, Felipe Carrillo Puerto, José María Iturralde Traconis, Dr. Álvaro Torre Díaz, and César Alayola Barrera, received their political initiation as *Alvaradistas*. The radical Carrillo, for example, had previously been run out of Yucatán by Ávila; now Alvarado recognized his rapport with the Maya *campesinos*, which, if skillfully handled, would bolster the legitimacy of the general's regime. He employed Carrillo in the countryside, first as an organizer (*agente de propaganda*) in his home district of Motul, later as one of the leaders of the pivotal *Departamento de Cooperativas* (Department of Cooperatives).[20]

This, then, was Alvarado's peculiar talent, an ability to forge a political coalition incorporating conservative planters as well as radical intellectuals and laborers, all working to advance a program that, despite its revolutionary rhetoric, was rather moderate in substance. Already, in a series of initial talks with representatives of the ruling bourgeoisie, Alvarado had reassured the big planters and merchants that expropriation was not on his mind. Rather, he sought to enlist their support in a variety of large-scale agricultural, commercial, and industrial ventures he had under consideration, which would recast traditional notions regarding the state's passive role in the regional economy but not to the exclusion of private enterprise.[21] In fact, it was only later, when he found Yucatán's former oligarchs reluctant to cooperate economically, that Alvarado began to employ sterner measures for the realization of these goals.

Alvarado's policy of elite collaboration to provide needed expertise in essential economic areas contributed in the beginning to the success of his regime and enabled him to introduce and consolidate his bourgeois revolutionary program. However, this strategy, continued by later Socialist governments, ultimately proved to be a costly mistake, serving in most cases further to enrich a few while dissipating the region's revolutionary drive from within.[22]

Salvador Alvarado: caudillo and ideologue

The director of this nascent populist coalition brought impressive political credentials to Yucatán. Born in 1880, the son of a modest printer in the northwestern state of Sonora, Alvarado went on to become a shopkeeper, druggist, and small farmer (*ranchero*). Like so many of the future revolutionary chiefs from Sonora, Alvarado felt suffocated by the corruption and privilege of provincial Porfirian society. Years later he would write:

I began to feel the need for a change in our social organization from the age of 19, when, in my home town Potam, Río Yaqui, I used to see the Police Commissioner get drunk almost daily, in the local billiard room, in the company of his secretary, the judge of the lower court, the tax inspector . . . and various businessmen or army officers, all people who made up the influential class of that small world.[23]

Finding his path for further advancement blocked, Alvarado joined the anarcho-syndicalist Mexican Liberal Party (PLM) in 1906. That same year, while proprietor of a small store in Cananea, headquarters of the North American Greene Copper Company, Alvarado became involved in the bloody Cananea workers' strike and was forced to flee to Arizona. The PLM's intense persecution by the Díaz regime led him to transfer his allegiance to the more moderate, broader-based *Maderista* movement in 1909. Alvarado's organizational and tactical skills elevated him rapidly in the military hierarchy during the revolutionary campaigns against Díaz and Huerta. In July 1914, with Álvaro Obregón he won a major Constitutionalist victory over the *Huertistas* at Guaymas. Promoted subsequently to division general by Carranza, Alvarado was named military commandant of the federal district following Huerta's defeat. After only two and a half months in Mexico City, however, the First Chief sent him to Yucatán.[24]

Alvarado's commission by Carranza was fraught with political consequences for both of these highly ambitious revolutionaries. No doubt Alvarado intended to use his appointment in Yucatán to promote an image for himself; perhaps he even viewed the peninsula as a springboard to the national presidency.[25] Repeatedly, he publicized his intention to make Yucatán a model of what the Mexican Revolution could accomplish, to transform the region into a revolutionary laboratory.[26] The First Chief had a different agenda. Since the beginning of the decade, Alvarado had been a bitter rival of Carranza's principal general, Obregón, in their native Sonora. Once the Constitutionalist campaign to reconquer the central plateau from the forces of the Convention began early in 1915, Carranza shrewdly realized that he would receive a double advantage by assigning Alvarado to Yucatán. First, by removing him from the scene in central Mexico, the First Chief would avoid flare-ups with Obregón or his cronies, who were then running Sonora. The *Obregonistas'* consolidation of power in the northwest remained a sticking point for the fiercely competitive Alvarado, who had lost the struggle for hegemony in his home region. An exacerbation of the Obregón–Alvarado rivalry was the last thing Carranza wanted to risk in the spring of 1915; in fact, prior to the great battles at Celaya and León, it was still conceivable that the opportunistic Obregón might be pushed into an alliance with the *Villistas.* Secondly, by putting Obregón's arch rival in charge of one of the two richest states in the country (his son-in-law, Cándido Aguilar, was already in charge of the other, Veracruz), the First Chief guaranteed himself a strategic source of income in case Obregón did enter into a pact with Villa. In short, Salvador Alvarado was Carranza's insurance policy against Álvaro Obregón's betrayal.[27]

Alvarado, of course, hoped to turn Carranza's dilemma to his own advantage, carving out a political base for himself in the peninsula. However, his intention to make Yucatán his great revolutionary monument reflects more than personal ambition. The general's ideological commitment to Mexico's social renovation was also a powerful motivation. Like a number of other petty bourgeois autodidacts who became caudillos, Alvarado found himself caught up in the revolutionary struggle as a "man of action" frequently called upon to act as a "man of words."[28] However, perhaps to a greater extent than other revolutionary chieftains, Alvarado relished the opportunity to exercise his intellectual pretensions and play the ideologue. Writing in the aftermath of the Revolution, historian Frank Tannenbaum observed that "he, perhaps more than any other Mexican who took an active part in the Revolution, attempted to formulate its program. But no

Mexican intellectual would admit that Alvarado was an intellectual or that he formulated the program of the Revolution."[29]

Alvarado's social thought – consolidated in several weighty tomes as well as numerous *folletos* (tracts) and articles – reflects the classic blend of modernization and moralizing that characterizes bourgeois reformers. Ironically, he fancied himself a socialist. On one occasion, in 1920, he went so far as to tell the national Chamber of Deputies that he had been, was, and would continue to be a bolshevik.[30] A voracious reader, Alvarado admired the European utopian socialists as well as New World socialist and social democratic thinkers, such as Henry George, W. E. Walling, and H. W. Laidler.[31] However, at most, Alvarado was prepared to experiment with forms of state intervention in the economy. Despite his early connection with Ricardo Flores Magón and the anticapitalist PLM, at no time did he embrace more than a philosophical commitment to the concept "that the worth of each man is proportional to that which is produced for the mass of the people."[32]

By "socialism," Alvarado seemed broadly to understand several basic concepts: first, that henceforth Mexico's riches (e.g., Yucatán's henequen) would be exploited for the benefit of the Mexican people and would not go to enrich the foreigners who invested directly or controlled Mexican production indirectly through marketing trusts and monopolies; second, that future generations of Mexican workers would be delivered, by means of government organization and legislation, from their condition as forced laborers and social pariahs; and finally, that it was the responsibility of a powerful state to effect these changes and eliminate all obstacles standing in the path of Mexico's future progress. However, Alvarado's extensive polemical writings – most notably the bulky three-volume study *La reconstrucción de México* (1919) – and his Yucatecan praxis suggest that his idiosyncratic, self-proclaimed state socialism was more precisely a detailed blueprint for state capitalism via a populist brand of bourgeois revolution.

The basic assumption that guided Alvarado as he formulated his revolutionary program for Yucatán was that although the demands of workers and *campesinos* were valid, they could – indeed, must – be met within the limits of the capitalist system. Consequently, the central goal was to eliminate obstacles to industrial capitalism and progress: conditions of slavery or peonage, the nonproductive great estate, and foreign imperialism. To combat such evils, a statist approach and a strong executive were favored;

nationally controlled industries were encouraged; and the medium-size, intensively cultivated, highly capitalized "small property" (*pequeña propiedad*) was preferred to the *ejido* in the agrarian sector. Item for item, Alvarado's ideological horizon was that of Obregón, Calles, and the nascent class of *jefes sonorenses* who in the 1920s and early 1930s consolidated Mexico's bourgeois Revolutionary state.[33]

In Yucatán, Alvarado sought not only to defend capitalism, preserving the right of private property, but also to implant it throughout the region, substituting the wage relationship for all forms of coerced or precapitalist labor. Foreign monopolists and local agents who speculated with the region's well-being were the enemies. The hard-working, productive planter or businessman had nothing to fear, provided he didn't abuse his workers. Alvarado's goal was to transform what he regarded as neo-feudal *hacendados* into modern capitalists, to convert slavelike *peones* and *obreros* into true proletarians. In the wholesome climate of capitalism that would emerge from these reforms, the rich and the poor would both be redeemed. In Alvarado's roseate vision, the responsible forces of capital and labor would come to regard their interests as complementary rather than conflictive: "Capital and labor, mind and muscle-power, idea and action, these things ought to work in unison, in a joint effort to promote progress and happiness for everyone."[34]

The laboratory of the revolution

In the light of more recent social movements in the twentieth century, Alvarado's philosophy of revolutionary reform appears rather conservative, not to mention utopian. However, this was prior to the Russian Revolution of 1917, and a sophisticated formulation of social property had not yet taken root in Mexico. For its period, Alvarado's program was progressive indeed. In a traditional plantation society such as Yucatán, the application of Alvarado's bourgeois reform spelled the end of oligarchical domination. Moreover, Alvarado made good his boast: Under his regime Yucatán *did* come to be regarded by the rest of the Republic as a pace setter, a social laboratory for the Revolution where bold experiments in political organization, state intervention in the economy, and labor and educational reform were carried out.[35] Beginning in late 1915 and continuing throughout his tenure in Yucatán, Alvarado received scores of queries and requests from other Constitutionalist governors and military commanders who expressed a desire to learn and follow the precedents of the *vía revolucionaria yucateca* (the Yucatecan revolutionary way) and, in some cases, solicited financial aid for their strife-torn states.[36] In this chapter, attention is given to a wide range of Alvarado's social reforms and to the strategy of political mobilization that guided his bourgeois revolution. The following chapter will examine the general's response to the central economic problems of land and the henequen industry.

To Alvarado must go the credit for shattering the formidable repressive mechanisms of the Porfiriato and for introducing and then legitimizing a nucleus of political, social, and economic reforms upon which later revolutionary regimes could build. That Alvarado was able to accomplish so much in only three years (1915–1918) is attributable in part to his organizational ability and drive. More likely, however, Alvarado owed much of his success in initiating revolution from above to the timing and circumstances of his arrival in Yucatán. As a divisional general – there were only ten at the time in the entire Republic – in charge of a large military force, Alvarado brought great extralegal powers to the weighty civilian responsibility, entrusted to him by Carranza, of ruling what was then perhaps Mexico's richest state. Moreover, his period of rule in Yucatán coincided with the preconstitutional phase of the Mexican Revolution, when, as Carranza's personal representative in the Republic's most isolated region, he enjoyed a measure of autonomy from Mexico City and freedom from constitutional restraints.

Alvarado's tenure in Yucatán also fortuitously coincided with a wartime export boom for henequen. In fact, from 1916 to 1918, Yucatán's chief industry experienced a veritable golden age in terms of production and earnings. These circumstances gave Alvarado control of political and economic institutions and great latitude for action as Yucatán's military governor in 1915 that subsequent civilian revolutionary governors could not count on in the 1920s and 1930s.

Looking back on his era in Yucatán, Alvarado would later boast that he had issued more than a thousand reform decrees and laws en route to transforming Yucatán into a revolutionary vanguard.[37] Perhaps most important, Alvarado did what his predecessors, Ávila and de los Santos, had been incapable of doing: He put an end to slavery in Yucatán. He changed the relations of production on haciendas, abolishing forced labor and in a modest way begin-

General Alvarado and his secretary in the Governor's Palace, Mérida, 1915.
(Reprinted from Gustavo Casasola, *Historia gráfica de la Revolución Mexicana,
1910–1970*, 2d ed., Mexico, 1973, vol. 3, p. 994. Casasola, INAH.)

ning the process of mobilizing the Yucatecan *campesinado*, thereby
hastening its proletarianization. When significant numbers of the
approximately 100,000 freed *peones*[38] exercised their newly won
right of movement and left the haciendas – in the majority of cases
only temporarily[39] – Alvarado silenced *hacendado* criticism by ar-
ranging for the immigration to Yucatán of over 21,000 contract

workers form other parts of Mexico, thereby helping to ensure that henequen production would keep pace with soaring prices.[40]

Alvarado's enforcement of Ávila's 1914 decree canceling debt labor also extended to the thousands of domestic servants, largely Maya women and children, who had labored through the generations in Mérida and the larger towns "without pay, without contract, without end."[41] When Alvarado learned that in many cases these indebted servants had been forced into prostitution by their masters, he moved to reform Yucatán's oldest profession, eliminating bordellos, outlawing pimps, and stipulating frequent medical inspections for women in the trade and heavy punishments for men with venereal disease who patronized them.[42]

Alvarado's approach to women's issues in general was revolutionary by the Mexican – and Western – standards of his time. To further his goal of liberating women from the influence of centuries of oppression and constraints of traditional religion, Alvarado called Mexico's first Feminist Congress in 1918 (two would be held in Yucatán that year), introduced coeducation in Yucatecan schools, reformed the civil code, and opened government employment to women. His measures in Yucatán influenced national policy and ideology and provided a foundation for later feminist activity in the region.[43]

Although he was generally broad-minded and progressive, Alvarado occasionally displayed a tendency toward authoritarian prudishness that did not win the approval of the *Yucatecos*. In the social sphere, he sought to impose his own rather inflexible Victorian morality on the region, striking down such traditional institutions and pleasures as the cantina (hard liquor), bullfighting, raffles, lotteries, and other forms of gambling and "vice" that would interfere with what Alvarado referred to as "the complete regeneration and splendid resurgence of the Indian race."[44] In place of these vices, which corrupted the youth, Alvarado was prepared to import such wholesome cultural innovations as the Boy Scouts.[45]

Needless to say, despite provisions for fines and imprisonment, it was much easier to eliminate these popular pastimes in print than in practice. Most observed in the breach was the new provision regarding alcohol. Alvarado was quite right in identifying alcoholism as one of Yucatán's social weaknesses. However, *Yucatecos* found it impossible to quench their thirst with 5 percent beer, and the clandestine liquor trade flourished, channeled, as it always had been, through the local power structure in each village or hamlet. Further attempts by Alvarado to threaten local officials and his own military subordinates, whom he (accurately) suspected of complicity, produced only temporary compliance with the unpopular edict.[46] Generally speaking, Alvarado's blitzkrieg upon the region's manners and mores resulted in defeat.

Considering the full panoply of his reforms, Alvarado probably misjudged the sentiments of his adopted region on only one other occasion. His harassment of the local Church, which at times spilled over into violent acts of persecution, never caught on among the deeply religious *campesinado* and lost him the respect of large segments of the urban elite and middle sectors.[47] Like so many of his generation of northern caudillos, "ideologically weaned on . . . secular missals which exalted the *Juarista* and anticlerical *Patria*," Alvarado contrasted the "secular heaven" of the modern capitalist state that would be Mexico's future to the "cavern of clericalism" that had been its feudal past.[48] For the first two years of his regime, he applied almost continuous pressure on the Church, exiling priests, ransacking and closing temples, transforming ecclesiastical buildings into public schools.[49]

Alvarado told the North American Ernest Gruening that his anticlerical displays served "the deliberate purpose of showing the Indians that the lightning would not strike – that the Constitutionalists were not the enemies of God as priests had told them."[50] Yet the public spectacle of Alvarado's mounted *federales* riding into neighborhood churches and desecrating altars did not enhance the general's popularity. Outraged planters and professionals, including members of Alvarado's revolutionary coalition, denounced these "sacrilegious acts" sponsored by a government that had degenerated into "a tribe of savages led by a modern-day Attila."[51] Counterdemonstrations, often instigated by the elite but made up in large part of *campesinos* and their wives, began to challenge Alvarado's anticlerical offensive. On 30 January 1916, for example, in the country town of Telchac, a crowd of 300, mostly irate *campesinas*, violently protested the local military commander's seizure of relics from the community church. Brandishing sticks and hoes, they blocked the road and forcibly unloaded the artifacts from a government mule train.[52] Early in 1917, no doubt in response to these popular expressions of dissatisfaction, Alvarado began to temper his anticlericalism, opening a number of churches and tolerating a small number of priests.[53]

A more successful strategem was Alvarado's occasional jailing of prominent planters for relatively minor transgressions, such as public displays of arrogance with their former slaves.[54] By providing a series of dramatic object lessons to the rural masses, by encouraging them to view religion and seigneurial privilege as the symbols of their exploitation, Alvarado hoped to rouse them from their lethargy and pave the way for a more systematic mobilization that he would control from above.

True to liberalism, Alvarado nurtured the hope that education and not the expropriation of property might contribute significantly to a solution of Yucatán's pressing social and economic problems. Repeatedly, he expressed the wish that, if for nothing else, he be remembered and judged for the more than 1,000 new schools he created in Yucatán – the majority of them in remote rural areas – and for the corps of teachers he trained or brought into the state from central Mexico and the United States.[55] According to one observer, by 1916 Alvarado's teachers outnumbered the soldiers in his army.[56] The general established several important educational precedents that Felipe Carrillo and the Socialist state governments under Cárdenas would follow and expand: the allocation of a much greater percentage of the state budget for public – and especially rural – education; the establishment of more normal schools and teacher-training programs, some of which would emphasize the preparation of Maya teachers for rural areas; and the responsibility of the state to provide "rational education," that is, a curriculum that would incorporate collectivist principles in teaching the skills necessary in the daily life of the village.[57]

Much less transcendental in their impact were Alvarado's attempts to establish "popular libraries" throughout the state and prescribe the reading of important books by high school students. Although packets of books were distributed by the state government, which ordered them from Mexico City, the libraries ultimately depended upon funding by the local *hacendados* or town councils, which even in the best of times proved unreliable.[58] Thus, the "great books" program was probably more significant for what it revealed of the liberal bourgeois attitude that guided Alvarado than for any important service it rendered. The general assigned books that he felt would mold the character of Yucatán's youth, instilling traits such as thrift, self-reliance, determination, and hard work. That pillar of Victorian and Edwardian Britain, Samuel Smiles, who had influenced Alvarado as a boy,[59] became required reading in the local schools.

Alvarado's introduction of the rural school as early as 1915–

1916 was certainly his most enduring educational reform and had important political consequences as well. Although ex-*hacendados* and their apologists continue to claim that the first country schools were formed on a number of large haciendas prior to and during 1910,[60] these early schools were imbued with an educational philosophy and purpose radically different from that of Alvarado's first secular, free, compulsory rural schools.[61] The rural schools created earlier, at the individual proprietor's initiative or through the *hacendados' Liga de Acción Social* in 1910, sought to domesticate their pupils – the children of their *peones* – in order to encourage them to be more obedient, efficient workers and shield them from contact with "unsettling revolutionary ideas."[62] Few actual classroom skills – certainly no arithmetic to "confuse" the issue of the *peón's hoch cuenta* (cumulative debt) – were taught and religious instruction was emphasized.[63] Alvarado's schools, by contrast, initiated a rudimentary literacy campaign – 12,000 *campesinos* learned to read and write Spanish[64] – and, more importantly, taught the former *peones* their constitutional rights as Mexican citizens, encouraging them to accept their responsibilities as free men. In effect, the rural school provided the essential ideological reinforcement for the political decree that had abolished forced labor and served – albeit in a very modest way – as an early focal point for mobilization in the *campo*. Under Alvarado there came to the fore the revolutionary agent who, after 1920, would lead political mobilization in the rural sector, the *maestro de escuela* or local schoolteacher.[65]

The rural *maestro* became, along with the *agente de propaganda*, a kind of revolutionary ombudsman.[66] These teachers and local agents – among them Felipe Carrillo Puerto and other future socialist leaders – became Alvarado's men-on-the-spot on the haciendas and in the pueblos. It was their duty to communicate, either directly to Alvarado or indirectly through his subregional military commandants or the local municipal officials, any violation of revolutionary legislation or labor abuses committed by *hacendados* or merchants against the common people.[67] And no abuse was too small to be overlooked. Alvarado publicly fined and humiliated the daughters of a prominent planter family when it was reported that, in violation of the general's edict against *besamanos*, they had coerced their former slaves into kissing their hands in the traditional style.[68]

It was by means of this communications network, which extended to even the smallest country hamlet, that Alvarado was determined to establish the precedent of a "retroactive revolution" in Yucatán. In other words, Alvarado sought to develop a realization in the minds of *campesinos* (and urban workers) that the Revolution would now redress all abuses and injustices suffered by them, whether they occurred in the present or years, even decades, earlier. The *jornalero* who once had lost a hand in a henequen press and the mechanic who had been scalded in a boiler explosion might now join the *peón* whose wages were unnecessarily low or held up without justification in bringing their cases before one of the state government's new Tribunals of Conciliation and Arbitration. If their complaints could be substantiated, monetary compensation, including awards for punitive damages, would be paid by their past or current employers. Unfortunately, in the absence of systematic union organization and strong mobilization in the countryside, which Alvarado was reluctant to encourage, the burden of disclosure was placed on the individual Maya *campesino*, who was then pitted in court against his powerful (and often articulate) former master or current employer. Not surprisingly, few cases were reported from the rural sector.[69]

As expected, the unionized urban workers of Progreso and Mérida were far more successful in invoking the principle of retroactive revolution.[70] Under Alvarado's aegis, the urban working class came of age in Yucatán. An atheist who had come from modest urban beginnings, the general had a cultural affinity for the anticlerical *obrero* (urban worker) that he could not hope to share with the often devout Indian *campesino*. Immediately upon taking control of Yucatán, Alvarado recognized the legality of the old guard unions and *sindicatos* (syndicates) – made up principally of railroad and port workers, service employees, and artisans – that, after some struggle, had emerged in the final years of the Porfiriato.[71] He then exhorted other workers to organize and obtain the benefits of the Revolution, mounting an intensive propaganda campaign in both the state capital and chief port. Backing up his words with patronage, the general gave subsidies of 20,000 and 10,000 pesos to the masons and ironworkers, respectively, to encourage them to unionize. In the first few weeks of his administration, typesetters, restaurant waiters, and beer, cigarette, and confectionary workers also formed syndicates.[72]

That same first month, on 4 April 1915, Alvarado hosted at his private residence in Mérida the formation of a branch of the national anarcho-syndicalist *Casa del Obrero Mundial* (House of the World Worker) (COM). By the end of 1915, only nine months after the general's arrival, the COM was firmly established as Alvarado's umbrella organization for the urban labor sector and had registered 418 old and new syndicates, including organizations in smaller urban centers such as Motul and Valladolid.[73] Through the COM, Alvarado encouraged worker participation in local and state political office. In June 1916, COM activists and high-ranking *Alvaradistas* collaborated to form the *Partido Socialista Obrero* (Socialist Workers' Party), a first attempt to institutionalize Alvarado's populist coalition. In their initial test the following September, the Socialists swept the elections for mayor and town council in the state capital. Significantly, the party's first directorate included a barber and two railway men in addition to two school teachers, a journalist, and a pharmacist. Rafael Gamboa, the fiery barber known as "Ravachol," was the party's first president. During Alvarado's administration, he would be succeeded as party leader by Carlos Castro Morales, a railroad worker, and Felipe Carrillo Puerto, a carter, railroad conductor, and jack of many trades.[74]

For those who still had not gotten the message that he intended to make the urban proletariat his chief civilian ally, Alvarado passed a radical labor law in December 1915 that immediately was recognized as one of the most progressive in the Republic and later served as one of the models for Article 123 of the new national Constitution of 1917.[75] The Yucatán labor law answered traditional demands on wages and hours, working conditions, child labor, and accident compensation; granted the right to strike; created a Department of Labor; supported mutualistic societies – which Carrillo Puerto would later develop into a network of consumer cooperatives – and provided for the labor tribunals that would administer the retroactive revolution on the *obrero's* behalf.[76] Under Alvarado's protection, urban workers successfully began to press wage demands on employers, utilizing the new tribunals as well as their right to strike. Mérida's underpaid bakers and cantina employees, for example, struck for a 100 percent salary increase. They were soon followed by the typesetters, cigarette makers, and beer and confectionary workers, all of whom had recently been organized by the government.[77] Meanwhile, under Alvarado's wing, the railroad workers and the 2,000 Progreso longshoremen were establishing themselves as a peninsular labor aristocracy; despite inflation and later severe recession, they commanded steady wage hikes throughout the 1915–1918 period.[78]

Revolution from above

At no point, however, did Alvarado lose control of the process of popular mobilization. Indeed, his policies of retroactive revolution and patronage of the urban labor movement clearly illustrate the populist strategy of mobilization from above that guided his bourgeois revolution. The general's program was geared to impress upon workers and *campesinos* that all of the benefits they received – for example, freedom from debt peonage, redress of old grievances, the right to organize and strike, salary increases – resulted directly from state action. In turn, the state demanded their support in its efforts to consolidate the Revolution in the face of potential opposition from the *Casta Divina* and its North American allies. Workers and *campesinos* would give their support by incorporating themselves into organizations created and controlled by the revolutionary government and by channeling their demands through the state apparatus. This meant that once old and current abuses had been redressed by the government, workers would strive, through state mediation, to conciliate their differences with employers rather than exacerbate them. In the process, the state would encourage a blurring of class interests and maintain a revolutionary coalition capable of standing up to the threat of retaliation by the oligarchy and its allies.

Consequently, General Alvarado's encouragement of organized labor had its limits. Like Carranza, Alvarado did not hesitate to close the COM in April 1916 when the regional branch, true to its anarcho-syndicalist ideology, sought a sphere of action beyond Alvarado's control.[79] And, like the First Chief, Alvarado threatened to shoot public employees when they invoked one of the basic rights of labor around which he had originally organized them – the right to strike.[80] As the state's control over workers' organizations became more pronounced, Alvarado sought to persuade the workers of the value of a "mutualist" approach based on government conciliation and cooperativism, rather than a "syndicalist" posture based on confrontation and the strike.[81] It became increasingly clear that the general favored the creation of urban syndicates and rural *ligas de resistencia* (resistance leagues) primarily as a means of legitimizing his government's authority. The state would give the masses a stake in the political process; however, it would not let them actively participate, let alone rule. One student, rather uncharitably, has characterized Alvarado's caudillo populism with the quip that, although Alvarado seemed favorably disposed toward some form of state socialism, "it was almost immediately obvious that . . . he considered himself the state."[82]

On the other hand, Alvarado was able to construct a successful organizational framework for his Yucatecan revolutionary coalition. In fact, by galvanizing the military, coopted members of the middle sectors and bourgeoisie, and large segments of the urban and rural working classes behind a nominally socialist or collectivist ideology, his Yucatán coalition was a prototype of the national populist state that Obregón and Calles would consolidate in the 1920s and, in certain respects, an early precursor of Lázaro Cárdenas's more elaborately corporatist PRM (*Partido Revolucionario Mexicano*) and the modern-day PRI (*Partido Revolucionario Institucional*). Like the PRI's founders, Alvarado recognized that if his multiclass coalition were to endure, it would have to be institutionalized. During his three-year regime, he created pilot institutions such as a state party and a network of local revolutionary organizations in the city and countryside that later would become constituent party units. An examination of this emerging political system reveals more specifically the proto-corporatist manner in which Alvarado carried out his revolution from above.

At the top was Alvarado and his Yucatecan Socialist Party (the name was formally changed to *Partido Socialista de Yucatán* in 1917), which increasingly staffed Alvarado's state administration. Both the state government and the Socialist Party enjoyed the support of the Constitutionalist Army of the Southeast, which Alvarado controlled in his dual capacity as state executive and military commander. In the cities and major towns, Alvarado's chief clients, the urban workers, were tied to the party through their affiliated syndicates and unions, which were renamed *ligas de resistencia* toward the end of the general's administration. Middle-sector intellectuals and professionals, along with some liberal *hacendados* and merchants, were directly coopted into the government bureaucracy; sick of the power and arrogance of the *Casta Divina*, many of these officials also joined the Socialist Party.

In the countryside, the organizational structure was looser and underwent a significant transformation about the middle of 1917. The Porfirian system of authority and control, centered on the *jefes políticos* backed by state, local, and private police, had been dismantled following Alvarado's invasion in March 1915. In place of the sixteen unpopular, high-handed district prefects, who in most cases had been planters or their proxies, Alvarado now stationed his most trusted officers, making sure that, in certain instances,

Yucatecos were appointed to these *comandancias militares*. Alvarado transferred complete local authority to these military chiefs; many of them took the general as their model and acted out their own reduced version of his populism in their rural domains.[83]

As bosses of their districts (*partidos*), the *comandantes militares* were entrusted with keeping the political peace, preventing the exploitation of workers on the rural estates, and implementing Alvarado's social and educational reforms. They were required periodically to write reports to Alvarado, briefing him on social conditions and providing a detailed statistical account of agricultural and livestock production in their districts.[84] To check their potential influence and promote the bureaucratic honesty that he insisted upon for his regime, Alvarado frequently transferred the *comandantes* from district to district. He encouraged their civilian subordinates – members of local municipal councils, revolutionary *maestros*, and *agentes de propaganda* – to report directly to him regarding the district's management.[85] Moreover, the general was quick to lecture, reprimand, fine, and even imprison subordinates who abused their administrative powers. A 1,000-peso reward was publicly offered to anyone producing reliable evidence of misuse of public funds. "We must show the people that the Revolution has the power to punish its bad servants," Alvarado explained.[86] Several *comandantes militares* from outlying *partidos* were hauled before revolutionary magistrates for bribery, embezzlement, extortion, and speculation in government-regulated maize. The military commander of Izamal was removed following local complaints that he had been bought by local planters and merchants. His counterpart in Tekax, on the other hand, was severely reprimanded for being too harsh on the local elite.[87]

By and large, however, these *comandantes militares* ruled honestly and firmly. Many were seasoned campaigners who had served with Alvarado in the north. Following their caudillo's example, they were scrupulously honest in their political and economic dealings at the local level. Like Alvarado, they came and went without setting down local roots.[88] Not surprisingly, the kind of isolated, violent *campesino* protest that had been set off by local abuses during the final years of the Old Regime did not materialize during Alvarado's military interregnum.

Although the countryside was tightly under his control, Alvarado was much less active in mobilizing the rural areas than he was in the cities. Having freed the slaves, he did little thereafter in a systematic way to organize them politically. He feared that excessive politicking in the *campo* might interrupt the steady flow of henequen revenues that lent harmony to his revolutionary coalition. Although he sent *agentes de propaganda* and *maestros* into the rural areas, Alvarado limited their political duties to instructing the *campesinos* about their constitutional rights and reporting any abuses against them by disgruntled *hacendados*. On several occasions, in fact, the general censured teachers and *agentes* for "overzealousness" and provoking the *campesinos*.[89] Whereas urban workers were immediately organized into syndicates, Alvarado deliberately refrained from organizing the rural workers during the preconstitutional period of military rule. In the manner of later corporatist regimes, he made sure to separate rural workers from their urban counterparts, who played an important role in the Socialist Party, thereby ensuring that each sector was dependent primarily on the state for its gains.[90] The first rural *ligas de resistencia* were formed in mid-1917 by radical political organizers such as Felipe Carrillo Puerto, Rafael Gamboa, and Felipe Valencia López. By that time, however, the preconstitutional period was over, and Alvarado's system of *comandancias militares* was giving way to civilian rule and partisan electoral politics under the guidelines of the new Mexican Constitution of 1917. Simultaneously, Alvarado was losing much of his power in the state.

Determined to see his policies continue, Alvarado desperately wanted to remain governor of Yucatán under the new national constitution. As early as October 1916, he had publicized his intention to run as a civilian in the November 1917 state elections. A month later he was declared to be an official resident of Yucatán and asked leave from his duties as regional military commander. However, because of a legal technicality (the general had not resided in the state long enough – five years – under the new constitutional provisions[91]) and, more importantly, because of Carranza's desire to dim the star of a potential rival, he never got the chance. Attempts to bend the rules were vetoed by Don Venus. Then, midway through 1917, Alvarado was suddenly "promoted" to chief of military operations for the entire southeastern portion of the Republic and directed by Mexico City to supervise *Carrancista* operations in neighboring Chiapas, Tabasco, and the Isthmus of Tehuantepec. For three months, from July to late September 1917, Alvarado was absent from the state. During the final year of his military command, after he had vacated the governorship in November 1917, Alvarado was able to visit Yucatán only for short periods.[92] Thus, for almost a full year and a half, at a critical moment of transition in the local revolutionary process, Alvarado was kept at the periphery of Yucatecan politics. In November 1918, President Carranza recalled him from Yucatán for good.

Prior to leaving for military duty elsewhere in the southeast, the general had added two final legitimizing touches to his political work, drawing up a state constitution that embodied his reforms, then designating *Yucatecos* to succeed him. Alvarado had no say in who would follow him as regional military commander; that privilege remained entirely with Carranza. However, the Mexican president did not interfere as he sought to influence the internal political realm. No doubt in an attempt to blunt the growing power of the more radical Felipe Carrillo Puerto, Alvarado divided the state's civilian power, formerly unified during his military rule, into two parts. Carlos Castro Morales, a railroad worker, union leader, and former president of the Yucatecan Socialist Party, received his blessing as candidate for governor, and Carrillo Puerto, already the most powerful civilian politician in the state, was sanctioned as the new head of the party.

Mobilization in the *campo*: the revolution moves left

Disquieting reports of Carrillo's preparations for the November state elections that would open the political process began to reach Alvarado in Chiapas during the fall of 1917. In March, Carrillo had taken the first steps toward the creation of a centralized network of rural and urban *ligas de resistencia* – the unification of the working class that Alvarado had avoided. Carrillo established the headquarters of this *Liga Central de Resistencia* in Mérida, then began to recruit additional political organizers to penetrate the isolated rural domains and mobilize agricultural workers. According to Carrillo's plan, *campesinos* in towns, villages, and haciendas would be organized into protective associations or *ligas*. Ideally, these *ligas* would work, with the government's assistance, to resolve the pressing social problems of country life, such as wages and working conditions, access to *milpa* plots and the recovery of former village lands, and the recrudescence of abuses by local bosses (*caciquismo*). Although the *ligas* would recruit local *campesinos* and select local officials, Carrillo intended that they be under the direct control of the *Liga Central* in Mérida. Ultimately, these rural *ligas* (and their urban counterparts based in the labor syndicates) would serve as the constituent units of a muscular, ideologically socialist party that would transform productive relations throughout the region.[93]

Carrillo Puerto directed the Socialist Party campaign, well aware that the party was in an enviable position. Although Alvarado was temporarily away, the federal forces within the state remained loyal to him and had been instructed not to interfere in the electoral process. The party's close relationship with the urban labor movement ensured the Socialists' success at the polls in the cities. Moreover, opposition to the party had been slow to organize. Minor elections for municipal officials had been permitted by Alvarado in June 1915 and September 1916 but had produced no real challenge to the general's Socialist Party. Now, even with the first full-scale elections of the new order at stake, and with Carrillo Puerto attempting to move the revolution to the left, opponents still seemed reluctant to commit themselves. No doubt, this was because most of the elite and middle class either feared Alvarado or were reasonably content with the populist reformism he offered. Finally, backed by generous funding from Avelino Montes and other smarting members of the *Casta Divina*, a twenty-eight-year-old, middle-class Yucatecan colonel in the Constitutionalist Army, Bernardino Mena Brito, formed the *Partido Liberal Yucateco* (Yucatecan Liberal Party) among the Yucatecan exile community in Mexico City and declared himself a candidate for governor.[94] The Liberals' initial platform spoke vaguely about revoking many of Alvarado's preconstitutional reforms and censured the Socialists' extremist efforts to "attract the support of the plebeian classes."[95]

Not surprisingly, the Liberals failed to secure significant support among either the *campesinos* or *obreros*. Party president Víctor Manzanilla, a planter, recruited heavily among the thousands of *braceros* whom Alvarado had brought into the state from central Mexico since 1915. The Socialists immediately charged that these *huaches* had been ordered to "provoke disorders and riots throughout the state, to disturb the peace and public tranquility." Manzanilla and six migrant workers were soon arrested by Interim Governor Álvaro Torre Díaz.[96]

Yet although the Liberals would strongly contest the prize of politics with the Socialists in later years, they were no match for Alvarado's revolutionary coalition in 1917. The results of the elections were never in doubt: The Socialists swept all offices, and Carlos Castro Morales succeeded Alvarado as governor. However, far more significant than the electoral result was the nature of the campaign itself and its implications for the future revolutionary process in the region.

The campaign was marred by a seemingly unnecessary, almost wanton, destruction of property and loss of life. In all, twenty were killed and scores seriously wounded. These episodes of political violence, popularly termed *atropellos*, included burnings, beatings, and assassinations – the last almost ritualistic acts performed with gun and machete. Virtually in every case, the victims were identified as "Liberals." The targets were mostly apolitical *campesinos* who had refused to join *ligas de resistencia*, though occasionally an hacienda administrator or influential merchant, such as Hoctún's Bonafacio Gamboa, was assassinated. As violence escalated the week before election day, Gamboa met a gruesome end at the hands of a Socialist band: "[A]fter suffering eight rounds and twenty-seven *machetazos*, [Gamboa] had his belly split open in cross-like fashion."[97]

To the Liberal leaders in Mérida, it appeared as if another race war was brewing, pitting the illiterate Indian masses against propertied whites and their *jornaleros*. As in 1847, the Maya *campesinos* were led predominantly by mestizo *caciques*, this time the organizers of Carrillo's Socialist Party. As Mena protested to President Carranza: "These ideologues operate without conscience and culture. They go from village to village and hacienda to hacienda, sowing the seeds of discord, inspiring ambitions of power among the ignorant with their empty promises . . . They are preparing the countryside for a new and disastrous caste war."[98]

Carrillo Puerto was singled out as a prime instigator of racial hatred and rebellion. A member of the Liberal Party in Valladolid claimed to have overheard Don Felipe tell some 200 *indios* who had come to the city from surrounding pueblos and haciendas:

Have your machetes and shotguns ready, for if Sr. Carlos Castro Morales does not triumph, you will kill all the whites [*dzules*] in the city. The whites have lorded it over you; today you are in a position to strike back. You have a right to everything: if merchandise is denied you at the price you feel you should pay, take it by force.[99]

The use of so much unnecessary violence reflects the type of rural mobilization that Carrillo's Socialist organizers had begun in mid-1917. Building on a small nucleus of seasoned Mérida-based *agentes de propaganda*, most of whom, like himself, had gained experience in the countryside under Alvarado, Carrillo recruited a number of local people who spoke Maya, had grown up with the problems of the *campo*, and, most importantly, had influence in their communities. Relatively quickly, these organizers won support for the Socialist Party in their home districts. In fact, in many cases, these *Carrillistas* used Mérida's backing to carve out local political and economic domains for themselves. For with the old Porfirian system of control dismantled and Alvarado's tight system of military rule now obsolete, there existed in many localities a power vacuum that made possible the consolidation of new revolutionary *cacicazgos*,[100] virtually as powerful as those of the Porfirian *jefes políticos*. This was especially true in the outlying districts on or beyond the frontier of the henequen zone – districts that, even under the most stable political conditions, suffered from unsatisfactory communication with Mérida.[101]

The dramatic political ascent of Socialist *cacique* Manuel ("Polín") González and several of his lieutenants in the southwestern district of Maxcanú is a clear case in point.[102] Previously a foreman on a local hacienda, Polín sensed opportunity knocking during the separatist *Argumedista* revolt. He left the estate to help Alvarado's Constitutionalists mop up around his home town of Halachó, and the general rewarded him with the *comandancia militar* of Maxcanú. González used the prestige and power of his military appointment, and the absence of authority that existed in this remote district following Alvarado's defeat of the oligarchy, to establish a *cacicazgo* that would endure until his violent assassination in 1921. Polín appears to have been an effective military boss, enforcing Alvarado's decree abolishing debt servitude and dealing sternly with reported cases of labor abuse on local estates. However, as he loyally carried out his caudillo's directives, González made sure to strengthen his own position. A local boy of Maya descent, he knew the neighboring pueblos as intimately as the hacienda he had worked for and now used his local connections to identify a core of dependable lieutenants – most notably the Euán and Vargas brothers – who brought their own men to him. Despite Alvarado's measure decreeing *El Estado Seco* ("The Dry State"), Polín built up a lucrative clandestine business in *aguardiente* (moonshine) that enabled him to pay off his circle of retainers and diversify his local operation into other more respectable lines of trade. Retaining Alvarado's trust, González was transferred from military commander to administrative inspector of the Maxcanú district as the preconstitutional regime began to be phased out. Then, late in 1916, he was elected one of four Yucatecan representatives to the Constitutional Convention at Querétaro.

As Alvarado's profile in the state lessened and his power began to wane during 1917, Polín González had little trouble moving to the left with the *Carrillista* faction, then consolidating its control of the party in Mérida. In the years ahead, González and other local power holders would play instrumental roles in Carrillo's Socialist Party and its consolidation of a centralized network of *ligas de resistencia*. The 1917 elections gave many of them an initial opportunity to exercise their new political clout. For Polín, the political campaign represented a chance to settle some old scores with factional rivals – many of whom he conveniently labeled "Liberals" – and to strengthen further his political and economic domain.

Carrying out their chief's directives, Polín's lieutenants proved themselves energetic campaigners. Based in the municipalities of Opichén, Maxcanú, Halachó, and Muna, Benjamín and Lisandro Vargas and Braulio, Bruno, and Juan Euán recruited support for the Socialist *ligas* and intimidated the Liberal opposition. The Vargas brothers and their band of recruiters hounded Liberal organizers from their homes in Halachó and Opichén, publicly roughed them up, and then transported them to the district seat of Maxcanú, where they were jailed. Only after the polls closed on 4 November 1917 were they released. The notorious Euáns of Opichén, popularly renowned as the *matones socialistas* (Socialist assassins), were Polín González's principal clients. Braulio served as chief of police, whereas Juan – described in Mérida's Liberal press as "a habitually drunken Indian, whose countenance is so horrid, whose instincts so savage, that it makes one tremble" [103] – was González's choice for president of the local *liga de resistencia*. With younger brother Bruno, they exercised powerful sway over the *campesinos* of Opichén, successfully enrolling the majority of the *municipio* in the *liga*. Throughout the election campaign, the Liberals accused them of committing an untold number of *atropellos*, including homicide and arson. Furthermore, a Liberal petition warned General Alvarado to take heed of the new social message that had begun to emerge through Socialist *caciques* such as the Euáns: "They influence the poor *jornaleros*, the majority of whom are illiterate, with deceitful promises of economic gain which in the long run they cannot fulfill." [104]

Without question, the 1917 elections radicalized the Yucatecan political process, introducing a greater level of rural mobilization and a new breed of political leadership at the local level and in Mérida. Yet although the stated goal of Carrillo's Socialist Party was to introduce democratic government through free elections, such was not the result. There had been no experience in the past that would prepare Yucatán's *campesinado* for representative government. On the contrary, until very recently, *campesinos* had been purposefully isolated, denied the vote, and kept ignorant of their rights and obligations as citizens. The character of the campaign as well as the voting results bore out this legacy of ignorance. The physical intimidation and bribery that characterized Yucatán's emerging system of revolutionary *cacique* politics produced in many rural villages and towns elected officials who lacked political experience and were incapable of fulfilling their duties to their constituencies. As Felipe Carrillo Puerto's brother Eraclio, an administrative inspector, reported from his own districts of Motul and Temax: "Many local governments here are composed of simple people who cannot be expected to govern in accordance with state law." [105] Numerous town councillors and even some state and federal deputies had been imposed by local bosses in whose interests they would now be acting; other posts were held by these *caciques* themselves. The military commander of Temax told Alvarado that at Cansahcab the municipal officials were "so ignorant that they barely know how to sign their names. They are men lacking in judgment, 'elected' by the *cacique* Carlos Poot Castillo so he can manage them at his whim and fancy." [106] In the Tixkokob *partido*, a group of *campesinos* complained that the new municipal president of Conkal was the administrator of a local plantation and "might very well be a pawn for the *señores* to oppress us." [107]

Ironically, in the weeks before the elections, Carrillo had instructed party organizers and officials at the district level to travel to the villages, haciendas, and remote *rancherías* and inform *campesinos* of the significance of the voting, of their responsibility to select capable leaders and not be intimidated or bribed to vote for candidates who might not represent their true interests. [108] Unfortunately, the officials Carrillo sent to convey this message were often the same *caciques* who, in the name of the Socialist Party, were responsible for the bribery and intimidation Mérida sought to eliminate. In the months following the elections and subsequently, during the 1918–1924 period, Carrillo would frequently send trusted cadres of socialist ideologues from Mérida into the *campo* to provide political education to local chiefs and *campesinos* alike, in the hope of democratizing the revolutionary process and eliminating the abuses of *caciquismo*. But in the absence of friendly federal support during much of that period, the Socialist Party would be forced to tolerate the heavy-handed behavior of its *cacique* allies in its struggle to maintain authority in the region. In retrospect, Salvador Alvarado, and not the Liberal leader Mena Brito, may have been the real loser in November 1917. Alvarado had not only failed in his personal bid to gain the governorship; he had lost control of the pace and direction of Yucatecan revolutionary politics. Already Carrillo and other radical Socialist leaders threatened to shatter the delicate multiclass coalition that he had taken such pains to assemble. Focusing their immediate efforts on the agrarian sector but ultimately projecting a unified mobilization of the popular classes, the *Carrillistas* were polarizing the political climate and alienating many of the progressive planters and professionals whom Alvarado had wooed into his populist alliance. It was clear from the way they managed the political campaign in 1917 that they would build a rather different coalition for the purpose of implementing a different ideological program.

Yet Alvarado's revolution and the populist coalition that underwrote it, although threatened, were by no means moribund late in 1917. Ultimately, the fate of Yucatán's bourgeois revolution, under Alvarado or his hand-picked successor, Governor Carlos Castro Morales, would hinge on the political posture that Carranza's federal government assumed toward it and on the performance of the monocrop economy. With henequen production and market prices soaring to unprecedented heights, rewarding Mexico City with handsome dividends, President Carranza declined to meddle in Yucatán's internal political affairs.[109] After all, such partisan conflict characterized the transition from military rule to civilian government throughout much of the Republic. Moreover, despite the threatening show of strength by the *Carrillista* faction of the Socialist Party, most members of the bourgeoisie remained *Alvaradistas* at the end of 1917. Ultimately, revolutionary politics and *cacique* violence in the backlands were a side show for the Mérida-based planters. The main event continued to be land and the profitable fiber it produced. Here, Alvarado's reforms had not hurt the planters' pocketbooks. Let us examine what may have been the hallmarks of the general's bourgeois revolution, his agrarian reform and transformation of the export sector.

5

The theory and practice of bourgeois reform: land and the export economy

The "small property" [*pequeña propiedad*] is the only foundation for the greatness and prosperity of a people.

—Salvador Alvarado

You could lead them around the world with a lump of sugar but could not drive them an inch.

—Thomas W. Lamont to Charles
Evans Hughes, 1922, on dealing
with Mexicans

Alvarado's agrarian program in the region must be viewed against the larger backdrop of Constitutionalist land policy, which was itself part of a current of bourgeois agrarian thought dating back to the Madero regime and, before that, to the liberal and positivist ideologues of the nineteenth century. Central to this ideological approach was its advocacy of the *pequeña propiedad* or small property, which came to be regarded as a panacea for the agrarian problem, identified early as the most important challenge facing the Revolution. Indeed, by 1912, the hacienda became for middle-class intellectuals what the Porfirian *científicos* collectively had been in 1909: the *cabeza de turco*, the emblem of all that the Revolution opposed. Contrasted to the image of the static, wastefully cultivated great estate was the notion of a dynamic, family-owned, intensively cultivated and capitalized, medium-sized *pequeña propiedad* that would develop the countryside and, by creating an internal market for nascent Mexican industry, energetically complement a burgeoning urban sector.[1]

The development of the Revolutionary notion of the *pequeña propiedad*, its subsequent enshrinement in the Constitution of 1917, and its central influence in shaping Mexican agrarian policy ever since all reflect, in large part, the thought and effort of its chief intellectual exponents, principally Luis Cabrera, his agrarian mentor, Andrés Molina Enríquez, and other progressive members of Carranza's corps of advisors.[2] In a series of speeches before the Chamber of Deputies late in 1912, Cabrera and other reform-minded intellectuals had first demanded an end to the traditionally liberal compromise solutions to the land question promised by the Madero government. They called for immediate large-scale state expropriation of unproductive haciendas and the simultaneous reconstitution of *ejidos* for the Indian pueblos that had been despoiled of them. Echoing the sentiments of other *Maderista* reformers, Cabrera told the Chamber of Deputies that although he favored the *pequeña propiedad* over the *ejido*, a systematic promotion of the former would not be possible until the problem of the Indian village was solved.[3] In broad outline, Cabrera and other intellectuals were proposing what was later to constitute the agrarian program of the Constitutionalist movement, and of Mexico as well, for several decades. Their identification of the hacienda as the root cause of misery in Mexican society strategically put the Revolution back on track, permitting bourgeois intellectuals and revolutionaries to articulate, perhaps for the first time, the interests of the rural masses.[4] By borrowing the concept of the *ejido* from the *Zapatista* agrarians, and later incorporating some provision of it into the seminal 6 January 1915 land decree that he wrote for Carranza, Luis Cabrera would blunt the impact of *Zapatismo* and no doubt contribute ideologically to the First Chief's ultimate triumph over the *Zapatista* and *Villista* forces of the Convention.

Surprisingly, few have emphasized the ideological consensus that existed in the Constitutionalist ranks on the agrarian issue, uniting most of Carranza's middle-sector advisors, epitomized by intellectuals such as Cabrera, and the predominantly petty bourgeois *ranchero* chiefs from the northern states – men such as Obregón, Calles, and Alvarado. Although worlds apart in temperament and geographical-cultural background, Cabrera and his colleagues shared a common vision with the men of the north. Each group viewed the oligarchical hacienda as its *bête noir* and regarded the *pequeña propiedad* as the cornerstone of Mexico's future. Within this common framework, there were differences – or, more accurately, varying degrees of emphasis. By and large, the Constitutionalist caudillos from the north had lived on the rim of Indian Mexico, primarily in the states of Sonora, Sinaloa, Chihuahua, and Coahuila. In certain ways, they were closer in their aspirations and notions of land tenure to the United States, with which they shared a border. Consequently, for them, the *pequeña propiedad* meant the right of each man to own, in fee simple, *at least* a decent-sized plot of land to farm and the opportunity perhaps to acquire a good deal more.[5] For example, the semirural, semiurban lower middle class that emerged as the leaders of the Revolution in Sonora – and, subsequently in the 1920s and early 1930s, throughout Mexico – aspired to a profitable, large-scale agriculture based on high investment, mechanization and irrigation, and production for export. Moreover, after generations of a savage guerrilla war contesting the river valleys of the Yaqui and Mayo, they remained unenthusiastic about Indian demands for a restitution or distribution of *ejidos*, either in Sonora or elsewhere in Mexico. One senses that the attitude of many Sonoran chiefs towards the *Zapatistas* and the nonnorthern Mexican peasantry in general was based on images previously held of the Yaqui: bandits, vandals, barbarians.[6]

The notion of the *pequeña propiedad* advanced by urban intellectuals such as Cabrera and Molina Enríquez was more complex. Products of the central plateau, they had grown up in the bosom of Mexico's Indian core and had come to know the basic institutions of hacienda, peonage, and pueblo.[7] For them the *pequeña propiedad* represented a double equation. Their long-term goal was an agrarian system predicated upon the intensively farmed, medium-sized property – a somewhat smaller and more productive unit than the hacienda but one that allowed for capital investment and the employment of an outliving labor force. This, in turn, triggered the second half of the formula, which called for the existence of a new *ejidatario* class. The haciendas would be expropriated and the *ejidos* would be reconstituted. However, the process was envisioned as an essential compromise: The hacienda would be partitioned, its cultivated nucleus earmarked for the former proprietor as a healthy-sized *pequeña propiedad*, its outlying lands going to the deprived neighboring pueblos in the form of individual subsistence plots. Custom, attractive wages, and an increase in population would draw the *ejidatario* to the *pequeña propiedad* to supplement his income. Ultimately, Cabrera and Molina Enríquez suggested, the ambitious *ejidatario* would enlarge his holding and become the proprietor of his own *pequeña propiedad*. In this sense, that is, for this type of enterprising individual, the *ejido* was viewed as a transitional phase. In later years, Cabrera would place increasingly less emphasis on the *ejido* and speak almost exclusively in terms of the *pequeña propiedad*. Like his agrarian mentor, Molina Enríquez, he believed that communal systems of land tenure should be utilized only until the members of Indian communities could adjust themselves to a freehold arrangement.[8]

On 6 January 1915, their backs pressed against the sea by the forces of Villa and Zapata, the Constitutionalists issued their long-awaited agrarian decree from Veracruz. In the process, the Revolution took an important stand on the land issue, one that would have significant repercussions in Yucatán. The 6 January decree constituted the first really systematic attack on the hacienda. There would be no turning back now: The decision had been made that the hacienda had to go, and the edict rendered this decision irrevocable. The law, authored by Cabrera, accorded instant recognition to seizures and distributions of hacienda land already carried out by military leaders and cleared the way for stepped-up expropriations in the future. In principle, the decree held that "all pueblos without lands, whether they traditionally held *ejidos* or not, now had a right to hold them to satisfy their agrarian needs."[9] All that remained to be worked out in the future was what constituted a pueblo or, as the Mexican Constitution later came to read in the 1930s, a *núcleo de población*.[10]

Secondly, the decree reflected the balanced equation that continued to guide Carranza's progressive bourgeois intellectuals. For although in principle the law provided for the dismantling of the hacienda, it did not, practically speaking, invite its immediate disintegration. In fact, the decree was kept intentionally vague on some points and hedged about with technical and procedural limitations on others.[11] The *hacendado* was given a right to appeal (and delay) expropriations and the right of compensation. Furthermore, Luis Cabrera's rather selective definition of who would be governed by the decree – communities of *acasillados* (resident *peones*), for example, were not pueblos and were completely excluded[12] – reflected a deep-seated personal reluctance to entrust Mexico's agrarian future to a *minifundista* interpretation of the *pequeña propiedad*.

Alvarado's agrarian strategy

Salvador Alvarado did a good deal of thinking on the agrarian question, and his writings and actions betray the influence of Cabrera and Molina Enríquez. Indeed, as he progressed from an ordinary military caudillo in the early 1910s to a pivotal revolutionary governor and polemicist during the 1915–1920 period, his outlook began to conform ever more closely to the position formulated by the Constitutionalist Revolution's middle-class intellectuals.[13] Alvarado was well aware of the great riches that continued to flow in from the henequen fields and had already transformed Yucatán from a near desert into perhaps Mexico's richest state on the eve of the Revolution. He would use the *oro verde* to promote a full agenda of reforms and enthusiastically spoke of making Mérida – only recently modernized by Olegario Molina – the New Orleans or San Francisco of the southeast.[14] Nothing would come of these visions of progress if the proverbial goose were killed or its productivity seriously impaired. For Alvarado, this meant a concerted policy to exempt producing *henequenales* from the agrarian reform he would initiate in the region.[15]

The general's reluctance to affect the henequen hacienda, based upon his belief that fiber production would suffer if the privately owned fields were expropriated and divided up or even threatened with tampering, did not constitute a repudiation of the middle class's campaign to replace the reactionary hacienda with the more dynamic *pequeña propiedad*. In fact, it seems more likely that Alvarado envisioned the henequen *finca* – in most cases substantially capitalized and employing a high level of modern technology – as, in principle, already pretty much conforming to the Constitutionalist notion of the *pequeña propiedad*.[16] The Yucatecan henequen plantation was, with rare exceptions, substantially smaller than the extensive northern and central Mexican haciendas with which Alvarado and the other men of the north were most familiar and upon which they seem to have based their conclusions regarding agrarian reform. Alvarado believed that once these plantations had been stripped of their "feudal tendencies," such as a reliance upon dependent labor, and equally important, once their proprietors had been liberated from their own condition of debt peonage vis-à-vis the Molina–Montes–Harvester trust, these *fincas* would constitute the progressive *pequeñas propiedades* upon which the region might reasonably plan its future development.[17] Echoing Molina Enríquez's message almost verbatim, Alvarado told *Yucatecos* that his agrarian reform aimed at developing the *pequeña propiedad*, "the only foundation for the greatness and prosperity of a people."[18] Then, in the tradition of Cabrera, he specifically detailed his intention to distribute, upon request, small plots or *lotes*, each of which would be farmed by an individual family. By means of hard work and thrift, these *lotes* might be expanded into healthy-sized *pequeñas propiedades* in their own right; more likely, Alvarado reasoned, their income would have to be supplemented by labor on the neighboring *grandes propiedades*.[19]

Certainly the henequen haciendas would not be entirely exempt from the agrarian reform that he would implement under the enabling provisions of the Constitutionalists' 6 January decree. Alvarado fully intended to pare down the plantations to a more efficient nucleus of operation, in the process restoring ejidal land to despoiled pueblos, as well as granting *lotes* to individual householders. In fact, Alvarado's State Agrarian Law of 3 December 1915 even holds out – in principle, if nothing else – the possibility of cultivated henequen land being expropriated to form *ejidos* for eligible pueblos, although it quickly adds that only 10 hectares, instead of the standard 20, would be distributed to *ejidatarios*. More to the point, however, the law makes it clear that expropriation of *henequenales* would become necessary only if uncultivated state and private lands proved insufficient. This, of course, was quite unlikely, given the abundance of uncultivated lands throughout the state, which Alvarado intended to distribute first.[20] Nevertheless, Alvarado was quickly swamped with requests from individuals and pueblos for choice henequen lands as well as the more usual demands for *milpa* plots. These *solicitudes*, usually addressed to Alvarado personally, were frequently quite specific. Often the petitioners were city folk who for some time had had their eyes on a particular piece of property and now made bold to claim it:

> Ignacio Soberanis requests his own small parcel of land [*su terrenito*], sown with henequen, due south of this city of Mérida, on the Kanasín road not far from the railroad line.
>
> The youth Miguel López Contreras, a *vecino* of Colonia García Ginerés [Mérida], petitions for a small *lote*, sown in henequen of full yield, on the lands of the Hacienda "Tanlúm."[21]

The record is clear, however, that in these and numerous other cases, Alvarado refused to touch *henequenales*, preferring instead to distribute *terrenos incultos* or, in regional parlance, lands not cultivated in henequen.[22]

For Alvarado, the guiding principle animating his policy toward the henequen hacienda, and agrarian reform in general, was the bourgeois notion of productive land use and its obverse, that of land waste. In his *Reconstrucción de México*, Alvarado divided society into four classes. Along with the traditional classifications of lower, middle, and upper classes, he added a fourth category, "the aristocratic, parasitic class," which he distinguished from the "hardworking and productive capitalist upper class." It would be this privileged and parasitic caste of monopolistic *hacendados* and merchants, in which he placed Mérida's *Casta Divina*, that Alvarado would attempt to destroy; other smaller producers had little to fear so long as they continued working their properties efficiently.[23] In fact, Alvarado made it clear on a number of occasions that certain export crops in the southeast, most notably henequen, rubber, and coffee, needed larger extensions of land to remain productive, and their producers would be entitled to them under special provisions of the agrarian reform provided they proved they could cultivate them.[24] Those who chose not to work their estates might be directly penalized by expropriation and ejidal division or indirectly coerced to cultivate their fields by a blistering tax upon idle property along the lines suggested by Henry George.[25]

Of these two alternatives, Alvarado clearly favored the latter. Although he judged the failure to work good land as an unconscionable act against society, he could generate little enthusiasm for the traditional Indian *ejido*: "Those men [*ejidatarios*] want only to sow their miserably small *milpas*, will eat nothing but corn, and cannot be persuaded to produce anything of worth for society as a whole."[26]

Largely to feed a hungry population during the 1915–1916 seasons and to relieve mounting social tensions, Alvarado had persuaded a number of *hacendados* to rent, or cede on a temporary basis, parcels of *milpa* land to groups or entire communities of *campesinos* – this in addition to the *lotes* he had distributed that conferred the right of ownership.[27] Ejidal distributions during this period were much rarer, largely because in these early years the process of awarding *ejidos* in Yucatán, and in Mexico as a whole, was a slow and convoluted one – not surprising, in view of Alvarado's and Carranza's coolness to the institution itself.[28] All told, Alvarado distributed several thousand hectares in the form of *ejidos* to twelve pueblos, plus many hectares more in the form of *lotes* to individuals.[29] Although he saw some limited use for the *ejido* as a means of restitution when pueblos blatantly had been cheated out of their lands by *hacendados*, in the Sonoran tradition he never advocated the *ejido* as more than a stopgap measure.[30] He was scornful of those who would divide land up *homeopáticamente*, in the fashion of an impulsive surgeon.[31] One detects in Alvarado's political writing and praxis the underlying assumption regarding land tenure that guided Madero and a generation of Porfirian intellectuals before him: The Spencerian, positivistic principle that the land must be worked by those who can most productively develop its potential – in other words, by those who can afford to buy and invest in it.[32]

Again, we see that Alvarado's dream was a respectably bourgeois one: He hoped that his agrarian reform would help sound the death knell of feudalism in Yucatán and set an example for all of Mexico. The aim of his land policy was *not* to eliminate the *hacendado* and transform the agrarian structure in the interest of the *campesino* by encouraging a new unit of production (the *ejido*) to replace the hacienda as the cornerstone of the henequen industry. Rather, Alvarado sought to clean up the hacienda system, eliminating slavery, refining agricultural techniques, updating equipment through improvement loans, and stripping the haciendas of excess acreage.[33] In the process, the *peón* would be converted into a responsible rural worker or, in some cases, a small property holder in his own right. Similarly, the *señor feudal* would become an *hacendado burgués* or – to use the euphemistic expression that has subsequently been adopted by the "Party of the Institutionalized Revolution" – a *pequeño propietario*, a prosperous modern farmer comparable to his counterpart in the United States.[34] Although he implemented a limited program of ejidal distribution in Yucatán, Alvarado, unlike his successor Carrillo Puerto, had little enthusiasm for the kind of agrarian réform envisioned in the *Zapatista Plan de Ayala*, centering on forms of communal land tenure. He had even less patience with *campesino* mobilization from below. Lest there be any doubt on this score, we should note that "inconvenient agrarian rebels like those who raised the flag of rebellion at Temax [late in 1914] were jailed."[35]

And yet, when we consider the narrow range of ideological possibilities open to Alvarado within the Constitutionalist camp, as well as the global economic conditions that influenced his thinking, we must appreciate the congruence of his reform strategy with the region's problematical structure of agrarian production. Clearly, it was not Alvarado's intention, either in the short or long run, to expropriate the henequen plantations and turn them over to worker control. On the other hand, the general was equally wary of a solution predicated upon the *minifundio* or *ejido*. Applying his formative experience with large-scale export agriculture in the northwest, he recognized that the Yucatecan plantations were highly integrated agro-industrial units that, to remain productive, must be kept intact. No doubt, his urban bourgeois orientation reinforced his appreciation that the production of henequen fiber was as much an industrial process as an agricultural one.[36] Perhaps the essential irony of Alvarado's agrarian ideology was that, in stressing the northern middle-class notion of the *pequeña propiedad* – a view by and large foreign to Yucatán – he was equipped to recognize the functional unity of the henequen plantation and to appreciate its need for a reliable work force, which, in turn, obliged him to formulate a strategy very much in accord with regional needs and priorities. This strategy, emphasizing access to *milpa* land, improvement of working conditions on haciendas and, most importantly, an increase in wages in direct proportion to a rise in the price of fiber, reflected a sensitivity to the Yucatecan environment. This is borne out by the virtually identical agrarian programs put forward by later Socialist state governments in the 1920s and 1930s prior to the arrival of Cárdenas. These Yucatecan successors of Alvarado were, like him, consistent in their preference for a solution weighted heavily toward wage increases, with less emphasis placed upon the division and parceling out of existing plantations, and in their espousal of a land policy granting *campesinos* access to *milpa* through either ejidal grant (*dotación*) or more traditional rental arrangements. Ironically, Alvarado, the Sonoran bourgeois revolutionary, was far more in tune with the position taken on the agrarian issue by regional spokesmen – that is, by Socialist leaders and the *campesinos* themselves – than were the agrarian socialists in the national capital who later formulated and implemented an ill-fated land policy in Yucatán under Cárdenas.

The federal government's response

Alvarado was never able to carry out the agrarian program he envisioned. However moderate it may have been, it overstepped the bounds of what his federal boss, Venustiano Carranza, deemed proper. As 1916 progressed, the First Chief gradually reneged on the national agrarian policy spelled out by Cabrera in the 6 January 1915 decree; simultaneously he reduced the power of Yucatán's local agrarian commission. The final straw came at the close of the year, when Carranza ironically instructed Alvarado not to issue any new ejidal grants to pueblos eligible to receive them under the provisions of his own Veracruz decree.[37] Repeatedly, though unsuccessfully, Alvarado tried to persuade Mexico City to rescind its instructions and even worked secretly to distribute additional *milpa* lands outside the henequen zone in an effort to redeem pledges he had made as well as to enable the state to feed itself.[38] This failing, he stepped up his program of providing *campesinos* with usufruct rights to *milpa* land, thereby keeping cereal production as high as possible despite poor harvests and holding agrarian discontent in check.[39] Late in 1916, for example, when Felipe Carrillo led *Motuleño campesinos* in a land invasion to secure access to maize fields that the local *hacendados* had denied to them, Alvarado upheld the invasion, working out a rental agreement with the owners on the *campesinos'* behalf.[40] Ultimately, however, the general told the *Yucatecos* that his land program had been thwarted by forces beyond his control – an obvious reference to Carranza, inasmuch as he was careful to point out that his agrarian reform had not encountered serious opposition from the *henequeneros*.[41]

Why was Carranza so opposed to even minimal land reform in Yucatán? Why did the national Revolutionary government repudiate the initiative of one of its regional caudillos, who was ostensibly following its agrarian guidelines? It is not enough to point to the First Chief's origins as a wealthy Coahuilan proprietor; other Mexican revolutionaries of landed background were willing to go much further on the agrarian question than Don Venus. The issue of North American influence on Mexico City must also be considered. Was the U.S. government, acting on behalf of Yucatán's oligarchy – the cordage trust's perennial ally – responsible for Carranza's sudden ultimatum in 1916 to halt land distribution?[42]

The Central and "Confidential" files of the U.S. State Department, as well as those of the Department of Defense, and records of the local U.S. consular post (Progreso) reveal absolutely no hint of North American coercion of Carranza on behalf of the planters. This is not to suggest that the United States shrank from applying pressure upon Mexico and Yucatán when its interests were threatened. We will see that the North American government was more than capable of threatening force and actually sending gunboats to get its point across when normal diplomatic channels did not produce the desired results. In addition, there was an almost unbroken succession of planter delegations to the United States during the 1918–1924 period, when economic conditions deteriorated and the ruling plantocracy mounted a sustained campaign both in Washington and in Mexico City against Carrillo's bona fide socialist government in Yucatán.

However, in 1916, the planters' prospects could not have been brighter. The onset of World War I had put a big premium on Yucatán's staple, and Alvarado showed no intention of significantly interfering with either their estates or the large profits the planters could now reasonably expect to receive. To be sure, there were occasional grumblings by planters who bristled at Alvarado's high-handed military style and arrogant manner. Many of the large planters and certainly the members of the *Casta Divina* deeply resented, even hated, Alvarado.[43] After all, by ending the slave-peonage system in the peninsula, the general had rudely stripped them of their accustomed prerogatives and shattered the paternalistic aura of their familiar world. He had stung them so deeply that not even increased profits could provide an adequate salve. Yet, early on, the members of the landed bourgeoisie learned to live with Alvarado, for they had come to the important realization that the general was by and large prepared to coexist with them, equating the continued prosperity of the henequen industry, and of the region itself, with the smooth operation of their privately owned haciendas.[44]

Furthermore, it is reasonable to assume that, by mid-1916, the North American cordage interests, always in close touch with the large *hacendados*, came fully to appreciate this fact and apprised Washington that Alvarado's agrarian program per se posed no real threat to the productive plantations that regularly supplied this country's cordage needs. And by this time, the U.S. consul in Progreso and a special agent of the State Department had already reached this conclusion and expressed it in a variety of dispatches.[45]

Of course, this does not completely dispose of the matter. Additional possibilities exist. For example, more subtle or covert pressure may have been applied on the Carranza government by the United States that subsequently went unrecorded in any major branch of the U.S. National Archives – rather unlikely, especially in view of the preceding analysis. Or perhaps Carranza, a conservative in agrarian matters anyway, responded to what he *perceived* to be the North American position by quashing additional land reform in the hope that this would further legitimize his newly recognized regime in the eyes of its powerful neighbor. Although traditionally regarded as the intensely nationalistic leader who stood up to Woodrow Wilson, it is important to consider that Carranza had relied and would continue to rely upon the United States and Wilson for diplomatic favors, arms shipments, and supplies should his regime be internally threatened – a distinct possibility in 1916.

Some writers have maintained that the First Chief's opposition owed more to his jealous defense of the prerogatives of the central government in the face of a serious challenge from a powerful regional caudillo than to any serious ideological differences with Alvarado or pressure from the United States. To be sure, Alvarado's growing regional power would prove so disconcerting to Carranza that in 1918 he would call him home for reassignment. Yet the related assertion that Carranza was merely waiting for the establishment of constitutional government to ensure the centralized development of agrarian reform policy is much less convincing.[46] It rather naively glosses over the pronounced ideological differences that separated Alvarado, Obregón, and many of the other Constitutionalist caudillos, and even Cabrera, from their nominal leader.[47] That such differences were clearly perceived by Alvarado is illustrated in an excerpt from a letter that Modesto Rolland angrily sent him following Rolland's failure, as Alvarado's envoy, to dissuade Carranza from his decision to prohibit further agrarian reform in Yucatán: "How difficult and frustrating is this struggle . . . with the conservatives who regard themselves to be revolutionaries . . . who are unable to grasp the social truth of a more just and pleasant world."[48]

However, although these differences in ideology are significant and affected to some extent the amount of *milpa* land that Alvarado might have distributed during his tenure in Yucatán, ultimately they reflect the differences that separate a traditional liberal (Carranza) from a bourgeois revolutionary (Alvarado). At no time was Salvador Alvarado himself prepared to alter radically the prevailing agrarian structure and, hence, Yucatecan society in general, by expropriating the henequen fields.

The henequen export sector: the rise of the *Reguladora*

If the prime concern of Alvarado's agrarian strategy was to keep the henequen plantation productively intact under progressive private ownership, the underlying motives were the general's desire to harness its wealth to his program of reforms in Yucatán and, increasingly, his need to satisfy Carranza's escalating demand that Yucatán finance the Constitutionalist cause elsewhere in the Republic. To raise the ever-increasing revenues that these projects would require, Alvarado moved to establish and rationalize government control of the henequen export sector. Though he permitted the *hacendados* to continue to own the plantations, he consolidated the state's control over the all-important marketing apparatus of the industry.

The general realized that only by forging a powerful state monopoly capable of dealing directly at least with the North American manufacturers and, ultimately, perhaps, with the final consumers (the U.S. and Canadian wheat farmers) could he shatter the hated system of collaboration that had flourished prior to his arrival. By keeping the purchasing price of Yucatán's fiber depressed, the North American cordage manufacturers and the select group of commercial agents and planters who were linked with them had succeeded in depriving the producers and Yucatecan society of millions of dollars – $80,000,000, according to Alvarado's rough estimate, since the formation of the International Harvester Company[49] – money that might now be used to create the progressive society he envisioned.

Like so many of the *norteño* chiefs, Alvarado was intensely nationalistic and, although he admired the efficiency and technological achievements of North American culture, the formative years he spent in Sonora near the border had made him keenly aware and bitterly resentful of the United States's massive informal empire in Mexico.[50] It is clear from his political writings that, by late 1915, Alvarado had become virtually obsessed with breaking the viselike grip that *los Trusts* – his consistent expression for Harvester and the North American cordage interests – had on the Yucatecan economy through their control of the henequen market. For Alvarado, this was reduced further to the more immediate and symbolic goal of driving Avelino Montes and the *Casta* out of business and Harvester and the lesser North American buyers out of the peninsula.[51]

In Alvarado's campaign to put an end to the trusts' informal empire in Yucatán by destroying their durable collaborator elite, the three major elements of his ideological program of "state socialism" are integrated. For by using the full powers of the state to challenge the control that the North American corporations had over the henequen market and, by extension, the regional economy, Alvarado attempted to disengage Yucatán from the unequal relationship that had existed as far back as the 1870s, when the tentacles of the henequen monoculture had closed around the region. Henceforth, Alvarado pledged, Yucatán's fiber would enrich Yucatecans (and Mexicans) rather than *gringos*. Moreover, the state would distribute the fiber's benefits at all levels of society, raising up the many who had been exploited in the past and humbling the few who had worked so closely with the foreigner to perpetuate this system of exploitation. Significantly, Alvarado hinted that in the process of saving the regional economy, not only the poor but the rich too would benefit and, it became clear, the latter far more than the former.[52]

The explanation was simple. Alvarado conceived of Yucatecan society as a grotesque pyramid of exploitation. At its base were about 100,000 *campesinos* – slaves – who were given only what was necessary to keep them alive and who, in turn, supported the 300 to 500 or so large and intermediate henequen *hacendados* who occupied the pyramid's middle level. Alvarado believed these planters were victims as much as villains and referred to them as "nothing more than the *mayordomos* of the trusts who were the real masters of the henequen industry."[53] In other words, the great majority of the region's *hacendados*, who might be operating their properties in an efficient and socially and technologically enlightened manner, were being prevented from doing so by the dozen or so super-planters at the top of the pyramid, whom Alvarado labeled as a *Casta Divina*, as much for their arrogance and cliquishness as for their complete domination of Yucatán's government and economy. In his view, this *Casta* came to exploit the smaller *hacendados* and control their production much as the latter dominated their dependent Indian labor force. For Alvarado, preoccupied as he was with fomenting a progressive middle sector of independent *pequeños proprietarios*, the liberation of the rank-and-file *hacendado* was at least as important as the liberation of the *peón*.[54] Indeed, he believed the success of the latter would turn on that of the former because in striking its bargain with the Harvester trust, the *Casta* had not only managed to impede the development of this potentially progressive middle-level planter group but had converted it into an agent for the repression of the masses. The trusts' symbiotic relationship with the *Casta* had resulted in fabulous profits for the partners and the demise of fair profits for the majority of *henequeneros*, who, in turn, had been compelled to reduce wages and worsen labor conditions on their *fincas*.[55]

Of course, Alvarado's view, colored as it was by the requirements of an essentially bourgeois–nationalist ideology, greatly distorted reality. As I have shown, although the vast majority of Yucatán's henequen producers and merchants remained outside this exclusive collaborator or *comprador* group and bitterly railed against it, the monopoly that Yucatán enjoyed in the world market, combined with incredibly low labor and production costs, permitted prices high enough to ease the qualms of most irate members of the region's agro-commercial bourgeoisie. In fact, prior to 1915, only the very small planters had been forced to the wall by the *Casta* and these only in times of real economic recession, such as the crisis of 1907–1908.[56] Thus, although there existed significant intraclass or intraelite fragmentation on the eve of the Revolution, the agro-commercial bourgeoisie was fully capable of closing ranks and maintaining solidarity in the face of a serious threat to its social and economic hegemony. (Such a threat never existed during Alvarado's tenure in Yucatán but would occur during the 1918–1924 period, when Carrillo Puerto took over the leadership of the Socialist Party.)

Alvarado, of course, did not perceive the problem in such class terms. He therefore found himself in the curious position of distinguishing between good and bad *hacendados* in order to aid the former by undercutting the latter. However, with henequen prices high and promising to climb much higher, Alvarado's strategy achieved real local popularity, gaining approval in all but the highest circles of planter society.[57]

This popular consensus was hardly surprising. To begin with, Alvarado made sure to keep the internal enemy – the *Casta Divina* – omnipresent yet ill-defined. In his speeches and decrees, he never referred to the *Casta* in any but vague terms, nor would he specifically define its size or identify its members with the exception of Montes.[58] This allowed for the possibility of a straw man whom *Yucatecos* at all levels of society, planters included, could safely oppose. Secondly, Alvarado chose to mount his attack in strongly regional terms. Repeatedly, the general contrasted the capacity for hard work and invention that had traditionally characterized the region's *henequeneros* to the crass opportunism of the relative parvenus of the *Casta* who had become their masters. Here Alvarado played to traditional prejudices in the *Yucatecos*, capitalizing on the fact that a number of the leading members of the *Casta* – most notably, Montes – had come to Yucatán from Spain:

> The true sons of Yucatán who so laboriously developed henequen's great riches, who built their own railroads and established stable banks, who constructed the wharves and founded the Port [Progreso] itself, have watched these past years how, with much less energy and ability the modern potentates of the Caste, the great *henequeneros* of today, have come to control all aspects of the region's economic life

through financial chicanery with the help of the North American trusts.[59]

Having identified the problem and marked the enemy, Alvarado wasted no time activating the mechanism that was ready-made to provide a solution, the *Comisión Reguladora del Mercado de Henequén.* The *Comisión Reguladora* had been founded in 1912 at the insistence of the *hacendados* themselves. The performance of the original *Reguladora* represented only the most recent of several unsuccessful attempts by Yucatán *hacendados* to combat the monopoly that Molina and Harvester had established shortly after the turn of the century. Essentially, the *hacendados* had conceived the *Reguladora* as another valorization scheme, similar to the one perfected a few years earlier in Brazil by the São Paulo coffee planters.[60] What distinguished the *Comisión Reguladora* from earlier *hacendado* schemes to purchase fiber and hold it off the market until a decent price could be obtained was the more active role of the state government. Unlike its predecessors, the *Cámara Agrícola* (1906–1910) and the *Negociación Exportadora* (1911), which were limited cooperatives voluntarily organized and financed by minority groups of *hacendados*,[61] the *Comisión Reguladora* was a government agency, supported by the overwhelming majority of Yucatán's *henequeneros* and financed by a state law sanctioning an extra impost on production. By the end of 1912, its membership included all but the largest planters who constituted the *Casta* and those very small producers who found themselves trapped in the web of debts and mortgages spun by Montes and his associates.[62]

However, because the 1912 *Reguladora* operated in an open market still controlled by the Montes faction, it had little hope of achieving even its modest goal of maintaining a reasonable and remunerative price. Nor did the state government, which was given only regulatory powers, possess the requisite political clout to ensure that the *Reguladora* fulfilled this limited economic goal. In fact, it is not even clear whether the *Maderista* governor in Yucatán was prepared to work against the Montes faction or whether he had been put on the *Casta's* payroll. Some suggest that Madero's national government was opposed to the *Reguladora* and supported the attempts of Montes and Harvester to cut off loans to the new agency.[63]

Consequently, the career of the first *Reguladora* was a brief one. Initially, the *Comisión Reguladora* filled its warehouses with

100,000 bales and tenaciously held them as world demand grew and the price rose to 15.4 cents per kilogram. Here, however, the trust drew the line. Working through his agents at the banks that held paper on some of the planters who had contributed to the *Reguladora's* growing stocks, Montes effected a forced sale of much of the stock, and the agency ceased purchasing shortly thereafter.[64] During the next three years prior to Alvarado's arrival, the *Reguladora* was loath to renew large-scale purchasing. Significantly, when it did, it was Montes who became one of the primary buyers of its fiber.[65] The coup de grâce was administered by separatist leader Ortiz Argumedo, who stole the remaining 5 million pesos of the *Reguladora's* tax-generated revenue as he fled the state early in 1915. Previously, Huerta's governors had dipped into the agency's war chest for 2 million pesos to finance their patron's counterrevolution, and Carranza had instructed Ávila and de los Santos to lift an additional 6 million to fight Villa and Zapata and "pacify" Yucatán.[66]

However, for better or for worse – and the consensus of the *hacendado* class is that it has been the latter – the creation of the first *Reguladora* established the precedent that, henceforth, the management of the henequen industry would come under the state's purview. Whereas the *Maderista* government of 1912 was content to invoke this principle to a limited extent, Alvarado, Carrillo Puerto, and later Socialist administrations would construe it much more broadly, assuming increasingly greater control over the marketing of henequen and, in the case of the *Cardenista* regimes of the late 1930s, in the area of production as well. Little wonder, then, that *hacendados* have come to rue the day they petitioned for the creation of the original *Reguladora*, which, in retrospect, they regard as a veritable Trojan horse of socialism. *Hacendado* writer Manuel Zapata Casares has rendered the point more fatalistically, borrowing a Spanish proverb: "Raise a crow and one day he'll peck your eyes out."[67]

Alvarado wasted no time in resurrecting the *Comisión Reguladora* in the spring of 1915 and revamping it to meet the requirements of his ambitious reform program. Much like the contemporary trust-busting Progressives of the United States whom he admired,[68] Alvarado initially imposed stricter government controls on the henequen industry, serving notice that under his administration the *Comisión Reguladora* would truly *regulate* the market. However, almost immediately, the general came to realize that the control exercised over production by the trusts and their local allies would nullify any halfway measures. Going far beyond the moderate North American Progressives, Alvarado determined that the only weapon powerful enough to combat monopoly was monopoly itself.[69]

First he moved against Montes and the *Casta*, persuading and then compelling all *henequeneros* to sell their fiber only to the *Reguladora*. With a stroke of the pen, Alvarado declared all debts and obligations backed by fiber void, in effect releasing a number of smaller producers from Montes's financial grip.[70] Having already bought and nationalized the state's railway system in 1915, Alvarado now imposed a transportation boycott on any *henequenero* who would not sell to the *Reguladora*.[71] He answered the protests of the large planters who traditionally had done business with Montes (Harvester) and Peabody by pointing out that the market still remained open and that they could sell fiber to whomever they chose. Of course, withholding railroad cars from the buyers' clients was equivalent to consigning their fiber to rot on the plantation. When Lorenzo Manzanilla and several other large coastal producers sought to circumvent Alvarado's strategy by shipping their henequen to Progreso via schooner, the general became infuriated and seized both the boats and the fiber.[72]

Late in 1915, Alvarado moved to rationalize the situation, making a concerted drive to enroll all *henequeneros* in the *Reguladora*, which he now rather euphemistically referred to as a "state-managed planter cooperative." *Hacendados* were obliged to sign five-year contracts with the *Reguladora*, pledging their entire fiber production to it. In consideration, Alvarado guaranteed them an *anticipo* (advance) of 8.8 cents per kilogram for their henequen delivered in Mérida, which the *Reguladora* would then sell for the best price obtainable on the international market. At the end of each year, the organization would liquidate its accounts, dividing its net profits with the *henequeneros* after extracting certain amounts for operating expenditures and, more importantly, for taxes in support of Alvarado's revolutionary programs.[73]

The members of the *Casta* resented any state incursion on their traditional preserve and, as they would do so many times thereafter, refused to cooperate with Alvarado. The small and medium growers, on the other hand, were only too eager to sign the general's contract, for it not only freed them from the *Casta's* control but provided them with their only source of credit. Moreover, the monetary terms of the contract were almost universally acknowledged to be very generous, especially with the prospect of skyrocketing fiber prices looming on the horizon.[74] By April 1916, therefore, Alvarado had succeeded in isolating the 49 producers (out of about 1,000) who had not yet signed contracts. Threats of property confiscation followed, and some disgruntled planters later confessed that they had been brought into the fold at gunpoint – not inconceivable, because Alvarado himself would admit that force had been applied to convince the more skeptical. By the end of 1916, membership in the "cooperative" approached 100 percent of the *hacendado* community.[75]

In his efforts to forge Yucatecan monopoly control, Alvarado was even less subtle in his dealings with the buyers than he had been with the producers. He was adamant not only that all henequen would be bought by the *Reguladora* but also that the *Reguladora* would be the sole agent of sale to the manufacturers in the United States. There would be no commercial intermediaries, either Yucatecan or North American. Accordingly, in 1916, the houses of Montes and Peabody and Company were legally prohibited from purchasing henequen once 90 percent of the *henequeneros* signed *Reguladora* contracts.[76] However, the buyers had seen the writing on the wall long before. After witnessing the humiliation of its agents and the fining and imprisonment of various producers who traditionally sold to them, Peabody closed its doors at the end of 1915.[77]

Following Avelino Montes's flight to Havana prior to Alvarado's arrival, Montes's firm had gradually been declining in importance in the export trade. The firm's decline had prompted Harvester to send a man to Mérida from the Chicago home office to look after their joint interests.[78] No sooner did the Harvester agent arrive in Yucatán than he was summoned by Alvarado and presented with the same ultimatum that his counterpart from Peabody had received earlier:

> The Government of Yucatán would not interfere with the International Harvester Co. in the sale of binder twine in the U.S. and Harvester could charge the American farmer any price it pleased, but Alvarado would not rest until he had driven Harvester out of business in Yucatán . . . Whatever sisal the Harvester Co. required would have to be bought through the Regulating Commission . . .[79]

In Chicago, the Harvester brass quickly appraised the situation:

> The Governor [Alvarado] regards us as a necessary evil in consequence of our large consumption of their sole product,

and he is anxious to sell us all the sisal we require, but we must "eat it out of his hand" and pay his prices for it.[80] Weeks later, early in 1916, Harvester terminated its business relations with the house of Montes, sent its agent home to Chicago, and began buying its henequen exclusively from the New York office of the *Comisión Reguladora* – just as Alvarado had instructed.[81]

By mid-1916, Harvester and the other cordage manufacturers were indeed eating out of Alvarado's hand, and expensively. With the supply of manila fiber and most African and Asian sisal choked off due to the exigencies of wartime transportation, Alvarado became increasingly able to name his price – and then raise it. The general moved to cement his hold on the bullish henequen market by negotiating an unprecedented $10 million line of credit with a consortium of North American bankers – strange bedfellows, indeed, for a self-styled bolshevik! Although the terms were rather onerous, calling for high interest rates and a substantial commission payment, they gave Alvarado the liquid capital he needed to keep Harvester and the other manufacturers over a barrel for as long as boom conditions prevailed.[82] He would now put the credit to work, salting away fiber stocks and keeping his producers happy with advances while he held the North American cordage industry to ransom. During Alvarado's administration, the price of henequen exported to the United States rose nearly 400 percent, from 13.2 cents per kilogram in 1915 to more than 50.6 cents (briefly) in 1918. Within a period of less than 12 months between 1916 and 1917, fiber quotations jumped over 100 percent. The result was that Yucatán's export earnings from henequen more than doubled during Alvarado's three-year period.[83] (See Table 5.)

As long as world market conditions reinforced the general's inclination toward a *política alcista* (policy of high prices), Alvarado's multiclass coalition remained unified and enjoyed a consensus of popularity. Henequen – millions of pesos' worth in taxes over the three-year period – footed the bill for the salaries of a greatly expanded bureaucracy that oversaw the general's burgeoning welfare state and promoted the new political organizations throughout Yucatán. Henequen raised wages in both field and shop and paid for Alvarado's thousand schools and hundred libraries. It facilitated Mexico's first feminist congresses and paved the way for its first effective labor tribunals.

As the Revolution prospered, so did the planters. In 1916, after

Table 5. *U.S. market prices for henequen, 1915–1925 (quotations in cents per kilogram, U.S. currency)*

Year	Average price	General market trends
1915	12.96	Alvarado assumes control of the *Reguladora*
1916	12.30	
1917	29.15	Wartime demand and *política alcista*
1918	42.35	All-time henequen bonanza
1919	14.30	Armistice; bottom falls out of market
1920	9.90	
1921	9.35	U.S. bankers dump surplus on already glutted market
1922	8.25	
1923	9.35	Beginning of modest recovery
1924	13.20	
1925	14.65	

Sources: *Cordage Trade Journal*, 1915–1925; Nathaniel Raymond, "The Impact of Land Reform in the Monocrop Region of Yucatán, Mexico," Ph.D. dissertation, Brandeis University, 1971, p. 55; Enrique Aznar Mendoza, "Historia de la industria henequenera desde 1919," *Enciclopedia Yucatanense*, Mexico, 1947, vol. 3, pp. 778–782.

its first year of operation, the *Reguladora*, which had already advanced the *henequeneros* 8.8 cents per kilogram for their fiber, now distributed an additional $3.7 million among them in profits. A year later, they would receive well over three times that amount ($12.6 million), and the year after that, their share of the profits doubled again. In other words, in 1918, the year Alvarado left Yucatán, the planters received $24.6 million in addition to their *anticipos*, which the *Reguladora* had by then increased to 15.4 cents per kilogram. Put another way, over the three-year period from November 1915 to November 1918, a few hundred *hacendados* received $81,900,569, or approximately 42 percent of Yucatán's total earnings from the sale of its henequen ($190,619,930).[84] This exceptional payoff enabled the *henequeneros* to dig themselves out from under the mortgages and debts that had previously mired their *fincas* while still living sumptuously and, in many cases, depositing surpluses in North American and European banks.[85] Several years later, in the wake of economic recession and resulting recrimination by *hacendados*, Alvarado mused: "And all that enrichment occurred during the black days of my ruinous administration and owed to my oppressive economic policies."[86]

Moreover, in addition to receiving the lion's share of the profits, the *henequeneros* found themselves aided by the general in other ways. He guarded against labor shortage by importing thousands of central Mexican contract workers. More stringent safety regulations were prescribed to protect *henequenales* from accidental fires − common during the dry season when neighboring pueblos cleared their maize plots by burning − and harsh penalties were decreed for arsonists.[87] Alvarado inaugurated a state-sponsored campaign to improve cultivating techniques and refine decorticating machinery in the face of a decline in the quality of Yucatecan fiber and the emergence of foreign competition on the world market.[88] Low-interest loans were made readily available to improvement-minded planters.[89]

Even the much publicized real estate tax that Alvarado introduced was not the burden on the *henequenero* that some writers have claimed, least of all a serious attempt to put into practice Henry George's single-tax theory. Prior to Alvarado's arrival, rural property went untaxed, and the rate on urban property was rather insignificant. As a result of Alvarado's new land tax, the urban rate was reduced still further and a yield of 400,000 pesos was realized from rural property by 1918. Far from signaling a significant redistribution of wealth or even the introduction of a more equitable tax structure to Yucatán, it did no more than shift some of the tax burden to the affluent *henequeneros* and penalize their failure to cultivate good land. The *henequenero* had little cause for alarm. In fact, the *Catastro* (office of property tax) records of Alvarado's government show that, more often than not, the general acceded to *hacendado* requests that property valuations be reduced and taxes lowered.[90]

With the flow of henequen revenues increasing at a geometric rate, Alvarado embarked upon more ambitious reforms of the Yucatecan economy. As early as the middle of 1915, the general signaled his intention to expand further the scope of the *Reguladora's* activities.[91] In the months ahead, Yucatán would generate enough income from henequen to meet the financial contributions demanded by Carranza and still implement a massive program of state intervention in the regional economy. This intervention would take several forms: the establishment of a *Comisión Reguladora* for the domestic commercial sector; the reorganization and modernization under state control of the region's only *cordelería* (cordage factory); and, most importantly, the creation of a vast, umbrellalike regional development corporation.[92] Had these reforms been carried through to completion and survived at least the first revolutionary decade (1915–1924), Yucatán might have taken a major step toward freeing itself from the worst social and economic effects of monocrop dependence.

Although its title suggests an organization parallel to the state's Henequen Regulating Commission, the *Comisión Reguladora de Comercio* was actually a subsidiary of the older *Reguladora*. This was perfectly logical because all wealth derived from henequen, and all other forms of economic activity – most notably commerce and the little industry that had managed to take root – were generated by, related to, or provided needed services for the henequen industry. Not surprisingly, many of the great planter families had successfully diversified their interests in commerce and, by dominating the import and wholesale trades, essentially controlled prices in the three basic retail lines – groceries, dry goods, and hardware. Although a number of immigrant families – Spanish, French, German and, increasingly, Lebanese – had made inroads into their preserve, the first three ethnic groups had been incorporated successfully through marriage into the regional bourgeoisie.[93]

Gouging was the rule, and hoarding and speculation were common in local business practice. Markups of 200 percent above cost were not uncommon, and 100 percent was standard on many retail goods.[94] The economic and social impact of this kind of mercantile system on the common people of a region that was unable to produce most of its foodstuffs, had no textile industry to speak of, and was geographically isolated from areas of production could be devastating, especially during periods of inflation and agricultural scarcity.[95] Consequently, the *Reguladora de Comercio* represented Alvarado's attempt to bring life's basic necessities – food and essential consumer goods – within reach of all of Yucatán's inhabitants.[96]

From the start, the venture was beset with opposition from private merchants[97] and quickly degenerated into a wasted effort. The organization's capital of 4.5 million pesos, raised via a loan from the *henequeneros* (which was promptly repaid),[98] should have been sufficient to enable the *Reguladora* to police existing commercial establishments for price gouging while simultaneously instituting an alternative chain of cooperative stores in Mérida and the smaller centers that would compete with the private merchants and distribute cheaper food and goods.[99] Such had been Alvarado's strategy for implementing the new *Reguladora*, and several years later Felipe Carrillo would energetically attempt to carry it out. However, so corrupt was the management of both *Reguladoras* – controlled almost exclusively by a group of large *hacendados* and merchants that effectively represented a rival clique almost as wealthy and powerful as Montes's *Casta* – that the money allocated disappeared before either of the new *Reguladora's* goals could be met.[100]

The first cooperative stores did not even begin to do business until 1918, after Alvarado had left Yucatán and Carrillo had shaken up the state bureaucracy and begun to implement a more radical program.[101] Nor were the private merchants adequately policed by the new agency or compelled to reform their shady practices. In fact, gouging continued, only now the officials of the *Reguladora* were equally guilty of the practice. Under the "controls" of the *Reguladora*, it was not uncommon for the price of sugar to rise 60 centavos within a twenty-four-hour period or for beans to double in price in less than a month's time. More often than not, the *campesinos* complained, officials of the *Reguladora* themselves became speculating middlemen, selling staple commodities wholesale to selected large merchants, who then imposed their own markups on the helpless consumer. Publishing a biting attack on the *Reguladora*, the Mérida town council revealed that the agency had sold corn to merchants at 18 pesos per sack and these, in turn, had commanded 30 to 35 pesos from the public.[102] Indeed, if most private merchants were threatened by their new rival, it was because they feared that Alvarado's government would re-create in the import and domestic commercial sector the same monopoly it held in the henequen export sector. Already, they observed – and here their protest was echoed by *campesinos* and urban workers – the *Reguladora* had abused the special importing privileges it had been granted, controlling the flow of goods in certain lines and raising rather than lowering prices. Comparisons were drawn with the old colonial practice of *repartimiento*, whereby profiteering magistrates would use their authority to impose a sale of goods on a subject population at exhorbitant prices.[103]

However, ultimately, the private merchants had little to fear, for by 1918 it had become clear that they and not the *Reguladora de Comercio* would be granted generous export licenses by the U.S. government's wartime Food Administration to bring badly needed food and commodities into Yucatán. Thus, in addition to its internal corruption and administrative difficulties, Alvarado's commercial *Reguladora* was also the victim of the preferential treatment that the U.S. government – no doubt influenced by the cordage interests and established North American exporting houses – accorded to Yucatán's mercantile elite.[104]

Alvarado's reorganization and renovation of *cordelería* La Industrial, at that time Yucatán's only substantial henequen manufacturing plant, suggests still another avenue explored by Alvarado in his attempt to mitigate the evils of the region's traditional syndrome of monoculture and economic dependence. In reincarnating La Industrial in August 1916, Alvarado sought to wean the agro-commercial bourgeoisie from its belief in the traditional international division of labor by which raw fiber was shipped to the United States and there manufactured into binder twine. Repeatedly, he impressed upon the *henequeneros* the slogan "Industrializar el henequén en nuestro propio país" ("Henequen must be industrialized in our own land") and argued that industrialization was the only sure way in the long run to stabilize prices for the fiber that would not be manufactured but exported *en rama* (in raw form) to the United States.[105] Meeting with reluctance and skepticism from most *hacendados*, who were content to enjoy greatly increased earnings on their raw fiber, Alvarado compelled a number of large *henequeneros* to resuscitate and manage La Industrial, a "privilege" for which they collectively would contribute 5 million pesos.[106] The manner of recruitment is suggestive of the lack of enthusiasm that later plagued the project. La Industrial under Alvarado never supplied more than a portion of Yucatán's or Mexico's cordage needs, let alone provide a surplus for export to the North American market. The consolidation of Yucatán's *cordelerías* would not take place until the early 1930s.[107]

Martín Luis Guzmán once wrote of Alvarado: "With every twenty words he outlined a plan which, if put into effect, would have changed the face of the earth."[108] In May 1916, Alvarado established a corporation for the economic development of southeastern Mexico, a state venture of such vast proportions that *Yucatecos* are still divided as to whether the idea was conceived by a genius or a madman.[109] Alvarado decreed that his *Compañía de Fomento del Sureste* would function for 100 years with an original capital of 100 million pesos, half of which, he suggested – apparently without having obtained Carranza's complete commitment

– would be defrayed by the federal government.[110] Merely to list the objectives of the new corporation is provocative, for, taken as a whole, they constitute a catalogue of the infrastructural goals and programs that subsequent Socialist state governments would press for over the next two decades, vainly petitioning the federal government for financial support. Basically, Alvarado decreed that the corporation would undertake all necessary public works in the states of Yucatán, Campeche, Tabasco, Chiapas, and the Territory of Quintana Roo. This would include the development of land and sea transportation and communications networks with the rest of Mexico and abroad, extensive oil exploration and exploitation, the establishment of a Yucatecan-owned and -operated steamship company (to go along with the state's control of its railroads, already accomplished by Alvarado), and the renovation and construction of new port works at Progreso.[111]

The actual record of the *Compañía de Fomento* was a mixed one. Public (i.e., *hacendado*) response to the scheme in Yucatán was not encouraging, and Alvarado's government found it difficult to sell the stock it held in the corporation.[112] More damaging to the venture was the Carranza government's refusal to contribute its share of the capital, resulting in the embarrassing reduction of the corporation's operating capital from 100 million to 5 million pesos, 2 million of which had been put up by the *Compañía de Fomento's* parent body, the *Comisión Reguladora*.[113] Still, Alvarado's development corporation managed to purchase its own "henequen fleet" of seven ships to transport fiber and foodstuffs to and from the United States, as well as to finance the construction of petroleum storage facilities in Progreso. In fact, it also mounted an unsuccessful search for oil but left reports that Pemex (*Petroleos Mexicanos*, the more recent national oil monopoly) later used to strike oil beneath the peninsula's limestone foundation.[114]

Clearly, Alvarado was ahead of his time in attempting to carry out so comprehensive a blueprint for regional economic development. Of course, the program could have been initiated only during a period of extraordinary prosperity, such as marked Alvarado's tenure in Yucatán. However, for the program to realize its monumental ambitions, continued economic prosperity and a stable political climate would be essential. But these conditions did not exist in Yucatán after 1918. Alvarado would watch helplessly from Mexico City as his grandiose plans – which would have freed Yucatán in large part from its reliance upon costly North

American transportation, energy, and technology – were beset with economic and political difficulties that the foreign cordage interests would quickly turn to their advantage.

We should keep in mind that Alvarado's *Comisión Reguladora*, although it influenced and became a prototype for other Mexican *comisiones* regulating other commodities, represented only one particular solution to the grave economic problems that gripped Mexico during its chaotic first revolutionary decade. Beginning early in 1915, with much of the Republic under military occupation, there cropped up a variety of agencies or commissions, usually known as *reguladoras de comercio*, to meet the growing crisis in supplying life's daily necessities, above all corn, beans, and charcoal. These agencies were most often organized by the local military authorities and had as their minimal goal control over the shipments and pricing of basic goods. The orientation and composition of these *reguladoras* varied as widely as the local conditions in which they emerged and were particularly influenced by the inclinations of the military chiefs who set them up. Unfortunately, in the majority of cases these *reguladoras* probably represented little more than an opportunity for the local boss and his cronies to monopolize local trade and keep all the gouging for themselves. But in other areas, such as Veracruz and Yucatán, these *comisiones reguladoras* constituted exciting socioeconomic experiments. In the city of Orizaba, Veracruz, *reguladoras de comercio* were actually run by powerful local unions that virtually socialized local trade for several months in 1915–1916. Then, acting pragmatically in the absence of effective local political and military authority, these workers moved from control of distribution to questions of production and, at some moments, even vied for the right to control the means of production. Orizaba workers claimed authority to review hacienda account books, inspect factory records and warehouses, and take over railroad stations. [115]

Yucatán's *comisiones* were a far cry from these "proto-soviets" in Veracruz. Among other things, the authority of Alvarado's army of occupation never lapsed or was effectively challenged in Yucatán; nor were *Meridano* or *Progreseño* workers ever as tough or independent as their counterparts in Orizaba. Although Alvarado's *Comisión Reguladora del Mercado de Henequén* proved itself to be hydralike in its ability to expand its activities and progressively extend its control over the state's economy, it never assumed a socialist orientation. The Yucatecan *Reguladora* established a monopoly over all banking and credit operations in the state and gained exclusive control of the henequen export sector. Through its offshoot, the *Compañía de Fomento*, the *Reguladora* promoted and extended its control over public works and infrastructural improvements as well as transportation and shipping. However, it never seriously threatened the private sectors of commerce and industry in attempting to rationalize consumption or evidenced any interest in expanding its control over actual agricultural production, either in the henequen zone or outside it. As Yucatecan economic historian Renán Irigoyen concluded, the political economy of Salvador Alvarado, epitomized in his *Comisión Reguladora*, was more a "transitional bridge between the final stages of economic liberalism and the onset of real state interventionism" than a serious prescription for state socialism.[116]

Yet Salvador Alvarado was the first revolutionary governor to suggest to the Mexican nation the possibilities for regional development that might issue from the creation of *empresas descentralizadas* – decentralized, state-supported economic ventures. In addition, Alvarado's skillful use of cooperativism – essentially a bourgeois phenomenon quite distinct from state socialism – represented an important early attempt in Latin America to balance between or mediate the interests of capital and labor. Beginning in the 1920s, cooperativism would be applied to a variety of state economic ventures by the Mexican federal government and, in subsequent decades, would constitute a basic element of the economic policies of many authoritarian corporatist regimes throughout Latin America.[117]

6

The breakdown of bourgeois revolution, 1918–1920

Bitterness will overflow and abundance will dry up . . . It will be a time of suffering, of tears and of misery.

—Prophecy of Napuc Tun

We have the advantage: They must sell to eat; we only have to buy hemp.

—U.S. Consul Gaylord Marsh to the Secretary of State, 1919

As he prepared to leave the state for reassignment late in 1918, Salvador Alvarado cast a dire prophecy. Challenging the great *hacendados* and merchants who, in the wake of declining henequen prices, suddenly began to denounce the monopoly powers of the *Comisión Reguladora* and demand the restoration of an open market, Alvarado wrote:

> Go ahead and deliver up the *Reguladora* and the state economy to your cruelest enemies; dissolve the *Cía. de Fomento del Sureste*; hand your railroads over to their foreign creditors and sell your ships overseas to the highest bidder; destroy the petroleum storage tanks and sell the parts for scrap iron . . . Close the schools and libraries if they are as harmful as you say; and then be sure to reopen the bars, the bullrings, the whorehouses and the gaming dens . . . Do all this and in one year I challenge the people of Yucatán and the entire nation to consider the results and compare them with the situation that exists today.[1]

Alvarado's prophecy would be borne out with frightening accuracy. Within a year, much of his reform program lay in shambles and Yucatán's incipient bourgeois revolution had run aground. The circumstances and events of 1918–1919 reveal the essential contradictions of Yucatán's condition of staple dependence within the global economy and powerfully illustrate the complex of relationships that bound the region to the United States and Mexico City, subordinating regional interests to those of the national and international metropolis.

One cannot help but be struck by how closely the success of Alvarado's revolution was tied to the fortunes of the henequen market. The effectiveness of his program rose and fell on the *Reguladora's* receipts from henequen. As long as fiber prices were high, Alvarado was able simultaneously to improve the wages and material conditions of the masses and ensure the continuing prosperity of the agro-commercial bourgeoisie. This moderate strategy produced an ideological consensus and a level of internal harmony within the region sufficient to construct a viable, if fragile, revolutionary coalition.

Moreover, enough surplus profit remained to support the substantial fiscal demands of Carranza's federal government, which, consequently, also found it in its interests to continue to sanction the operations of Alvarado's closely regulated regional economy. In addition to depending upon a measure of benign neglect from Mexico City for the implementation of his reforms, Alvarado also realized the importance of Carranza's support should Yucatán have to withstand diplomatic and economic pressures from the U.S. government, acting in behalf of the powerful cordage lobby, or be faced with a renewed campaign of economic warfare and price manipulation emanating from the cordage manufacturers themselves.

Regarding the North American response to revolutionary activities in Yucatán and, in particular, to Alvarado's transformation of the traditional system of henequen marketing and export, it is fair to say that Alvarado was able to proceed in the face of U.S. disapproval – and do so with near impunity – only so long as the world market, artificially buoyed by the contingencies of World War I, supported high prices for henequen. While this fortuitous conjuncture existed, from 1915 to 1918, Yucatán temporarily altered the terms of its dependent and unequal relationship vis-à-vis the United States. In effect, the traditional terms of trade that for so long had worked against Yucatán were suddenly reversed, and the monocrop region found itself holding the whip hand in what, for the moment, had become a seller's market. Since the earliest days of monoculture in the 1870s, the North American corporations had based their monopolistic or oligopolistic strategy upon the region's desperate need to sell its only commodity. Now, ironically, the logic of the situation had changed, for wartime America desperately needed its daily bread, and there would be no bread if the midwestern wheat farmer could not bind his sheaves. Henequen had become more than big business: It was crucial to the war effort. According to the U.S. Office of Naval Intelligence, any obstacle that threatened America's supply of fiber for binder twine was now "as crucial to the United States as the Tampico oil strikes which affected the fuel of the allied fleet."[2] And with the Philippines and other sources of production cut off, it was the North Americans who were forced to buy at least as much as the Yucatecans were obliged to sell.

In order better to appreciate how the declining fortunes of the fluctuating monocrop economy wreaked havoc with Alvarado's revolutionary program following World War I, let us first examine how the general used booming wartime conditions to his advantage against the North American cordage trust and its allies in Washington.

The North American response: dealing from weakness

The sea lanes and wartime shipping had been unreliable since 1914. Moreover, a severe drought in the Philippines and inadequate capacity in the emerging centers of production in Africa and Asia had led cordage manufacturers and U.S. government officials to conclude, in 1915, that it was not practical to seek fiber supplies elsewhere: "The world cannot supply any other fiber in commercial quantity in less than six years at the very least."[3] The United States would have to content itself exclusively with Yucatecan henequen, which it ordinarily favored anyway. For although overseas fibers were of a higher quality, henequen was far cheaper and more reliable, due to the peninsula's proximity and its reputation for political tranquility.

Suddenly, in March 1915, Alvarado had brought the Revolution to Yucatán and thrown the henequen industry into disarray. The predictive capacity that the cordage interests had enjoyed in the fiber business ever since they had gained control of the henequen market over a generation ago was now gone. First, the manufacturers were faced with the prospect of being unable to secure reliable shipments of fiber at any price. To their horror, they learned of naval blockades, transportation shutdowns, and even a rumored threat that the *hacendados* intended to burn their own fields. Then, mercifully, the agrarian situation had stabilized and they were offered all the henequen they wanted – but only after their agents had been ousted by the new revolutionary government, the marketing system had been transformed, and the purchasing price had soared to unheard of levels.

The manufacturers fought these changes every step of the way. International Harvester, with by far the most to lose, formulated the strategy of their counterattack. For Harvester found itself in an increasingly vulnerable position during the 1915–1918 period. Following the entrance of John Deere and Company and other smaller independent concerns into the harvesting machine field, beginning around 1910, Harvester's business had slumped badly and its monopoly position in the manufacture of binders, mowers, and rakes – its major lines – quickly vanished.[4] This disturbing trend only heightened Harvester's resolve to take a firmer stand on other fronts, such as the binder twine field, which continued to be an important secondary line of business.

Over the years, International Harvester and its constellation of satellite manufacturing firms had built up a formidable lobby in Washington. Now, in 1915, they were determined to bring all of their power to bear in an attempt to regain their former prerogatives. During Alvarado's three-year tenure, the North American cordage industry, in addition to utilizing its traditional allies in the peninsular bourgeoisie, enlisted the aid of all three branches of the U.S. government. In vain, it took Alvarado's *Reguladora* into the U.S. state and federal courts, seeking to enjoin it, under the terms of the Sherman Anti-Trust Act, from operating in this country.[5] Meanwhile, the manufacturers arranged for powerful spokesmen in both houses of Congress to draw attention to the *Reguladora's* harmful activities and to initiate hearings in the Senate for the purpose of establishing the guilt of the Yucatecan agency and devising a means of combating it in the interests of the American people. Thousands of pages of testimony and months later, in February 1917, a Senate subcommittee did indeed find that the *Reguladora* was a "harmful monopoly" and recommended that the Justice and State Departments take whatever action they found advisable to dissolve the *Reguladora* or at least curb its power, and that the manufacturers and farmers find some substitute for Yucatán's henequen in binder twine.[6] Both the State and Justice Departments had already been working quietly in the manufacturers' interests against the *Reguladora* and had been – or soon would be – joined by other executive departments, most notably Commerce, Agriculture, the Navy, and the powerful wartime Food Administration.

The manufacturers' basic strategy through all of these channels was to appeal to the reason of the Yucatecan revolutionary government, making it realize the long-term benefits of a symbiotic commercial relationship with them that should not be foolishly jeopardized for short-term gain. Rhetoric failing, the manufacturers would pressure Yucatán on a variety of fronts: economic, diplomatic, and legal. The diplomatic channel would entail working through Carranza's federal government in Mexico City but would not exclude cruder forms of gunboat diplomacy when words failed to persuade the Mexican president. It became clear that more than diplomatic protocol was involved in the North Americans' desire to work through Mexico City. Early on, they perceived that, up to a point, Carranza's stake in keeping a tighter reign on Alvarado and Yucatán coincided with their own interests. They found him more ideologically disposed to consider their demands than Alvarado.[7] Moreover, until October 1915, Washington held as a powerful trump card U.S. recognition of Carranza's government. This was no small inducement, and it served to make Carranza more responsive to at least the earlier demands of the cordage lobby.[8]

The first objective of the manufacturers was to restore the regular flow of raw henequen, which had been disrupted by Alvarado's conquest of Yucatán and the subsequent period of political readjustment. Initially, the cordage interests were confronted by Carranza's blockade of Progreso, implemented by the Constitutionalists in March 1915 in their effort to crush Ortiz Argumedo's separatist revolt. The First Chief's strategy had been to seal Yucatán off by sea while Alvarado's Army of the Southeast overwhelmed the insurgency by land. Meanwhile, however, the North American cordage factories were already short of fiber as they attempted to meet the expanded wartime demand. Immediately, the manufacturers petitioned the Wilson government to prevail upon Carranza to open the port and allow their ships to move the henequen for which they had already contracted.[9] Wilson instructed Secretary of State William Jennings Bryan to warn Carranza that unless the port was reopened, not only would further arms shipments to the Constitutionalists be canceled but the United States would be forced to reopen Progreso with a naval force in order to save the Mexicans from themselves:

> Go into Yucatán rather fully with Carranza and explain how indispensable the sisal is . . . as the food supply of the world may be said in a large measure to depend on it, and that we are justified, as friends of Mexico, in keeping her out of the deep trouble that would ensue if he interfered with the trade.[10]

Bryan concurred, reasoning that should it come to a gunboat, "we are in a position to restrain the use of force within the smallest possible range, just as we did at Veracruz."[11] The First Chief, however, aware that Yucatán would shortly be taken anyway, deferred to Bryan's request and lifted the blockade.

Yet, Harvester and its allies feared the advance of Alvarado's army in the region far more than the blockade and remained restive. Rumors abounded that either Alvarado or the *henequeneros* would fire the plantations (the latter out of spite). One of the cordage companies urged the State Department to "have Yucatán declared a neutral territory."[12] Throughout March and April 1915, other manufacturers called upon Washington to take some action to ensure that fiber shipments were not interrupted and the American farmer deprived of his wheat crop. Later that summer and fall, when Alvarado withheld railroad cars from Avelino Montes and the buyers, the trickle of letters and cables became a torrent.[13] Harvester and Peabody advised their clients and allies to complain to the State Department, and lending weight to the petitions of farmers, twine dealers, manufacturers, and buyers were those of congressmen and officials from a variety of U.S. government departments and agencies, and even a memorial from the British ambassador representing the Canadian wheat farmers.[14] Yielding to this effective lobby, the State Department instructed the Department of the Navy to send a gunboat to stand off Progreso for a few days, amidst almost continuous pressure on the Carranza government. The Navy was to keep the gunboat offshore, where it would work a "moral effect . . . on the authorities of Yucatán'" and "until [they] have given definite assurances . . . and taken steps to carry them out, that they will provide adequate railroad facilities for all American dealers without discrimination by favoring the *Comisión Reguladora* or anyone else."[15]

Because no evidence can readily be found in either Mexican or Yucatecan archives suggesting even the rumor of a threat on the part of Alvarado or the *hacendados* to burn the henequen fields, one suspects that this episode of gunboat diplomacy was prompted less by a fear of burned fields and more by Alvarado's takeover of the railroad system and his obvious intention to oust Montes–Harvester and Peabody from the state. Carranza had already given his assurance to Washington that Alvarado would not damage private property, and Alvarado clearly guarded against violent measures upon his arrival.[16] On the railroad matter, however, Carranza proved more sticky. On the one hand, Carranza's ambassador to Washington, Eliseo Arredondo, emphasized the First Chief's willingness "to have the whole [henequen] crop go to the United SStates and to afford all necessary facilities, so that the exportation may take place without any impediment from our part." [17] He pointed out that the failure to deliver henequen, which was the main source of state revenue and a large contributor to the National Treasury, created as great a hardship for Yucatán and Mexico as it did for the North American buyer. However, the matter was not so simple. For, as Arredondo explained in a note of formal protest to Secretary of State Bryan:

> We feel that the activities of the International Harvester Co., through its agent Montes are going too far . . . Harvester through Montes has been making undue use of the good name of the Department of State, with no other purpose than to foster its own interests . . . Montes has been making all kinds of threats in order to force his own prices and has even gone to the extent of saying he will bring complaints to the attention of the State Department whose influence and support he claims to have, and if his terms are not met, intervention by the U.S. Government might follow. [18]

Certainly, the Wilson government's haste in summoning a gunboat gave credence to Montes's claim of influence and suggests the effectiveness of Harvester's brand of informal empire based upon tested collaborator networks. Ultimately, Carranza, after hasty consultation with Alvarado, formally complied with Washington's ultimatum: Railroad cars were subsequently provided to move the fiber purchased by Harvester, Peabody, and the other buyers. [19] However, Alvarado remained undeterred in his campaign to forge a government henequen monopoly and Montes, Peabody, and the others soon realized the futility off their struggle, closing their doors by the beginning of 1916.

These buyers' assessment of the events proved to be more realistic than those of the U.S. government. Encouraged by past concessions regarding the movement of henequen, Washington now escalated its demands. In October 1915, with Alvarado's *Reguladora* having established virtually complete hegemony over Yucatán's henequen industry, Secretary of State Robert Lansing moved to nip the new state monopoly in the bud. He cabled his agent in Mexico City: "Immediately take up the [henequen] situation with General Carranza and urgently request him to send appropriate instructions to Yucatán's authorities. Say to him that this Government will appreciate it if he will at once direct the reestablishment of an open sisal market in Yucatán."[20] However, with henequen booming and no sign of a price ceiling in sight, Carranza had no intention of dissolving Alvarado's *Reguladora*, whose *alcista* policy was in part responsible for the dramatic price hikes. An open market was the last thing he desired; rather, he was content to give the *Reguladora* all the leeway it needed, then skim off a substantial portion of the *Reguladora's* receipts in federal taxes and mandatory loans.[21] Moreover, the State Department had already played its trump card, recognizing his de facto government months before. In November 1915, State Department Special Agent J. R. Silliman, who from his vantage point in Mexico City was more in touch with the situation, informed Washington of its reduced options:

> *First:* The easy, friendly and practical way of accepting the situation and coming to the best possible terms with the Company [the *Reguladora*] which is in absolute control, which is backed by the state and the recognized de facto government, and which is desirous of selling whether to distributors like the Harvester Company or direct to the manufacturers.
>
> *Second:* The difficult, unfriendly and slow way of freezing out the Company by refusing to buy.[22]

There was, realistically, no third option for the United States by the end of 1915. Gunboat diplomacy was falling into disrepute, even among the British, who found it simply no longer got the job done. Overt displays of violence were now regarded as admissions of failure, anachronistic nineteenth-century tactics inadequate in the management of twentieth-century empires that often did not include formally annexed colonies. Of course, on special occasions and when severely provoked, the United States would again resort to armed intervention, as when Pershing "invaded" northern Mexico in vain pursuit of Pancho Villa. However, the United States had too much property and other investments at stake in Mexico – especially its mushrooming oil empire along the Gulf Coast – to warrant an ugly incident with the nationalistic Constitutionalists.[23] Consequently, for the better part of the next three years, with the war dragging on and the price of fiber soaring higher and higher, the North Americans were obliged to choose the first option even as they contemplated and prepared to take the second.

Equally galling for the cordage interests and their government were the Senate subcommittee hearings. The subcommittee's finding, released in January 1917, that the *Reguladora* was a monopoly surprised no one, especially because the *Reguladora's* U.S. representative, Víctor Rendón, had gone on record to state that this was precisely the intention of its guiding force, General Alvarado. Alvarado used the lengthy hearings for his own purposes, parrying the manufacturers' propaganda and presenting the Yucatecan case as favorably as possible. Before the senators, he paraded a string of sympathetic *hacendados*, all of whom argued that increased production costs necessitated higher prices and testified – with real or feigned indignation – that Harvester and Montes had fixed and depressed prices in order to control the henequen industry, to the detriment of farmers in Yucatán and the United States.[24] Spending thousands of dollars to pay lobbyists and journalists.and to campaign in the North American press, Alvarado pitched his case to the tenor of the times, which was decidedly Progressivist and sensitive to the threat of trusts and monopolies.[25] Yes, Alvarado's propagandists admitted, the *Reguladora* was a monopoly of sorts, but it was first and foremost a government regulatory agency designed to bust the truly pernicious Harvester trust, which utilized local agents to perpetuate a regime of slavery and poverty in Yucatán while subjecting farmers and consumers to price gouging at home. Then, in the wake of the hearings, the *New York Times*, the *Chicago Herald*, and other leading dailies ran headlines such as "Fight Harvester with $10 million," "Envoy from Mexican State Gives Facts of Alleged Unfair Monopoly," "Oust Harvester Company: Two Big American Companies Driven Out, Says Dr. Rendón, Defending New Organization."[26] Suddenly, Alvarado and his *Reguladora* were regarded by many middle Americans as underdogs with courage enough to stand up to the Morgans, McCormicks, and Rockefellers and actually carry the day. Meanwhile, the hearings themselves had accomplished nothing. As long as wartime conditions and demand persisted, the *Reguladora* would continue to inflate prices with impunity. Given the nature of the *Reguladora's* legal and political status, Congress and the courts could do little more than rant against its activities and pricing policy.

    Herbert Hoover and the powerful U.S. Food Administration also found that dealing with the *Reguladora* could be a frustrating, if not downright humiliating, experience. The Food Administration was set up late in 1917 to implement needed wartime controls over distribution and speculation in food and collateral commodities – such as sisal and binder twine. It continued to function through the Armistice, until July 1919. The Food Administration was immediately concerned that the increasing price of twine would lead to prohibitive grain harvesting costs for American farmers that might impair the final phase of the war effort.[27] Under its director, Herbert Hoover – who had early acquired the informal titles of "Food Czar" and "Food Dictator" – the administration entered into negotiations, first with the cordage manufacturers and then with the *Reguladora*, in an effort to obtain prices pegged to production costs plus a reasonable profit. The October 1917 Washington conference between Hoover and the manufacturers resulted in an agreement whereby the twine makers would purchase their entire fiber requirements through the Food Administration. It was also agreed that the manufacturers would not sell their twine at a price greater than the cost of the raw material plus the conversion cost and a reasonable profit. The reasonableness of the profit would now be determined by the Food Administration, inasmuch as there had justifiably been considerable protest from American grain farmers that Harvester and the smaller companies, far from acting in the wartime spirit and shaving their profit margins in the face of the *Reguladora's* price offensive, had consolidated or actually increased them.[28]

With the *Reguladora*, however, Hoover's agency made no headway. Late in 1917, the price stood at 42.9 cents per kilogram and, after prolonged negotiations with the *Reguladora's* New York agents, the Food Administration found the *Reguladora* unwilling to budge beyond a reduction of 1.1 cents per kilogram. Moreover, the *Yucatecos* would accept no price formula and were not swayed by the recent manufacturers' agreement to buy through the Food Administration. Negotiations dragged on, with Hoover making it clear that the U.S. government would not be the victim of extortion when vital commodities were concerned.[29] Hoover's assistant, Mark Requa, went even further, asking for troops to compel the *Yucatecos* to accept a fair price. The State Department counseled patience, arguing that intervention would disrupt fiber production rather than guaranteeing an adequate supply at a fair price. Moreover, a policy of confrontation would disrupt trade in other necessary Mexican commodities, such as oil.[30] From Mexico City, Ambassador Henry Fletcher was more cautious, suggesting that "an attempt be made to obtain . . . [a price] reduction in connection with shipments of gold and foodstuffs from the United States,"[31] exploiting Yucatán's inability to feed itself. The Food Czar, his patience stretched to the limit, apparently favored this approach, for he immediately called a halt to the negotiations. Traditionally reserved but now very much unbuttoned, he thundered to the State Department:

> We do not feel we have any right to submit the American people to the humiliation of this government's signing a contract so abundant with graft and robbery . . . We propose we should keep the embargo on food to Mexico until the Mexican Central Government comes on its knees to receive help and . . . then put our demands as a quid pro quo. I trust you are in agreement with this programme.[32]

The State Department was not, simply because the farmers and manufacturers could not wait for such an embargo to take effect. That very month the manufacturers informed Hoover that they had become desperate: Unless fiber was shipped immediately, it would be impossible to manufacture sufficient twine for the 1918 harvest, which promised to be a bumper crop, substantially greater than the preceding three. Reluctantly, Hoover returned to the bargaining table and settled on the *Reguladora's* terms. All in all, Yucatán would deliver 340,000 bales of henequen at 41.8 cents per kilogram New Orleans (42.9 cents New York), and the Food Administration guaranteed to make food and gold shipments in return.[33] The wheat and small grain harvest in North America was saved. But it would be the last really successful sale that Alvarado's *Reguladora* would ever make.

In fact, contrary to alarmist North American reports, Alvarado exercised considerable moderation in formulating the *Reguladora's* pricing policy. Market quotations for henequen were traditionally pegged 6.6 to 11 cents lower than those for manila, allowing for the superior quality and increased transportation costs of the rival Philippine fiber.[34] At the height of the wartime boom, in the spring of 1918, the price of manila would skyrocket to 66 cents per kilogram, averaging 64.9 cents during 1918. During the same period, henequen momentarily climbed to 50.6 cents per kilogram, averaging 42.4 cents for that peak year.[35] Thus, although it is true that the price of henequen was considerably inflated and bore less correspondence to actual production costs than to what a wartime market would bear, the fact that Yucatecan fiber was not pegged to manila, with quotations soaring as high as 55 to 59.4 cents, attests to a restraint on Alvarado's part that went unnoticed by his North American critics. The *Reguladora* had Hoover over a barrel in November 1917, and had it insisted on the traditional 11-cent spread in relation to manila, the Food

Administration would not have been able to refuse, given the manufacturers' desperate straits.[36]

It is interesting to examine, in this light, the allegations made in an extremely controversial State Department memorandum concerning Yucatecan speculation on the world fiber market in 1917. In a "confidential" intradepartmental memo dated 6 February 1917, Leon J. Canova, head of the Division of Mexican Affairs, briefed Secretary of State Lansing regarding the *Reguladora's* rumored intention "to make money not only by controlling [henequen] prices, but by manipulating the market." Henequen quotations were up about 22 cents above normal and, thus far, manila had been disposed to rise by a similar proportion. The *Reguladora*, Canova suggested, did not dare raise its prices higher; rather, it intended

> to buy short on Manila, drop the price on sisal hemp [i.e., henequen], forcing Manila down, and, when it reaches bottom, buy long on Manila, raise prices on sisal, and make a killing both ways. This manipulation may be repeated from time to time, to fatten the purses of the men in control of the *Comisión Reguladora*.[37]

The reality proved to be far different from Canova's projection. There is simply no evidence in the trade journals, among the records of the *Comisión Reguladora*, or even in those of the cordage interests that hints at Yucatán's intention to speculate on the world market in the manner that Harvester did prior to the Revolution. Nor does a careful examination of price trends for henequen or manila during 1917–1918 betray such an intention. Furthermore, although in future years the Yucatecan government considered the possibility of establishing an agency in the Philippines and coordinating a unified strategy among fiber-producing regions, it had made no move to do so during this period. In sum, it is unlikely that Yucatán possessed either the ambition or the expertise to engage in the kind of speculative venture referred to in Canova's memorandum.

The North Americans take the offensive

The negotiations between the *Reguladora* and the Food Administration, which began in the spring of 1918, reflected the inevitable shift of power in the fiber market that was already taking place as the war wound down and the 1919 grain harvest promised to be, at best, a mediocre one. Whereas the *Reguladora* had avoided a firm contractual agreement late in 1917, it now attempted to compensate for its deteriorating position with the best one it could negotiate. Hoover, on the other hand, was now slow to negotiate and relished the prospect of driving a hard bargain. Transcripts of the proceedings in Washington reveal the Food Administration apparently reneging on a series of verbal agreements made in previous months specifying that at least 700,000 bales would be sold at the former price of 41.8 cents per kilogram. Moreover, Hoover's representatives hinted none too subtly that, should the opportunity arise, the United States would look to buy elsewhere. Understandably miffed and accusing the Food Administration of acting in bad faith, the *Reguladora* representatives announced Yucatán's intention to sell elsewhere.[38] Hoover regarded this as mere bluff but later found that the *Reguladora* had found prospective buyers in Argentina. Furthermore, he discovered that the purchase price would be significantly lower (35.2 cents per kilogram) than that offered to the United States. Hoover charged unjust discrimination and once more began using food shipments as a lever in the discussions. The bargaining became increasingly bitter and, in mid-April, the United States again interrupted the negotiations.[39]

The Food Administration and the manufacturers had agreed to wait as long as possible in making purchases, hoping not only to push the price down but also to force the *Reguladora* to the wall in the process. An elaborate system had been worked out whereby stocks of fiber would be transferred between factories, with Harvester using its stock to supply a number of less well-endowed satellites.[40] Hoover revealed to the State Department and the manufacturers that, for the moment, he intended to force the price down at least to 33 cents while negotiating for an amount large enough to carry the factories through the end of 1919. "And once the contract is made," he emphasized, "we will have the upper hand!"[41]

The negotiations were finally concluded in mid-June, and the resulting agreement stipulated that a substantial quantity of fiber – 500,000 bales – would be delivered, but at a slightly higher price than Hoover had wanted. The *Reguladora* received 37 cents per kilogram for the first 100,000 bales and 34.8 cents for the remaining 400,000, figures that implied parity with the Argentine quotations.[42] The manufacturers contented themselves with the knowledge that they now enjoyed a fiber surplus that would effectively place them beyond the control of the *Reguladora*. Moreover, time was now on their side, and their position would improve with each passing month.

By mid-1919, the Food Administration was ready fully to press its advantage on an increasingly impoverished and embattled *Reguladora*. The waiting game began. The State Department instructed its embassy in Mexico City that the Food Administration, having already supplied the needs of the manufacturers for the 1919 harvest, was "no longer interested in the purchase of sisal in any quantity, but requested this information be treated as confidential."[43] As he watched the unsold fiber pile up on the Progreso wharves, the U.S. consul observed that the time had come "to discipline the *Reguladora*": "This state has run riot for two years and a forced normalization of prices, wages and minds . . . would no doubt benefit Yucatán as well as reduce the cost of twine to the American farmer."[44] The "normalization" began in earnest in 1919.

The breakdown of Alvarado's revolutionary coalition

Once henequen prices began to plummet, Alvarado's regional revolutionary edifice became increasingly vulnerable and soon collapsed under the weight of sustained pressures from within and without. Not surprisingly, a rather early casualty was Alvarado's fragile populist coalition, which quickly showed signs of schism and then shattered amid bitter recriminations, widespread defections by the bourgeoisie, and, ultimately, the rejection of Alvarado himself by the coalition's ascendant left wing. The handwriting had been on the wall since the middle of the bonanza year of 1918. For even as henequen earnings were climbing to an all-time high of $91 million, Alvarado and the *henequeneros* knew that Yucatán would be facing serious difficulties in the near future. Alvarado himself suspected that the 1918 bonanza might one day be remembered not as henequen's finest hour but as its *canto del cisne* – its swan song – one last crest before an inexorably final decline.[45]

The war in Europe was ending, and Alvarado and the planters realized that the postwar market would not support the high prices Yucatán had been asking and commanding in wartime. They knew the manufacturers were already stockpiling large quantities of fiber and twine for the immediate postwar period. Moreover, they reasoned that the peacetime market would also be affected by the advent of competitive large-scale sisal production in other parts of the world, most notably in the British and Dutch colonial possessions of Africa and the Far East. Labor costs in these areas were now much cheaper than those of revolutionary Yucatán, and soil conditions supported sisal of much higher quality than that of the henequen that grew in the peninsula.

By early 1919, the new downward price trend had clearly been established. (See Table 5) Fiber quotations fell even faster than they had risen several years before, dropping 300 percent in 1919. The price of fiber f.o.b. Progreso fell from nearly 44 to 13.2 cents per kilogram and earnings shriveled from $91 million to $37 million.[46] The year of victory that restored peace to Europe and the world brought only defeat and economic hardship to Yucatán.

The agro-commercial bourgeoisie, however, had grown skittish long before this, and toward the middle of 1918 its leaders had decided upon a course of action. By that time, Alvarado's *Comisión Reguladora* had become the object of almost daily attacks in the local press by large planters and merchants who resented the agency's monopolistic control of banking and the export sector. It was obvious, they argued, that the *Reguladora's* unrealistic pricing policy had been primarily responsible for the collapse of the fiber market and the debasement of the local currency. Led by representatives of the old buying firms, including Montes and Peabody, the large producers clamored for the return of the open market, where henequen would once again be sold and not left to rot in the government's warehouses. By and large, they were not asking for the return of a pure free-market situation. The consensus was that some regulation was needed to discourage speculation and that the best solution would be the return of the old, toothless 1912 *Reguladora*.[47] No matter that Harvester and Montes would return and the old marketing arrangements would be resurrected: There would be enough for them all, provided business was again transacted and money injected into the regional economy. As it was, in the absence of sales, even their capital resources were almost gone. In their view, the Socialist Party government, both in its refusal to lower prices and wages and in its stepped-up drive – under the emerging firebrand, Felipe Carrillo – to organize *ligas de resistencia* to secure the workers' new benefits, was bringing them to the brink of ruin.[48]

The planters were especially sensitive to Carrillo's rapid rise to prominence within Alvarado's Socialist Party. Quite accurately, they perceived that Carrillo Puerto, the uncompromising exponent of a far more threatening agrarian socialism, represented the other face of the Revolution in Yucatán. They noted that, by mid-1918, Alvarado and the more moderate elements in the Socialist Party were either unwilling or unable to restrict the political activities of Carrillo and other agrarian agitators. More importantly, they realized that Carrillo's promise of land might become substantially more attractive to the *campesinado* if fiber prices continued to fall on the world market and recession became chronic in Yucatán.

As early as April 1918, then, a number of the wealthiest *henequeneros* had formed the *Asociación de Hacendados Henequeneros* to press their political and economic grievances before Carranza and the federal authorities in Mexico City. Although the declared goal of the new organization was the reinstitution of an open henequen market, the *Asociación's* real purpose transcended those of a narrow planters' lobby. In fact, by allying itself with the conservative Yucatecan Liberal Party, which represented the "wealthier classes"[49] and had already begun to wage a power struggle with the Socialist Party for control of the state – the *Asociación* betrayed its real aim, which was to end Socialist hegemony in Yucatán. As its representatives, the *Asociación* chose Lorenzo Manzanilla and Enrique Aznar, the former an ultra-conservative member of the *Casta* who had never been reconciled to the Alvarado regime, the latter an ex-*Argumedista*. In August 1918, the pair presented the case of the great bourgeoisie before Carranza, the secretary of the interior, and the Supreme Court in the form of a series of briefs that blamed Alvarado and the Socialist Party for the difficult economic and political situation in the peninsula.[50] Their immediate prescription was a simple one: The *Reguladora* no longer functioned in the interests of Yucatán – which, as large fiber producers, they equated with their own interests – and should be abolished.[51] They reasoned that the *Reguladora* was the key to Alvarado's influence in the region and, once it was gone, all residual traces of his control would quickly disappear.

Alvarado, now advising the current governor, Castro Morales, from the sidelines, desperately tried to stem the tide of dissension and economic recession in Yucatán. At his urging, a "Study Committee for the Economic Reorganization of the State" was established with representatives from the diverse groups in his fading coalition – the state bureaucracy, labor, and the agro-commercial bourgeoisie – to formulate a strategy to meet the economic crisis.[52] Speaking before the committee, Alvarado suggested, "It's not always possible to move forward," and counseled a temporary lowering of wages, prices, and freight rates, plus a decrease in government spending to soften the immediate blow. He indicated that as long as unsold henequen continued to pile up on the wharves and in the warehouses, a temporary restriction on current production would be a necessary palliative. However, he argued that the only viable long-range solutions to the problem of over-production would be the opening of new markets in Europe, South America, and Japan and the development of new Mexican industries capable of using the region's raw fiber.[53]

The Study Committee accepted, in principle, the validity of Alvarado's propositions but, in failing to implement them, underscored the fatal schism that had already developed within the general's revolutionary coalition. The strategic decision to ignore Alvarado's proposals was made by Governor Castro Morales at the instruction of the president of the Study Committee and the Socialist Party, Felipe Carrillo, who chose to place the hard-fought wage gains of the working classes before all other considerations.[54] In addition to driving a wedge between Carrillo and Alvarado that would never be removed, the decision symbolically represented the Sonoran general's replacement by Carrillo as the leader of the Revolution in Yucatán – now fully a Yucatecan revolution and bound on a socialist course.

The federal government's response: settling accounts

Following Alvarado's departure in November 1918, with henequen sales and prices depressed, Carranza grew impatient with Yucatán's autonomous style of political and economic development, now distinctly less tasteful – because more radical – under Carrillo Puerto. Don Venus had been more willing to overlook Yucatecan "socialism" under Alvarado when the region was contributing a million pesos per month to his treasury.[55] Now, besieged by lobbyists from Mérida and diplomats from Washington seeking an open market, Mexico City was receiving more headaches than monetary gain from Yucatán's state-controlled henequen monopoly. In 1918, Carranza's policy toward Yucatán had been accurately summarized by an American visitor who wrote: "Mexico . . . justly regards Yucatán as the goose which lays the golden eggs, whose laying abilities are not to be lightly interfered with."[56] A year later, the federal government was actively interfering, suspecting that its goose was now withholding her golden bounty. Heeding the petitions of the great *henequeneros* and the demands of the U.S. diplomats, Carranza made it clear that he supported their call for an end to the *Comisión Reguladora's* monopoly, which then became a foregone conclusion. In July 1919, Yucatecan planters were freed from their exclusive contracts with the state agency.

Three months later, in October 1919, when the *Reguladora* declared bankruptcy and announced a liquidation of its assets, the federal government moved to exact a final pound of flesh. Charging that Yucatán owed the federal treasury 200,000 pesos in back export taxes, Carranza's finance minister, Luis Cabrera, attached Yucatán's railroad and embargoed all shipments of fiber in Progreso until the debt was paid.[57] The state immediately posted a bond to cover the duties; however, when economic conditions continued to deteriorate and the state's debt increased, Cabrera foreclosed on – and later sold – Alvarado's entire henequen fleet, thus depriving Yucatán and all of Mexico's southeast of an independent merchant marine capable of competing with foreign shipping interests.[58]

The importance of such a fleet had painfully been driven home some months before, when Alvarado's plan to finance a binder twine factory in Buenos Aires with Yucatecan and Mexican capital had been defeated by the North American cordage interests working through the U.S. Food Administration. Significantly, the Food Administration was represented in that instance by none other than H. L. Daniels, formerly the head of Harvester's Fiber Department, and now serving as director of the wartime agency's Division of Chemicals, Sisal and Jute. Learning of the Mexican bid to erect a binder twine plant in Argentina, Daniels had immediately formulated a preventive strategy, advising the State Department that "it would be wise to rely on our control of the shipping situation to prevent exports of sisal from Yucatán to [the] Argentine," then stipulating that "our Consul in Mérida advise me through the State Department, by wire immediately, in the event of any ships departing from Progreso loaded with any considerable amount of sisal for any destination other than the United States."[59] Shortly thereafter, its fleet under embargo, the Yucatecan government scrapped the project.

It is striking that the Carranza government – which had previously reneged on its promise to help finance Alvarado's *Compañía de Fomento del Sureste* – did not now at least scale down Yucatán's tax burden to make it commensurate with the decline in fiber prices. Such a hard fiscal line is even more difficult to square with

Yucatán's impressive record of fiscal service to the Republic and the Constitutionalist movement. Forgotten was the continuous flow of revenue during the 1914–1918 period, which many regard as having been the chief source of Carranza's finances. Cabrera would himself later boast that Yucatecan henequen had enabled Carranza to defeat Villa in the pivotal battles of Celaya and León.[60]

Indeed, Carranza's own records report that, from 1916 to 1918, Yucatán set an example for the other states, giving the federal government about 12 million pesos (about $6 million) in the form of taxes and levies alone.[61] No sooner had he arrived in Yucatán than Alvarado had been ordered by Carranza to send $100,000 to the Constitutionalist agent in New York City.[62] More crucial, perhaps, to the success of Carranza's movement was the amount provided the First Chief in loans and the credit base these loans allowed Carranza to establish in the United States. There is evidence that Alvarado sent at least 20 million pesos in *Reguladora* funds directly to Mexico City and, undoubtedly, much of another 30-million-peso interest-free, forced loan from the *henequeneros* went to Carranza.[63] At the height of the henequen boom early in 1918, President Carranza made an unbelievable demand upon Yucatán, ordering the *Reguladora* to deliver $15 million to the Mexican government within a month's time so that Cabrera might inaugurate the *Banco Único* that he and Carranza had promised. The *Reguladora* had nowhere near that much money on hand but Don Venus was adamant, insisting that Yucatán liquidate a large block of sisal at the highest price obtainable in order to raise the funds. The *Reguladora's* director, Manuel Zapata Casares, sailed immediately for the capital and after much pleading was granted a twelve-month period of grace. The project would collapse with the henequen market the following year.[64]

The North American cordage interests had long before recognized the vast financial reservoir that Carranza had in Yucatán's *Comisión Reguladora*. Peabody and Company told the American Secretary of Commerce:

> There is no doubt that it is through this "Reguladora" that Carranza is getting a large portion of his sinews of war . . . You see what a gold mine Yucatán is for Carranza: [henequen] costs him nothing except his own fiat money, and he turns it into gold in New York.[65]

In fact, the U.S. consul speculated in 1918 that the *Reguladora* contributions to Carranza's administration were so great that both the state and federal governments were embarrassed to make the actual figures public, fearing an outcry of protest in Yucatán.[66]

Keeping socialism in check

Mexico City's subordination of Yucatán extended to the political sphere as well. Following the expiration of Alvarado's term as governor, Carranza had also relieved the general of his duties as military zone commander, replacing him in November 1918 with General Luis Hernández. Hernández had been handpicked by the First Chief for his loyalty and obedience and sent off to Yucatán with explicit orders to put a brake on the much expanded activities of the Socialist Party.[67] Carranza had learned, with great uneasiness, that under its new leader, Felipe Carrillo, the party was bidding to transform itself into a mobilized party of the masses, organizing units, or *ligas de resistencia*, in all of the state's pueblos and hacienda communities and among workers in urban industries and crafts. The idea of forming syndicates and *ligas* had originally been Alvarado's and, Carranza reasoned, as long as the general remained the paramount military authority in the state, active propagandizing and widespread *liga* recruitment would continue.[68] Carranza had received numerous complaints from members of the opposition Liberal Party to the effect that Alvarado's federal troops had not only ignored Socialist violence but also had, upon occasion, actively abetted it.[69] For Alvarado, this had been a dangerous game, for by encouraging the radical wing of the Socialists during a time of economic recession, he was creating opportunities for the kind of popular mobilization that he had previously been careful to prevent. Like other populist caudillos in Latin America, Alvarado unintentionally created the conditions for a more radical social movement that he could not control and that ultimately displaced him.[70]

More immediately, however, under General Hernández and his successor, Colonel Isaías Zamarripa, the political balance swung sharply to the right as Carranza systematically carried out a campaign of harassment and repression against Carrillo's Socialist Party and its *ligas*. Carranza's replacement of Hernández with Zamarripa in July 1919 suggests the single-mindedness with which the Mexican president pursued his goal to crush Carrillo's revolution in Yucatán. In stripping the almost 30,000 *campesino* members of the *ligas* of all arms, including the ancient shotguns they used to hunt game, and in stationing federal troops on the henequen plantations, General Hernández had effectively blocked Carrillo's attempts to mobilize the rural sector and mitigated the threat that his new brand of socialism posed to the ruling bourgeoisie.[71] However, although he objectively aided the Liberal Party, Hernández had attempted to maintain at least an air of impartiality and, in mid-1919, had advised Carranza that he "wished to remain neutral in the upcoming state elections in order to give guarantees to all parties."[72] No sooner had he communicated this to Carranza than the president summoned him to Mexico City, leaving his subordinate, Colonel Zamarripa, in charge in July 1919. Zamarripa's reputation for cruelty was well established, and Carranza was looking for a proven enforcer to unleash on Yucatán.

To his ideological opposition of Carrillo Puerto's nascent socialist movement, Don Venustiano had by now added an intense personal dislike of Carrillo himself. Only weeks before, Carrillo had been among the first to declare his support for General Álvaro Obregón's candidacy in the 1920 presidential elections – going so far as to issue Obregón a red membership card in Yucatán's *Liga Central de Resistencia*. Support for Obregón meant open repudiation of Carranza. For although Don Venus could not be reelected under the provisions of the 1917 Constitution, he was already making plans for a relatively unknown diplomat, Ignacio Bonillas, to succeed him in the presidential chair. Although Carranza had not yet publicly declared Bonillas to be his candidate, he had made it clear that he would not favor Obregón. For years now, the popular, independent-minded Obregón had been distancing himself from his aging former chief, whom he perceived to be out of touch with Mexico's pressing social problems. Now, certain of a powerful base of support in both the Constitutionalist movement and the nation at large, Obregón formally challenged Carranza's hegemony by declaring his candidacy in June 1919 for the upcoming elections. Carrillo's attachment to Obregón, therefore, sealed the fate of the Yucatecan Socialist Party in Carranza's mind.[73]

The liquidation of Carrillo's Socialist Party became Carranza's obsession. Summoning Colonel Mena Brito from New Orleans, where he was now serving as Mexican consul general, Don Venus encouraged the Yucatecan Liberal leader to coordinate party opposition in the 1919 state elections, promising the Liberals a different outcome than 1917: "I am prepared to send one, two, three, ten battalions if necessary . . . I've already tolerated their [the Socialists'] crimes and outrages long enough . . . I hope you will help me get rid of this nuisance once and for all."[74]

The period of intense persecution that immediately followed is remembered to this day by many *Yucatecos* as the notorious *Zamarripazo*. Carranza's colonel symbolically inaugurated his application of the *mano dura* (mailed fist) by publicly flogging *campesinos* in the plaza of Motul, Felipe Carrillo's home town.[75] In the months ahead, Governor Castro Morales found himself hard pressed to expand upon or even continue a number of Alvarado's moderate reforms. In the area of land reform, for example, the clock was actually turned back. For although one *ejido* of 300 hectares was distributed among fifteen *vecinos* of Petecbitún in 1919, many more *campesinos* who had previously obtained *terrenos incultos* from Alvarado now found themselves dispossessed of them by Zamarripa's federals.[76] Surprisingly, even General Hernández took issue with Carranza's blockage of agrarian reform in Yucatán. Candidly, he wired the president that the land question was the principal cause of agitation and unrest in Yucatán, and a failure to act would ultimately prove to be counterproductive for the Constitutionalists.[77]

For close to a year, Zamarripa continued his vendetta against Carrillo's Socialist Party, vandalizing *liga* headquarters in Mérida and throughout the state, looting its treasuries, arresting and killing its members, and virtually crippling the operations of the badly needed worker consumer cooperatives, which the *ligas* sponsored locally in order to better feed and clothe the majority of Yucatán's population during the worsening economic crisis.[78] Meanwhile, reports of abuses on the haciendas proliferated, with *jornaleros* complaining of the reinstitution of *fagina* (forced labor) obligations, payment in scrip, and a return to the conditions of the *época de esclavitud*.[79] The situation became so bad in 1919 that Socialist Governor Castro Morales was forced to recant his support of Carrillo's *ligas* in order not to bring down greater retribution upon the state by the federals, who now held a virtual monopoly on physical violence in the peninsula.[80] Consequently, by the end of 1919, Carranza had succeeded in driving the Socialist Party underground and Felipe Carrillo into exile in New Orleans. No one was surprised when the Liberal Party swept the state congressional elections. The Socialists, realizing the futility of action, boycotted the voting.[81]

Carranza's draconian policy toward Yucatán was most damaging because it compounded the region's traditional economic dependence upon the United States. By refusing to provide Yucatán with federal economic support at the height of the postwar crisis plaguing the henequen industry, and instead draining the region of its remaining financial and infrastructural assets and exacerbating partisan political conflicts, Mexico City further weakened Yucatán and made it increasingly difficult to break the hold of monoculture and economic imperialism, which, despite Alvarado's efforts, continued to characterize the region's structural relationship with the North American corporations.

The fall

Wittingly or not, in granting the *henequenero* lobbyists their petition for an open market in the summer of 1919, Carranza had also accommodated Harvester and the manufacturers, who had continued since 1915 to press the same demand through the channels of the State Department. On more than one occasion since 1918, the large planters had sent envoys to Chicago and Washington to coordinate a joint strategy with the North Americans.[82] Late in 1918, the U.S. consul in Progreso confided to the secretary of state that a number of "my friends" among the "better class" of *Yucatecos* "are reporting to Washington."[83] Nor was it coincidental that these envoys and informants – men such as Lorenzo Manzanilla and Enrique Aznar – were members of the *Casta Divina* and alumni of the old collaborator networks that had served the cordage interests so well prior to 1915.

Part of the new joint strategy entailed mounting an intensive media campaign against the *Reguladora* in both North American and Mexican newspapers, magazines, and trade journals. This time, however, the massive propaganda drive against the *Reguladora* in the United States was not answered as effectively as it had been in 1915 and 1916, when Alvarado's agents were able to operate on a generous budget during boom conditions. The campaign moved into high gear in November 1918 with an article syndicated in the *Cordage Trade Journal* and a great number of smaller newspapers throughout the American wheat belt. Headlines read: "$86,000,000 Extorted During Last Three Years From American Farmers. Justice Department Powerless. Food Administration Now Fighting Profiteering Monopoly of the Mexican Government."[84] The major thrust of this and other articles was that not only were American and Yucatecan farmers being swindled, but the illicit profits were being used to disseminate socialist and International Workers of the World (IWW) propaganda throughout Mexico and Latin America.[85] Not surprisingly, the argument was virtually identical – even in small nuances of phrasing – to the one in the briefs presented before Carranza and the Mexican Supreme Court by the *Asociación de Hacendados Henequeneros*. In each case the authors were Manzanilla and Aznar.[86]

But a dissolution of the *Comisión Reguladora's* marketing monopoly was not the sole objective of the North American cordage industry. The manufacturers hoped to bankrupt and so discredit the *Reguladora* that it would never again be resurrected against them. In the process of breaking the state agency, they would secure all the henequen they needed at closeout prices and would teach the majority of Yucatán's producers a lesson in the realities of the international economic division of labor. The strategy employed by the North Americans and their allies from the *Casta Divina* was two-pronged. While the large planters continued their propaganda campaign, Harvester and the manufacturers, released from their agreement to buy solely from the Food Administration in May 1919, continued to wait the *Reguladora* out. Periodically, they would feign interest in buying fiber and later back off, allowing unsold stocks to accumulate and public pressure upon the local government to build.

They did not have long to wait. The *Reguladora* had at first stubbornly attempted to hold firm at its average 1918 price of 41.8 cents per kilogram. But it lacked funds to finance the continued operations of its producers and to meet the increased storage costs of its expanded stocks, let alone sustain the expenses of Alvarado's expanded social program, and so gave ground and sold at about 33 cents. Harvester then instructed its New York agents to buy cheaply and only new fiber; they were forbidden to touch the 800,000 bales of stock that continued to depress the market. At this point, in July 1919, the Castro Morales government – responding to federal and regional pressure and perhaps believing ingenuously that a reestablishment of the open market might normalize the situation and induce sales – canceled its mandatory contracts with the producers but maintained its price at 33 cents per kilogram. Harvester reacted by reverting to a policy of near abstention, the final play to bring the *Comisión Reguladora* down under the weight of growing debt and public disapproval.[87]

Discontent had become extremely vocal and widespread, running through every level of society. The *Reguladora* had not made a major sale in months and could no longer guarantee its currency emissions. Inflation was rampant and increasing by the day – in fact, as often as the *Reguladora's* money depreciated. Urban workers and merchants were most immediately affected by the depreciated currency, although the Progreso longshoremen, buoyed up by recently won wage hikes, were best able to cope with the inflationary spiral. Throughout 1919, *Meridano* and *Progreseño* merchants refused to accept anything but hard currency – or U.S. dollars, which had become rare specimens in Yucatán – causing a good deal of hardship among those paid in paper, most notably laborers and public employees, whose condition bordered on desperation. By mid-1919, General Hernández had added his voice to the chorus of protest, demanding that his troops be paid in metal.[88].

The *hacendados*, especially the small and medium producers, were similarly in dire straits. Those still doing business with the *Reguladora* went for long periods without payment for their fiber and lacked cash to pay their workers. The *jornaleros*, in turn, had been deprived of the protection that Carrillo's consumer cooperative program – now systematically harassed by Carranza's federals – might normally have provided them. The thousands of central Mexican laborers whom Alvarado had brought into Yucatán several years earlier were now leaving in droves. *Campesinos* speculated about the prospects of the coming harvest and joked nervously about eating the pulp of the henequen plant.[89]

As the price of henequen continued to fall rapidly during the second half of 1919, small and medium *hacendados* encumbered with debts found production costs overtaking them and began to remove some of their fields from cultivation. In other cases, entire haciendas were abandoned. Many of the smaller *henequeneros* feared or actually found themselves in danger of losing their *fincas* to wealthier members of their class. More often than not, they expressed a particular dread of Avelino Montes, who had returned to Yucatán and, along with Peabody and the other independent buyers, was back in business on the open market.[90] In fact, by late 1919, Peabody was lamenting that Montes, employing many of his former tactics, including loan sharking, had managed to gain a "practical monopoly of the New York market" and was once more driving other buyers out of business.[91]

Early in October 1919, public demonstrations and violence signaled the *Reguladora's* demise. On 6 October, Mérida's merchants, supported by representatives of all classes, closed their doors and demanded an end to the *Reguladora* and its worthless paper currency – which, under Alvarado, had once been the most stable in Mexico.[92] Mobs roamed the streets, smashing windows and looting. The Governor's palace was circled and, when Governor Castro could not be found, his house was fired and his son stoned. The mob dispersed only when federal forces fired into it, killing some and wounding many. The next day, the State Congress voted to suppress the *Reguladora* money and, although the agency lingered in existence for some months longer, for all intents and purposes it was now moribund.[93]

Harvester and the cordage interests were determined, however, to drive the price still lower. In engineering this, they capitalized on the misfortunes of the American and Canadian banking consortium whose loans had been primarily responsible for keeping the *Reguladora* monopoly functioning for as long as it did in the face of such powerful opposition. Back in 1916, four banks – the Equitable Trust Company of New York, the Royal Bank of Canada, the Interstate Trust and Banking Company of New Orleans, and the Canadian Bank of Commerce – had agreed to furnish Alvarado's *Reguladora* with a $10 million line of credit, at a substantial rate of interest with a sizable commission tacked on, and the entire arrangement backed by fiber as collateral.[94] Now, with the liquidation of the *Reguladora*, these same bankers, with 800,000 bales of fiber on their hands, were desperately seeking a way to maintain their position in the henequen industry and salvage their investment. The result was the formation of the ERIC Corporation – the title was an acronym for the names of the individual banks – a latter-day version of the original 1916 Pan-American Commission Corporation, which agreed to market Yucatán's henequen but on much more exacting terms than those of the original agreement.[95] The ERIC came to hold most of the old *Reguladora's* surplus production and, when it was no more successful than the *Reguladora* had been in enticing Harvester to buy, the bottom rapidly fell out of the henequen market. At this point, Peabody and Company suggested that the *Yucatecos* consider any method of disposing of the stock, "whether as fuel or otherwise."[96] Ultimately, in a desperate effort to cut their losses and violating the spirit, if not the letter, of their agreement with the state government, the bankers dumped most of the henequen in Harvester's lap roughly at cost. This meant that the price on the Yucatán market had skidded all the way down to 9.9 cents per kilogram, ironically the very price engineered for Harvester by Montes in 1912, which had sparked the furor leading to the creation of the original *Comisión Reguladora*.[97]

The ERIC's sale to Harvester unleashed a wave of protest in Yucatán and Mexico City and caused considerable consternation in the United States. Rumors began to circulate in business and political circles that Harvester had been in collusion with the ERIC from the beginning, although the bankers immediately denied the charge.[98] Speaking on behalf of the exporting houses in New Orleans and New York that traditionally did business with Yucatán and were now suffering due to the depressed state of the henequen market, Consul Gaylord Marsh offered the following opinion:

> The International Harvester Co. may have no participation in the ERIC but the general impression is that it has. Harold McCormick, head of the International and son-in-law of John D. Rockefeller, is said to be a large stockholder, and perhaps a director of the Equitable Trust Co. If this be true, it is difficult to conceive that the policies of the banks may not be dictated largely by the International Harvester Co.[99]

By mid-1921, according to speculation in the North American business community, Harvester had withdrawn from its alleged partnership with the ERIC and successfully covered the tracks of its former participation.[100] However, protests from Mexico, U.S. exporting firms, and Harvester's rivals in the cordage business compelled the State Department to order a secret investigation. After a careful examination and many inquiries, Special Agent R. S. Sharp reported that although "no conclusive evidence of proof" existed of Harvester's connection with the ERIC, there were numerous "inferences" that the company might be camouflaging its involvement through the Royal Bank of Canada or, more likely, the Continental and Commercial Trust Company of Chicago, in an effort to prevent antitrust action in the U.S. courts.[101] Referring to an early study that Harvard Professor William Z. Ripley had made of Harvester in his *Trusts, Pools and Corporations*,[102] Sharp noted the company's former predilection for working through agents (e.g., Montes) and dummy firms in order to "acquire in a secret way, the control of . . . other concerns which competed in the manufacture of twine and harvesting machines."[103] Harvester had been known to operate these concerns without disclosing such control for extended periods of time. This tactic originally had been extremely useful in lines such as fiber and twine, which, around the turn of the century, were highly competitive and as a result ordinarily offered a small rate of profit. Now, Sharp suggested, Harvester was again digging into its old bag of illicit tricks.[104]

There were other inferences as well. The long-time director of Harvester's Fiber Department, H. L. Daniels, had served during the war with the Food Administration and, through this office, had brought an antitrust suit against the ERIC's predecessor, the Pan-American Commission Corporation, which had allied itself with the *Reguladora* against Harvester's interests.[105] Now, Sharp found it strange that Daniels, once again heading Harvester's fiber operations, had not seen fit to register the slightest protest when the ERIC had contracted to shore up Yucatán's bankrupt *Reguladora*.[106] Moreover, Sharp linked Daniels with Franklin Helm, a New York entrepreneur who was financially involved with the New Orleans bankers in the ERIC Corporation. Sharp speculated that Daniels and Harvester had located Helm and designated him as their contact with ERIC through what the special agent termed the "Chicago connection" – the Continental and Commercial Trust Company of that city.[107]

Finally, Sharp emphasized that, although he had "no evidence of Harvester being financially interested as far as capital goes," at the very least, "as a heavy borrower, it was quite likely that the ERIC was being bankrolled by the International Harvester Company."[108] Moreover, he had learned from informants in New Orleans that the ERIC had been created in such a way as to be ready to liquidate on a moment's notice. "In other words, it seems to me that it is a price-fixing proposition from which all interested parties can get out quick."[109]

The blame

Intrigue or no intrigue, the principal factor behind the demise of the *Reguladora* and Alvarado's bourgeois revolution was Yucatán's structural relationship to the world market. For as a Mexican writer has expressed it:

> The Revolution's defense of the *campesino* and its desire to provide him a salary that would cover the basic necessities of life were beside the point when it came to improving Yucatán's position in the international market. For what concern was it of the controlling North American cordage trust whether the Yucatecan henequen worker ate meat twice a

week or protected his children from pellagra? Why should the cordage manufacturers accept a rise in the price of henequen just because Yucatán now chose to abolish slavery? Why should it matter in the slightest to them that the *peón* was now an agricultural worker protected by the revolutionary labor code?[110]

Under Alvarado, Yucatán had dared to rebel against the low prices dictated by the North American corporations that controlled the world's hard fiber market. After some initial successes during the war years, the region was soundly defeated in the war's aftermath. In fact, the Armistice inaugurated a period of decline for the regional henequen industry from which it has not yet nor is ever likely to recover. The price that Yucatán paid for its wartime bonanza was a very high one. For having attempted to fix the price of its product, the region was forced thereafter to accept the unconditional terms of the cordage interests. Following their brief flirtation with Alvarado, the large planters again took up their former position as the manufacturers' agents and spokesmen, agreeing to the onerous prices that the cordage trust chose to mete out. Worse still, Yucatán had been made to agree, partly as a result of its formal financing agreement with the banks and partly due to the exigencies of a glutted market, to restrict periodically its future production, even as its African and Asian competitors were dramatically increasing their own productive capacities.[111]

This, in fact, was the saddest consequence of Yucatán's failed rebellion. Whereas Yucatán had covered 100 percent of the world's sisal demands in 1900 and 88 percent in 1916, by 1922 this figure had slipped to 75 percent and, by 1929, had fallen all the way to 53 percent. (See Table 6.) Once lost, Yucatán's hegemony would never be regained. Several years later, in 1933, the peninsula would claim only 39 percent of the demand and, by 1938, the year following Cárdenas's massive land expropriations, a paltry 23 percent.[112]

Lamentably, the economic consequences of Yucatán's declining position in the world market would soon work subtle attitudinal changes upon even the region's Socialist leaders. Dr. Álvaro Torre Díaz, who had formerly been secretary of the state under Alvarado and, as such, the general's chief Yucatecan aide, commented as governor of the state in 1930 that "Yucatán's henequen had *always* been marginal in the global fiber picture and therefore had to adjust itself to the prices established by those in a position to dictate them."[113] Speaking in 1932, during the worldwide de-

Table 6. *Yucatán's loss of the world fiber market, 1880–1950*

Year	World production (tons)	Yucatecan production (tons)	Yucatecan production as percentage of world production
1880–1900			100
1901	105,600	105,600	100
1908	139,952	137,452	98
1915	211,109	186,109	88
1922	122,138	92,138	75
1929	229,000	121,456	53
1933	286,429	113,011	39
1938	349,965	80,065	23
1949	560,000	93,491	17
1950	600,000	90,128	14

Source: Luis Echeagaray Bablot, *Irrigación, crisis henequenera y condiciones agrícolas y económicas de Yucatán,* Mexico, 1956, p. 49.

pression, Yucatán's secretary of finance identified the colonial character of the region's dependence with a fatalistic candor that would have shocked Salvador Alvarado: "In the past Yucatán has sought to impose conditions upon its buyers. This has hurt Yucatán and compromised the prosperity which henequen once brought us. The seller can never impose conditions upon the buyer, just as the debtor can never set the terms for his creditor." [114]

It is indeed ironic that the economic thesis of Olegario Molina should find restatement twenty-five years later, and in a far more fatalistic form, by the minister of a Revolutionary government. And in its restatement, Yucatán as a primary producer is not even compared to a seller but to a debtor, whose obligation consists of complying with whatever terms his creditor might choose to establish. It is perhaps even more surprising that the minister's statement – made roughly a decade after Alvarado's sojourn in Yucatán – should represent such an unmistakable repudiation of Alvarado's bold, if unsuccessful, attempt to free Yucatán from its subordinate position in the world economy.

Not surprisingly, the indictment of Alvarado's henequen policy was put in its harshest form by Alvarado's former allies, the bourgeoisie. Almost immediately, the planters blamed Alvarado for the region's economic ills, which had already begun to appear chronic by the early 1920s. *Diario de Yucatán*, which would continue to fight the *hacendados'* battles in future decades, singled Alvarado out as the outsider who, in order to further unrealistic pipe dreams, had left behind a sad legacy of bankruptcy, misery, and hunger. "What has come of his revolution?" the paper asked in the midst of the postwar depression:

> His schools and libraries have disappeared; alcohol, prostitution and idleness have returned; and so have the foreign monopolies and corrupt governors. Meanwhile, the *peón* has lost the security he once enjoyed and his high salary to boot. Hunger and sickness are again life's daily reality for him and his family. [115]

But, was Alvarado the culprit? Subsequent generations of writers, emerging from the worst effects of the depression of the 1920s and 1930s, have tempered the indictment, and the official Revolutionary Party (PRI), led by its Yucatecan wing, has appropriated the general for the Revolution's pantheon of heroes – along with native son Felipe Carrillo Puerto. In retrospect, perhaps the most highly prized of Alvarado's achievements is his determined stand in blocking International Harvester's attempt to maintain its control over the peninsula. Henceforth, some form of state or federal control would be built into the henequen industry and Harvester, despite its powerful position as Yucatán's chief buyer, would never again enjoy hegemony comparable to that of the prewar period. [116]

Ultimately, the fundamental issue in the indictment of Alvarado is the wisdom of his wartime fiber pricing policy. His critics argue that the general's determination to impose inflated prices on Yucatán's North American buyers artificially stimulated outside competition that undermined the region's preeminent position in the world market, finally ruining the Yucatecan economy. Yet it is unreasonable to hold Alvarado's *política alcista* responsible for the region's economic decline following the general's departure. One Mexican writer suggests that to censure Alvarado for having raised Yucatán's henequen industry to such heights that it might reasonably stimulate envy and competition is absurd. "With equal logic might one censure Henry Ford for his development of the auto industry which similarly aroused a worldwide desire of imitation." [117] Moreover, the great planters' charge that Alvarado's prices provoked the United States to seek markets elsewhere, leading to Yucatán's loss of the fiber market, [118] is untenable on rigorously historical grounds. To be sure, the cordage lobby and the U.S. government were infuriated by Alvarado's policy and did look to invest elsewhere. However, the manufacturers and the U.S. government had already become determined to ensure that the United States would not have to rely upon any single source for its hard fiber needs some years *before* Alvarado's arrival. We have seen that even before the turn of the century, Harvester began directly to finance or subsidize sisal and flax experimentation schemes in the continental United States, other parts of the Americas, and the Philippines. Shortly after 1900, Harvester was joined in these endeavors by the U.S. government, which sponsored experimentation in North America, Hawaii, and Puerto Rico. Prior to Alvarado's entry into Yucatán in 1915, Harvester had invested in additional fiber schemes in the Dominican Republic, Ecuador, and various British, German, and Dutch colonies in Africa and Asia – to name only those ventures that have surfaced in the major archives, press, trade journals, and secondary accounts.[119] Many of these new areas had, independently of North American capital, begun to grow sisal fiber at the turn of the century, ironically, in large part because Yucatán's own *hacendados* had found it profitable to sell henequen shoots abroad.[120] By 1918, in fact, competitors already accounted for 20 percent of the world market, which means that – allowing for the five to seven years that sisal normally needs to enter into production – Yucatán's future rivals had already decided to offer competition some years before Alvarado came to the peninsula.[121] Yucatán lost its hegemony because the end of World War I now allowed for the shipment of fibers from other areas to the United States and because the fiber produced elsewhere was of superior quality and often produced at lower cost.

Finally, although Olegario Molina and Avelino Montes – no doubt to justify their relationship with Harvester – had called for volume production at low prices to prevent foreign competition,[122] Alvarado had little reason to apprehend a serious foreign threat to Yucatán's near monopoly in 1915. Certainly, he had no incentive (as Molina and Montes did) to condone greatly reduced prices to Yucatecan producers at a time when the region produced upward of 90 percent of the raw fiber consumed in North American binder twine, and it seemed inconceivable that it would not continue to do so in the years ahead. If Alvarado, the nationalist revolutionary, may have gone too far to the other extreme in setting Yucatán's fiber prices, this, too, is understandable, in view of the insistent demands for redress against the North American cordage trust that greeted the general following his arrival in the region. Moreover, Alvarado was astute enough to realize the fallacy of the U.S. Senate's charge that, by fixing high prices, he had violated the law of supply and demand that governed the market in normal times. He knew that the law of supply and demand had never obtained in the henequen market because the market had never been structured as a situation that fostered transactions among equals. Speculations and manipulations had always been the rule since henequen's rise in the late nineteenth century, and especially since International Harvester was formed at the turn of the century. Alvarado also appreciated that the North American corporations, backed by their government in Washington, had always sought to break Yucatán's position as the market's exclusive supplier and would continue to do so, irrespective of his pricing policy. [123] It was – as the Senate subcommittee chose to phrase it, borrowing the very euphemism that Alvarado had employed – all part of the continuing U.S. commitment to "regulate" the market.

This being the case, Alvarado reasoned that he had nothing to lose and more than a little to gain by challenging the controlling North American interests at a fortuitous juncture when the world market had been suddenly – and perhaps only momentarily – stood on its head in favor of primary producing regions like Yucatán.

PART III

The socialist revolution, 1920–1923

7

Felipe Carrillo Puerto and the rise of Yucatecan socialism

He who understands will become ruler over our people.
                                    —The Book of Proofs of the Maya

At his gesture and at his command,
Sixty thousand voices raised,
Sixty thousand spirits joined,
Repeating
The Red Commandments.

                                    —Elmer Llanes Marín ("Felipe
                                    Carrillo Puerto")

The mass of white-clad *campesinos* pressed around the tall, light-skinned visitor from Mérida. From their pueblo, Umán, the *campesinos* and their guest (the latter still attired in the dark suit of the city) had walked several kilometers into the countryside until they came upon an open space in the checkerboard of small, newly sown cornfields. In the distance beyond the corn was a jagged horizon of thorns, interrupted here and there by sooty smoke-stacks. These marked the huge decorticating factories, which consumed the spiny plants harvested from the desertlike expanse and transformed them into golden fiber. The visitor addressed the throng of peasants in their native Maya:

The *campesinos* of Yucatán have not had to shed their blood to share in the Revolution's triumphs. They have not seen their pueblo strafed with machine gun fire or their fields overgrown with weeds because there were not enough hands left to cultivate them. And because *you* have not felt any of the misery of war, perhaps you do not fully appreciate the significance of what General Alvarado has done today in giving the members of this pueblo their own plots of land. However, you should know that even as you savor this satisfying moment, you have not won completely. In the days ahead your enemies will attempt to snatch this victory from you. In fact, the time is not distant when you will be told that these *milpa* are no longer yours, that the Constitutionalist

Revolution has failed and you must leave the land. But I swear to you it is then that you must prove that this land was not delivered to tired old women but to men who know how to defend it. Do this and tomorrow your children will not accuse you of being cowards. It may be necessary for each and every one of you, when the time comes, to muster the courage to go to Mérida and demand from General Alvarado a rifle to defend the land he has given you today . . . Go to the Governor's Palace and demand the right to defend what is yours . . . Do not be afraid, you will be welcomed. How many times have I seen you, with your pants rolled up, squatting timidly in the streets outside the Palace gates. Come in and the General will receive you; if he's not there, go to his home and freely speak your minds. Now that you have asked for and received your lands, you must be vigilant . . .

The visitor paused to give his point emphasis, then continued:

And if you want to see what it takes to be a revolutionary, come to my pueblo . . . There the *señores* once took our lands; indeed their *henequenales* pressed right up against the plaza of our village. But that's all finished. Now we know how to deal with those who take what is ours. The Revolution has taught us . . .

You, too, must learn who your true friends are. The *hacendados* will tell you that things were better in the old days, when they paid you 1½ *reales*, gave you a little medicine and a *copita* once a year, and beat you the rest of the time for being drunkards and lazy-good-for-nothings. They will mock you: "Why do you send your children to school? Will they become doctors or lawyers or engineers? Send them instead to cut henequen where they can bring some money into your home!" In this and other ways do they seek to destroy this revolution of ours. But the time has come to show them what proud and hard-working men you are. Attend to your fields and you will offer no better proof of their lies!

As the speaker concluded his talk, he was swallowed up by the white mass. "Viva el General Alvarado! Viva Don Venustiano! Viva la Revolución!"

"Y viva el pueblo trabajador de Umán!" ("And long live the hard-working people of Umán!") responded the visitor.[1]

As Alvarado's premier *agente de propaganda*, Felipe Carrillo Puerto would inspire many such gatherings in the countryside during that summer of 1916. Invariably, the message was the same. Carrillo's exhortations of the *campesinos* revealed his grasp of the difficulty of waging social revolution in Yucatán. Would-be revolutionaries would have to confront an almost total absence of political mobilization in the *campo*. Carrillo made it clear that precisely because the villagers had not participated in the Revolution and Alvarado's agrarian reform, their triumph was partial and tenuous. It was not enough to be given land by influential outsiders; the demise of the revolutionary government could mean the loss of that land. One day the *campesinos* would have to fight the enemies of the Revolution to keep their *milpa*. Meanwhile, to preserve their gains, they had not only to cultivate the land diligently but also to organize and arm themselves. Carrillo told them that rather than put their faith in leaders, they ought to look to themselves.

Not surprisingly, Carrillo's active dedication to rural mobilization would try the patience of his immediate superior, General Alvarado, and offend the political sensibilities of President Carranza. It is unlikely that Alvarado, who rarely chose to deal personally with country people, would have welcomed the impromptu visits that Carrillo was encouraging the *campesinos* to make. Of course, it never came to that. The First Chief saw to it that Alvarado's promise of moderate land distribution flickered and died before 1916 was out, and there is no indication that any *campesinos* ever camped out on the general's doorstep seeking guns. However, Carranza's 1916 "stop decree" did not deter Felipe Carrillo, who, along with a small group of other agrarian agitators, was determined to keep the land issue alive and use it to politicize the region's agrarian sector. Indeed, until they were chased out of Yucatán by Carranza's federals in 1919, Carrillo and his circle (which included former *agentes* Rafael Gamboa and Rafael Cebada) would traverse the state, building up contacts with local chiefs and exhorting *campesinos* to form *ligas de resistencia* for the purpose of pressing the land question. By the time Alvarado reluctantly left the state in 1918, Don Felipe – as he was increasingly called – was being acknowledged as Yucatán's premier revolutionary by *campesinos*, Socialist bureaucrats, and worried *hacendados* alike. The last especially had never entertained any illusions about Carrillo. Divided as they had been in their reaction to Alvarado's moderate reforms, they recognized that the Sonoran's mild bourgeois revolution, which had been imported from without, was now being pushed inexorably to the left and, in the absence of outside influences, would soon be transformed into a serious socialist revolution from within. Almost overnight, the powerful members of the regional bourgeoisie stopped their incessant squabbling and closed ranks in the face of the serious challenge that their revolutionary *paisano* posed.

Carrillo gets an education

Carrillo had begun his career as a home-grown revolutionary rather inauspiciously. Like so many of the Revolution's leaders, he was a member of the "noncommissioned" or petty bourgeois class, which especially resented its lack of opportunity under the Old Regime. Born in the heart of the henequen zone, in the prosperous town of Motul on 8 November 1874, he was the second of fourteen children. Carrillo's father, Justiniano, was a modest merchant who had moved to Motul from the turbulent southeastern frontier during the Caste War and supported his large family with a small neighborhood grocery attached to a bustling billiards parlor. Carrillo was essentially an autodidact who never got beyond his primary schooling. While still in his teens, he was given a small parcel of land by his father in the neighboring village of Ucí and began his working life as a *ranchero*. In addition to developing his physical stamina and learning the difficulties of commercial cultivation in the region's harsh soil, Carrillo, the town-based mestizo, drew closer to the social problems of Yucatán's Maya majority. Because almost everyone spoke Maya in the interior of the state, Carrillo learned the language as part of his daily round in the small pueblo. But he learned more than "city Maya," the patois of Maya and *castellano*, which was used to bargain with *dzules* (whites) in the marketplaces of Motul and Mérida. Felipe Carrillo learned the idiom of the *campo*, and in the process he received an apprenticeship in an entire culture. In school he had been taught about the Maya past, of the glories of a classical age that now seemed very remote and abstract. Now he learned the concrete Maya reality: the customs, the agricultural techniques, the songs, prayers, and legends, the sorrows and frustrations of Yucatán's agrarian underclass. Sensing that he grasped these things, the people of the pueblo affectionately began to call their young neighbor *Yaax Ich* – "Green Eyes."

The extraordinary difficulty of making a living as a small farmer in Yucatán's plantation economy around the turn of the century forced Carrillo off the land. In rapid succession, he pursued brief

PARTIDO LABORISTA MEXICANO

C. FELIPE CARRILLO PUERTO
GOBERNADOR DE YUCATAN
ASESINADO EL 3 DE ENERO DE 1924, POR ORDENES DEL TRAIDOR
ADOLFO DE LA HUERTA, EN CONNIVENCIA CON LOS
GRANDES LATIFUNDISTAS DE LA PENINSULA

Picture issued by the Partido Laborista Mexicano bearing the title: "Felipe Carrillo Puerto, Governor of Yucatán, assassinated on January 3, 1924, on orders of the traitor Adolfo de la Huerta, in connivance with the large landholders of the peninsula." (Reprinted from John W. F. Dulles, *Yesterday in Mexico: A Chronicle of the Revolution, 1919–1936*, Austin, Tex., 1961, p. 233. © 1961 by John W. F. Dulles.)

careers as a cattle herder, circus hand, butcher, railroad conductor, woodcutter, back-country carter and mule driver, small retail merchant, stevedore (while in exile in New Orleans), journalist, and finally, agronomist. These various lines of work enabled him to crisscross the Yucatán peninsula (and, when necessary, to range outside it), to maintain contact with large numbers of *campesinos* and local brokers, to sharpen his command of Maya, and generally to expand and refine his political consciousness and savvy.[2]

Along the way, Carrillo suffered many setbacks. The earliest of these are depicted in revealing (if romanticized) accounts of his assistance to exploited villagers and *peones acasillados* during the Porfirian *época de esclavitud*. Still a *ranchero* at eighteen, Carrillo responded to a request for help from *campesinos* of the nearby village of Kaxatah. A stone barricade had been erected by a local planter near the entrance of their pueblo that restricted passage to their cornfields. Acts such as this, which subordinated the surviving villages to the henequen plantations, were common in Yucatán in the 1890s. Carrillo set out for the hacienda of Dzununcán, where he appealed to the *peones* to assist him in dismantling the wall. Although at first the hacienda residents regarded him with suspicion, they were eventually won over by his command of their language and customs and by the sympathy that many of them had for the plight of their kin who still lived in Kaxatah. As Carrillo began personally to tear down the wall, he was joined by a number of the *acasillados*. The *patrón* acted swiftly when he learned of the defiant act. Only the intervention of Carrillo's father, who emphasized the youthful age of the offender and paid a stiff fine, saved Carrillo from more than a few days in the Motul jail.[3]

Several years later, Carrillo again challenged the oligarchical regime. Now a muleteer who conducted business between the local estates and communities, he had witnessed the severe corporal punishment of *peones* for supposed lapses in discipline. Angered by these abuses, occasionally against people he knew, he once more conspired to infiltrate the haciendas, this time to smuggle out flogged victims.

> The visits were frequent. Waiting for the right moment in the evenings when vigilance was most slack, and a whistle would be given by a *peón* accomplice, Felipe would steal into the hacienda compound, drape the beaten man over the back of his mule, and carry him to safety.
>
> Although Felipe ignored the risk of personal harm should

he be trapped inside the hacienda gates, he was severely punished on at least one occasion. Lingering to instruct a group of *acasillados* about their human rights, Felipe was surprised by the *patrón*. The *hacendado* was infuriated by this invasion of his personal domain and ordered the young trespasser to receive, in front of his assembled *peones*, the 25 lashes customarily applied to those audacious enough to speak of liberty, individual rights, and emancipation.

Following the public flogging, the *patrón* handed Carrillo over to the *Jefe Político* of Motul for formal jailing.[4]

Shortly after the turn of the century, Carrillo organized a small group of fellow carters and muleteers into a cooperative to sell meat in the Motul district. The plan was to eliminate the middlemen who, working with larger suppliers in Mérida and Progreso, had previously controlled the trade and subjected the rural populace to unfair markups. The cooperative was initially quite successful, due in great part to the connections and goodwill that Carrillo had built up in his previous work in the district. The partners even began to discuss the possibility of branching out into other commodities as well as into neighboring *partidos*. They never got the chance. Efforts were made by merchants in Mérida and Motul to harass the cooperative and its customers through the local *jefe político*. Physical violence was threatened and local taxes were suddenly increased. Embittered but further educated in the operation of the Porfirian political economy, Carrillo liquidated the venture.[5]

The setbacks continued. Carrillo made attempts in 1906 to establish an antiregime paper, only to be jailed again by the local establishment. Then, with Díaz defeated in 1911, he discovered to his chagrin that he had backed the wrong *Maderista* politician, passing over the victor of the gubernatorial race in Yucatán, Tabascan-born José Mária Pino Suárez, for the more popular native son, Delio Moreno Cantón. A year later, he nearly paid for this mistake with his life, narrowly averting an assassination attempt plotted by disgruntled *Pinistas* in league with certain *hacendados*.[6] Imprisoned by Madero's and Huerta's governors and then hounded out of the state by Ávila, Felipe joined the *Zapatistas* late in 1914.

Here, at last, was a revolutionary movement that seemed to appreciate his agrarian sympathies and was able to make use of them, training him — virtually on the spot — as an agronomist and commissioning him a colonel in the cavalry. Later he served as Zapata's agrarian commissioner for the important town of

Cuautla, assisted by a seventeen-year-old agronomy student named Fidel Velázquez, who would later win a national reputation as the perennial general secretary of the Mexican Workers' Confederation (CTM). Carrillo was influenced by the anticapitalist doctrine that pervaded *Zapatismo* in 1914–1915 through anarcho-syndicalists such as Antonio Díaz Soto y Gama and other former PLM members who had caught on as Zapata's intellectual advisors.[7] By mid-1915, however, he had learned of Alvarado's invasion of Yucatán and was ready to return to his *tierra natal* (native soil). As Carrillo confided to his friend and fellow agronomist, Marte R. Gómez: "Alvarado is distributing lands among the Maya *campesinos*. I would be quite content to remain here, helping *campesinos* receive their lands, but the *Morelenses* have Zapata and I will not be missed. My duty is to return to Yucatán."[8]

Yet as he left the central plateau, Carrillo was skeptical of Alvarado's intentions. He had only contempt for the general's predecessors, Ávila and ʾde los Santos, who, he felt, had used the Constitutionalist Revolution as a pretext for exploiting Yucatán without improving the lot of poor country people. Only the "bandit Zapata" had dedicated himself to returning land to the tiller, and for that he remained the sworn enemy of Constitutionalism. In a letter to his younger brother Acrelio, which he wrote en route to Yucatán, Felipe sarcastically aired these doubts:

It gladdens me, dear brother, that you are so convinced of the "justice" of General Alvarado's cause – Alvarado whom the press already regards to be a saint . . . But tell me now, what do you mean by justice? I suppose that he has already returned the *ejidos* to their rightful owners . . . I suppose, little brother, that the large merchants have stopped shamelessly robbing the public . . . that new schools have been created to teach our young people that they must not exploit or be exploited . . . I suppose, dear Acrelio, that in our state the priests no longer contribute to the enslavement of humanity. From what you tell me all Yucatán must be beside itself with happiness . . . Unfortunately, my little brother, past experience tells me that they are not so deliriously happy as you suggest.[9]

Carrillo's spirits were certainly lifted when he reached Yucatán in August 1915 and saw for himself the beginning that Alvarado had made. However, no sooner had he gotten settled in Motul than he was jailed by Alvarado on the basis of his reputation as a troublemaker. It seems that the general was made suspicious of the *agrarista* by some of the planters and merchants who had been recruited into the revolutionary regime. Of course, Carrillo's stint in Morelos and his reputation as a *Zapatista* would not have endeared him to Alvarado under any circumstances. As a *Carrancista* officer, he was obliged to arrest enemy agents entering Constitutionalist zones without a pardon. Almost immediately, however, Alvarado foregave Carrillo this heresy because he needed his considerable talents in the countryside.[10] Following his amnesty and the introduction of Alvarado's short-lived agrarian reform, Carrillo was selected by his pueblo, Motul – much as Zapata had been chosen in Anenecuilco – to head the community's fight to regain its former lands.[11] Carrillo quickly established himself as a powerful force in local and regional politics, displaying singular organizational abilities and prominence as an agrarian leader. Thus, the very talents that had aroused Alvarado's mistrust were the credentials that prompted Alvarado to commission Carrillo an *agente de propaganda* charged with promoting the government's mild agrarian reform.

Carrillo's dedication to rural organization was extraordinary, and his rise in Alvarado's party was meteoric. From late 1915 until his expulsion by Carranza's federal troops in November 1919, Carrillo traveled endlessly throughout the state, promoting local agrarian committees, organizing *ligas de resistencia*, cultivating local chiefs, and recruiting political organizers, and all the while actively campaigning for Socialist candidates. His efforts were first rewarded in September 1916, when – after being back in the state for only several months – he was elected an alternate delegate to the Querétaro Constitutional Convention behind Polín González. A mere five months later, in March 1917, he replaced gubernatorial candidate Carlos Castro Morales as Socialist Party president, a position he would relinquish only in death seven years later.[12]

Perhaps to divert Carrillo's attention from the kind of grassroots mobilization of *campesinos* that by 1917 had already resulted in at least one land invasion and the prospect of work stoppages on henequen haciendas,[13] Alvarado named the *Motuleño* one of the leaders of his problem-ridden *Departamento de Cooperativas* later that year. Given his own previous experiment with cooperatives, Carrillo was a strong exponent of Alvarado's plan to create a chain of cooperative stores in Mérida and the major rural centers that would replace gouging private merchants and distribute cheaper food and goods to workers and *campesinos*. However, Carrillo soon discovered that the project had thus far accomplished nothing more than the further enrichment of its directors – large *hacendados* and merchants – and had actually worked to inflate retail prices. With what remained of the dwindling funds allocated for the project, Carrillo and his trusted advisor, Roberto Haberman, created the first cooperative stores late in 1918, not long after Alvarado departed Yucatán.

Carrillo regarded the viability of the workers' stores as the first major test of his ability to bring socialism to Yucatán. The test proved to be a failure, for the stores were undone by the monocrop region's pressing wartime need to import food and provisions from the United States. Despite a shrewd, pro-Ally public relations campaign, directed at the U.S. Food Administration through the American consulate in Progreso, the State Department would not support, nor would the Food Administration grant, the generous wartime export licenses that the coops needed to stock their shelves and remain open.[14] Just as the Food Administration had already favored Yucatán's commercial elite over Alvarado's *Reguladora de Comercio*, it now accorded preferential treatment to these same large merchants over the *Reguladora's* successor, the *Departamento de Cooperativas*. The conservative U.S. consul, who surprisingly had been swayed enough by Carrillo's rather superficial anti-German propaganda to recommend the granting of licenses, candidly admitted late in 1918 that the stores were going under "for a reason which may be better known in Washington than locally. I assume that the rather liberal treatment by the United States of private merchants in the matter of exports was a prominent factor."[15] The death knell of these consumer cooperatives was definitely sounded in 1919 when Carranza's federal troops under Colonel Zamarripa looted the surviving stores, drove them out of business, and ultimately hounded Carrillo and other radical Socialist leaders out of the peninsula.

Carrillo's dilemma

Don Venus's attempt to impose his puppet, Ignacio Bonillas, on the presidency had brought the Republic to the brink of civil war and ultimately cost the aging president his life. National opposition to him had formed early in 1920 throughout the state of Sonora, where Carranza's chief rival, Obregón, had joined forces with Adolfo de la Huerta and Plutarco Calles in issuing the *Plan de Agua Prieta* on April 23. The plan called for Carranza's overthrow and the guarantee of fair presidential elections, which General Obregón was sure to win. Less than a month later, the rebellion had spread nationwide, most of the federal army had deserted to the rebels, and Carranza, in fleeing Mexico City, had been hunted down and killed.

As usual, the shock waves of national rebellion had barely registered in Yucatán. After weathering Carranza's purge of Yucatecan socialism in exile, where he linked the Socialist Party's cause to the *Plan de Agua Prieta*, Carrillo returned to Yucatán in June 1920. Still a socialist committed to profound structural change, he remained adept at working through the maze of formal and informal political networks that, in organizing peasants and enlisting the support of *caciques* at the local level, had previously started him on the road to political power. In the two years (1920–1921) that followed the triumph of the Agua Prieta movement, Carrillo Puerto bided his time, entrusting the interim governorship to his close twenty-eight-year-old friend, Manuel Berzunza, while he turned his attentions, as president of the party and its *Liga Central de Resistencia*, to resurrecting what little remained of the former network of *ligas de resistencia*. He appreciated that he would have to begin again, almost from scratch, the difficult task of mobilizing Yucatán's agrarian sector, for the *campesinado* had been virtually reduced to a state of numbness by the concerted regime of terror and repression employed by Carranza's officers.

Two years later, in January 1922, as he personally claimed the governorship from his proxy, Berzunza, the potential for waging a radical social revolution in Yucatán had not substantially improved; indeed, Don Felipe realized that the terms of his dilemma had become even more pronounced. His Socialist Party of the Southeast,[16] essentially Alvarado's old coalition minus the general's former bourgeois allies who had defected en masse, had been beset with political and economic problems since the late 1910s. Carranza had almost driven the party and its constituent *ligas* completely out of existence in 1919. Moreover, Don Venus had disarmed Yucatán's *campesinado* in every sense, stripping it of its guns and driving many of its major agrarian leaders into exile. Then, although political opposition from the center had subsided in 1920 with the victory of Carrillo's ally, Obregón, Yucatán had suffered severe economic woes. The postwar depression of the henequen market hung over the region like a black cloud. Money to sustain even Alvarado's moderate agrarian reform and social welfare programs, let alone implement the more radical measures

that Carrillo had in mind – such as an expropriation of the henequen plantations – had dried up. However, as 1922 began, there
was minor cause for optimism, because the henequen industry
showed tentative signs of rejuvenation for the first time in over
three years. Increasingly, Yucatán's socialist revolutionaries were
becoming aware that their prospects of success hinged upon the
fluctuating market fortunes of the capitalist system that they
sought to overthrow.

At this crucial juncture, Governor Carrillo, intent upon implementing plans for a socialist revolution that he had been nurturing
now for the better part of a decade, took stock of the objective
conditions within the region, and at the national and international
levels as well, and weighed his various policy options. He realized
that whereas the members of Yucatán's powerful agro-commercial
bourgeoisie, although still divided, had tolerated Alvarado's moderate reforms, they could now be counted upon to present a much
more unified front against him. He knew that his regional revolutionary coalition was, at best, a fragile one. His support from
the urban labor movement, which was never the focus of his efforts
or interest as it had been under Alvarado, was increasingly tenuous. Carrillo's attempts to manipulate union politics and restrain
constantly escalating wage demands during the postwar economic
crisis infuriated many of the region's several thousand well-paid
stevedores and railroad workers. Late in 1921, members of these
hostile unions came close to assassinating him in a dramatic
bombing attempt.[17]

Carrillo believed that because Yucatán was overwhelmingly an
agricultural region, the agrarian sector would provide him with
the base of power he needed to wage a successful revolution from
above. However, although he had been developing cadres of full-
time agitators and propagandists as well as training activist *maestros*, Carrillo realized that a thoroughgoing mobilization of the
countryside would be a slow and demanding process. He was well
aware that even after almost two years of Socialist Party rule,
during a time when economic crisis had created significant privation and rural unrest, political mobilization had still not progressed very far for a variety of reasons. A primitive road and
communications network continued to plague Yucatán and had
been allowed to deteriorate further during the economic recession.
Carranza's reign of terror in the rural sector had largely nullified
previous *Alvaradista* attempts at organizing *campesinos*. Furthermore, the majority of these former efforts had been restricted to

recruiting the *campesinos* of the pueblos, or free villages. Alvarado's *agentes* and *maestros* had made fewer inroads into the hacienda communities where the great majority of Yucatán's *campesinos* actually lived or worked much of the time.

Carrillo had no way of knowing how much more time he would be granted to galvanize the *campesinado* into an effective force through his centralized network of *ligas de resistencia*. In addition to the low levels of political education and mobilization, the military capability of such a force was virtually nil, because the Yucatecan *campesinos*, whatever their numbers, still lacked sufficient guns and ammunition and any semblance of military training. Although, after his defeat of Carranza, President Obregón had approved the return of some of the shotguns previously confiscated by Carranza's federals, these ancient pieces in most cases were barely sufficient to knock pheasant out of the air, let alone be effective in open combat or guerrilla campaigns.

Nor could Governor Carrillo have taken heart from a variety of petitions from *campesinos* imploring the Socialist government to teach them basic self-defense techniques. As the president of the *liga de resistencia* of a small Maya pueblo confessed in 1922: "The truth is, *Sucúm* [Brother] Felipe, we don't know how to fire a pistol at a simple target."[18]

The lukewarm support that Obregón and General Plutarco Calles – Obregón's principal ally against Carranza and now his minister of the interior (*Gobernación*) – gave to *campesino* rearmament raised serious questions about their future commitment to Yucatán's revolutionary effort. Carrillo wondered whether these Sonoran caudillos were likely to sanction his plans to expropriate the valuable henequen plantations, which produced sizable federal revenues. He recalled Carranza's flat ultimatum to Alvarado in 1916 to halt his modest agrarian reform. That move had been prompted, many believed, by intense pressure on Mexico City by Yucatán's wealthiest *hacendados* and, some speculated, with the support of the U.S. government and the cordage interests as well. Would Obregón, if subjected to similar pressure, step in and thwart his agrarian reform?

Such was Carrillo Puerto's dilemma: He appreciated the difficulties of waging social revolution from above and realized that only a mass movement, mobilizing social groups and classes around a coherent revolutionary ideology and carefully orchestrated agenda, had any prospects of success. However, the creation of a broad revolutionary base would take time, more time than he probably had, considering the powerful opponents and obstacles arrayed against him.

Carrillo Puerto: the popular image

Traditional interpretations of Carrillo Puerto have not recognized the existence of this dilemma. Today in Mexico, Felipe Carrillo is recalled as a popular champion, a revolutionary exemplar, through a widely accepted historical image painted with hues of charisma and righteous rebellion. The traditional view stresses Carrillo's service with the *Zapatistas* and his undisputed Marxist sympathies, invariably documented with mention of his correspondence with Lenin and other international socialist luminaries.[19] Having established his ideological credentials as an *indigenista* and an agrarian socialist, these accounts go on to emphasize his personal appeal for the Indian masses that facilitated the creation of the *ligas de resistencia*.[20] These *ligas*, it is held, assured Carrillo a dedicated peasant militia of 60,000 to 90,000 strong – the figures vary but, by any account, clearly the largest force of its kind in the Republic.[21]

However, in treating Felipe Carrillo, historiography rapidly gives way to hagiography and myth making. The manner in which Carrillo met his death – executed by insurgent federal troops during the de la Huerta rebellion in January 1924 – has been given a higher priority in the historical record than the struggles and strategies that gave meaning to his political life. Carrillo Puerto has, alternately, been declared a "revolutionary martyr," a secular "saint of the proletariat," the "Mexican Allende," a pacifist "Gandhi of the Mayas," and even "Yucatán's Abraham Lincoln," the man who freed the region's *peones* from a de facto slave system.[22] His defeat and death have become central issues in modern Yucatecan history and a half-century later continue to preoccupy intellectuals and inspire novelists and playwrights within the peninsula and without.[23]

Over the past several decades, historians have been reluctant to perform the exercise in revisionist historiography that would free Carrillo from the burden of his saintliness. The extensive body of apocryphal lore that has grown up around Carrillo's origins, personality, political career, and death has flourished under the guidance of the Party of the Institutionalized Revolution through regular airings, gradual accretions, and occasional prunings. By sanctifying Carrillo and inducting him into the National Revolutionary Pantheon, along with Morelos's Zapata, Michoacán's Primo Tapia, and others, the modern Mexican state has sought to appropriate for itself a measure of legitimacy that the myth confers in an otherwise hostile and resentful region.

But it does not demean the man or dimish his accomplishments to demystify his political persona and assert his standing as an astutely pragmatic revolutionary leader, very much in the caudillo mold. Indeed, when he became governor in 1922, Carrillo Puerto was a seasoned Mexican politican who had fashioned an effective party machine and held, at one time or another, every other major political post in Yucatán.[24] But before examining the manner in which Carrillo attempted to resolve his political dilemma – to bring a socialist revolution to an economically depressed and poorly mobilized society – let us take a closer look at his ideological formation. For it is in the delicate interplay of idea and event, in the relationship between Carrillo's revolutionary ideology and his actual practice, that we come fully to appreciate the shrewdness and courage of his leadership as well as the formidable obstacles that blocked his socialist experiment in Yucatán.

A home-grown Yucatecan socialist

Whereas Alvarado, a self-styled revolutionary theorist, wrote numerous articles, tracts, and a succession of weighty tomes, Carrillo Puerto wrote little and published even less. There is no indication that Carrillo ever took himself seriously as a revolutionary intellectual, and an occasional article, the texts (and less reliable accounts) of some of his speeches, and his gubernatorial *informes* (reports) of 1922 and 1923 make up his entire written legacy. Moreover, as a master politician and propagandist, Carrillo often tailored his speeches to meet the exigencies of the moment or to evoke a certain response from a particular audience. He might alter his political rhetoric depending upon whether he was addressing a gathering of *campesinos* in Maya, haranguing a workers' congress in Mexico City or Motul, or directing his remarks to the U.S. business and diplomatic community in Washington and Mérida. Consequently, perhaps to an even greater degree than with Alvarado, an evaluation of Don Felipe's ideological orientation must lean heavily on an analysis of his social programs and his political direction of the revolutionary process.

Carrillo's speeches and writings draw more consistently and vividly upon the experiences he gained over two decades of organizing *campesinos* than upon any individual source of doctrine. Nevertheless, throughout his life, Carrillo exposed himself to a variety of political doctrines, conscientiously searching for ideological precepts to guide his actions. It is likely that he was first introduced to the basic principles of socialism as a boy by his village priest, a Spanish refugee with a reputed anarchosyndicalist background.[25] As a young man he read a chapter of Marx's *Capital*, Proudhon, and other European leftist thinkers. Yet prior to joining the *Zapatistas*, Carrillo still operated within the liberal mainstream of Mexican politics, attacking *Porfirismo* in the *Maderista* press and even translating the 1857 Constitution into Maya while serving time in prison in 1911. Carrillo's father, Justiniano, had fought in the *Juarista* ranks that had driven Maximilian's imperialists out of the peninsula and raised his children on liberal ideals.[26]

Carrillo had broadened his ideological horizon with the *Zapatistas*, reading and discussing anarchist and socialist works with fellow agronomists and gradually developing a Marxist world view. Brief periods of exile in New Orleans, where he worked on the docks and fraternized with militant North American workers, augmented his political education. When Carrillo returned to Yucatán from Morelos in 1915, he was clearly sympathetic to socialist ideology; by the time he returned from North American exile in 1920, he regarded himself as a Marxist and a communist (although, unlike Alvarado, he never bragged about being a bolshevik).[27]

Carrillo and other Yucatecan socialists appear to have owed much of the rudimentary political education they received to Roberto Haberman, the Rumanian-American leftist who advised the Socialist Party of Yucatán in the late 1910s, briefing its leaders on the history and organization of working-class movements in Europe and the United States. Haberman would later recall Carrillo's original naiveté in these matters. Upon hearing from Haberman how labor organizations conducted business abroad, Carrillo exclaimed: "If other labor groups have conventions and statutes, let us have them also!"[28] Thus was born, according to Haberman, the first Socialist Workers' Congress at Motul in 1918. "Compañero Roberto's" role at the Motul Congress was a pivotal one. A member of the Socialist Party of the United States, Haberman stressed to the 200 delegates representing 26,000 members of the Socialist Party of Yucatán the importance of linking their struggle against the oligarchy and North American imperialism to an international socialist movement. Recognizing that the majority of the delegates were probably *Alvaradistas* imbued with the general's utopian populism, Haberman patiently began to sow the seeds of a more revolutionary ideology. He broke down complicated Marxist concepts such as the theory of surplus value, paraphrasing Marx through a skillful use of concrete local illustrations:

> You build magnificent houses, yet you live in huts that are not even fit for your animals; you cut thousands of *pencas*, yet others profit from the fiber; . . . when you are sick there are no doctors and your families die of hunger or must ask their neighbors for charity . . .
>
> For your labor on the hacienda you earn approximately 5 pesos, which is only half of the wealth which you produce, because the statistics reveal that each worker yields a product of 15 pesos per day . . . Let us suppose that the bosses must spend 5 pesos each for taxes, machinery, transportation, and the like: every day they take 5 pesos away from each of you, and from every hundred of their field hands they extract at least 500 pesos. You all know how well this enables them to live here and travel overseas . . . [29]

At a time when Marxist texts were still scarce in Mexico, the potential impact of agents like Haberman in diffusing ideas was great. Under Haberman's tutelage, Carrillo and his Socialist colleagues embarked upon a program of reading during 1917–1919 that included Marx, Engels, and Lenin. However, the *Carrancista* purge in 1919 that exiled Carrillo also removed Haberman, and he never returned to the peninsula.

It seems doubtful that local Socialist leaders ever penetrated the labyrinthine complexities of dialectical materialism. Don Felipe and his lieutenants never really had the time fully to assimilate, let alone act upon, the Marxist–Leninist literature they read avidly in the late 1910s and early 1920s. Thus, although he would later lift entire passages from the *Communist Manifesto* and place them on Socialist Party placards, conclude all political meetings with a singing of "The International," and print the resolutions of the Third International of Moscow on the letterhead of party stationery, Carrillo Puerto was never a sophisticated socialist ideologue. [30]

Carrillo would proudly proclaim his administration "the first socialist government in the Americas." [31] However, his was a pragmatic socialism tailored to the needs of Yucatán's social landscape, eschewing doctrinaire influences from abroad. To be sure, Carrillo's government borrowed European songs and slogans and studied the social programs of the Russian Revolution. Yucatecan Socialists corresponded with Lenin and his ministers and were particularly impressed with the Soviet school system, which became an important model for Socialist Party educators. Yet at the outset of his administration, Carrillo emphatically stated his party's intention of establishing an independent socialist regime: "We do not intend to imitate Soviet bolshevism. But we certainly will create a system in which the workers alone will have the right to dispense and receive justice."[32]

In line with this desire for autonomy, the party resolved in 1921 to correspond with the Moscow Third International without actually joining it. Carrillo argued that the worldwide socialist movement, with which the Yucatecan Socialist Party of the Southeast identified, now embraced a constituency much greater than that included in the Eurocentric International. Carrillo and the party had come a long way since 1918, when Roberto Haberman had stressed the importance of internationalism. Of course, another factor that entered into the party's decision not to affiliate with Moscow was the displeasure that Obregón's government in Mexico City had shown when the issue was first raised.[33]

Unlike Alvarado, Carrillo never reneged upon his socialist declarations as his political career evolved. He could, if the occasion demanded, adopt a conciliatory posture, as when he sought export licenses for his worker cooperatives in 1919 and endeavored to convince the U.S. diplomatic and business community that his brand of socialism was compatible with North American commerce and the Allied war effort. However, a year later, when given the opportunity as a federal deputy backed by General Calles to address a workers' demonstration in Mexico City, Carrillo would thunder:

> If the merchants monopolize provisions and you lack bread, then go to the stores, tear down the doors and loot all the goods. Let's dynamite the Chamber of Deputies, shut down the Senate and finish with the Supreme Court. Enough peaceful demonstrations! Enough empty talk! The principles of the bolsheviks should be implemented. Let's wave the red flag . . . Instead of ringing the bells on Sunday, let's melt them down for bronze coins. If we must, let us tear down and destroy to build the higher ideals of communism. The distribution of land, a rise in wages, these things can only be brought about by force, not peaceful demonstrations.[34]

Thus, like any good politician, Don Felipe was not above the uses of rhetoric and polemic to further his political goals or his personal career. In his inaugural speech of January 1922, however, Governor Carrillo stated the ultimate goal of his Socialist regime. Speaking in Maya from the balcony of the Governor's Palace to an audience made up largely of *campesinos* who had journeyed to Mérida by train or on foot to hear him, Carrillo introduced a theme that would recur frequently in future orations:

> *Compañeros!* Today we put an end to the politics of the Socialist Party and begin the difficult task of working together as socialists . . . The moment has come to demonstrate to the *señores* that we know how to govern; that we are the builders and not they; . . . that without the workers neither this palace . . . nor anything else useful to modern man would exist; . . . that labor existed before capital, and that, for justice's sake, those who produce everything have the right to possess everything, not just a minority of it.[35]

The inaugural speech in effect reiterated the resolutions of Yucatán's Second Workers' Congress, held at Izamal in August 1921. The Izamal Congress, presided over by Carrillo, called upon the Yucatecan government and its *ligas* to step up efforts to socialize the means of production throughout the state, including all public utilities and services that were still in private hands, and to work for the implementation of agrarian and industrial communism. It also reminded the government and its *ligas* of Marx's dictum that "the emancipation of the proletariat was the responsibility of the proletariat itself."[36]

Yet, Carrillo Puerto was too shrewd a politician to believe that the socialist millennium would be ushered in quickly or easily. Upon returning to power in 1920, Carrillo had recognized the importance of formulating a patient and deliberate strategy. Over the long term, such a strategy would require a popular mobilization of the rural and urban proletariat, but the rural masses were a long way from being able to emancipate themselves. Over the short term, therefore, the first step would be to use every possible means to place Socialists in public posts, then to pass laws in favor of the working class.[37] Thus, although the rhetoric and the ultimate goals of the socialist program called for a mounting ground swell from below, Carrillo's strategy implied, at least for the present, a revolution made from above. And to help bring about this revolution from the top down but, more importantly, to protect it from its enemies inside and outside the peninsula, he would have to recruit and maintain powerful allies at both the federal and regional levels – allies who in most cases did not share his revolutionary commitment. In the months ahead, Carrillo and the Socialist leadership in Mérida would find that in hammering out a pragmatic strategy, they ran the risk of compromising their ideological principles.

Caudillos and *caciques*: Mérida and Mexico City

Carrillo's political career – his successful rise to power and the ultimate demise of his socialist regime – is most easily understood when viewed within the context of caudillo politics. In Carrillo's own career, first as a local agrarian *cacique* and later as a regional caudillo, we can identify many of the essential characteristics of *caciquismo* and *caudillaje*: the rise to power from a local or subregional base; a consistent tactical use of violence (or the threat of violence); a predilection for working through informal political networks structured by the bonds of kinship and personalistic patron–client arrangements; the timely manipulation of ideological symbols; and the performance of a mediating or middleman role in dealing with both state and national structures and with local *campesinos*.[38]

Contrary to the popular mythology that has depicted Carrillo Puerto as a pacifist by nature and imbued him with the gentle qualities that befit a martyr executed along with twelve of his "disciples,"[39] the documentary evidence reveals a pragmatic regional chief who did not shrink from the use of violence or political homicide in gaining or maintaining himself in power. In his early career, Carrillo's marksmanship had protected him from at least one assassination attempt and, along with his bold leadership of peasant land invasions, won him a reputation as a man of action.[40] More importantly, under Carrillo Puerto's orders, brother Wilfrido's small but efficient force of secret police (*Policía Judicial*), working in alliance with local power brokers, violently and systematically quelled dissent throughout the region, smashing the rival Yucatecan Liberal Party and its conservative press, disbanding competing parties in Campeche, and ultimately establishing the Socialist Party of the Southeast as the only party in the peninsula by late 1922.[41] En route to establishing a monopoly of force within the region, which would enable him to implement a socialist program, Carrillo did not hesitate to strong-arm and terrorize his opponents.[42] In 1919, *Carrancista* minister Luis Cabrera had attempted to reconcile Carrillo's undisputed commitment to improving the quality of life in Yucatán with the often ruthless methods he employed as he led the Socialist Party in its struggle for power:

> Don Felipe Carrillo . . . is . . . an authentic visionary, an idealist who truly believes in the just cause of his people. His tenacity and pluck are renowned . . . He is the true author of the Yucatecan Socialist Party . . . And yet, like all visionaries who are blind to all that is not their ideal, he cannot see the justice of allowing another political faction to exist in Yucatán. He who is not enrolled in the leagues of resistance must perish; for – as Christ said – he who is not with him, is against him . . . Carrillo and the masses who make up the Socialist Party will never grant those who have exploited them for so long the right to survive . . . They will never agree to reinstitute the democratic process . . . [43]

Carrillo's foundations as a regional caudillo were firm and tested. In Motul, he constructed a tightly knit faction of close relatives and intimate friends that later formed the heart of his party organization and state administration.[44] No major revolutionary leader utilized the bonds of kinship more fully than Carrillo: According to one estimate, 142 members of his extended family took positions in the state government, in addition to scores of long-standing friends (e.g., Manuel Berzunza, his proxy as governor during the 1920–1921 period). A minimum of 14,000 pesos per month was paid in salaries to members of his immediate family alone.[45] Of the three brothers who accompanied Carrillo to the *paredón* (firing squad), Wilfrido was chief of the secret police, Benjamín secretary of the *Liga Central de Resistencia* (and formerly a federal deputy), and Edesio jointly the municipal president and president of the *liga de resistencia* of Motul. Other siblings, who managed to avoid execution, ran the state's *ligas feministas* (Elvia), directed the state-owned railroads (Gualberto), and headed the state treasury (Eraclio). A son-in-law controlled the Mérida *ayuntamiento* (town council).[46]

Nor did Don Felipe neglect to cultivate informal patron–client networks in his dealings with the national power structure, now controlled by the two caudillos who would establish a Sonoran dynasty, Álvaro Obregón and Plutarco Elías Calles. In 1919, Carrillo had become the first regional leader to declare his support for Obregón, incurring President Carranza's wrath for his boldness. This farsighted move enabled him to eliminate his last serious rival at the regional level, Governor Carlos Castro Morales. Castro

Morales, who had pledged himself to support Carranza and uphold the formal, "legally constituted process,"[47] paid for backing
the wrong horse with years in political exile. Carrillo, on the other
hand, had found himself a powerful benefactor. Following the
Agua Prieta rebellion, Carrillo, although continuing to support
Obregón, went out of his way to secure General Calles, Obregón's
minister of the interior (*Gobernación*) as his principal patron. Carrillo had sensed that Calles, generally assumed to be more radical
than Obregón, would be a force in national politics for years to
come. This was important, for Carrillo and the Yucatecan Socialists had become suspicious of Obregón's commitment to land and
labor programs shortly after his election in 1920. They believed
Calles would more readily offer "moral and material support for
the maintenance of a socialist government in Yucatán,"[48] a view
shared by other leftist politicians of the time. At the least, Carrillo
sought to ensure that Calles (and *Gobernación*) would place no obstacles in the path of his social programs. Most importantly, as
Carrillo confided to the visiting José Vasconcelos in 1922, he
understood "support from Calles" to mean "federal troops on request."[49] Accordingly, Carrillo lavished gifts on Calles's personal
secretary and contributed 100,000 pesos to Calles's campaign for
the presidency in 1923.[50]

Both Obregón and Calles rewarded Carrillo for his loyalty and
service, first by supporting him as he turned back a renewed
challenge to his hegemony by Salvador Alvarado in September
1921 and then by giving him a free hand to implement his programs in Yucatán and, increasingly, throughout the entire southeast.[51] Beginning in 1920, for example, *Carrillista* agents backed
by 1,500 regular and irregular Yucatecan troops invaded neighboring Campeche, organized *ligas de resistencia* and, splitting the
existing majority party in two, established the hegemony of the
Socialist Party by early 1921. Following the explicit orders of
Calles, federal troops remained as spectators, and subsequent
Campechano protests against this violation of state sovereignty fell
on deaf ears. Less dramatic and decisive political incursions were
made into Chiapas and Tabasco (and feelers were even sent to Cuba
and Guatemala) as Carrillo attempted to enlarge his sphere of
action and give substance to his party's hitherto formal pretensions
of being *El Gran Partido Socialista del Sureste*.[52] In 1921, Carrillo
answered a call for aid from workers' groups in Tampico and the
Laguna region, selling them corn at cost and sending along several
agentes de propaganda to communicate the party's message.[53]

Don Felipe transcended his image as a regional leader early in 1922, when he led the party into the so-called *Partidos Coaligados*, a loose political federation that would later evolve under Calles's direction into the nationally based *Partido Nacional Revolucionario* (PNR). By late 1923, as he seemed prepared to embark upon a major expropriation of henequen plantations, there was some talk both within the region and outside that Carrillo might now be contemplating a national following and a run at the presidency. Despite Carrillo's own declaration of support for Calles's candidacy, these rumors could not have pleased the man whose protection Carrillo had sought and enjoyed, the man whom Yucatecan socialists referred to as *el amo* (the boss).[54]

Caudillos and *caciques*: the Yucatán *campo*

Generally speaking, Yucatán was able to avoid the anarchic violence that disrupted and dislocated the Mexican society and economy from 1910 to 1920 – the violence of free-ranging revolutionary armies and caudillo bands. On the other hand, the popular characterization of twentieth-century Yucatán as *el país tranquilo*, a society rendered docile and passive by the bloody and traumatic nineteenth-century Caste War,[55] is clearly a myth. Over a thirty-year period after 1910, low-level factional *cacique* violence became institutionalized into the political and social fabric of the countryside. Moreover, at least during intervals of the 1918–1924 period, such violence could be especially intense. In some parts of the state, settlement patterns were severely, if usually only temporarily, affected as band violence uprooted large communal segments and, in some cases, depopulated entire villages and hamlets.[56] Indeed, atrocities as grisly as any reported elsewhere in revolutionary Mexico were carried out in Yucatán, although mercifully they tended to be isolated episodes. Yet, on several occasions, as during the state elections of 1917 and 1921, there was nervous speculation in Mérida's cafés and press about the possibility of another Caste War.[57]

The continuation of factional violence under Carrillo Puerto suggests that his revolution often failed to destroy traditional mechanisms of social control in the rural areas. Rather than restructure political and socioeconomic relationships in the countryside, the programs of the revolutionary regime and the formal administrative apparatus created to implement them often used and were used by local power brokers to consolidate and legitimize informal control. In other words, a new class of *caciques* replaced the old one.[58]

In fact, Don Felipe made *caciquismo* one of the bulwarks of his regime. As he had begun to do in 1917, Carrillo allied himself with a variety of local bosses, most of whom came from petty bourgeois or rural proletarian backgrounds (e.g., hacienda foremen and overseers, *rancheros*, artisans, and *peones*) and a number of whom had gained local reputations for their exploits as social bandits. Some had begun to establish local followings during the first sporadic uprisings surrounding the Madero rebellion (1909–1911). However, in virtually every case, these strongmen actually carved out their *cacicazgos* following the relaxation of Alvarado's military rule and the opening of the political system in mid-1917. Some of these incipient *caciques* began their careers as "white guards" – retainers and henchmen of Porfirian *hacendados* – when the local *jefes políticos* were higher-level enforcers for the planter oligarchy. The majority of these men had little opportunity for advancement under the Porfirian regime, based as it was on the large estate, henequen monoculture, and a harsh dependent labor system. Most seem to have reconciled themselves to the rather meager prospects of life on the margin, in the interstices, or directly within the orbit of the large estate. A few, however, attempted to improve their life chances and give vent to their frustrations through banditry. In sweeping aside the custodians of Porfirian social control in the countryside, Alvarado created new opportunities for these men that they more easily exploited following the general's departure in 1918, during the intensification of conflict between Carrillo's Socialist Party and the Liberal Party.[59] Table 7 is a listing, no doubt incomplete, of the major *caciques* active in Yucatán during the 1917–1924 period.

As Carrillo Puerto advanced in his political career, and especially as he toured the state promoting the *ligas de resistencia*, which, he envisioned, would one day become the backbone of the party, he sought to identify and enlist the support of these incipient power brokers for the Socialists. Similar efforts by agents of the Liberals gave the routine factional conflicts of *cacique* politics an intensely "ideological" flavor, especially during the period of Carranza's persecution of the Socialist Party (1918–1920). More often than not, however, regional politics served merely as a pretext, an overlay for deep-seated local rivalries over land, cattle, commercial rights, and the accession to local power that would

Table 7. Caciquismo *in Yucatán,* 1917–1924[60]

Name	Occupation	*Municipio*	*Partido*
Loreto Baak[d]	Bandit	Santa Elena	Ticul
Donato Bates	*Ranchero*		Valladolid
Juan Campos	Bandit		Temax
Pedro Crespo	Ex-officer, state militia	Temax	
Agustín Espinosa[a]			Acanceh
"Los hermanos Euán" ("The Euán brothers," Braulio, Bruno, and Juan)		Opichén	Maxcanú
Bartolomé García Correa	*Maestro*	Umán	Hunucmá
Manuel González ("Polín")[c]	*Mayordomo;* military officer	Halachó, Opichén, Maxcanú	Maxcanú
José Ma. Iturralde Traconis	*Maestro*	Valladolid	Valladolid
Felipe Lara		Cenotillo	Espita
Humberto León	Barber	Halachó	Maxcanú
Manuel Mendoza Rosado[d]		Santa Elena	Ticul
Lino Muñoz		Progreso	Progreso
Anaceto Moreno[b]		Yaxcabá	Sotuta
Miguel Ortiz		Muna	Ticul
José Jesús Patrón		Xochel	Izamal
Carlos Poot Castillo		Cansahcab	Temax
José Pío Chuc	*Ranchero*	Hunucmá	Hunucmá
José D. Presuel			Valladolid
Juan Quijano Pérez	*Mayordomo*	Conkal	Tixkokob
Enrique Poveda	Military officer; small merchant	Tekax	Tekax
Ignacio Solís[a]			Acanceh
"Los hermanos Vargas" ("The Vargas brothers," Lisandro and Benjamín)[c]		Opichén	Maxcanú
Demetrio Yamá ("El Tuerto," "Wall-eye")[b]	*Peón*	Yaxcabá	Sotuta

Note: The main occupation of the *cacique,* when known, and the location of the *cacicazgo,* as can best be determined (i.e., *municipio* and/or *partido*), appear following the *cacique's* name. Matching letters following the names indicate strong evidence of a dual or multiple *cacicazgo.*

assure the winning faction control over these economic resources. A Liberal faction, for example, would literally drive its Socialist rival out of town, the latter taking refuge in a friendly (i.e., Socialist-controlled) pueblo nearby. The victors would then seize lands and goods and often take over the losers' jobs on neighboring haciendas. Then the political balance of regional politics would shift, the Socialists getting the upper hand, and the division of spoils would be reversed.[61] The editorial writer of Mexico City's *El Universal* portrayed the local struggle late in 1920 as a "grotesque tragedy," with political affiliation almost incidental:

> Burnings, looting, murder . . . it's all happening there! The so-called political parties are no more than bands of gangsters. They do not compete like politicians in civilized lands . . . using the spoken and printed word, but rather brandish guns, torches, and machetes, caught up in the brutish mentality of troglodytes.[62]

By early 1922, however, the issue was no longer in doubt. Backed by Obregón and Calles, Carrillo Puerto had effectively employed various forms of patronage to come to terms with all factional leaders of consequence and put the Liberals out of business. He had instructed General Alejandro Mange, his loyal military zone commander, not to interfere with his Socialist allies as they enforced their political authority within their informal domains. Upon occasion, however, state police and federal troops did intervene in *support* of local Socialist bosses, and there is evidence that the party itself sent small shipments of guns to a favored few in 1920.[63] Generally speaking, after 1921 Carrillo seems to have condoned the practice of controlled violence for limited political ends, although impressing upon these *caciques* the importance of braking indiscriminate acts of criminal violence and banditry, especially against the henequen plantations, whose continued production was so central to the regional economy. Carrillo stepped up his campaign against lawlessness after formally taking office in 1922, when, with fiber prices again on the upswing, it was especially imperative to ensure the social peace. Particularly egregious behavior by local *caciques*, such as the assassination of *hacendados* and *mayordomos*, brought some form of immediate retribution from Mérida. Usually the guilty *pistolero* was jailed and the existing *cacicazgo* dissolved in favor of a rival faction.[64]

To ensure the loyalty of more discreet and sensible bosses, Carrillo Puerto elevated a number to the state legislature (e.g., Braulio Euán, Bartolomé García Correa, Demetrio Yamá, Manuel González, Juan Campos) and awarded others the plums of civil government and agrarian office to hold themselves or bestow as they saw fit. Many, in addition to being municipal presidents, were also entrusted with the presidency of their local *ligas de resistencia* (e.g., Lino Muñoz, Loreto Baak, Pedro Crespo, Felipe Lara, Juan Campos, Donato Bates).[65] The Liberal, *hacendado*-controlled press raged against what it viewed as Carrillo Puerto's "communist republic," maintained by a "bloody system of political rule in the countryside, dictated by the personal whim of *caciquillos*." Even more infuriating to them was the spectacle of "barely literate Maya *pistoleros*" taking up seats in the state legislature in Mérida: "rude assassins who walk our streets and ride about in chauffered automobiles with total immunity from the law!" Here, the editorial writer of the conservative *Revista de Mérida* lamented, was a macabre, plebeian version of the Porfirian Peace, with all the evils of the old *jefe político* system but none of its dignified stability.[66]

Moreover, Carrillo had been careful, whenever possible, not to impinge upon the established economic preserves of his local allies. Don Felipe's government was inundated with memorials from *campesinos* protesting against abuses that, in most cases, they explicitly linked to individual *caciques*; for example: illegal sales taxes (*alcabalas*); unwarranted exemptions from the payment of taxes; clandestine liquor traffic – especially rife since the puritanical Alvarado decreed Yucatán to be *El Estado Seco* in 1915, legislation that Carrillo had not seen fit to repeal; irregularities in the implementation of agrarian reform, including personal control of the best *ejido* lands; violations in landlord–tenant arrangements; the use of unpaid communal labor (*fagina*); corruption in the management of Carrillo's rural consumer cooperative stores, often in collusion with monopolistic merchants; and embezzlement of *liga* dues – to name only the most frequent complaints.[67] Carrillo's response was invariably to promise redress and, in many cases, he made good on his promise. Yet the frequency of such memorials suggests either an inability or, in certain situations, an unwillingness to act. In the case of the contraband liquor trade, one of the local bosses' most lucrative sidelines, it was common knowledge that the law would not be enforced. Indeed, one of the rising young men in Carrillo's inner circle, Bartolomé García Correa, soon to become governor in his own right, was acknowledged to be one of the worst *contrabandistas de aguardiente* in the western part of the state.[68]

In addition to respecting the existing sources of the *caciques'* income, Carrillo Puerto extended preferential economic treatment to his most favored clients. Thus, García Correa received a juicy concession to establish a badly needed electric plant; Lino Muñoz got a sizable land option in the state's best grazing area; and free passes and railroad privileges to move goods were bestowed generously upon these allies, although they were denied to the great *hacendados* who attempted to resist Don Felipe's agrarian reform and new wage tariffs. Moreover, it seems clear that the petitions that these influential chiefs brought on behalf of their pueblos and individual supporters – requests for ejidal grants, increased wages, and additional hacienda employment – were received much more favorably by the governor than those that filtered up to him from less politically favored petitioners.[69]

In return, Carrillo's clientele group recognized his absolute authority within the state and performed a variety of services for its patron, who, by 1923 was being commonly hailed as *El César Rojo* ("the Red Caesar").[70] Not only was violence selectively brought to bear against opponents of the regime to ensure Carrillo's Socialist Party a political monopoly within the region, but the *caciques* doubled as informal ward bosses, guaranteeing through a variety of incentives and coercive techniques the enrollment of local *campesinos* in the *ligas de resistencia*. Occasionally, local bosses organized *ligas* themselves. More common was the combination of initial contact by cadres of propagandists and rural teachers followed up, when needed, by the strong-arm tactics of a local boss.[71] Merchants and *hacendados* were also forced to join *ligas* and obtain Socialist Party membership cards. Most merchants and planters regarded *liga* membership as equivalent to buying protection for their future. Those who refused to join found their fiber embargoed and their stores boycotted. Without a red card, it became practically impossible to run a business in Carrillo's Yucatán, especially in the countryside.[72] The result was a dramatic rise in *liga* recruitment over the course of Carrillo Puerto's governorship. By the end of 1922, there were approximately 73,000 *ligados* in 417 leagues. A year later, on the eve of the de la Huerta revolt, the membership rolls had swelled to well over 80,000.[73]

In short, Carrillo's network of *ligas de resistencia* was not a massive grass-roots mobilization in spontaneous response to his charismatic leadership, but rather a skillful reaccommodation by the Socialist Party government of existing *cacique* power bases. This is not to suggest that Carrillo preferred to work with corrupt *caciques* and *pistoleros* rather than with the *campesinos*. He was undeniably committed throughout his life to bringing structural change to Yucatán. But in the early 1920s his nascent Socialist regime was embattled and his options were few. Unlike General Alvarado's regime, which combined military and civilian power, his government was based solely upon civilian rule and, in the absence of guaranteed federal military support, was vulnerable to attack from within and without. He sought alliances with local *caciques* because he knew how they operated, having grown up among them, and because they were ready-made allies with controlling ties in the *campo* at a time when time itself would determine the fate of his socialist experiment.

The socialist program

From mid-1920 until the end of 1923, the *cacique* alliances that underwrote an expanding network of *ligas de resistencia* allowed Felipe Carrillo to implement a broad revolutionary program in Yucatán. Under Carrillo's leadership, the *ligas* first began significantly to penetrate the hacienda communities as well as the free villages. Early in 1923, for example, the Socialists destroyed what was then referred to as *el último reducto de esclavitud* (the last bastion of slavery), the Catmís sugar plantation located in the remote southeastern corner of the state. Labor conditions at Catmís during the Porfiriato had been notorious, reflecting the worst aspects of the *enganche* system, including the exploitation of Yaqui deportees. The plantation had gained even greater notoriety in March 1911, when a bloody *jacquerie* occurred during the *Maderista* rebellion, the *peones* exploding in a brief, cathartic rage, destroying machinery, and brutally carving up the *hacendado* and members of his family.[74] Thereafter, conditions on the plantation had slipped from public view, and it was only in 1922 that Carrillo learned from one of his *agentes* that the harsh conditions of the Old Regime had been virtually reestablished by the new *hacendado*, who had managed to enlist the support of the local *cacique* (nominally, a Socialist and conveniently placed as the community's *comisario municipal*). The violations of the 1918 Labor Law were flagrant: The houses of the sugar workers resembled the former barracks of slave-peonage, "human beehives inhabited by 30–50 people, including many families."[75] Roofing was inadequate, water scarce, medical attention and facilities nonexistent. On the plantation resided 200 children of school age, yet no school had been provided. It was

reported that workers were forced to cut and grind cane a minimum of eighteen hours a day and were recompensed in scrip.

Carrillo acted immediately, deposing the *cacique* and creating a
liga de resistencia. Within the first four months of its existence,
enrollment increased from 80 to 200 workers, effectively mobilizing Catmís's entire labor force.[76]

There were other haciendas with labor conditions approximat-
ing those at Catmís in the early 1920s, though probably none so
geographically removed or highly publicized.[77] Generally speaking, although Alvarado had done away with the slave-peonage
system, it was not until the Socialists consolidated their power
during the Berzunza–Carrillo years that an initial attempt was
made to organize the Yucatecan field hand and transform him into
a unionized agricultural worker. Of course, abuses continued to
be documented in later years, especially following Carrillo
Puerto's death,[78] and the process whereby the rural worker was
proletarianized and politically organized reached its conclusion
only under President Lázaro Cárdenas in the late 1930s, and even
then imperfectly. Yet under Carrillo Puerto, great strides were
made. Alvarado's precedent of retroactive revolution was continued, only now the *campesino* was given the protection he had lacked
under Alvarado and was actually encouraged to come before the
Tribunals of Conciliation and Arbitration with his grievance. The
fact that many more Maya *campesinos* actually did come forward to
plead their cases before magistrates in regional centers and in
Mérida also speaks well for Carrillo's campaign to instill the beginnings of ethnic pride and class consciousness in the rural
masses.[79]

Carrillo's educational program clearly reinforced these new attitudes. His notion of the *escuela racionalista* (rational school)
linked the educational process with the socialist notion of class
struggle. Salvador Alvarado, in introducing this concept, had
been primarily concerned with raising the *Yucateco* from pariah to
wage earner. Education would transform an oppressed and shift-
less *peón* into a productive *obrero* with skills and attitudes appropriate for modernizing capitalism. Carrillo, influenced by the
pedagogy of Spanish anarchist Francisco Ferrer Guardia as well as
by the new revolutionary schools of the Soviet Union, challenged
the assumptions of the bourgeois school, which he felt still functioned like the Porfirian school before it, to coopt, control, and
domesticate the *campesino*. Carrillo and the Yucatecan Socialists
sought a "true socialist school, created to nourish the masses," an

institution that would train "men apt for life and liberated from all dogmas," struggling to transform society.[80] The Socialists envisioned a school that would change the Yucatecan *campesino* from a pariah to a class-conscious worker "who will no longer want to work for the bosses but who will know how to profit from the price of [his] labor."[81]

In applying the principles of Ferrer's *escuela racionalista* at all levels of Yucatán's education system, from primary school on up to the new *Universidad Nacional del Sureste*, which he created in 1922, Carrillo provided a brief glimpse of the kind of class-oriented pedagogy that would later emerge at the national level under Cárdenas with the introduction of the *escuela socialista* (socialist school). The first *escuelas racionalistas* were created by the Socialists in 1922 and their guidelines called for an end to all rewards and punishments, examinations, diplomas, and titles and an emphasis on knowledge that could be acquired from manual work in the fields, shops, laboratories, and work areas of the schools themselves. Furthermore, all schools would be "based on liberty," that is to say, off-limits to priests and other religious personnel, and coeducational. Prospective teachers for these *escuelas racionalistas* would attend a brief course in government normal schools, where they would study labor history, Marxist economic theory, and Articles 27 and 123 of the 1917 Constitution. They would then be expected to instruct all Yucatecan children in the principles of socialism, which would be required learning in the state's private schools as well. Moreover, in order that the new revolutionary society might benefit from its past errors, Carrillo stipulated that all teachers would be obliged to emphasize that man's previous attachment to individualism had been a serious social mistake. In the future, if society were to run smoothly, the individual would have to subordinate himself to the will, and for the good, of the collectivity.[82]

Led by the conservative editor and publisher of the *Revista de Yucatán*, Carlos R. Menéndez, a significant uproar developed over Carrillo's introduction of *educación racionalista*. In addition to opposition from members of the traditional elite (many more of whom now sent their children out of state or abroad to be educated) and some middle-class professional families, the experiment suffered from the inertia and passive resistance of some public school teachers.[83] More difficult still to overcome was the relatively high cost of building, equipping, and staffing the kind of *escuela–taller* (school–workshop) that the ambitious rational concept demanded. (It appears that much more actual school building took place during the economically prosperous Alvarado period.) Ultimately, Carrillo's defeat in 1924 led to a shelving of the program until the Cárdenas regime resurrected it in a slightly different form during the mid-1930s.[84]

Had it not been so costly and presented in the combative and dogmatic class rhetoric that alienated an important sector of the literate, educationally concerned population, Carrillo's rationalistic approach to pedagogy would have had much to offer Yucatán. Almost everyone favored some reform of the decrepit, nineteenth-century curriculum, and most concurred with Carrillo's principal assumption that, in order to be relevant and effective, education had to be "más pragmática y menos verbalista" ("more pragmatic and less verbose").[85] Moreover, Carrillo's attachment to the rational concept led him to introduce a number of additional educational programs that proved highly popular: for example, his creation of *escuelas granjas* (farm schools) to develop new and better methods of crop cultivation and diversification; his plans for the development of *escuelas industriales* (industrial schools), which would encourage the growth of characteristic artisan industries in the individual pueblos; the introduction of special night schools to educate urban workers and teach hacienda *encargados* and *mayordomos* improved management skills; and his adoption of experimental literacy techniques, which geared reading and writing skills to meaningful "central experiences" in the rural worker's life, most notably his relationship to the land.[86]

Carrillo's progressive reforms in the areas of birth control, women's rights, and divorce also drew an indignant, though futile, protest from the traditional element in regional society. About the same time that his rational education curriculum was being introduced early in 1922, the *Liga Central* and its *ligas feministas* were distributing North American Dr. Margaret Sanger's pamphlet on contraception in the public schools and marriage registries and introducing sex education classes in Mérida's schools. Carrillo's government lent its full support to these campaigns. Pointing out the great need to instruct the men and women of the proletariat in such matters, the Socialist Party paper exclaimed: "Many children! To pour into the world year after year more future slaves of misery, hunger, and exploitation is the bourgeois ideal, and only works to favor the selfish interests of the ruling class."[87] Later in the year, the *Liga Central* organized as part of its regular Monday night cultural program a series of presentations by Socialist teachers on "The Need to Instruct the Children in School and at Home on the Facts of Life." Urban workers and rural *campesinos* were brought into Mérida, where they were told that it was their duty to learn and then educate their children properly about the functions of their bodies. They were also encouraged to avail themselves of the mobile "sanitary brigades," made up of Socialist doctors and medical students, which the party was now deploying to instruct them on preventive techniques and to attend to the current problems of venereal and other contagious diseases. Nevertheless, it is not surprising that, given Yucatán's traditional agrarian culture, the Socialists had far greater success promoting their *escuelas granjas* than their sex education classes.[88]

Then, in December 1923, shortly before Carrillo's regime fell, Yucatán's already liberal divorce law, stipulating a six-months' residence period in the state, was further liberalized. Divorce was awarded virtually on demand to either party on the grounds of irreconcilable breakdown, and foreigners could obtain one after only a month's residence – provided they hired the services of a Socialist lawyer (i.e., one duly enrolled in one of Carrillo's *ligas*). Yucatán quickly became a haven for well-to-do North Americans seeking a painless release from the bonds of matrimony and was an especially attractive option for those adventurous enough to combine minimal legal trammels with the exotic thrill of visiting the "lost Mayan cities of communist Yucatán."[89]

But there was more involved here than priming the pump of the state's infant tourist industry. Had that been the extent of it, the agro-commercial bourgeoisie, already gaining a firm grip on the new hotel, transportation, and service lines, might have been won over and supported Carrillo's divorce decree. Rather, its members appreciated that Carrillo was waging a relentless campaign against all facets of the Old Regime over which they once held sway. The entire area of women's rights and male–female relations was an especially sensitive one and a symbolic front in the Socialists' struggle with the former rulers of this traditional, characteristically *macho* society. And it was here that Don Felipe struck some of his earliest telling blows. Alvarado had refused to mobilize working-class women. Carrillo, on the other hand, entrusting the organization of the women's sector to his sister, Elvia, and Rosa Torres, both socialist–feminists, had already organized eighteen *ligas feministas* by September 1922 and increased the total to forty-five by March 1923.[90]

In retrospect, it appears that Elvia Carrillo Puerto, who had already become known as *La Monja Roja* ("the Red Nun") in Mexico City for her fierce and tireless dedication to both the Revolution and the women's movement, may have been one of Mexico's most interesting and unsung revolutionaries.[91] Married at thirteen, widowed at twenty-one, and decorated as a "Veteran of the Revolution" shortly thereafter, Doña Elvia founded Yucatán's first women's organization in 1912 when she organized *campesinas* around Motul. Although she read the great revolutionary writers – Marx, Lenin, Gorky – like her brother, she never became a theorist. She would, however, attend over forty workers' congresses and establish a score of feminist organizations during her long career. By 1919, she had founded in Mérida what would become her political legacy, the *Liga Rita Cetina Gutiérrez* (named after one of Yucatán's greatest educators). The *liga* would expand its activities throughout Mexico and direct the Socialists' drive to mobilize women in the Yucatán peninsula. In 1922, backed by the members of the *Liga Rita Cetina* – whom opponents now labeled *sufragistas bolcheviquis* – and by her brother, the governor,[92] Elvia Carrillo became Yucatán's and Mexico's first woman state deputy (and Rosa Torres became a *regidora* – councilwoman – of the Mérida *ayuntamiento*) at a time when women elsewhere in the Republic still lacked citizenship. In 1923, she took part in the Pan-American Women's Congress held in Mexico City and led the radical faction that supported resolutions for birth control, child care centers, support for single mothers, and increased vocational training for women.

These and other more strictly class-oriented objectives made up the essential program around which Elvia's and Rosa Torres's *Liga Rita Cetina* mobilized Yucatecan women in the region's cities, towns, country villages, and hamlets during 1922–1923. The records of the *Liga Central* in Mérida show that although the new *ligas feministas* crisscrossed the entire state, enrolling more than 55,000 working women, organizing efforts were particularly successful outside the henequen zone, in poor areas far removed from Mérida (e.g., in the *partidos* of Valladolid, Tizimín, and Peto), where great numbers of women regularly joined their husbands and sons in the daily work routine.[93] Among the myriad themes and slogans that the *ligas feministas* sought to instill in recent converts, the following seem most representative:[94]

"La fecundidad de la mujer es la maldición del pobre."
(Woman's fertility is the curse of the poor.")

"La mujer que no hace política organizada con los obreros, no obtiene su reivindicación." ("The woman who does not make common political cause with the workers will not receive redress of her own just grievances.")

"La independencia económica es la base de todas las demás." ("Economic independence is the basis of all other freedoms.")

Although the *ligas feministas* lent their full support to Carrillo's rational education, birth control, "defanaticizing," and divorce programs, the governor was not always able to reciprocate by granting their demands. In June 1923, for example, Elvia's petition for mandatory child care centers and increased wages for working women was turned down by Carrillo, who responded that although these demands were just, the government did not immediately have the means to finance them in preference to more pressing socialist objectives. The feminists in Yucatán would make greater headway with their petitions for child care during the Cárdenas period in the late 1930s.[95]

The more than 470 *feminista* and regular Socialist *ligas de resistencia*, in addition to defending and advancing their material interests, also came to provide essential social services that the Church and state for political and/or economic reasons could often no longer provide. Under Carrillo Puerto, more and more local *ligas* adopted colorful political names and flamboyant slogans that indicated the developing sense of pride that characterized the regional revolutionary movement and hinted at the friendly level of competition that existed among the *ligas*. Most often these names celebrated regional, national, and international heroes of the left, as well as historical revolutionary events or movements, for example, *Liga Nachi Cocóm, Liga Ricardo Flores Magón, Liga Emiliano Zapata, Liga Carlos Marx, Liga Máximo Gorki, Liga de los Mártires de Chicago,* and so on.[96] Rural *ligas*, often led by a local *cacique*, might organize the local fiestas that in former times had been directed by *cofradías* (religious brotherhoods). For a time, many of the *ligas* had helped to man Carrillo's ill-fated consumer cooperatives. The *Liga Máximo Gorki* of Itzimná, on the outskirts of Mérida, established an experimental agricultural farm on recently acquired *ejido* land.[97] Mérida's *Liga Edmundo G. Cantón* organized a popular baseball team that barnstormed the peninsula on behalf of the Socialist regime.[98] A Progreso *liga* made up of stevedores opened a successful socialist night school, whose seventy-three students volunteered their time and labor to make repairs on the town hall. The night school movement caught on among a number of other urban *ligas* and was encouraged by the *Liga Central* as a means of combating illiteracy. Literate *ligados* who taught at least two of their fellows to read and write would be inscribed on a list of honor to be displayed at the local *liga* headquarters.[99]

Members' dues supported these local projects as well as the activities of the Socialist Party of the Southeast and its *Liga Central* in Mérida. The party received 20 percent of the income of the local *ligas*. Beginning in 1918, *ligados* paid an initial two-peso membership fee and 1.5 pesos in monthly dues. The postwar economic depression prompted the party to reduce the membership fee to 1 peso and monthly dues to 50 centavos. To bolster revenues, Socialist government employees were asked to contribute a percentage of their wages to the party, according to a sliding scale based on salary level. Party members out of work were excused from dues, but failure to pay them without a valid excuse resulted in expulsion from the party.[100]

During Carrillo's administration, the Socialist Party of the Southeast and the state government became so fully integrated that it was difficult to tell where the one ended and the other began. The governor remained leader of the party and president of the *Liga Central de Resistencia*. The local *ligas* were now, practically speaking, the constituent units and instruments of both the party and the government. Whereas General Alvarado, the bourgeois populist, had sought the unity of government, party, and syndicate for the pupose of conciliating class differences, Carrillo, the Marxist revolutionary, utilized this organizational framework as a powerful weapon in the class struggle.[101]

Yet Carrillo regarded the *ligas* as more than a political instrument. Ideally, they would reach out and touch every aspect of regional life. Shortly before his death, Don Felipe elaborated this holistic vision:

> The *liga* is more than a political party, more than an educational institution, and more than an instrument of local government. It is all of these combined. It is an instrument for the rejuvenation of the Maya and his culture; it gives him the power he needs to carry out a broad social program . . . The *ligas* are Yucatán . . . They are an instrument for spiritual growth.[102]

It was in this spirit, as a vehicle for the *campesino's* liberation and the renaissance of his culture, that the *ligas de resistencia* were most innovative. Under Carrillo's direction, *liga* officials worked first to

Assembly of the *liga de resistencia*, Temax, 1923.

wean the Maya *campesino* away from the traditional institutions of the Old Regime. Local leaders were instructed to paint all church (and public) buildings red. In keeping with Carrillo's commandment that *Yucatecos* should "flee from the Church as if from a plague," a manipulation of symbols was to be encouraged for ideological purposes. Thus, the red equilateral triangle, the logo of the Socialist Party, would replace the cross, and "socialist marriages and baptisms" – complete with red floral arrangements and orchestrations of "The Marseillaise" and "The International" – would supersede the traditional Catholic versions of these sacraments.[103] Ernest Gruening, who visited Yucatán during Carrillo Puerto's governorship, was impressed by the *campesinos'* "homage to the color [red] that . . . represented the symbol of a *new religion*."[104] Carrillo, on the other hand, was under no such illusion. Unlike Alvarado, he had not underestimated the strength and vitality of the people's folk Catholic tradition. His strategy had been to work within the tradition and merely substitute new Socialist symbols for time-worn Catholic ones. On a variety of occasions in the Socialist press and at party events, the representatives of the Church were denounced but the message of Christianity was affirmed. Marxism and Christianity were held up as two ideologies that sought the betterment of the collectivity. In an open letter to Archbishop Martín Tritschler y Córdoba, published in the party paper, *El Popular*, Don Felipe took the monsignor and his subordinates to task because "none of you have been true to your great mission . . . of imitating our beloved master and lord, Jesus Christ, one of the world's first socialists, who imbued working people with love and duty."[105]

Because he perceived that the Church in Yucatán posed no political threat to the Revolution, as it did elsewhere in Mexico, he adopted a more moderate policy toward it than his rabidly anticlerical predecessor. The result, he proudly boasted, was that the *Liga Central* was "more vitally a spiritual institution than the Church ever was."[106] Yet, many of the Socialist leaders and local *caciques* were not as restrained in their campaign against the clergy as Carrillo and engaged in destructive acts reminiscent of those of Alvarado's federals. Quite likely, Carrillo's politico-religious syncretism, served up as it was by *caciques* and party middlemen, confused or angered large numbers of Yucatán's devout *campesinos*.[107]

More successful was the encouragement that the party gave to the teaching of Maya language and art forms. Every effort was made to instill in the *ligados* a sense of pride in the great cultural tradition to which they were heir. Local officials were responsible for scheduling weekly cultural programs on these themes, to be known as *lunes rojos* ("red Mondays"). According to Socialist accounts, the Monday night functions became popular events on the local calendar. Close to 1,000 regularly attended in Mérida, and it was not uncommon for 200 to 500 *campesinos* to appear in the municipal seats and larger villages.[108]

Liga chiefs were also called upon to organize communal work details to begin construction on serviceable roads to the largely inaccessible, classical Maya ruins of Chichén Itzá and Uxmal, both of which Carrillo was now working to restore in collaboration with a team of archaeologists from the Carnegie Institution.[109] For his own part, Carrillo Puerto commissioned and desseminated local editions of the *Chilám Balám* and *Popul Vuh*, the sacred books of the Yucatecan and Quiché (highland) Maya, the latter of which had been relatively unknown in this peninsula. Moreover, to bind himself more directly to this usable past, Don Felipe propagated the notion among his subordinate chiefs that he was a direct descendant of Nachi Cocóm, the Maya noble who, like Cuauhtémoc, had fiercely resisted Spanish conquest and come to be regarded as a symbol of regional pride and autonomy. The claim was based on the fact that Carrillo's ancestors had come from Sotuta, the approximate locale of the old *cacicazgo* of the Cocomes. Tenuous to begin with, the claim was severely undercut by Don Felipe's six-foot frame, green eyes, and distinctly white appearance – hardly the best advertisements of Maya ancestry.[110] Of course, Carrillo appreciated that rational and factual content need hardly be the stuff from which useful mythology is fashioned.

Carrillo realized the importance of myth as an essential element in the organizing process and in sustaining the Yucatecan *campesinado* during what might be a long political battle. One of the greatest obstacles to revolutionary change was routine itself. Like latter-day Mexican politicians, Don Felipe knew that well-chosen myths, with their promise and optimism, could mobilize *campesinos* burdened by ceaseless drudgery. Moreover (and also like his successors), he appreciated that myths required constant attention and reinforcement. Carrillo's repeated use of Maya myths and symbols was calculated with great care. He hoped to reclaim for the

Communal project for road improvement, *liga de resistencia*, Temax, 1923.

Indian masses the revolutionary tradition they had established in conquest times (Nachi Cocóm), which developed through a series of rebellions during the colonial period (e.g., Jacinto Canek, 1781) and culminated in the mid-nineteenth-century Caste War. Carrillo Puerto astutely realized that, given the Indian *campesino's* economically impoverished and culturally despised position, the development of ethnic pride would also work simultaneously to promote class consciousness.

In view of the close relationship that Governor Carrillo established with the Maya *campesinos*, it seems ironic that his government would stumble in its relations with the urban proletariat, the traditional ally of Marxist revolutionaries. In many respects, Carrillo's attitude toward the longshoremen, railroad workers, electricians, service workers, and artisans who formed the urban labor movement constituted a virtual mirror image of Alvarado's policy. Carrillo's cultural background and political experiences in Yucatán and Morelos promoted in him a warmth and affinity for *campesinos* that he never developed for the urban workers. Whereas Alvarado had early signaled his intention to make the urban proletariat his chief civilian auxiliary, Carrillo Puerto had opted to use the agrarian sector as his power base. Under Alvarado's patronage and during a period of economic boom, the organized working class of Mérida and Progreso had prospered and grown accustomed to high wages, whereas material conditions in the agrarian sector had improved much more slowly. Now, during an extended period of economic recession, the urban workers refused to halt their escalating wage demands and bristled at attempts to lay off temporarily members of an already inflated work force. Moreover, far from collectively evidencing any solidarity with the *jornaleros* of the agrarian sector, many made no secret of their contempt for the *campesinos*, whom they regarded as masses of "imperfectly civilized Indians." [111]

Governor Carrillo especially resented the powerful and independent *Federación Obrera* that controlled the Progreso wharves and, along with the *Liga Obrera de Ferrocarrileros*, refused to affiliate with the party's *Liga Central de Resistencia*. Both organizations had been formed at the end of the Porfiriato, and in each case, the founders included Spanish anarchists and anarcho-syndicalists who had settled in the peninsula. These stevedores and railroad workers jealously guarded their autonomy and, although they had cooperated with Alvarado, now resisted Carrillo's attempts to incorporate them into his regional political machine. [112] Carrillo's close links with his national patrons, Calles and Obregón, obliged him to promote organizing efforts in the peninsula by the *Confederación Regional Obrera Mexicana* (CROM), led by *Callista* Luis Morones. Morones had already acquired a reputation for corrupt bossism that would only darken with time; moreover, the CROM had long since abandoned the anarcho-syndicalist approach of direct action that the leaders of these unions still favored.[113] Thus, the double prospect of tighter control by the state, coupled with Morones's campaign to turn them into CROM affiliates, threatened and angered these railwaymen and dockworkers, who had proven their ability to look after themselves. The Progreso stevedores had independently established a close relationship with the equally autonomous and combative longshoremen of Veracruz. By 1921 there was, practically speaking, a Gulf union of dockworkers, although never formalized.

As economic conditions deteriorated, tensions between the governor and the unions grew. Following the great henequen bust of 1919, government advisors had recommended that only 500 stevedores be retained to handle the reduced commercial traffic, whereas arrangements in 1922 provided work for the *Federación Obrera's* full 2,000 members. A variety of complaints were brought before Carrillo by disgruntled businessmen and travelers regarding the high tariffs and unreasonable attitude of the Progreso longshoremen. The *Federación Obrera*, it was charged, would divide and subdivide the work of loading and unloading freight into a mosaic of tasks and then overcharge on each of them. One member union raised and lowered freight from the ship's hold into a lighter; another transported it from the lighter to the dock; a third raised or lowered it onto or from the pier; a fourth moved it on the pier; still others moved it on land. Visiting Progreso in the early 1920s, foreign traveler Thomas Gann marveled at the *Federación's* edict that forbade passengers to carry hand baggage the quarter-mile from the custom house on the pier to the railway station, then exacted $10 for the privilege. He left muttering that the port might aptly be renamed "Retrogreso"![114]

Similar problems plagued the state-controlled railroads. By late 1921, the *Ferrocarriles Unidos de Yucatán* was deeply in debt to a group of British bankers and owed 50,000 pesos in back wages to its featherbedded work force. In a manifesto to the Yucatecan proletariat, Carrillo called upon the railroad and port workers to police themselves and pointed out that their failure to do so would price Yucatecan fiber off the market and place a heavy burden on their fellow workers throughout the state.[115] When they refused to act voluntarily, he moved to undercut them, promoting a rival railroad league (*Liga de Resistencia Torres y Acosta*) with firmer ties to the party, then moving to infiltrate and coopt the renegade Progreso unions.[116] Failing to undermine the cohesive *Federación Obrera*, he set about building a road from Mérida to Telchac (near Motul), where he proposed to establish a rival port, to be manned by the loyal *campesinos* of his home district.

Finally, in mid-1922, the conflict between Governor Carrillo and the unions exploded in violence. By May, the independent *Liga Obrera de Ferrocarrileros* realized that its rival, the *Carrillista Liga de Resistencia Torres y Acosta*, with which it had peacefully coexisted, was now stepping up its organizing activities, determined to drive the *Liga Obrera* out of existence. When the inevitable riot broke out on the railroad shop floor, killing several leaders of the *Carrillista* league and wounding many more of its members, Don Felipe intervened in the conflict. About 100 of the independent union's leaders and members were arrested; one of the leaders was subsequently killed in prison. Making common cause with the embattled railwaymen, the Progreso longshoremen called a general strike, which effectively represented a test of the Socialist Party's strength.[117]

The notorious *huelga de junio* (strike of June) lasted ten days but never succeeded in paralyzing the capital or chief port. Both sides enlisted the support of outside allies. The stevedores of Veracruz lambasted Carrillo and threatened to foment a nationwide dock strike. Yucatán's conservative press, led by Carlos R. Menéndez's *Revista de Yucatán*, supported the walkout and, some observers charged, even drafted the manifestos of the strikers. The Socialist Party, simplistically blaming the conflict on a conspiratorial alliance between a reactionary bourgeoisie and its *sindicatos blancos* (scab unions), recruited the support of Morones's CROM, which sent agents from Mexico City. Street scuffling and gang-style violence marred the duration of the strike.[118]

Ultimately, Carrillo's Socialist Party busted the strike and survived the challenge of its authority. The settlement terms were lenient for the stevedores: They retained their automomy but were forced to sign a pact obliging them "absolutely not to obstruct the work of the Socialist Party of the Southeast nor the government derived therefrom." Carrillo's plan to challenge their power by building a rival port at Telchac would eventually expire after his death early in 1924.[119] The "instigator" of the conflict, the old

Liga Obrera de Ferrocarrileros, was not as fortunate; it was summarily replaced by its *Carrillista* rival, the *Liga de Resistencia Torres y Acosta*.

In retrospect, it seems that Carrillo, intent as he was to establish an omnipotent single party apparatus in Yucatán, resented the threat that the autonomy of these unions posed as much as if not more than their abuses of power, which had harmful economic consequences for the agrarian sector. Like Alvarado, Carrillo ultimately responded to this threat in what has proved to be the tried and true Mexican Revolutionary fashion, confronting the leaders of these maverick unions with an ultimate choice between cooptation or coercion.[120] To the members of those unions that did cooperate and formed *ligas* affiliated with the Socialist Party, Carrillo invoked the principle of retroactive revolution and, whenever possible, sought to implement the broad provisions of Alvarado's Labor Law, which had been updated in its language by Carrillo in 1919 to suggest the inevitability of class struggle.[121]

But what of the financial cost of waging such a social revolution? Could a monocrop region tied to a weak international market afford these and other more radical reforms of the agrarian and henequen export sectors? It is to the economics of Yucatán's ill-fated socialist revolution that we now turn.

8

The ideology and praxis of a socialist revolution: agrarian reform and the henequen industry

> The fortune and misfortune of men can be explained if we remember what connection they have to the land.
>
> —Abreu Gómez, *Canek*

> Without question, the land must be the focal point of our revolution.
>
> —Felipe Carrillo Puerto

Like his close friend and predecessor, Manuel Berzunza, Governor Carrillo soon found that his generous impulses toward his working-class allies and the immediate scope of his revolution would be severely limited by the continuing economic crisis that plagued Yucatán's henequen industry. All revolutions cost money, and socialist revolutions, postulating a radical transformation of a region's social and economic foundations, are especially costly. Moreover, as Carrillo Puerto quickly came to realize, it avails the revolutionary nothing to expropriate and socialize the means of production when those means have ceased to be profitable. If his Socialist regime was to transform and improve the quality of life for the region's masses, it would have to do more than merely capture the means of production; it would have substantially to re-create them and perhaps create new productive capacities as well.[1] Such a task was especially difficult for a region dependent upon a single commodity, even under favorable market conditions.

The task was extraordinarily formidable in 1922. Yucatán's economic fortunes had reached their nadir late in 1921, shortly before Carrillo assumed office. Just before vacating the governorship in January 1922, Berzunza shocked the party faithful by revealing in his annual *informe* the extent to which the henequen industry and the regional economy had fallen since the halcyon wartime period. As bad as 1919 and 1920 had been for the industry, 1921 was worse. Receipts from the export of henequen had fallen by 55 percent, and because all major taxes and revenues were pegged to the price of fiber – which had plummeted from 13.2 cents per kilogram at its highest point late in 1920 to less than 2.2 cents per kilogram at its lowest point in 1921 – the state government's income had fallen in like proportion. The state was forced to operate with well over a million fewer pesos and, despite the fact that expenditures had also been slashed, Yucatán was operating in the red for the first time in memory. However, far more depressing than the export and tax figures was Berzunza's report that henequen production in 1921 was down 332,478 bales from 1920. This alone had cost the state 24,447,350 pesos in export earnings; more importantly, it had seriously weakened Yucatán's future productive capacity, because many existing fields had been abandoned and the prescribed ratio of new plantings had not been met.[2]

The consequences of Yucatán's economic crisis were everywhere apparent. The failure to sell significant amounts of henequen on a still-glutted market meant that, as in the worst days of 1919, there was not enough money within the region to sustain the existing economic services and enterprises of a population of 337,000. More than fifty bankruptcies were reported in urban commerce, with large and medium firms as well as the usual number of small, marginal businesses represented among the casualties. Many more liquidations seemed imminent in Mérida and Progreso, and scores of *tiendas* (small general stores) had gone under in the pueblos and hacienda communities. The planters quipped that "these days a tour of the Maya ruins means a visit to our henequen haciendas."[3] Pueblo leaders and hacienda owners alike petitioned the government for reductions or exemptions from property taxes, because they were unable to meet their current obligations. In several instances, to avoid tax payments, small *hacendados* actually turned their property over to neighboring *campesinos* or attempted to persuade the government to accept land in lieu of cash.[4] The impoverished Socialist government, in virtually every case, rejected these offers and continued to press its demands for money. Yet for varying periods in 1921 and 1922, it found itself behind on rent payments on its buildings, unable to pay the civil servants, policemen, and teachers on its payroll, and defaulting upon its "traditionally sacred" pension obligations to the few remaining "heroes of the Caste War."[5] Dedicated revolutionary *maestros*, who had begun their service in remote rural areas chafing under the political restraints of the more conservative Alvarado regime, now wistfully recalled some of the material advantages of those early days: "Forget the free railroad passes which enabled us to more efficiently carry out our work . . . At least Alvarado gave us enough to get by on!"[6]

Such symptoms of economic privation were, of course, attended by severe political and social consequences. The months immediately prior to Carrillo's election as governor were probably the bloodiest of Yucatán's entire Revolutionary history. During 1921 Carrillo was involved in the final stages of consolidating his alliances with subregional *caciques* and using them to eliminate the Liberal opposition. Contemporary accounts leave little doubt that political violence was compounded in the rural areas by the hunger and want produced by deteriorating economic conditions. Outside the henequen zone, in the remote districts of Sotuta, Espita, and Valladolid, whole *rancherías* (hamlets) and haciendas were evacuated as *cacique* bands engaged in large-scale rustling, looting, burning, and killing. In the Sotuta area, for example, eyewitnesses reported that dead bodies were piled high, to be picked apart by *zopilotes* (vultures) and then thrown into *cenotes* (deep wells).[7] On the western fringes of the henequen zone, near Opichén and Maxcanú, bandits alternately proclaiming themselves Socialists or Liberals plied their trade in the open road on anyone who happened by. In the process, a number of local hacienda administrators, foremen, and workers were assaulted and killed, often by means of a stylized form of beheading.[8] The rural correspondent of Mérida's *Revista de Yucatán*, echoing the fears of the local bourgeoisie, observed (again, with characteristic contempt) that "here in the countryside they're killing each other like dogs."[9] Not long after, an entourage of prominent *Yucatecos* complained to President Obregón that "the lawful citizen has no other guarantee than his own revolver."[10] Outgoing Governor Berzunza was forced to agree with these critics of his Socialist regime. He concluded his 1922 *informe* with the frightening observation, "We are faced with nothing less than the complete paralyzation of business and the dislocation of society."[11]

Confronted with this violence and misery, Carrillo Puerto had become sensitive to the economic constraints that would impede the fulfillment of his comprehensive program early in 1922. Accordingly, in a widely publicized interview with the national press following his inauguration, Carrillo was careful to distinguish between more costly infrastructural and economic goals, which would be achieved only gradually, and more immediate political and social objectives.[12] In the former category, he listed an extensive road building campaign linking haciendas, *rancherías*, and pueblos with *cabeceras* (municipal seats) and *cabeceras* with Mérida; a renovation of the state's aging rail system and the creation of new lines connecting the interior with both the northern Gulf coast and the eastern Caribbean coast; the construction of many more country school buildings; the promotion of self-sufficiency in food staples (as of 1918, Yucatán produced only 30 percent of its food supply);[13] the industrialization and modernization of the henequen industry; and the resumption of the search for oil, suspended by Alvarado, which would make Yucatán less dependent on Mexico and the United States for its energy needs.[14] It is a tribute to Carrillo that, despite the limited time and meager finances available to him, he managed to resuscitate La Industrial and sponsor the establishment of other cordage plants; win recognition from Obregón as Mexico's premier road builder; found a regional university and contribute to the physical growth of Yucatán's school system as well as introduce innovative curriculum changes; and launch a combined Yucatecan–North American venture that located oil deposits in the peninsula. (The oil scheme subsequently caved in when W. R. Grace and Company, the U.S. firm that had agreed to supply the capital and technology, withdrew from the project, fearing that its socialist partner would nullify the existing contract and expropriate the venture once it became reasonably profitable).[15]

Of all the social and political goals that Carrillo earmarked for immediate attention, the most important was his publicized intention to distribute *ejidos* to all of the state's major pueblos within the first year or two of his administration.[16]

Carrillo Puerto's agrarian program: a continuing debate

From his earliest days as an agrarian agitator under Alvarado, Carrillo had demonstrated that the focal point of his social vision was land. During Carrillo's regime, the pace of agrarian reform accelerated to the point where, by 1924, Yucatán had distributed more land than any other state, save perhaps Zapata's Morelos.[17] Yet, surprisingly, Carrillo's land reform and his closely related policy regarding the management of the henequen industry remain the least understood of his programs.[18] To date, the prevailing explanations of Carrillo's agrarian reform have, by and large, been variations of two opposing theses, each of which attempts to adduce an ideological interpretation of Carrillo's activities on the basis of isolated statements that he made without viewing these statements and actions within their total political, social, and economic context. The central point of controversy is Carrillo's attitude toward the henequen industry and his position regarding the expropriation of the henequen hacienda.

According to the first view – by far the more popular one – Carrillo, like Zapata with whom he had worked, was essentially a conservative in agrarian matters, as much the bitter opponent of the highly capitalized, modern henequen plantation as he was the proponent of the traditional Indian village and its communally owned *ejido*.[19] This interpretation holds that Carrillo sought to turn back the clock and restore the *campesino's* former way of life in Yucatán, complete with its village-oriented culture centered on maize-and-beans autarky.[20] Proponents of this view regard Carrillo as an *agrarista–indigenista*, noting that he even adopted for the Yucatecan Socialist Party the anarchist cry of *Tierra y Libertad* ("Land and Liberty"), which became associated with *Zapatismo*. They quote Carrillo's celebrated statement that "henequen is a link in the Indian's oppressive chain of servitude, and it's time we finished with this cactus!"[21] to establish his antipathy to henequen monoculture and the great estate. Carrillo would achieve this end, they reason, by expropriating the *henequenales* and distributing *ejidos* on the *Zapatista* or central Mexican *minifundista* (small plot) model. The extreme expression of this view positing Carrillo's opposition to the henequen industry and his support of an *indigenista* economic autarky based on corn and beans naively suggests that "Carrillo Puerto believed that if the Indians refused to cultivate henequen, the capitalist class – *hacendados*, merchants, manufacturers and foreign imperialists alike – would have to emigrate from the peninsula, leaving the Maya master once again of his own land."[22]

The other major interpretation, virtually the antithesis of the first, suggests that Carrillo Puerto, however much he may have been a champion of the Indian *campesino*, never sought to undermine the henequen industry or even seriously proposed altering the existing system of private ownership. Put another way, it argues that Carrillo, despite his reputation as an agrarian socialist, acted much more in the modernizing bourgeois revolutionary tradition of Salvador Alvarado than in the conservative peasant tradition of Emiliano Zapata.[23] This view writes off Carrillo's famous invective against henequen as merely a mixture of propaganda and pique and contends that on the basis of his other statements and existing accounts, which make no mention of the distribution of *henequenales*, expropriation was never his intention. For "although Carrillo emphasized land distribution to form *ejidos*, which he felt was the 'fundamental contribution of the revolution,' land reform progressed without affecting henequen fields." [24] Carrillo differed from General Alvarado in his much greater commitment to the *ejido* as an institution. Both agreed, however, that until other sources of production could be developed and the regional economy successfully diversified – which both regarded as, at best, a tremendously difficult long-term proposition – Yucatán would be forced to protect and develop its existing fiber assets by every means possible. According to this "pro-henequen" interpretation, Carrillo, like Alvarado, quickly came to realize that expropriation would only further weaken the henequen industry, already beset by severe economic crisis.

Some writers press the comparison with Alvarado even further and suggest that Carrillo also centered his agrarian strategy on a wage solution. These authors place less emphasis on the massive ejidal distribution that he carried out, contending that Yucatán's *campesinado*, although it still looked to land to provide a supplement to wages and for residual cultural or ritual needs, was primarily concerned with obtaining better *jornales* (wages) and working conditions on the plantations. [25] Moreover, they suggest that Yucatán's *campesinos* were never preoccupied either with owning their own commercial-sized henequen properties or with collectively managing expropriated plantations.

It is surprising that neither of these interpretations goes much further than analyzing Felipe Carrillo's ideology, independent of chronological events and the dynamic social, political, and economic structures that shaped them. But if we rely on either of these interpretations, how do we account, on the one hand – in accepting Carrillo's alleged opposition to henequen – for his concerted efforts to resuscitate La Industrial and further industrialize the henequen industry? Or the extensive credit program he began in 1922, assisting *hacendados* to rehabilitate and strengthen their plantations? Or his creation of schools that same year to train *campesinos* and hacienda managers in modern techniques for the cultivation and improvement of henequen fiber? On the other hand, if we accept that where henequen was concerned, Carrillo applied virtually the same solutions as Alvarado, how do we square this strategy with his acknowledged commitment to socialize the means of production? More importantly, how do we explain the significant number of ejidal *dotaciones* (grants), including henequen land, actually distributed by him and Manuel Berzunza during the 1921–1923 period?

At the level of ideology, there is some merit in each of the traditional interpretations. Carrillo was strongly influenced by his encounter with *Zapatismo* and the Indian heritage of rural Yucatán, yet his thinking was hardly shaped by a nostalgic desire to turn his back on the twentieth century and commit himself to a restoration of preindustrial peasant society. He realized, as Alvarado had before him, that Yucatán's present dilemma and its limitations for resolving it were, in large part, shaped by its henequen monoculture. Yet Yucatán could not afford to neglect henequen and, if other economic alternatives and productive relationships were to be cultivated, henequen would provide the means to cultivate them.[26] Thus, like other twentieth-century socialist revolutionaries, Carrillo Puerto had made a synthesis, bringing modern political theories and techniques to bear upon the backwardness and social injustice of his own land. Through his own rather rudimentary understanding of Marxism–Leninism, Carrillo hoped to provide *Yucatecos* with a new way to perceive their society and the means to integrate it fully into the twentieth-century world. His idiosyncratic socialism sought simultaneously to allow Yucatán's *campesinos* to preserve their immediate folk traditions, recover a sense of their past, and gain a belief in change through faith in the power of the working class.

The essential point, however – and one that the conventional interpretations have failed to emphasize – is that Carrillo *was a committed socialist*, and this certainly applied to his agrarian strategy. As an ideology, the "socialism" that emerged during the first revolutionary decade developed out of the anarcho-syndicalism of *Magonismo* and the PLM and tended to blur with the blend of *agrarista* and *indigenista* currents that was *Zapatismo*. Therefore, in experiencing many of these influences and reflecting their impact in his social program, Carrillo was rather typical of the Mexican Revolution's earliest socialists. However, although he quickly became a proponent of the *ejido*, he never lost sight of his goals to collectivize its operation and, ultimately, to socialize the entire notion of property relationships in Yucatán. Carrillo's strategy was predicated upon an intimate lifelong knowledge of the region's particular agrarian structure and the relations of production generated by it.

Carrillo knew, for example, that twentieth-century Yucatán did not possess the basic dichotomy of free villages and dependent hacienda communities that essentially characterized central Mexico. It will be recalled that such a pattern had not existed in the region since Yucatecan fiber had acquired a virtual monopoly of the world market in the late nineteenth century, and the fiber export boom had revolutionized land and labor relations in the countryside. To stimulate henequen's boom, more and more land had been required for fiber production. Invariably the hacienda's gain was the pueblo's loss, and more often than not within the henequen zone, the quantity (and quality) of the villagers' land were forcibly reduced to the point of extinction. Increasingly, the *campesino* was compelled to intensify and lengthen the time he spent working in the planter's fields, in some cases actually moving onto the estate and becoming part of the *hacendado's* resident work force. Other *henequeneros* found it more convenient, because the labor force was dependent in any case, to maintain a numerically smaller resident population, which meant fewer expenditures and obligations in the long run. Prior to the Revolution, this transformation in the relations of production on haciendas had, in effect, worked a boundary change on the mode of production itself, turning Yucatán's henequen zone into a de facto slave society. The Revolution had eliminated this slavery, to be sure, but after the first revolutionary decade, it was abundantly clear that because the pueblo's traditional lands (*ejidos*) had disappeared and the *hacendado* had begun to abolish the custom of making small food plots available to his *peones acasillados*, the general trend for villager and resident worker alike had been an increasing reliance upon wage labor and an increasing proletarianization of rural life.

Don Felipe realized that through the Porfiriato and the first revolutionary decade, this proletarianization of the agrarian sector had not been completed. A number of pueblos, mostly outside the henequen zone, had managed to retain at least a portion of their lands, and some planters continued to provide some form of subsistence plot, if only to keep a ceiling on wages and ensure that *acasillados* would not leave their estates at the first opportunity. However, Carrillo recognized that the majority of Yucatán's villagers, hired out on a semipermanent basis by nearby henequen plantations that over time provided their only significant source of employment, increasingly functioned and came to regard themselves as rural wage earners rather than as peasants. Moreover, the individual nature of the tasks on the henequen plantation – itself closely resembling a factory in the field – did much to reinforce these emerging attitudes. Even outside the henequen zone, the proletarianization of the Yucatecan villager was well advanced. The economic influence of henequen was so pervasive that many villagers in the corn and cattle zones commuted to work inside the henequen zone or performed a variety of henequen-related functions in their own villages.[27]

Carrillo was determined to meet the needs of this emerging rural proletariat, in addition to shaping and raising its aspirations in accordance with his own ideological objectives. He realized that, despite (or because of) the party's earlier halting efforts at rural mobilization, the consciousness of most *campesinos* would be limited to an understanding of oppression at a rather basic level. Their grievances would center primarily on low wages and secondarily on the inflated prices of essential commodities, the inaccessibility of coveted *milpa* plots and, where these were available, the difficulty of retaining them (i.e., eviction, high rents, etc.). Moreover, he knew that, even assuming that money – always in short supply in the early 1920s – did exist for the purpose of bringing in the engineers and personnel necessary to implement the costly systematic expropriation of the henequen plantations that he had in mind, it was highly unlikely that the *campesinos* would enthusiastically endorse such a program. Severely affected by the postwar economic crisis that had wiped out the wage gains achieved under Alvarado, they were now most concerned with maintaining a level of work on the plantations sufficient to sustain them and their families at the subsistence level. And even assuming that they had the capital and the desire, they still lacked the expertise to operate collectively the henequen plantations on which they worked. Finally, each day of economic crisis rendered Carrillo's goal of expropriation and worker management more unthinkable, for as the price of henequen continued to fall, the number of fields that ceased to yield a profit or were gradually removed from production steadily increased. Under these conditions, socialization would be tantamount to rescuing the financially pressed *hacendados* by attaching their former millstone ever more tightly around the neck of an already overburdened *campesinado*.[28]

Therefore, Carrillo knew that he would have to bide his time. His strategy would be governed by opportunities created or denied him by changing economic and political conditions.

Agrarian reform: the first phase

Carrillo sought to implement his land program in two successive although potentially overlapping phases. The first phase, virtually completed before his death, centered on his inaugural promise to distribute *ejidos* systematically to all of the state's pueblos. These distributions were not restricted to the corn and cattle zones, as had especially been the case with previous regimes, but occurred throughout the state (see Figure 6). Moreover, those ejidal distributions that took place within the henequen zone frequently included land cultivated in henequen. Don Felipe's inclusion of *henequenales* in this first phase and, to a much lesser extent, Berzunza's earlier decrees involving some henequen land – both of which have gone unnoticed – seem to have been deliberate tactics and were not employed merely for the purpose of rounding out uneven ejidal parcels. To some extent, Carrillo sought to establish a precedent, launching, in effect, a trial balloon to gauge federal and international responses to the expropriation of privately owned henequen plantations. A more important motive seems to have been his desire to strike selectively at a number of the largest *hacendados* who had abused *campesinos*, failed to comply with his mandatory wage increases, or obstructed previous ejidal distributions.[29]

As president of the Socialist Party of the Southeast, Carrillo had already presided over a significant program of land distribution during the Berzunza governorship, which issued almost 150,000 hectares to twenty-six pueblos from February to December 1921.[30] Now, beginning with the first *dotación* (grant) bestowed several days after his inauguration, an even more ambitious schedule was carried out. From January 1922 until Carrillo's death early in 1924, over 23,000 *campesinos* in seventy-eight additional pueblos received 438,000 hectares in *dotaciones*[31] (see Table 8). These new ejidal villages were representative of every ecological niche and zone of production throughout the state. Carrillo immediately sought to institutionalize the agrarian reform process, setting aside Thursday of each week for declarations of new ejidal grants plus actual deliveries of land. These *jueves agrarios* (agrarian Thursdays), as they became known, were colorful occasions and the best sort of advertisement for Don Felipe's homegrown variety of socialism. Joined by a small entourage of engineers, agronomists, and party leaders, Governor Carrillo would, by some com-

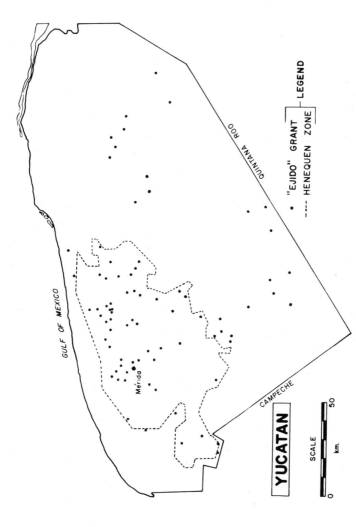

Figure 6. Agrarian reform by provisional decree, 1922–1923. (*El Popular*, 2 Jan. 1923; Archivo General del Estado de Yucatán, Ramo de Tierras, legajo 1 [1917–1929], "Relación de la reforma agraria"; National Archives, *Records of the Department of State Relating to the Internal Affairs of Mexico, 1910–1929*, 812.52/1110.)

Table 8. *Agrarian reform by provisional decree, 1922–1923*

Pueblo	Partido	Date of provisional delivery	Hectares	Recipients
Muxupip	Motul	17 Jan. 1922	5,920	296
Tinúm	Valladolid	19 Jan. 1922	6,060	?
Umán	Hunucmá	30 Jan. 1922	15,040	1,024
Chablekal	Mérida	3 Feb. 1922	4,820	241
Cuzamá	Acanceh	10 Feb. 1922	4,540	227
Pustunich	Ticul	16 Feb. 1922	2,700	125
Yotolín	Ticul	9 Mar. 1922	1,060	53
Mocochá	Tixkokob	16 Mar. 1922	2,060	103
Caucel	Mérida	23 Mar. 1922	5,880	294
Hunucmá	Hunucmá	30 Mar. 1922	23,180	1,159
Citilcúm	Izamal	6 Apr. 1922	2,440	122
Sudzal	Izamal	20 Apr. 1922	3,006	150
Maxcanú	Maxcanú	27 Apr. 1922	24,580	1,229
Papacal	Mérida	4 May 1922	3,200	160
Río Lagartos	Tizimín	11 May 1922	2,380	119
Cepeda	Maxcanú	15 June 1922	3,504	146
Kiní	Motul	22 June 1922	3,144	131
Pocoboch	Tizimín	1 July 1922	2,064	86
Cucholoch	Maxcanú	7 July 1922	2,856	119
Dzonothchel	Peto	27 July 1922	1,128	47
Nolo	Tixkokob	3 Aug. 1922	1,872	78
Kinchil	Hunucmá	11 Aug. 1922	8,000	375
Tixpehual	Tixkokob	17 Aug. 1922	3,894	166
Tixcuncheil	Motul	24 Aug. 1922	1,248	52
Huhí	Sotuta	31 Aug. 1922	8,184	341
Progreso	Peto	7 Sept. 1922	1,320	55
Zavala	Sotuta	14 Sept. 1922	1,176	49
Ticúm	Tekax	21 Sept. 1922	2,916	84
Chicxulub	Tixkokob	28 Sept. 1922	4,944	206
Quintana Roo	Espita	5 Oct. 1922	3,720	155
Tesoco	Valladolid	12 Oct. 1922	1,882	78
Dzidzantúm	Temax	19 Oct. 1922	9,864	511
Muna	Ticul	26 Oct. 1922	25,752	1,073
Halachó	Maxcanú	2 Nov. 1922	19,416	809
Pencuyut	Tekax	9 Nov. 1922	2,664	111
Xalau	Valladolid	16 Nov. 1922	1,992	83
Ixil	Tixkokob	23 Nov. 1922	4,704	196
Sitilpech	Izamal	30 Nov. 1922	2,928	122
Chapab	Ticul	7 Dec. 1922	9,912	413
Mama	Ticul	21 Dec. 1922	6,624	276
Sucilá	Espita	18 Jan. 1923	4,296	179
Tixmeuac	Tekax	25 Jan. 1923	7,440	310
Telchaquillo	Acanceh	1 Feb. 1923	2,880	120

Table 8. (cont.)

Pueblo	Partido	Date of provisional delivery	Hectares	Recipients
Tzucacab	Peto	8 Feb. 1923	3,288	137
Suma	Temax	15 Feb. 1923	4,608	192
Bolón	Hunucmá	22 Feb. 1923	2,520	105
Chuburná	Mérida	1 Mar. 1923	2,248	177
Kanasín	Mérida	8 Mar. 1923	7,248	604
Kantunil	Izamal	15 Mar. 1923	6,336	264
Ticumuy	Acanceh	29 Mar. 1923	7,720	330
Tekit	Ticul	5 Apr. 1923	14,712	613
Dzilám González	Temax	12 Apr. 1923	6,480	424
Temax	Temax	19 Apr. 1923	13,682	690
Tixkokob	Tixkokob	26 Apr. 1923	4,980	249
Cansahcab	Temax	3 May 1923	8,260	780
Mexatunich	Motul	10 May 1923	1,000	50
Koptá	Motul	17 May 1923	680	34
Kancabchén	Motul	24 May 1923	540	27
Tanyá	Motul	31 May 1923	810	54
Kancabal	Motul	7 June 1923	495	33
Acanceh	Acanceh	14 June 1923	6,382	501
Tekantó	Izamal	21 June 1923	4,000	365
Tixkochóh	Izamal	28 June 1923	1,260	63
Tahmek	Izamal	5 July 1923	7,000	350
Cenotillo	Espita	7 July 1923	10,488	437
Ucí	Motul	12 July 1923	1,460	146
Ticul	Ticul	13 July 1923	16,239	1,616
Hocabá	Sotuta	17 July 1923	4,206	370
Cosgaya	Mérida	18 Aug. 1923	744	62
Hoctún	Izamal	23 Aug. 1923	7,250	374
Komchén	Mérida	25 Aug. 1923	3,156	263
Telchac	Motul	30 Aug. 1923	2,300	230
Dzitjá	Mérida	1 Sept. 1923	864	72
Tepakán	Izamal	13 Sept. 1923	4,700	235
Tahcabó	Tizimín	1 Nov. 1923	1,396	50
Molas	Mérida	8 Nov. 1923	2,664	111
Tizimín	Tizimín	22 Nov. 1923	16,900	845
Sucohó	Tizimín	22 Nov. 1923	2,616	109
X-Kinil	Tekax	6 Dec. 1923	2,160	90
Totals			438,866	22,525+

Sources: El Popular, 2 Jan. 1923; Archivo General del Estado de Yucatán, Ramo de Tierras, legajo #1 (1917–1929), "Relación de la reforma agraria"; National Archives, Records of the Department of State Relating to the Internal Affairs of Mexico, 1910–1929, 812.52/1110.

bination of travel, usually including train, horseback, mule-drawn *plataforma* (flat car), and foot, arrive at the selected village, there to be greeted enthusiastically by the new agrarian benefi-ciaries. After story telling, a festive meal, and a series of toasts and mutual compliments, the new *ejidatarios*, accompanied by the governor's party, would make their way to the fields scheduled for delivery. There, amidst great emotion and almost endless oratory, they would receive their ejidal patrimony. Whenever possible, Carrillo himself would bestow the land and deliver the word, usually charging the *ejidatarios* with their new rights and duties in much the same fiery way that he had mobilized *campesinos* in 1915 and 1916. When he was not able to attend, he sent trusted seconds like "the two Rafaels" (Cebada and Gamboa), Maya speak-ers like himself who had also begun their careers as agrarian agi-tators under Alvarado.[32]

The systematic thrust of Carrillo's agrarian reform is revealed in his ingenious series of decrees throughout 1922–1923 that made "pueblos" of each of the state's major population centers, exclud-ing Mérida. Under the terms of Obregón's 1922 Agrarian Code, only towns and villages (i.e., pueblos) possessed the standing (*categoría política*) that enabled them to receive *ejidos*. Yet some-thing had to be done, Carrillo reasoned, for Yucatán's multiplicity of small urban centers (*villas*) and rural settlements (*rancherías*) that, despite the inappropriateness of their current classifications, had at one time or another also lost their lands during the course of the hacienda's expansion. Thus, with a sweep of his pen, Don Felipe equalized their standing under the terms of the agrarian reform and made possible redress via ejidal grant (*dotación*) or restitution (*restitución*).[33] Subsequent *hacendado* protests that urban centers such as Progreso and Izamal were hardly villages, although logically irrefutable, were juridically unavailing. Indeed, so in-tent was Carrillo on carrying out a definitive ejidal distribution that he made agrarian reform mandatory, dispatching agents to force *dotaciones* on pueblos that had shown themselves indifferent or even ill-disposed to receive them.[34]

The speed of the agrarian process similarly provoked consider-able attention and controversy. Previously, during the Carranza regime, pueblos had been obliged to initiate their own *solicitudes* (petitions for agrarian reform), then wait at least several years for state and federal agencies to take action on them. When Berzunza took office in 1921, scores of original *solicitudes* from the 1915–1920 period still had not even been processed by the state's *Comi-*

sión Local Agraria (CLA), let alone turned over to the governor for his "provisional decree." Under Berzunza, much of this backlog was immediately attended to,[35] and Carrillo's first ejidal *dotaciones* represented long overdue action on these cases as well.[36] But Carrillo was bent upon speeding up the agrarian process still further. Rather than content himself with waiting for the majority of Yucatán's pueblos to work up enough nerve to initiate *solicitudes*, Carrillo instructed his government's propaganda and agrarian departments to preempt the initiative, working actively with local leaders to speed up the land distribution process. Then after the CLA – now staffed with Carrillo's trusted subordinates – had arrived at a decision regarding the size and location of an ejidal *dotación*, Carrillo himself would expedite matters by approving the grant immediately, often the same day he received it. Once Carrillo had signed the provisional decree, he remanded the *expediente* (file) over to the CLA which, in turn, instructed the agrarian committee of the pueblo in question to make "provisional delivery" of the lands. This final step was invariably acted out with considerable ceremony during one of Carrillo's *jueves agrarios*.[37]

However, more noteworthy even than the speed with which Carrillo dispatched the provisional decree was the promptness of the actual provisional delivery of land. Traditionally, the governor's provisional resolution had merely been just another step in an extended journey of bureaucratic inconvenience that the *cam-*

Agraristas receive their ejdal grant.

pesino was forced to make and that often ended with the frustration of his demand or a crippling delay in its implementation. Even if the state governor chose to act on the CLA's recommendation for ejidal *dotación* – and he often did not – it would then be sent to Mexico City for further approval by the *Comisión Nacional Agraria* and, ultimately, the president's signature, signifying the "definitive resolution" of the case and instructing delivery of the *ejido*. Not only could the pueblo's *solicitud* be nullified at any point in this interminable chain, but even the president's definitive decree offered no real guarantee that the lands would be promptly delivered. As a final line of defense – indeed, at any point in the process – the *hacendado* had recourse to the *amparo*, a federal court injunction that, if invoked, could seriously delay or derail the agrarian process. During the course of Mexico's agrarian reform, it has not been uncommon for pueblos to wait years, even decades, for such bureaucratic and legal *trámites* (procedures) to be concluded. Many are waiting still.[38]

Carrillo Puerto's stratagem was, whenever possible, to bypass the national agrarian bureaucracy and complete the process at the regional level. To a large extent, he was remarkably successful, especially when henequen fields were not at stake. Rather than wait for the federal agrarian authorities and President Obregón explicitly to confirm his provisional decrees, Carrillo had authorized his state-controlled CLA to proceed with an immediate, although theoretically tentative, distribution of the *ejidos*. *Campesinos* were settled on the land and cautioned to defend it as well as till it. In return, they became loyal supporters of the Socialist regime.

Carrillo's rapid-fire approach had practical drawbacks and negative political and social consequences as well. By invoking the provisional decree to make deliveries he was often overly hasty, distributing lands before a careful study of local conditions and competing claims could be made. As a result, existing rivalries were exacerbated and new ones created, most frequently pitting *cacique* against *cacique*, *liga* against *liga*, and town against town.[39] Other instances were reported in which new "Socialist" *ejidatarios*, manipulated by local *caciques*, invaded the modest neighboring properties of relatively defenseless *rancheros* or small *hacendados*.[40] Finally, Carrillo received a number of complaints from groups of *acasillados* and their *hacendados* – some clearly without foundation but others pressing what appear to be quite legitimate grievances – that recent ejidal distributions had stripped their *fincas* of land traditionally set aside for workers' *milpa* plots or for supplying wood needed to fire the boilers of the hacienda's decorticating plant.[41] However, the records show that once informed of local conflicts and inequities relating to land distribution, Carrillo in most cases immediately worked to rectify them.

At any rate, tactically speaking, there was sound logic in Carrillo's aggressive approach. He reasoned that the Obregón government, which had explicitly committed itself to do more in the agrarian sector than Carranza had done, would be hard pressed to veto his distributions and would be more likely to acquiesce in them once the *campesinos* had actually been given the land. His assumptions were quickly proven correct when the first of a series of *amparo* suits, brought on grounds of the procedural unconstitutionality of Carrillo's distributions, was thrown out by the Mexican Supreme Court early in 1923.[42]

However, in subsequent suits, usually argued by the *hacendados* on much the same procedural grounds but specifically protesting the distribution of henequen fields, injunctions were granted to stop the delivery of that portion of the ejidal grant actually cultivated in henequen.[43] Obregón had specified in his 1922 Agrarian Code that productive "agricultural units" growing certain cash crops, including henequen, were to receive special exemption from the regular provisions of the agrarian reform, provided these *pequeñas propiedades* did not exceed 500 hectares. By way of remedy, the federal government and its courts would recommend that, in place of the affected *henequenales*, the planters substitute nearby *tierras incultas* or *monte* land in the amount originally specified by the ejidal decree.[44] Late in 1922 and throughout 1923, Carrillo and Berzunza watched as, one by one, the Supreme Court nullified the *dotaciones* that represented their first attempt to expropriate henequen fields.[45]

However, an expropriation of the henequen plantations does not seem to have been a central objective of what Carrillo viewed merely as the first stage of his agrarian program. It should be noted, for example, that no attempt was made to define the hacienda communities as villages and thereby distribute *ejidos* to *acasillados*. The Constitutionalists had made no provision for these resident workers to share in the agrarian reform, either in Article 27 of the 1917 Constitution or in Obregón's Agrarian Code of 1922 – and there would be none until Lázaro Cárdenas revamped the Agrarian Code in 1934. Carrillo realized that he would have to work slowly and indirectly, bending the existing system in subtle ways to achieve his ends. Thus, during the first phase of his agrarian strategy, he bided his time, operating within the guidelines of Obregón's moderate Agrarian Code, attempting only to redress the obvious grievances of some pueblos that had been despoiled of their lands during the Porfiriato and to satisfy the basic desire and need for land that other Yucatecan villages shared with their counterparts throughout Mexico in the early 1920s. He recognized that land constituted only one of the grievances of the *campesinos* within the henequen zone, and for the majority of increasingly proletarianized villagers – as well as for the *acasillados* – it was secondary to the issue of wages. But for many of the remote, propertyless pueblos outside the henequen zone, land had long been the central demand, and Carrillo saw that an ejidal distribution essentially following the central Mexican model would satisfy the most basic needs of these impoverished maize farmers.

Yet, even in the distant pueblos on the periphery of the state, Don Felipe was not prepared to abandon these new *ejidatarios* entirely to the pattern of individual parcelization and *minifundismo* that was already beginning to characterize the ejidal villages throughout much of central Mexico. Almost immediately on the heels of land distribution, Carrillo sent teams of agronomists and propagandists into the corn and cattle zones to introduce strategies and techniques for the cooperative cultivation and marketing of the *ejidatarios'* crops. Carrillo was convinced, for example, that large-scale producer cooperatives might restore Yucatán's former capacity to produce cane sugar in the southern and southeastern parts of the state.[46] Similarly, he advocated the creation of large-scale cattle cooperatives, especially among the new *ejidatarios* in the rich grazing areas of central and eastern Yucatán.[47]

Carrillo recognized that large producer cooperatives would be less applicable in distant and isolated pueblos devoted solely to maize production. However, even here he attempted to encourage *milperos* to form collective marketing organizations to bargain more effectively with local merchants. Moreover, in an effort to move closer to his long-range goal of enabling Yucatán to feed itself, Carrillo dusted off the Constitutionalists' little-invoked *Ley de Tierras Ociosas* (Idle Lands Law), which allowed *campesinos* waiting to obtain their own *ejidos* to work lands left uncultivated by neighboring haciendas. After the first year of his administration, Carrillo was able to report that, whereas levels of maize production had steadily declined over the preceding decade, some 640 hec-

A family of agrarian beneficiaries on a cattle cooperative.

tares of new *milpa* land had been harvested in 1922, and a more substantial increase in production could be expected in 1923.[48]

Thus, in each of the cases mentioned, Carrillo sought to diversify and, ultimately, to collectivize regional production in areas not suitable for the cultivation of henequen. Although he restricted himself to selling his new *ejidatarios* only on the notion of large, state-subsidized producer cooperatives, it is clear, certainly in the case of sugar, that he envisioned the state-supported cooperative as both an incentive and an important first step toward the formation of socialized, worker-managed collective farms.[49]

Within the henequen zone, Carrillo Puerto's strategy was even more dependent upon a waiting game. He distributed *ejidos* to a number of pueblos and, although some *henequenales* had been affected, these had not been extensive and had come at the expense of a few selected targets, in each case one of the region's largest *hacendados*. They could not be said, therefore, to have significantly weakened further an already depressed industry. Moreover, the federal government seemed systematically intent upon nullifying these expropriations.

Indeed, far from being "antihenequen," Carrillo seemed bent upon doing everything within his limited financial means to maintain the productive capacity of the plantations and stimulate the industry in the midst of its economic crisis. In the style of Alvarado, he made sizable loans (approximately 1 million pesos' worth) to planters to maintain their fields, make new plantings, and improve the quality of their fiber through the acquisition of more modern decorticating machinery.[50] Also like Alvarado, he tightened security measures and authorized stiff penalties to guard against the careless burning of *henequenales* by *milperos*, in addition to directing the Socialist *ligas* and town councils to provide immediate aid when fires did break out.[51] In various instances, Carrillo went out of his way to advise planters how they could continue operations in the face of impending agrarian distributions. For example, he issued a circular decreeing that until his government could determine how much uncultivated land the henequen haciendas required to provide wood for their rasping plants, *henequeneros* would be allowed to cut on affected land, following its delivery and prior to clearing by the *ejidatarios*. Moreover, these new *ejidatarios* were enjoined from cutting wood on their new *ejidos* for sale to the railroads if local planters needed it, and specific provisions were made, in some cases, to substitute vacant land elsewhere if ejidal land was urgently required by *henequeneros* to obtain wood.[52]

Carrillo also indirectly looked after the planters' interests in undertaking a number of measures designed to strengthen the long-term prospects of the henequen industry. In 1923 he set up a school to train prospective hacienda administrators and foremen, thereby hoping to ensure a skilled group of future technocrats to manage the productive aspects of the industry.[53] A year earlier he had resurrected Alvarado's defunct cordage plant, La Industrial (now La Nueva Industrial), and subsidized the creation of newer *cordelerías* such as Mayapán and San Juan. Carrillo encouraged these factories to operate around the clock as he renewed Alvarado's campaign for industrialization, now more necessary than ever, considering the glut of raw fiber on the market.[54] In conjunction with the *hacendados' Liga de Acción Social*, Carrillo's government sponsored contests for the invention of new machinery for the manufacture of finished henequen goods, especially those that utilized the waste materials discarded at the decorticating plants.[55]

Yet Governor Carrillo did not expect that these efforts at industrialization, aimed largely at a small domestic market, and other long-range attempts to develop new raw fiber markets in Russia, Europe, and South America[56] would significantly reduce Yucatán's current surplus stock. He had been forced, early in 1922, to implement the first restrictive measures on production in the fifty-year history of the henequen industry. It was predictable that with money in especially short supply and sales increasingly infrequent, the measure would be very unpopular with the *henequeneros*, large and small alike. The former were rankled because the decree was designed to place the greatest restrictions on the largest producers in an attempt to keep the smaller planters from going under completely.[57]

Carrillo moved to mitigate the planters' disappointment in a variety of ways. First of all, he increased the loan fund already available to tide them over the period of restriction. Once again, this worked to the advantage of the smaller producers, whose only other recourse to cash or credit was Montes and his associates. Without apologizing for his restrictive policy, Carrillo told the *hacendados* that quite likely they had not seen the last of restriction, so they had better adjust to it by supporting his government's attempts to match regional supply with present and projected trends in world demand.[58] Carrillo's prophecy would be borne out as the temporary downward movement in fiber prices of the late 1910s and early 1920s became a secular trend in the late 1920s, 1930s, and early 1940s and restrictive decrees became a regular feature of the region's economic life.[59]

Secondly, Carrillo raised the price a substantial 1.1 cents per kilogram on the quotas of fiber that producers would deliver to the government's *Comisión Exportadora* (Carrillo's new name for what had essentially been the reincarnation, in July 1921, of Alvarado's former *Reguladora* monopoly).[60] And finally, in an attempt to build faith, Carrillo named one of the *hacendados'* own, Tomás Castellanos Acevedo, as the new managing director (*gerente*) of the *Exportadora*. This was a highly controversial move and drew great criticism from the radical wing of the Socialist Party. Castellanos Acevedo was recognized in Yucatecan society as a financial genius and had been the prime mover behind the first *Reguladora* of 1912. However, it was felt that his nickname, *El Financiero*, also suggested a predilection for commercial speculation and a nose for business transactions of more dubious repute. He had served Olegario Molina well as Mérida's *jefe político* and, as recently as 1918, had been harried out of the state by General Alvarado for instigating the creation of the politically subversive *Asociación de Hacendados Henequeneros*.[61]

Yet El Financiero was not the first "reactionary" to serve in

Carrillo's administration. Ricardo Molina and Felipe G. Cantón had previously served the Socialists, the former as an overseas agent for the *Exportadora*, the latter as a consultant for the government's project to develop a viable tourist industry.[62] In each case, Carrillo had been forced to turn to these prominent members of the regional bourgeoisie because they possessed technical expertise in essential economic areas that his Socialist advisors could not provide. Carrillo's incongruous alliance with "that renowned technocrat, El Financiero,"[63] seems to represent one instance in Yucatán's revolutionary experience in which elite recruitment actually benefited the revolutionary regime. Castellanos worked to ensure that the *Comisión Exportadora* did not repeat some of the "unfortunate excesses" of Alvarado's *Reguladora*, most notably an unrealistic pricing policy and an unnecessary hostility vis-à-vis Yucatán's North American buyers. Moreover, in addition to mediating disputes with the *hacendado* community, Castellanos also served as a valuable liaison with the international banking community, securing several important loans at good terms that removed some of the burden from the financially straitened Socialist regime.[64]

Thus, where the henequen zone was concerned, Carrillo had primarily concentrated upon satisfying land grievances and – within the limits imposed by a strained economy – had done so while simultaneously attempting to maintain the productive capacity of the plantations and hold the line against further deterioration of agricultural wages. Following the beginning of the recession in 1919, hacienda *jornales* had been the first to be cut back and, by 1920, the rural worker's real wages were estimated to be about what they had been in 1915 before Alvarado's arrival.[65] During the 1919–1921 period, prior to the Berzunza governorship, agricultural wage levels had not been controlled but rather left to fluctuate at the discretion of the *hacendados*. The Socialists had subsequently reinstituted Alvarado's former policy of pegging the worker's *jornal* to the price of henequen while carefully guarding against the kinds of labor abuses (underpayment, the use of scrip, forced communal labor, etc.) that had recurred under the brief rule of the Liberals during 1919–1920. Moreover, as we have seen, Carrillo had attempted to lower the inflated tariffs commanded by urban labor unions in an effort to distribute the Revolution's gains more equitably among all sectors of the working class while keeping the production and marketing costs of Yucatán's henequen as competitive as possible in a steadily deteriorating market. Yet as long as the price of henequen remained so depressed, there was little his Socialist government – or any government, for that matter – could do to improve the position of Yucatán's emerging rural proletariat, let alone socialize the means of production.

Changing conditions: the regional economy

Toward the end of 1922, however, positive indications on the world fiber market, coinciding with the consolidation of several trends that had been developing over a longer term, gave the Socialists more cause for optimism. In fact, it seems that by mid-1923, Carrillo had already begun to think in terms of implementing the second, culminating phase of his agrarian strategy, which would turn on the socialization of the henequen plantations.

Throughout Carrillo's political career in Yucatán, he had witnessed great fluctuations in the region's export economy. At first, the developments had been upward and exhilarating. At their highest point in 1918, Yucatán's henequen earnings had soared above the $91 million mark, representing more than a sixfold increase over the export figures for 1912. During the subsequent postwar years, however, the acceleration of the downward trend had been even more striking, and in 1922, henequen receipts were one-fifteenth of what they had been five years earlier:[66]

Year	Henequen exported (in tons)	Value of earnings (in U.S. dollars)
1919	141,414	37,581,495
1920	154,249	30,184,291
1921	100,905	11,878,348
1922	63,979	6,192,557

Carrillo and the Socialist revolutionaries had no way of knowing in 1922 – as we perceive today with the benefit of hindsight – that what appeared to be only a temporary downward trend in the world fiber market would become a more or less permanent condition and that Yucatán's former dominance as a supplier of that market had disappeared forever. Rather, the Socialists (like their more conservative predecessors of the late nineteenth and early twentieth centuries) were determined to ride out the immediate crisis, and, when afforded the right economic opening, to initiate their long-term revolutionary strategy.

Indications began to appear late in 1922 that the long-awaited break in the crisis was near. In July, the *Comisión Exportadora's* agents in New York and Chicago had informed Castellanos Acevedo that the original 800,000 bales of Yucatecan henequen stock, which had been a blight on the market since 1919, were nearly exhausted. North American cordage manufacturers were now planning large fiber purchases to meet a demand for twine generated by a projected bumper grain harvest. Carrillo's decree restricting production had been discontinued some months before, and now the Socialist government announced that a loan fund of 1.5 million pesos would be made available to planters over the next year and a half to stimulate production further.[67] Moreover, anticipating large sales, the *Exportadora* also declared another price increase to planters, in the form of a package arrangement that would raise the *henequeneros' anticipos* (advances) a generous 5.5 cents per kilogram over the coming two-year period.[68] The results of these measures were immediately felt: Production increased dramatically from 461,515 bales in 1922 (the low for the decade, as revealed in Table 9) to a much more respectable 612,768 bales in 1923.

These positive economic signs were viewed as significant revolutionary portents by Carrillo and the Socialists. The radical reforms they had originally promised had bogged down in the economic trough of late 1921 and early 1922. Infrastructural programs such as Carrillo's road building campaign and the restoration of the Maya sites had virtually ground to a halt. There had barely been enough money to train political cadres, continue regular ejidal distributions, and support a minimal educational program, largely because many of the Socialist organizers, agronomists, and teachers had agreed (or been compelled by circumstances) to offer their services at a reduced salary or go for periods without any pay at all.[69] More ambitious goals, such as the expropriation of the henequen plantations, had been shelved indefinitely. In the midst of severe economic crisis, socialization of the plantations had been not only prohibitive in cost but unpopular as well, among both Socialist leaders and *campesinos*. But now, as fiber prices rose, sales were made, and production perked up, Carrillo and his advisors began to take a new hard look at the prevailing political climate and the policy options open to them.

Carrillo was confident that, if and when he did decide to imple-

Table 9. *Trends in Yucatecan henequen production, 1913–1923*

Year	Production (in bales)
1913	950,000
1914	964,862
1915	949,639
1916	1,168,076
1917	733,832
1918	798,862
1919	782,712
1920	936,136
1921	565,424
1922	461,515
1923	612,768

Source: National Archives, Department of State Consular Post Records: Progreso, *Correspondence, 1924,* vol. 7, 861.3, A. P. Rice to Bureau of Agricultural Economics, U.S. Dept. of Agriculture, 20 May. (Figures taken from U.S. Consulate, Progreso, and Peabody and Co. files.)

ment what would amount to a sweeping agrarian revolution from above, he would be able to persuade the *campesinos* in the henequen zone of its benefits. He did not subscribe to the contemporary notion that the Yucatecan *campesino* was by nature a primitive, a reactionary opposed to change.[70] If he clung to traditional beliefs and an established routine, it was because a history of bitter experience and oppression had impressed upon him the importance of being cautious. Yet Don Felipe had already found that the Yucatecan *campesino* was prepared to question the existing order when he was convinced of the advantages to be gained by doing so. Outside the henequen zone, for example, Socialist agronomists had successfully introduced more modern systems of maize cultivation by convincing the *milperos* to use improved strains of seeds. At first the *campesinos* had been reluctant, but when they saw that the experiment produced better yields, they enthusiastically adopted the new system. Similarly, Carrillo's government had had good success in encouraging *campesinos* to organize producing and marketing cooperatives and to support the new *escuelas granjas* by sending their sons to be trained in the new methods.[71]

Carrillo therefore saw no reason why the *campesinos* in the henequen zone, an incipient rural proletariat, would not support an attempt to socialize the plantations and collectivize production.

Of course, he realized that such a program, to be successful, would have to be introduced to rural workers in a way that would gain their trust and implemented, in large part, by the *campesinos* themselves. To promote effective *campesino* participation would require a lengthy transitional period during which the workers of the henequen zone would receive both political education and training in modern agricultural techniques and management. On the basis of his speeches, limited writings, and the thrust of his other social programs, we can deduce that Carrillo had in mind a systematic expropriation of the existing henequen plantations, which would then be kept intact and turned over to the workers who resided on them or commuted to them from nearby villages. There is no indication that Carrillo, mindful as he was of the immediate and potential productive capacity of these economic units, ever contemplated breaking them up and reaggregating them into new economic units based on the central Mexican models of the *ejido* and the *pequeña propiedad* (as President Cárdenas actually did, with disastrous effects, a decade later). Rather, he would convert the plantations into collective farms, owned and operated by the *campesinos* who had traditionally worked them. Moreover, such a solution did not preclude the possibility that the workers might allocate themselves the small *milpa* plots they traditionally coveted to satisfy food and cultural needs.[72]

The Socialists take hold of the region

In assessing the potential support of the *campesinado*, the Socialists were aware that they now possessed a monopoly of political power and violence within the region. Virtually all traces of the former Liberal opposition had been eliminated as Carrillo's Socialist *ligas*, backed and often led by local *caciques*, held sway in even the most remote rural hamlets. To ensure further the social peace and protect Yucatán's traditionally turbulent southeastern border, Carrillo made a point of personally inviting to Mérida, at his government's expense, the most prominent chiefs of the scattered Indian bands of Quintana Roo. For decades, the members of these small, impoverished, indigenous groups, collectively known as *los rebeldes*, had grimly and often fiercely resisted rule by Mérida and Mexico City. Scarcely a season passed in which they were not mentioned in the local press for robbing and killing the *dzules* (whites), mostly *chicleros* (chicle gatherers) and itinerant peddlers, who ventured into their isolated domains. The resistance of some of these tribal fragments dated back to the mid-nineteenth century and the final days of the Caste War, when the *dzules*, aided by Maya auxiliaries (*los pacíficos*) and troops from central Mexico, had reclaimed the Yucatán peninsula from the *rebeldes* and driven them into the dense forests on the frontier.[73] Now, the rude *caciques* of these bands, men such as the legendary warrior "General" Francisco May, traveled periodically to Mérida, there to pose proudly for pictures and chat in Maya with their new friend and ally, *Sucúm Felipe*. Amidst promises of future revolutionary benefits and gifts of Western-style clothes, modern household utensils, and a limited number of shotguns, these Indian chiefs assured the governor that there would be no more violence on the frontier.[74]

As a consequence of the Socialist consolidation of regional power, Yucatán's *hacendados*, and the *Casta Divina* in particular, had been rendered politically impotent. Olegario Molina, as we have seen, not only postponed returning from Havana but transferred a sizable portion of his economic empire to Cuba, investing in land, Cuban sisal, and a variety of other commercial ventures. Avelino Montes had remained in Yucatán but was determined to keep a low profile; accordingly, he turned over the active management of his commercial interests to his son, Alberto. Collectively speaking, the larger *hacendados* gave every impression of being cowed by Carrillo's Socialist Party. In an attempt to curry favor with the new Socialist governor in January 1922, a number of the wealthiest planters had bid to host Don Felipe's inaugural celebration on their *fincas*. Humberto Peón had won the distinction and, along with other *henequeneros* who were "instructed" to attend, was forced to entertain not only the local Socialist brass but a battery of distinguished international guests including the renowned Italian anarchist, Leon Marvini, and Lenin's appointed representative, Comrade Dr. D. H. Dubrowski.[75] *Diario de Yucatán's* social columnist joked, rather unsympathetically, that the planters, in order to regain some of their lost prestige and project at least the illusion of their former power, might consider forming a local branch of the North American Ku Klux Klan. Decked out in white and armed with official new titles (e.g., *El Gran Brujo* – "the Grand Wizard"), they might pound their breasts and vent their rage clandestinely throughout the countryside.[76]

The large proprietors, although carefully avoiding any statements or posture that might imply active involvement in regional politics and provoke the Socialists' anger, did express their opposition and attempt resistance in other more indirect and subtle ways. Indeed, they had a variety of axes to grind. They were not convinced that the Socialist government was doing everything in its power to reduce the exorbitant tariff schedules imposed by the Progreso longshoremen's unions. Moreover, they had complained futilely to President Obregón in September 1922 that in addition to the high cost of handling and moving henequen in and out of the port, there were no less than nine state and federal duties on the product, which ate up their profits. ("Do you think, Mr. President, that there is a fiber anywhere in the world as weighted with taxes as ours?")[77] Furthermore, they resented the cost and inconvenience of bringing *amparo* suits against the government and wondered how long Obregón would continue to uphold their private ownership of the *henequenales*. And even if the Socialists did not move immediately to expropriate their fields, they stood to lose an increasingly greater share of their profits to the workers in the form of wage increases. In response to all of these grievances, they employed a variety of tactics – bribes to agrarian reform officials, layoff of workers, payment in scrip, removal of fields from production, failure to make new plantings[78] – some of which, as we have seen, brought immediate reprisals from Carrillo's government.

The medium and small planters, finding themselves in a much more vulnerable financial position, could not afford to be rebellious. In most cases, they were faced with the sad dilemma of how, and to whom, they would become further indebted. They had the option of continuing to mortgage their properties to Montes and a small circle of other large planter creditors, or they could accept the loans that Carrillo's *Exportadora* was eager to press upon them, thereby signing away all rights to their future fiber production for years to come. Generally speaking, the small planters seemed much less reluctant to go into debt to the Socialists. In fact, late in 1923, amidst erroneous rumors that a free market might be reinstituted, they petitioned Carrillo's government to preserve the *Exportadora*, arguing that only a government monopoly would protect them from becoming "the economic satellites of the larger producers allied with foreign imperialists."[79]

Rapprochement with the United States and Mexico City

Of course, the larger planters had never been content merely to limit themselves to protests at the regional or even national level. In 1921, for example, sensing the futility and perhaps even the risk of protesting, either in Mérida or Mexico City, the Socialists' reestablishment of a state henequen monopoly, they sent a five-man commission directly to Chicago to approach Harvester and the other cordage manufacturers about the possibility of receiving North American economic and diplomatic support.[80] The planters were destined to be disappointed; market considerations and a concerted Socialist policy of rapprochement with the North Americans worked against them. There would be some sentiment among the U.S. buyers early in 1922 for carrying out a temporary boycott of Yucatecan henequen in order to kill off the *Exportadora* before it could become firmly established, but ultimately the scheme would be abandoned.[81]

By and large, Harvester and the lesser manufacturers were content to preserve the status quo, which was now very much in their favor. The price of fiber remained low and the supply was regular, mostly due, prior to 1923, to the continuing glut on the market caused by surplus Yucatecan stock and to the postwar emergence of competing sisal from the British and Dutch colonies in Africa and Asia. A U.S. State Department study in 1922 revealed that North American buyers, and Harvester in particular, were now buying an ever-increasing portion of their fiber from non-Yucatecan sources. According to the study, Harvester's purchases of Filipino manila, which in 1919 had broken the back of Alvarado's *Reguladora*, were being continued in somewhat reduced amounts in the postwar period, along with occasional lots of Asian and African sisal.[82] However, U.S. government fiber experts had been quick to remind the cordage manufacturers that although they might now diversify their fiber purchases, they would continue to regard Yucatán as their primary source of supply because of its close proximity and henequen's low price. Indeed, in 1923, one of these experts pointed out to manufacturers that 80 percent of the raw fiber used in the manufacture of binder twine in the United States still came from Yucatán.[83] And another warned that if price was no longer the greatest problem, "the principal danger for the American grain grower . . . is . . . the possibility of the collapse of the industry in Yucatán to such an extent that there will be totally inadequate supplies of fiber to produce the binder twine necessary for harvesting the crop."[84] The message for Harvester and the other manufacturers was clear: Go easy. This was not the time to attempt, by means of either economic sanctions or diplomatic pressures, to engineer a change in the management of Yucatán's fiber industry for the sake of making it more ideologically palatable for their own tastes or those of their traditional allies, the large planters.

Moreover, Carrillo and his new "fiber technician," Tomás Castellanos Acevedo, were doing everything in their power to promote better relations with the North American buyers than had ever previously existed with a Yucatecan revolutionary government. To a large extent, the Socialists had no choice. Yucatán's dependence on regular fiber sales at the best prices obtainable on a buyer's market promoted a sudden surge of "good will" and the kind of rapprochement in economic dealings with the North Americans that the bourgeois reformist regime of Alvarado had never encouraged during boom conditions. It also seems clear that Carrillo – much as he had done in waging a pro-United States propaganda campaign in the interests of the workers' cooperatives in 1918 – was now attempting to build North American confidence in him as a sane political leader. He hoped that this trust might later reduce foreign opposition to his social program, particularly the future changes he was contemplating for the agrarian sector. In this public relations work, El Financiero was an extremely capable ally and a particularly effective front man in negotiations with the North Americans. Repeatedly, he spoke of "working to harmonize, in so far as possible, the relationship between Yucatecan production and North American consumption."[85] Invariably, at these international dealings in high finance, and in terms that the North American businessmen could understand, Castellanos personally vouched for the integrity and "decided perseverance" of his boss, whose policies in marketing fiber were dedicated solely to the "economic progress and social well-being {of the people of Yucatán}."[86]

By and large, the North Americans were pleased with the Socialists' management of the henequen industry from 1921 to 1923. In fact, the reports of two separate U.S. government investigations conducted by the Departments of Commerce and Agriculture generously praised the pricing policies of Carrillo's *Comisión Exportadora*. The Agriculture Department report candidly admitted that it was not disposed to view with favor a closed monopoly in the marketing of an important primary commodity. However, judging from the results in actual practice, "it {the *Exportadora*} has been much more satisfactory than any method of marketing henequen during the past 15 years at least."[87] The Department of Commerce report independently concurred, concluding that not only had prices to binder twine manufacturers been more stable and in line with those of other hard fibers, but the Yucatecan producers had received a larger percentage of the final price under Carrillo Puerto than they had at any time since 1914.[88]

Not that the manufacturers and the U.S. government had been completely free of fears that Carrillo Puerto might attempt to reinstitute a regime comparable to the one presided over by Alvarado during the war. The *Comisión Exportadora* bore many frightening resemblances to its former incarnation, not the least of which was heavy financial backing by basically the same consortium of North American bankers that had propped up Alvarado's and Castro Morales's *Reguladora*. Although the bankers had adroitly changed their consortium's name several times – the Pan-American Commission Corporation had become the ERIC Corporation in 1920, which, in turn, became the Sisal Sales Corporation in 1922 – the terms of their partnership with the official Yucatecan henequen monopoly had remained basically the same.[89] Early in 1922, State Department Special Agent R. S. Sharp had not been able to restrain his cynicism in a confidential report appraising the terms of the renewed partnership between the bankers and the recently formed *Exportadora*:

> The ERIC has a deal on with this new outfit [the *Exportadora*] by which they [the ERIC, now the Sisal Sales Corporation] have absolute control of the entire . . . crop of sisal, and at all times they hold the sisal in pledge for unpaid promissory notes . . . In other words, these banking institutions . . . have got Yucatán tied up tighter than a bow knot, because they fix the purchase price by contract and they fix the sales price by contract. They catch you coming and going and in addition to that they get a final kick at 'em under the sales contract, because in addition to all that they have gotten before in the shape of increased prices by reason of this control and manipulation, they get 6% commission on the gross amount of all sales made by them for the account of the Comisión Reguladora [sic: *Comisión Exportadora*]. Of course, in the end the American farmer pays the bill . . .[90]

However, some months later, by early 1923, the Socialists had effectively dispelled North American fears. Not only had they kept prices stable but, thanks to Castellanos Acevedo's financial skill, they had independently floated loans providing them with enough capital to buy back much of the surplus stock mortgaged to the bankers, thereby giving Yucatán greater control over its future pricing strategy.[91]

Other potential sources of conflict between the Socialist henequen monopoly and the North American cordage interests were similarly ironed out with a minimum of strain. Early in 1922, for example, Castellanos Acevedo and Carrillo took great pains to ease the somewhat irrational fears of U.S. diplomats and manufacturers that Yucatán's negotiations with potential European buyers represented a German or a communist (i.e., Russian) plot to corner the entire henequen market.[92] The Yucatecans were at a loss to pinpoint the basis for such North American paranoia, inasmuch as the German and Russian cordage industries were still in their infancy and, more importantly, recent trade figures had conclusively documented the firm control of shipping that U.S. interests had achieved following the loss of Yucatán's own henequen fleet in 1919.[93]

The North Americans made some contributions of their own to this conciliatory spirit. Several times during the 1921–1923 period, when Peabody, joined occasionally by other allies, petitioned that coercive action be taken against the Yucatecan government's henequen monopoly for infringing upon its rights as an independent trader to purchase and move fiber, the State Department urged the company to seek redress in the Mexican courts. The U.S. government was joined by the International Harvester Company and its numerous satellites, which advised Peabody to show restraint and accept the inevitability of a closed market, at least for the time being.[94] It should be remembered that a similar grievance, pressed vigorously by both buyers and manufacturers, had come close to triggering armed intervention and the prospect of war in 1914–1915.

If the times had changed with regard to Yucatán's relations with the North American buyers and their government, the same could be said of the region's improved relationship with the Mexican federal government. Here, too, trends that had been developing in the early 1920s seemed to augur well for a realization of the social programs of the Yucatecan revolutionaries. However, Carrillo and the Socialists appreciated that the key factors here would be restraint and a gradual realization of their revolution. For although Obregón and Calles had thus far responded dependably to Carrillo's cultivation of them as benefactors, they had also given a number of unmistakable cues to their client, directing him to move cautiously and with respect. They had backed him up as he consolidated his base of power in the southeast, and Obregón had singled him out for praise as Mexico's "model governor" following his initial road building efforts and distribution of *milpa* land.[95] However, when he had prematurely attempted to strike at the most powerful *hacendados* by expropriating portions of their *henequenales*, Obregón had quietly but firmly rebuked him, impeding and ultimately nullifying these distributions in the courts.

Agrarian reform: launching the second phase

Determined to move slowly but always with his main goals in view, Carrillo presented two major pieces of agrarian legislation in November and December 1923, the import of which has thus far not fully been appreciated. Perhaps this is because the letter of neither law is particularly compelling; only the implications are far-reaching. However, in light of the events that unfolded in the weeks immediately following the decrees, it appears that the significance of Carrillo's legislation was not lost on the *hacendados*. Threatened by what they accurately perceived to be harbingers of an underlying intent to transform the existing agrarian structure, the large planters and their allies, when presented with a strategic opportunity, would mobilize against Carrillo's Socialist regime.

Within the short span of a week (28 November–4 December), Governor Carrillo established legal precedents for a mandatory redistribution of henequen's future profits to the workers; the expropriation of entire haciendas, including henequen plantations; and the collective ownership and operation of these economic units by the workers. The wording of these decrees was often subtle and conciliatory, predicated upon assumptions that the federal government was likely to approve. An initial reading of the first decree, issued on 28 November and entitled *Ley de Incautación y Expropiación de Haciendas Abandonadas* (Law Enabling the Expropriation of Abandoned Haciendas),[96] suggests that Carrillo was merely updating and extending Obregón's own 1920 Law of Idle Lands. The guiding principles behind the 1920 law had been the complementary bourgeois notions of the *pequeña propiedad* and the importance of productive land use that continued to animate Obregón, Calles, and the Sonoran dynasty that ruled Mexico throughout the 1920s and early 1930s. To hit at the unproductive hacienda, Obregón had provided that idle lands could be denounced and then cultivated by prospective individual small holders for prescribed periods of time (in most cases, one year) without payment of rent.[97] Interestingly, Carrillo had been one of the few governors to make extensive use of Obregón's edict, employing it in 1922 and 1923 to open up wider areas to maize cultivation. Now it appeared that with his new law, Don Felipe was proposing to restore abandoned hacienda lands to production and provide badly needed income to the rural workers who had been laid off when hacienda operations had ceased.

However, two important facets of the new law suggested radical departures from Obregón's earlier legislation. First, more than temporary usufructuary privileges would be involved; rather, the lands would be expropriated at nominal compensation. Second, and equally important, the abandoned hacienda lands would be turned over to the workers for collective operation. Indeed, Carrillo concluded his *considerandos*[98] – after being duly persuasive regarding the social obligation of combating waste and augmenting agricultural production – by observing that "the greatest of rights was *la existencia colectiva*," the right to a collective existence based upon the collective ownership and management of property.

The logic behind Carrillo's legislation was consistent from both an ideological and a strategic standpoint. The decree would immediately punish those larger *hacendados* who were using boycott tactics (e.g., work suspensions, planting cutbacks) against his government. Moreover, in the wake of the severe economic crisis, many haciendas would now be abandoned and ripe for picking just as prices were beginning to rise and expropriation and worker control were becoming brighter alternatives. Medium and smaller *hacendados* were especially vulnerable. Many faced outright expropriation of their bankrupt *fincas*. Others, in order to keep them running, would be forced to accelerate the mortgaging of their future fiber crop in order to receive badly needed government credit, thereby falling under de facto Socialist control. Moreover, Carrillo knew that once the property and productive capacity of the rank-and-file planters were under Socialist control, the larger planters would lose a valuable source of economic and political support and would themselves become more vulnerable to future attack by his government.

Carrillo's second piece of legislation underscored the gradualist nature of the Socialists' strategy. Essentially, it provided that 25 percent of all henequen receipts funneled through the *Exportadora* would be turned over to the workers as profits and as credit designed to stimulate henequen "cooperatives."[99] The decree represented the partial fulfillment of a promise Carrillo had made to the henequen workers in his *informe* of January 1923.[100] Noting the recent improvement in fiber prices, he had reassured the *campesinos* that the henequen industry was *una riqueza pública* (a public source of wealth), and not just the patrimony of the wealthy *hacendados*. It would now be the special responsibility of his government, in managing the *Comisión Exportadora*, to give the workers their long-awaited compensation:

> The bitter trials and occasional triumphs of our henequen industry symbolize and reflect the sweat, sacrifice, and hard work exerted by the workers who created it. With this thought in mind, my government will do everything in its power to maintain and strengthen the industry and not vacillate in redistributing an increasing share of its material benefits to the workers.

Here again, however, Carrillo attempted to disguise his true intentions. A quarter share of the profits to start with (over and above that portion of the government's tax revenues that went into its various social welfare programs) did not seem excessively radical. Moreover, Carrillo's explicit emphasis on cooperatives, notwithstanding the fact that he was ultimately pointing toward the establishment of collective farms,once again kept him in line with the federal government's official program. Cooperativism, as a means of balancing or incorporating the energies and demands of labor within an overarching capitalist framework of increasing production without altering the distribution of wealth, has traditionally been one of the characteristic economic institutions adopted by bourgeois revolutions. In their advocacy of the cooperative as a major solution to the complex problems of rural Mexican life in the 1920s and 1930s, the Sonoran caudillos sought to give further form to their ideological conception of reform capitalism. And for the time being, Yucatán's socialists found it convenient to cooperate, camouflaging their agrarian program with the rubric of their powerful national patrons.

9

The failure of revolution from within, 1923–1924

Yucatán is not a self-contained and self-supporting state . . . Any revolutionary movement in Yucatán is doomed to certain failure without strong material aid from outside.

—U.S. Consul to the Secretary of State, 1919

Mexico needs its heroes to survive.

—Rodolfo Usigli, *El Gesticulador* ("The Impersonator")

Less than two weeks after the new expropriation laws were decreed and certainly before any concrete attempts to put them into effect, Yucatán's Socialist government was overthrown. Felipe Carrillo Puerto was a marked man, fleeing eastward across the peninsula in a desperate attempt to make his way to Cuban exile. Little more than a month after the appearance of the decrees, Carrillo and his most trusted aides had been captured and executed, and Yucatán was once again under the rule of a Mexican army of occupation.

The demise of Carrillo Puerto has become a furious controversy in Yucatecan revolutionary historiography. A half-century later, the events surrounding Carrillo's death continue to preoccupy scholars and literati within the peninsula.[1] Explanations for his overthrow fill countless volumes and articles and fall into three potentially overlapping theories (presented here in descending order of plausibility). The first holds that Carrillo's death warrant was bought by the large henequen *hacendados* he was threatening with expropriation. It has been suggested as a corollary that the conspiracy was abetted by the North American corporations whose control of the henequen market Carrillo sought to break.[2] In the second view, Carrillo, essentially a pacifist, allowed himself to be martyred rather than shed the blood of his numerous poorly armed Maya supporters.[3] A third camp holds that Governor Carrillo, consumed by his passion for North American journalist Alma Reed, gave up any prospects of a fight with insurgent federal troops and was captured in his impetuous flight to join his lover.[4]

Most historians have judged the last view to be a bit too fantastic.[5] The martyr version is almost as improbable, because Don Felipe consistently revealed himself as more a pragmatist than a pacifist. Moreover, these polemics over the details of the making of a revolutionary martyr overlook another puzzle, one closer to the heart of the politics of revolution in Yucatán. If Felipe Carrillo Puerto had the organizational backing and military support of the *ligas* – that is, of the legendary "60,000 strong" – how was he so easily defeated by a decidedly smaller federal force, and how was his Socialist regime so quickly dismantled following his death? In order to make sense of all the puzzles of Carrillo's death, we will focus on the vital interests of each of the major actors in the demise of Yucatecan socialism.

Hacendados and insurgent federals

If they still lacked a motive late in 1923, Carrillo's recent agrarian legislation provided the wealthier *hacendados* and propertied classes with an immediate reason to seek his removal. As far as they were concerned, it was now only a matter of time before the Socialists, armed with these new precedents, would initiate a rapid expropriation of their plantations and businesses.[6] Moreover, in addition to being animated by a compelling motive, they were almost simultaneously given the proper instrument and the perfect timing to rid themselves of their socialist nemesis. Once again, as in 1919, forces and events from central Mexico would significantly alter the trajectory of revolutionary history in Yucatán.

On 3 December 1923, only one day after the publication of Carrillo's expropriation decree, Guadalupe Sánchez, the powerful divisional general in Veracruz, pronounced himself in support of Adolfo de la Huerta and against the government of President Obregón. He was soon joined in rebellion by well over half the first-line generals of the Mexican army. De la Huerta, formerly the third member of the Sonoran triumvirate that had supplanted Carranza and taken command of the Constitutionalist Revolution following the Agua Prieta rebellion, had fallen out with Obregón and Calles for a complex set of personal and political reasons, the exact ideological significance of which is still somewhat in doubt. For the most part, it seems that Don Adolfo resented being pushed aside by President Obregón, who, in the latter part of 1923, had designated General Calles his immediate successor.

Moreover, de la Huerta resented the manner in which Obregón's government had conducted Mexico's debt negotiations with the United States, which he felt had served to humiliate him as Mexico's chief negotiator.[7]

De la Huerta's challenge to his former Sonoran allies did not in the long run interfere with the consolidation of their dynasty. Within five months, by late April 1924, the rebellion was quelled. Perhaps its greatest casualty was Yucatecan socialism.

As the rebellion erupted and the Republic's most notable generals and civilian *políticos* were forced to calculate their allegiances and choose sides, early fighting broke out in Veracruz and the Gulf region. Once again, Yucatán found itself cut off from the national capital. Learning of the revolt only days later on 9 December, Carrillo never hesitated in expressing his government's support of Obregón. In the pages of *Tierra*, the official organ of the party, he exhorted *Yucatecos* to unite against the "traitors" in Veracruz.[8] Several days later, he declared martial law and, doubting the continued loyalty of the largely non-Yucatecan federal garrison stationed in the peninsula, urgently requested the *ligas* to prepare themselves for combat.[9]

Meanwhile, the *hacendados* were formulating their own strategy. Following a series of formal meetings and informal gatherings of cliques of the largest producers, a decision had been made to wait and see which side would gain the upper hand in the struggle and then come to terms with it. The *Delahuertista* insurgents consolidated their control over the peninsula with a speed that profoundly shocked Yucatecan society. Yet as rebel federal troops bore down on Mérida, the large planters and merchants made no secret of their preference to deal with the insurgents and sent representatives to parlay with them. For the first time in over two years, the conservative press printed ringing denunciations of Yucatán's one-party system, predicated, in their view, upon a violent Socialist brand of *caciquismo*.[10]

Moreover, the platform of *Delahuertismo*, broad enough in latitude to attract the support of substantial landowners throughout Mexico, had special appeal for the embattled *hacendados* of Yucatán. For although de la Huerta had included a provision for ejidal distribution in his *Plan de Veracruz*, he immediately hedged this with the powerful caveat that grants (*dotaciones* and *restituciones*) would proceed only *cuando fueran legales* (when they were legal). Furthermore, it was clear that his principal emphasis would be placed on the bourgeois notion of the ample, highly capitalized, productive *pequeña propiedad*. Like Obregón, he would grant exemptions in favor of costly export crops such as henequen and, in cases in which properties would be affected for *ejidos*, he promised real rather than theoretical indemnification. It was no coincidence, therefore, that included among the supporters of Adolfo de la Huerta's incipient national movement were a good number of veteran northern revolutionaries and assorted intellectuals who had rejected the *ejido* as a final solution to Mexico's agrarian problem in favor of the *pequeña propiedad*: for example, Antonio I. Villareal, Enrique Estrada and, significantly, Salvador Alvarado.[11] Not surprisingly, then, did the Yucatecan *hacendados* reason that they had much less to fear under future *Delahuertista* rule than they did from the present Socialist regime of Obregón's governor.

The planters also realized that the timing of this conjunction of regional and national political events was of the greatest importance in determining their long-range prospects. Yucatán's temporary isolation from the rest of Mexico could affect them in either of two ways. On the one hand, the political situation might work to strengthen the Socialists' hand, assuming they could maintain themselves in power. Cut off from Obregón's temporizing influence, Carrillo might opportunistically use the national crisis as a *cortina de humo*, a protective smokescreen behind which to socialize the henequen plantations,[12] much as Zapata had used Morelos's isolation during the 1914–1916 period to carry out large-scale expropriations of the sugar plantations. On the other hand, the *cortina de humo* might equally be made to work to their own advantage, providing the *Delahuertistas* triumphed and they could strike a bargain with the insurgents that would immediately put an end to Carrillo, Yucatecan socialism, and the government's henequen monopoly.

For a variety of reasons that we will examine shortly, circumstances and events favored the *Delahuertistas* and their new allies within the regional bourgeoisie. Carrillo's eleventh-hour attempt to coordinate a common defense effort with *Obregonista* leaders in Tabasco and Campeche was nullified by the speed of the insurgents' advance through southeastern Mexico. Despite efforts to keep the federal garrisons stationed in Yucatán and Campeche loyal to Obregón by distributing $150,000 worth of state revenues and *Exportadora* funds among the officers, the troops in Campeche rebelled, and on 12 December 1923 Carrillo was instructed by Obregón to dispatch the Yucatecan garrison to put down the insurrection. [13] All that now remained to defend the state was Carrillo's small, poorly armed police force (approximately 200 men) and the civilian *ligas de resistencia*, whose state of military preparedness was virtually nil. [14] Within hours of its departure for the relief of Campeche, Yucatán's federal garrison had itself mutinied, deposing its trustworthy commander, Colonel Carlos Robinson. Now led by Hermenegildo Rodríguez and Juan Ricárdez Broca, these insurgent federals allied themselves with the *Delahuertista* force controlling Campeche and set off for Mérida to depose Carrillo Puerto. Given advance warning of the impending arrival of the mutinous troops, Governor Carrillo evacuated Mérida in about thirty minutes, accompanied by a detachment of state police, ex-Governor Manuel Berzunza, and a small party of Socialist stalwarts that included several of his brothers. [15]

Over the next nine days – perhaps the most closely chronicled in Yucatecan history [16] – Carrillo fled eastward across the state determined to reach Cuba, from where he would sail to the United States and ultimately link up with the *Obregonista* forces south of the border. He was hotly pursued by the *Delahuertistas*, equally determined to make sure that he did not leave the peninsula. The Socialists commandeered special trains to aid their escape and, when the railroad tracks ran out at the edge of thick bush in the eastern part of the state, horses and mules were obtained from government partisans. At various points along the railroad route, Don Felipe was forced to ask local officials for municipal funds to bribe his police escort, whose members threatened to turn him in unless they received their long-overdue back pay. These local treasuries yielded only a pittance, often less than 10 pesos each. Ultimately, Carrillo and his companions were forced to sell their small arms in order to pay off the constables and send them back to Mérida. At Espita and later at Tizimín, the rail terminus, Carrillo bade all but his closest companions to depart and look to their own safety, which, after strenuously objecting, all but twelve of them did.

The remainder of the flight – subsequently reported by former participants and local writers in a style reminiscent of the apostles' description of Christ's road to Calvary – was filled with additional trials, humiliations, and betrayals. The party was told by the local boss in Valladolid that they would not be welcome there. Traveling on foot across the Quintana Roo border to the northern coast, they found the local Indians suspicious and uncooperative; later, they were sold a small motor boat that proved to be unseaworthy as they were about to make a last attempt to elude their pursuers. Finally, they were captured on 21 December, betrayed by the manager of the El Cuyo estate, who had originally represented himself to be a *Carrillista* and offered his services. Subsequent oral testimony has revealed that the man, Mario Ancona Cirerol, was a member of one of Yucatán's wealthiest planter families, other members of which would soon hold important positions in the new *Delahuertista* regime. [17]

This raises the larger question of planter involvement in the final act of Carrillo's tragedy, the denouement that played itself out in Mérida's Juárez Penitentiary between 23 December 1923 and 3 January 1924, when Carrillo and the twelve were led to the *paredón*. Not surprisingly, those writers who have required explicit and irrefutable documentary evidence – equivalent to the proverbial "smoking pistol" – before they will accept planter culpability in Carrillo's death, have not found it. However, for most writers and for the majority of *Yucatecos* today, it is widely accepted as a part of their revolutionary past that the large *hacendados* played an important role in Carrillo's execution. Indeed, most historical accounts and literary representations of the events hold that, ultimately, the planters were prepared to pay the *Delahuertista* officers more money to liquidate Carrillo than the Socialists could muster to keep him alive. [18]

The arguments of these writers are difficult to refute, because they suggest answers to important questions that otherwise would be difficult to explain. For example, we have seen that *Yucatecos* and their Mexican rulers had always rather strictly adhered to the regional maxim prescribing "Al enemigo que huye, puente de plata" ("Let the enemy be granted a safe road into exile"). [19] Thus, the Constitutionalist generals, including Alvarado, had not harmed Montes during the 1914–1915 period; Carranza and Zamarripa had permitted Carrillo to escape in 1919; Obregón had granted safe conduct to Castro Morales in 1920; and Carrillo had not harmed the major Liberal leaders in subsequent years. There was no logical reason why the *Delahuertista* officers should so desperately have sought to keep Carrillo from leaving the peninsula late in 1923 or executed him at the beginning of 1924. Indeed, to kill him as they did, after abusing him and subjecting him to a kangaroo court, was to create a popular martyr and invite the kind of public outrage that would only be detrimental to their safety and future prospects for ruling the region. Better, it would seem, especially after so easily defeating him, to let him sail peacefully away to Cuba.

The weight of the evidence suggests that Carrillo's death warrant was worth a tidy sum to the *hacendados*, substantially more than the 100,000 pesos that the Socialists had guaranteed to raise for Don Felipe's liberation. The purchasing price most commonly quoted is 200,000 pesos, a plausible figure, inasmuch as the *Unión de Productores de Henequén*, the body representing the largest planters, had collected and earmarked a war chest of 1 million pesos explicitly for "support of the de la Huerta rebellion."[20] At least 50,000 pesos seems to have been offered as an immediate down payment to the insurgent general, Hermenegildo Rodríguez.[21] And, if there is any consensus arising out of the conflicting accounts of Carrillo's death, it is that not only were the *Delahuertistas* hard pressed for money to finance their campaign but both of the insurgent leaders, Generals Rodríguez and Juan Ricárdez Broca, displayed an active desire to use the revolt as a means of establishing personal fortunes.[22] Neither of these opportunistic officers, unlike their divisional superiors (e.g., Alvarado, Estrada, and Sánchez), seems to have answered Don Adolfo's call to revolt for ideological or political reasons or because of personal animosity toward Obregón and Calles.

Moreover, the specific individuals presumed to have made the payoff clearly had special grievances against Carrillo. Some accounts name *henequeneros* Felipe G. Cantón, Felipe G. Solís, and Pastor Campos as the three who raised and delivered the 200,000 pesos to Ricárdez Broca and Rodríguez.[23] Others suggest that the blood money came from a larger ring of conspirators, which included the aforementioned trio plus Gerardo and Lorenzo Manzanilla Montore, Arturo Ponce Cámara, Arcadio Escobedo, Amado Cantón Meneses, and Enrique Cantarell.[24] An examination of the files of *amparo* suits brought against Carrillo's government for its early expropriations (*afectaciones*) of henequen fields (and *monte*) suggests that the Manzanillas, Felipe G. Cantón, and Felipe G. Solís had been special targets of the Socialists and that the other alleged conspirators were planters belonging to powerful family networks[25] who had either been similarly singled out by Carrillo or had a great deal to lose if the state government mounted a future campaign of expropriations in the henequen zone.[26]

According to the testimony of former participants, it was common knowledge, in both elite and government circles, that a dozen or so *hacendados*, including the planters mentioned above, were openly plotting against the regime several days before the insurrection reached Yucatán. Once he had ascertained the identity of the conspirators, Governor Carrillo dispatched a government official to inform one of their number, Arturo Ponce Cámara, that they would be given a grace period of eight hours to leave Mérida and join the opposition in Campeche. That same day, however, Mérida was overrun by the insurgent federals and it was the Socialists, not the *hacendados*, who were forced to flee. Once flushed out by Carrillo, these *henequeneros* were obliged, as a matter of future survival, to do everything they could to ensure against the possibility of Carrillo's return to power in the event *Delahuertismo* was ultimately defeated.[27] Moreover, this was neither the first nor the last time that the large planters would resort to assassination or other forms of violence in order to maintain their privileged position. The 1915 Ortiz Argumedo rebellion and the 1936 riots preceding Cárdenas's sweeping agrarian reform both represent episodes in which mass violence with great loss of life was directed or provoked by the ruling oligarchy to improve or protect its interests.[28]

Several of the alleged conspirators of 1923, not to mention their close relatives, friends, and business associates, went on to play important roles as economic advisors and bureaucrats in the short-lived *Delahuertista* regime, which ruled Yucatán from late December 1923 to April 1924. In gauging the significant influence that the large *hacendados* exerted upon their military allies, it is enough to note that the rebel regime presided over the reinstitution of an open henequen market, outlawed the Socialist Party and its constituent *ligas*, and brought Carrillo's systematic program of ejidal distribution to a virtual halt.[29]

Caciques *and* campesinos

Even assuming, as the evidence seems to warrant, that Carrillo's capture and execution were engineered by *Delahuertista* officers in league with influential *hacendados*, how was this effected so easily if the governor had the support of the legendary 60,000 behind him? The *ligas de resistencia*, the cornerstone of Don Felipe's political edifice, were conceived with a basic organizational flaw that proved fatal when the far-flung network was put to a severe test. In the absence of a thorough political mobilization of the masses, Carrillo had attempted to consolidate his power through local power brokers. Consequently, many of the more than 400 *ligas* that existed in the region on the eve of de la Huerta's revolt in 1923, which gave Carrillo his 60,000 to 90,000, were in reality paper organizations, nominally kept behind him by local *caciques*, with highly inflated membership lists. (After all, Yucatán's population at the time, including infants and children, was only 300,000.) Such an organizational arrangement was well suited to maintain control against internal threats, because it possessed a virtual monopoly of force within the region and its use of violence had been condoned by the Obregón government. But it remained vulnerable to a swift attack from without by a powerful, well-equipped force and/or by defecting federal troops from within the region – both of which occurred in December 1923.

When push came to shove during the de la Huerta revolt, the majority of the irregular bands led by *caciques* proved unreliable; in fact, remarkably few of them mounted even token resistance against the insurgent federals. According to one Mérida newspaper, Carrillo's "Socialist *caciques* fled shamelessly with their tails between their legs."[30] Braulio Euán was the exception proving the rule. From his large western *cacicazgo* in the country around Opichén and Maxcanú, he summoned 200 men for Carrillo Puerto and mounted guerrilla forays on insurgent federals in the area for some time after his caudillo's execution.[31] More common, however, was the behavior of the Vargas brothers and Miguel Ortiz in nearby Muna. These *caciques* found in the de la Huerta revolt an opportunity to liquidate their factional rivals and seize their property. To gain their ends, they had armed the local *campesinado* and declared for Carrillo in the name of Muna's *liga de resistencia*. However, later, when the *Delahuertista* troops closed in, they left the area with their immediate inner circle of supporters, abandoning the local *campesinos* to their fate. Hangings and reprisals followed in the Muna plaza. A short time later, the trio of *caciques* signed on with the *Delahuertistas* to hunt down Socialists and confiscate their property.[32] A number of other local chiefs, such as Loreto Baak, a seasoned campaigner and popular social bandit, immediately took their bands over to the insurgent federals.[33] A contemporary participant has gone so far as to suggest that several of Carrillo's more influential local allies – who remain unnamed – betrayed him, conspiring with a handful of powerful henequen *hacendados* to buy his death warrant from the federals.[34]

Fifteen hundred armed *campesinos* declared for Carrillo in his hometown of Motul, but few assembled spontaneously elsewhere throughout the state, lacking reliable leadership.[35] The fact that these *ligas* declined so rapidly in number and membership and lost sight of their initial social goals in the aftermath of Carrillo's assassination is further proof of the incomplete mobilization that was carried out during the Carrillo Puerto regime, in large part due to the lack of time and an inhibiting internal communications network.[36]

Supporting this "structural" argument is the compelling circumstantial factor of timing. The immediate outbreak of the revolt was unexpected and the speed with which the insurgents traveled through the peninsula worked to exacerbate the internal weaknesses of the regime's defense system, predicated primarily on the *ligas* and a rather small state police force. Less than twenty-four hours after the revolt broke out in Campeche, the rebels had taken Mérida and Progreso, affording Governor Carrillo little time to mobilize his widespread network of poorly armed agrarian *ligas*. In moving first against the peninsula's only significant urban centers, the well-armed insurgents hit Carrillo where he was weakest. The small size of the urban labor movement, coupled with its lack of enthusiastic support for Carrillo, rendered it an ineffective ally in the face of outside invasion and forestalled desperate eleventh-hour plans to form "red workers' battalions."[37]

However, the most tragic revelation that has emerged from Carrillo's failed defense of the region is the stark fact that he had ordered his local leaders to begin full-scale military training and emergency mobilization of the *ligas* only *one day* before the revolt actually broke out in Campeche. In the circular issuing this order, references are made to the lack of organization and discipline that continued to plague the *ligas*.[38] One is left to wonder whether Carrillo's excessive delay in ordering full-scale military preparedness was due to some combination of enemy surprise and colossal oversight (not likely, because Carrillo had expressly taken up the matter of possible military defection with Obregón weeks earlier in Mexico City); to a principled unwillingness to shed *campesino* blood, as traditional accounts hold (why, then, did he ultimately call for mobilization?); or to a growing realization (and resignation) that a defense predicated upon the organizational capacity and military skill of the *ligas* would likely be futile, more so in light of his recent unsuccessful attempt to secure arms shipments from the federal government.[39]

We know that in August 1923, several months before the de la Huerta insurgency, Carrillo told a gathering of Socialist supporters that Obregón's recent praise of Yucatán's "numerous and powerful workers' groups" (i.e., the *ligas*) had greatly exaggerated their actual strength. "Numerous they may be, but they are not very powerful," Governor Carrillo had candidly observed.[40] Even after several years, Carrillo knew that the *ligas* still lacked a unifying class consciousness and any real military training. He went on to confide:

> *Compañeros*, we must consider that there might soon come a time when, for some reason, perhaps due to a relatively insignificant event somewhere else in the Republic, the political situation may change drastically and suddenly, almost overnight, our regime might find itself turned out of power. To guard against this, we must mold the workers into an economic and political force capable of withstanding the threats and hardships which a new regime might pose. Otherwise we will find that all that we have worked for will be overthrown, just as we discovered to our dismay in the terrible time of Zamarripa.[41]

Four months later, when his Socialist regime was actually overtaken by the very political situation that he had foreseen, Carrillo knew that his government could not depend upon the workers' *ligas*. Rather, it would rise or fall on a counterattack against the *Delahuertistas*, waged not with massed troops of poorly armed *ligados* but with small, mobile *cacique* bands. No doubt, he also appreciated that the lack of organization hampering the *ligas* was attributable to poor leadership provided by the local *cacique* – often the founder or president of the *liga* or else the gray eminence behind its activities. The *cacique* depended upon and preferred to exert his force through his smaller band of hand-picked lieutenants and seasoned fighters (*luchadores*). Consequently, these *caciques* were usually not interested, even when guns were available, in arming and training the rural masses who technically comprised the membership of the *ligas*. Governor Carrillo received scores of petitions from groups of *ligados*, asking that they be given back the shotguns they originally lost to Carranza's federals. In addition, he received many more requests to dispatch government instructors for the purpose of teaching *campesinos* how to defend themselves, especially against the bandits (*ladrones*) and rival *caciquillos* who regularly preyed upon them.[42]

The federal government

It is also possible that, in waiting so long, Carrillo might have harbored the faint hope that Obregón and Calles would, if they could, bail him out with arms and reinforcements. This, of course, raises the final larger question of the federal government's abandonment of the Carrillo Puerto regime. Carrillo had visited Obregón and Calles some weeks before the revolt erupted, seeking federal military guarantees for his region in the event of invasion and requesting modern rifles to arm his *ligados*. Obregón had hedged and ultimately denied these requests, minimizing the threat to Carrillo's socialist revolution and arguing that the federal government might be forced to attach its defense priorities to other regions of the Republic that he judged to be more vulnerable than Yucatán. Carrillo immediately returned to Mérida and began negotiations in the United States for the purchase of guns and ammunition – negotiations that were still in progress when the revolt broke out.[43] Ultimately, Obregón did in fact withdraw Yucatán's federal garrison in an attempt to strengthen his deteriorating position in Campeche. Yucatecan writers have charged Obregón and Calles with doing little to aid their loyal governor before and during the insurgency and nothing to rescue or ransom him once he fell into enemy hands.[44] In the absence of hard evidence, we can only speculate about the possibility of a betrayal and the motivations behind one. Certainly, we must consider Carrillo's imminent plans to expropriate the henequen plantations in the face of Mexico City's determined resistance to such a move. Obregón was particularly reluctant to anger the North Americans in the wake of the recent Bucareli Conferences in Mexico City, which had led to U.S. recognition of his government and eased tensions between the nations. The president chose to emphasize agrarian reform only in those areas where North American landowners and market interests would not seriously be affected and where his own substantial properties would not be threatened.[45] Moreover, when we add the threat that Carrillo Puerto's substantial power as a regional caudillo and his growing reputation as a national figure was beginning to pose for Calles and Obregón, we have the basis of a plausible argument as to why these national leaders might have chosen to desert their former client. Following Carrillo's death, Obregón concertedly purged influential *Carrillistas* from positions of power within the Socialist Party of the Southeast, a fact that further substantiates the argument.[46]

Indeed, historians are now beginning to view the Obregón–Calles period, commencing in the early 1920s, as the first significant moment of institutionalization and centralization in the larger development of Mexico's Revolutionary corporatist state.[47]

This was a time when, in order to promote national unity and forge a modern bourgeois state, the central government began systematically to undercut the power and autonomy of the regional caudillos. In certain instances, Mexico City regarded these regional strongmen as being too progressive or extreme. Such was the case with Adalberto Tejeda in Veracruz, Francisco Múgica and Primo Tapia in Michoacán, and Carrillo Puerto, each of whom approximated, in varying degrees, the radical, popular style of leadership that would only later emerge at the national level with Lázaro Cárdenas.[48] In other instances, as with the Cedillo brothers in San Luis Potosí or the Figueroas in Guerrero, the federal government was critical of regional bosses for not being progressive enough, for applying a rude and anachronistic nineteenth-century political style to twentieth-century conditions.[49] In either case, whether it perceived them to be forward- or backward-looking, Mexico City found these independent regional chiefs out of step with its Revolution and, therefore, politically expendable.

The North Americans

Even if the direct involvement of the great *hacendados* in Carrillo's demise seems a virtual certainty, the accomplice role that some writers have ascribed to the planters' traditional allies, the North American corporations, and have even extended to include the U.S. government, is far less certain. Yucatán's relations with the North American cordage interests and their government had undergone a gradual improvement under Carrillo, a by-product in part of the reestablishment of firm North American control over the fiber market and in part of a more conciliatory attitude by Yucatán's Socialist government. On the eve of the de la Huerta revolt, although International Harvester and the other cordage manufacturers would have preferred an open or "free market," they had shown themselves amenable to the prospect of continued coexistence with the Yucatecan government's monopoly agency, the *Comisión Exportadora*. Nor is there any evidence, despite any misgivings that Obregón might have had, that either the corporations or the U.S. government were showing any serious panic in the face of Carrillo's agrarian legislation of November and December 1923. They not only doubted Yucatán's ability to implement radical changes in the face of Mexico City's more conservative stance on agrarian reform but also refused to believe, despite the high level of *hacendado* discontent and the occasional flurry of Marxist rhetoric, that Carrillo was seriously considering such a sweeping program of expropriation in the foreseeable future. The feeling was that Yucatán's Socialists had learned a painful lesson in 1919. Cognizant of the still fragile condition of the export economy, the Socialists would not risk the dangers to long-term fiber-producing capacity that socialization might entail.

Moreover, ultimately, it was only performance that counted with Harvester and the manufacturers. As long as they were receiving cheap fiber at regular intervals, they had few serious qualms about the Yucatecan Socialists, their *Comisión Exportadora*, or the bankers who financed them in North America and were quick to stifle any suggestions of a campaign against the legally constituted government, whether emanating from irate *hacendados* or from independent buyers such as Peabody.[50]

Indeed, it was only *following* Carrillo's assassination and the establishment of a *Delahuertista* government that the situation took on a different complexion. And here we must distinguish the aggressive attitude of the corporations from the more restrained policy of the U.S. government. The problems began when, prior to declaring an open henequen market, the insurgent federals seized control of the *Comisión Exportadora* on 22 December 1923 and appointed Arturo Ponce Cámara and several other *hacendado* merchants to manage the monopoly for the new government. However, several months before, Harvester and the North American manufacturers had contracted with the U.S. agents of Carrillo's government for their entire fiber supply to meet the needs of the 1924 grain harvest. Since mid-1922, in fact, *all* fiber transactions had been consummated through Hanson and Orth, representatives of the Sisal Sales Corporation, Carrillo's North American bankers. Yet now, with the Socialists' defeat, the *Carrillista–Obregonista Exportadora* had lost control of the fiber supply in the peninsula. No amount of friendly cajoling by Castellanos Acevedo, El Financiero (who had escaped to New York), or Hanson and Orth was likely to persuade Harvester and the cordage manufacturers to shut down their factories and wait patiently for Obregón to defeat de la Huerta and deliver the purchased fiber. Militarily, it appeared that Yucatán and the southeast would prove to be the last bastion of *Delahuertismo* and, with each passing month of insurgent rule, the manufacturers grew more desperate for fiber.[51]

Castellanos Acevedo, officials of the Obregón government in Mexico City, and representatives of the North American bankers

(Sisal Sales Corporation), who continued to maintain a lien on some of the fiber for which the Socialists had contracted with Harvester and the manufacturers, did everything in their power to dissuade the latter from buying henequen from the *Exportadora* as long as it remained in rebel hands. *Obregonista* agents warned would-be entrepreneurs that any Mexican national who attempted to sell the fiber that was being stockpiled in Progreso's warehouses would be liable to punitive fines and worse, once "constitutional government" was restored. Mexican shippers and stevedores moving rebel fiber would likewise find themselves *persona non grata* following Yucatán's pacification.[52] For its part, the Sisal Sales Corporation refused to make any deals with Arturo Ponce and the several other henequen commissioners sent to New York by the de la Huerta regime to negotiate a settlement. Moreover, the consortium of bankers issued a reminder to all prospective purchasers that its contract made it the exclusive agent of the original *Exportadora* and warned that shipments made to any other consignee would be attached by the courts.[53]

The money-starved *Delahuertistas* were determined to wring revenue from Yucatán's henequen industry and, if they could not exploit the existing monopoly, they would attempt to profit from revenues obtained within an open market, the arrangement that the large *hacendados* expected them to adopt anyway. At this point, late in February 1924, the rebels' shortage of funds would dovetail nicely with the planters' pressing need to sell fiber and the manufacturers' desperate need to buy it. Reports from Harvester's twine factories indicated that enough fiber remained from old stocks and more expensive foreign sources to keep these plants running only through March; after that, the binder twine supply for the 1924 wheat harvest was in great jeopardy unless large supplies were forthcoming.[54] In a confidential memorandum to the secretary of state, Harvester's attorney, Chandler P. Anderson, observed that a number of the largest planters had managed to avoid going into debt and mortgaging their fiber to the *Exportadora* and were now in a position to sell henequen to the manufacturers on a free market. He urged the U.S. government to press the case for an open market before the Obregón government, which continued to be the only government recognized by the United States. However, he concluded by serving notice that the manufacturers were determined, with or without Obregón's sanction, "to provide the necessary money to carry out a program which will result in a free market."[55]

Obregón's government stubbornly refused to permit the export of any fiber that might profit the rebels' cause. The manufacturers had at first attempted to be reasonable. In January, for example, the Peoria Cordage Company proposed a novel escrow arrangement whereby fiber could be shipped to the United States and payment made into an account earmarked for the "winning side." Neither of the contending Mexican factions would countenance the plan, each claiming exclusive legitimacy to govern and enjoy the revenues from Yucatán's henequen.[56] By mid-February, however, Peoria's stand had stiffened, reflecting the frustration and growing aggressiveness in the industry as a whole. "Permit me to remind you," Peoria's president, E. C. Heidrich, wrote to Secretary of State Charles Evans Hughes,

> that in 1915 the Wilson Administration took action on a basis that was even less secure. At the time, International Harvester Co. had a contract for 100,000 bales sisal, the contract having been made with the Yucatecan Monopoly, and our own Government insisted that Carranza fulfill that contract . . . When he refused, the Gunboat "Georgia" was ordered from Galveston to Progress [*sic*], with instructions to offer the money in payment of sisal, and if not accepted the money was to be dumped on the docks and marines were to go ashore to protect the tars, and the tars were to load the sisal on vessels that were standing at Progress at the time.[57]

When the State Department reminded Heidrich that the marines never actually landed and that a threat had sufficed to convince Carranza to move the fiber, Heidrich reiterated the need for similar action now, noting a "perfect parallel with the current situation . . . [because] once again an arm of the Mexican Government is impeding sisal shipment and . . . the fulfillment of contracts with U.S. binder twine manufacturers."[58] Heidrich was not alone in demanding action. Plymouth Cordage's president, Augustus P. Loring, called upon his close friend (and stockholder), Massachusetts Senator Henry Cabot Lodge, to press for intervention. He noted that the Mexican courts had never given adequate redress in suits against "the soviet in Yucatán"; only direct political action seemed to get results. There was some satisfaction to be gotten, he noted, from the fact that "the decent people shot the Soviet leaders."[59]

On 26 February 1924, Yucatán's *Delahuertista* government abolished the discriminatory tax that had favored the *Exportadora* and declared an open market. Immediately, Harvester sent John

Barrett, its buying agent, to Mérida to purchase fiber on which no government lien existed. By this time, the local economy had been reduced to a state of exhaustion. No sales had been made in almost two months and, in addition to the 50,000 bales of fiber backed up in the warehouses of Progreso and Mérida, another 10,000 were stored on the plantations, with several thousand more being produced each week.[60] Within his first several days in Yucatán, Barrett bought up 45,000 bales; in all, he would purchase 75,000 bales during the *Delahuertista* period, which paid substantial duties to the rebel generals ruling Yucatán. Barrett made no attempt to diversify his purchases, dealing solely with several of the largest planters who had traditionally been Harvester's best clients and totally ignoring those smaller producers who also had some fiber to sell.[61]

However, Harvester had entered the Yucatecan market at its own risk. Earlier, Chandler Anderson had approached the State Department about providing future protection for Harvester's investment in fiber should the *Obregonistas* retake Yucatán and impose stiff penalties on the company for trading with the enemy. Secretary of State Hughes had replied that beyond the protection afforded by international law, the U.S. government would provide no guarantees.[62]

The manufacturers did find the U.S. government more helpful on the problematical issue of shipping. Obregón's threats regarding future reprisals for shippers moving enemy goods had prompted the regular steamship line to suspend service with Progreso while the port was in enemy hands.[63] However, International Harvester was not about to be denied, especially after it had just gone to the trouble of contracting entirely new lots of fiber. Harvester found a ready supporter in Herbert Hoover, now secretary of commerce, who pleaded the case of the manufacturers and the North American farmers before the State Department.[64] Early in March, Secretary of State Hughes agreed that securing an adequate supply of binder twine would be among the nation's first priorities and instructed the American ambassador in Mexico City to "add that further delay in the shipment of sisal which might be caused by acts of the Mexican Government may be accompanied by far reaching effects the significance of which will be fully appreciated by the Mexican Government."[65] By mid-March, the State Department had worked out an arrangement with the National Shipping Board to send U.S. government-owned and -operated vessels to Progreso to move Harvester's fiber. And ultimately, the secretary of state was correct in his assumption that, when the time came, "the Mexican Government would never venture to interfere with the movement of an American government vessel."[66]

Thus, in 1924 as in 1915, the U.S. government, backing up the cordage manufacturers, made it clear that where North American interests and diplomatic attitudes toward Yucatán were concerned, the essential issue continued to be accessibility of fiber. When business operated as usual and henequen was forthcoming, the North Americans did not overly concern themselves with Mexico's or Yucatán's internal politics. When fiber was delayed or withheld, the manufacturing interests rather quickly lost their patience and, although the U.S. government remained somewhat more restrained, it ultimately moved to apply some form of pressure on behalf of those corporations.

Of course, the context and nature of the North American response also changed somewhat over time. In 1915, the gunboat style of diplomacy had been more in vogue than it was in 1924. Moreover, there were a number of other variables that the State Department considered in adopting a more moderate position in 1924. Demand was not quite as great, nor were the manufacturers' stocks quite as low as they had been during the early World War I period. Alternate sources of supply, although costly, were more abundant in 1924. Furthermore, the United States now formally recognized Mexico, whereas only de facto recognition existed in 1915, and it had only just been conferred. The de jure recognition had largely been the result of the recent and sensitive Bucareli Conferences, the successful results of which both nations were now anxious to preserve. By 1924, the United States had built up much greater investments in Mexico, displacing British, German, and other foreign investors in oil and other key extractive and manufacturing industries, and the Bucareli agreements were a major step toward protecting this powerful economic position.[67]

Indeed, following World War I, the United States was undergoing a major transition in its economic development to a corporate form of capital expansion based on the multinational firm. A more modern and conciliatory diplomacy had to be fashioned to protect this economic expansion in Mexico, Latin America, and the developing world in general. Personified by men like Dwight Morrow and Thomas Lamont, this new style of business diplomacy was already emerging in the mid-1920s. Among other things, it was characterized by an emphasis on the importance of not violating the formal political sovereignty of client nations and a belief that international business arrangements should rely on good faith rather than on force whenever possible. Morrow, while U.S. ambassador to Mexico, held that investments resulting in violent sanctions were a failure, an attempt "to save some planks from a shipwreck."[68] Lamont, who, in addition to carrying out diplomatic assignments was for years a partner in J. P. Morgan and on the board of directors of International Harvester, echoed Morrow's maxim that "there is no international sheriff"[69] and censured diplomacy by gunboat as "unrighteous, unworkable, and obsolete."[70] Maximization of profits remained the economic goal, yet the diplomatic means of promoting it would now undergo alteration. Rather than have the United States impose its will on the Mexicans, U.S. diplomats now sought to educate them in the workings, benefits, and culture of a shared international capitalism, which emphasized a blurring of national economic boundaries, a less aggressive national state, the shift from a collectivistic to an individualistic orientation, and a commitment to economic modernization rather than the social redistribution of wealth. With what would be left of the Mexican Revolution, Morrow, Lamont, and the new diplomats reasoned, American business interests could indeed be reconciled.[71]

Aftermath: the cultivation of a revolutionary myth

The sudden manner in which Felipe Carrillo Puerto was defeated and then killed, interrupting a struggle to bring social justice to Yucatán's Maya *campesinos*, would have assured him a privileged position in Mexican Revolutionary mythology even if the official party (PRI) had not taken such an active interest in the care and grooming of his memory. Indeed, in Carrillo's case, the temptation to mythologize is almost irresistible: A progressive leader — revolutionary to some, prophet to others — is foully done to death by members of the reactionary establishment, who purchase his death warrant for the proverbial "thirty pieces of silver" to keep him from preaching a new social gospel to the poor and outcast. Along the way, he suffers repeated betrayals, is subjected to the abuse and mockery of his captors, and is ultimately martyred with exactly twelve of his followers.

Precisely because, over the past several decades, a gradually evolving regional myth has been read back or superimposed upon the events, it has become almost impossible to distinguish Carrillo's actual participation in events from the apocryphal stories about him. For example, did Carrillo, several weeks in advance of his fall, fatalistically vow "not to shed a single drop of blood in defense of my government except my own"?[72] Did he, in desperate flight, actually refuse to destroy the rail or telegraph lines because "my government is one of construction"?[73] Did he, although vehemently protesting the illegality of his trial, and later, when approaching the *paredón* (firing squad), declare that none of his companions should suffer his fate, because he alone was responsible for all that his accusers sought to "impute about my government and my party"?[74] And did he, in fact, blurt out in the instant before the fusillade the paternal words that have since become his epitaph: "No abandonéis a mis indios" ("Don't abandon my Indians")?[75] None of these questions can be answered with any degree of certainty, so much have man and myth become fused.

It is an interesting exercise, however, to trace the development of the elaborate martyrology that has grown up around Carrillo. Initially, the recollections of Don Felipe and the religious imagery that served to fuel the regional myth were provided almost exclusively by close friends, relatives, and local intellectuals, often former Socialist colleagues. However, over time, as Yucatán's Socialist Party lost its autonomy and became the regional machine of Cárdenas's national *Partido Revolucionario Mexicano* (PRM) and, subsequently, of the modern PRI, these ideological tasks were increasingly appropriated and zealously carried out by spokesmen of the official party in Mexico City and Mérida.

It is not surprising that in a region pervaded by such a hardy and resilient tradition of folk Catholicism, the controlling symbols have remained basically religious ones. Seeking to relegitimize Socialist rule following the defeat of *Delahuertismo* in April 1924, Carrillo's successors seem to have concentrated their emphasis upon his execution (martyrdom) and gone on to promise, through the party's agency, to achieve his ultimate vindication (resurrection). To be sure, the Yucatecan Socialists and, later, the national Revolutionary governments did not restrict themselves to the use of religious symbols. Almost immediately, Carrillo was commemorated with phrases such as "the unforgettable comrade of the working man," which is emblazoned on the wall of the National Chamber of Deputies in Mexico City. However, more often than not, he was described as "the immortal apostle (alternately rendered as "martyr" or "saint") of the national proletariat."

In a special memorial issue of a popular magazine, distributed widely throughout the region by the Socialist Party immediately following the ouster of the *Delahuertistas*, the future trend of religious symbolism was clearly established:

> Even the most faithful of his followers denied him three times in his hour of travail, yet did he continue his work, spreading his social doctrine throughout the countryside, ultimately to sanctify it with his own blood . . . Today, however, in the wake of our triumph, the sepulcher swings open and his resurrection is at hand.[76]

Nazarene images pointing up the monumental significance of Carrillo's sacrifice for Yucatán would henceforth be employed to legitimize the rule of the official regional or national party. Subsequent governors and party leaders to a man have claimed for themselves Carrillo's mantle and, anointed as his lineal disciples, have promised to give concrete form to his revolutionary gospel. Carrillo's rhetorical style and content have often been imitated and, when convenient, latter-day Revolutionary governors have toured the state, as he used to do, and occasionally have spoken to the *campesinos* in Maya.

However, almost immediately, the Christlike imagery that Carrillo's political successors began to propagate, began subtly to recast his essential political style, "cleaning up" his personality, as it were, as befitting a proper martyr. After all, Jesus of Nazareth has traditionally been portrayed as a man of peace, not a violent revolutionary; as a gentle teacher, not a political power broker: "Felipe Carrillo was not born for the violence of this period, just as Christ was not born for that of his own time . . . In a society which tolerated the base and the hypocritical, his gentleness and honesty seemed almost childlike."[77] Other Socialist writers joined the chorus by characterizing their recently fallen leader with terms such as *dócil, tranquilo, gentil,* and *utópico.*[78]

Subsequent generations of local and national politicians, writers, and school teachers have reinforced and perpetuated this passive, sacrificial image.[79] The longtime editor of Yucatán's official party newspaper, who has written a number of basic school texts, recalls Carrillo's "noble sacrifice": "that tragic dawn in January . . . when Felipe and his twelve disciples purified with their martyrs' blood and passion our Revolutionary ideals."[80] Another regional party spokesman, commissioned over the past decade to write a number of official histories of the state, cautions against explicit New Testament comparisons, yet still concludes, "like

Jesus of Nazareth, his path led him to the martyr's cross, to the stake of the seven sorrows, to the wall of the five words: 'No abandonéis a mis indios.'"[81]

In light of the recent, almost constant, political discontent in Yucatán's agrarian sector, the perpetuation and constant reinforcement of this exaggerated, ahistorical image of Carrillo Puerto by the spokesmen of the party appears increasingly to be merely part of a concerted campaign of regime maintenance. There is no question that the PRI, in appropriating Carrillo in its propaganda as Yucatán's representative in its unofficial Pantheon of Revolutionary Heroes, in periodically commissioning works of art and sculpture commemorating him, in renaming a number of regional schools and towns (including the capital of the new state of Quintana Roo) after him, and only recently in naming an industrial park and the first worker-owned decorticating plant in his honor, has sought to shore up what little remains of its tarnished popularity and legitimacy in an increasingly hostile region.[82] It would also seem – indeed, many left intellectuals are sure of it – that in portraying the region's greatest political hero and most legitimate personification of the Revolution as a passive and self-sacrificing figure, the regime would be in a better ideological position to defuse rebellious tendencies among Yucatán's restive *campesinos* and command the kind of patience and deference it needs to promote its moderate programs of regional economic development.[83]

Recently, the imagery of the Carrillo Puerto myth has been opportunely invoked on two separate occasions, each of which not only suggests its continuing vitality but also provides insight into the ideological flexibility of the regime and its skillful manipulation of symbols to enhance its legitimacy. The first of these episodes took place in Mexico City.[84] To prepare Yucatecans and Mexicans for the fiftieth anniversary of Don Felipe's death – *El Año de Carrillo Puerto* (1974) – the federal government unveiled an impressive bronze statue of *El Apóstol y Mártir de la Revolución* on 30 August 1973. The event, attended by a personal representative of President Luis Echeverría Álvarez and a host of national and Yucatecan dignitaries, was seized upon as an occasion to curb peninsular regionalism, promote much needed harmony between the federal government and Yucatán, and publicize the economic goals of the "Institutionalized Revolution." One of Yucatán's federal deputies, when called upon to orate, dutifully emphasized the magnitude of Carrillo's sacrifice for all Mexicans, drawing upon the same religious symbolism that has been the rhetorical standard for the past half-century. His speech was immediately followed by a message from President Echeverría, who pointed out that Carrillo, in addition to sacrificing his life for the social goals of the Revolution, had realized, ahead of his time, that "only by sowing the seed of economic progress along with that of social justice" would "a new era dawn for both Yucatán and Mexico." The speeches that followed, alternating Yucatecan and Mexican speakers, praised the Mexican president, comparing him with Yucatán's great martyred governor, and underscored the wisdom of achieving social justice through "economic liberation." One means of obtaining such liberation, it was pointed out, was a firm commitment by Yucatecan entrepreneurs to the development of the peninsula's eastern coast as a deluxe resort area. (What was not emphasized, however – and naturally enough – was the substantial personal investment in the future of Mexico's new "Gold Coast" that had already been made by the Echeverría family.)

The death of Yucatecan student leader Efraín Calderón Lara (*El Charras*) in February 1974 also illustrates the regime's manipulation of the still potent Carrillo Puerto myth.[85] Prior to 1974, law student Calderón Lara had not been regarded very differently from any number of other up-and-coming student leaders throughout Mexico. He skillfully built up a constituency among the students and blue-collar workers that most observers felt would serve him as a power base from which to launch a traditional political career in the Revolutionary Party.[86] Yet, unlike most others, El Charras was not receptive to the efforts made by the regime to woo him. More importantly, despite repeated warnings, he refused to stop organizing nonunion construction workers on sites owned or controlled by important party backers. In mid-February, as his efforts to organize workers into independent unions outside the party's corporatist labor sector were beginning to produce results, Calderón Lara was kidnapped and brutally murdered. On 14 February, amidst rumors that he had been tortured by a goon squad (*matones*), which had only meant to scare him but had gone too far, the remains of his body were found in a vacant field alongside the Escárcega–Carrillo Puerto highway in Quintana Roo after they had been picked over by vultures. Calderón's student comrades claimed that the *matones*, although paid by the interested industrialists, had included members of Mérida's regular constabulary and had been directed by the chief of police himself. Barricading themselves in the buildings of the *Universidad de Yucatán*, the students briefly traded pistol shots with police rifle and machine gun fire, then were forced to submit. The episode continued to smolder for some months but had long since subsided as the anniversary of Carrillo Puerto's death approached in early 1975.[87]

However, on that day, 3 January 1975, groups of students marched through the streets of Mérida, carrying placards and photos of the dead student leader. It was their hope that by reviving his memory, the contradictions of the Revolutionary regime and the injustices that it continued to tolerate in the labor and agrarian sectors would be brought into full view. The demonstration remained a peaceful one and competed for the public's attention with a number of speeches and cultural events sponsored by the State Committee of the PRI. The following day, Mérida's press, although failing to print any of the students' comments, contained summaries of a variety of speeches by regime spokesmen. Several paid tribute to Efraín Calderón Lara, who like Carrillo Puerto had been martyred for his beliefs. One party official observed that Don Felipe would have been proud of young Efraín, in the way that a venerable teacher smiles with satisfaction upon a loyal disciple.[88]

The students were outraged. Previously, they and El Charras had been alternately dismissed or attacked by the media as irresponsible Marxist extremists. Now their former leader, no longer a threat to the regime, could, like Felipe Carrillo Puerto, be posthumously coopted and converted into one of its heroes. Raised to believe that Don Felipe had been Yucatán's greatest revolutionary, a number of these students now found themselves in the position of having to repudiate his memory in order to dissociate themselves from the policies of the Party of the Institutionalized Revolution.

Perhaps equally ironic and representative of the current political reality is the fact that, by and large, it has been Carrillo's fairweather allies (the rural *caciques* and their successors) and the descendants of his most bitter opponents (the *hacendados*) who have, in conjunction with the Revolutionary regime, been highly instrumental in fashioning and perpetuating the historical myth of Felipe Carrillo Puerto. As with Emiliano Zapata, the number of local politicians and notables who claim to have fought the good fight with Don Felipe or to have had some intimate connection with one who did continues to multiply geometrically. And in the half-century that has elapsed since Carrillo's celebrated martyrdom, the local bosses and members of a number of the wealthiest planter families he threatened with expropriation have found their way into the highest circles of the regime. Once there, they have themselves taken a hand in manipulating the protective symbols of the regional revolutionary myth that, although now a bit frayed, still confers a measure of legitimacy upon those who respectfully conjure it.

EPILOGUE

Without revolution, 1924–   :
Yucatán's legacy of frustration

Everywhere in Yucatán I searched for the legacy of Felipe Carrillo
and nowhere have I found it.

–Vicente Lombardo Toledano, 1934

To divorce one's wife is simple; to divorce one's mistress
impossible.

–Mexican proverb

Early in 1934, Vicente Lombardo Toledano, soon to become the
foremost Mexican labor leader and Marxist ideologue of his day,
made a brief trip to Yucatán. He came to the peninsula primarily
to gather regional support for a new national workers' confederation. But he also came, by his own admission, to pay homage to
one of the heroes of his youth upon the tenth anniversary of the
man's death. "I have come to find the legacy of Felipe Carrillo
Puerto," Lombardo told *Yucatecos* upon his arrival.

Several weeks later, Lombardo left the region, somewhat embittered by what he had found:

I have asked the official leaders about Carrillo's doctrine of
class struggle and they have answered by pointing to the
busts and statues of Felipe which seem symbolically to popu-
late the Yucatecan landscape – almost as thoroughly as the
images of Kukulkán[1] once did . . . in centuries past. I question these leaders about socialist organizations and revolutionary change and they offer me pamphlets enumerating the
regulations of the Leagues of Resistance. I inquire about new
customs and ways of living . . . and they introduce me to
men dressed in red shirts . . . who spend most of their time
resting in the shade of the plaza and betray an air of pain and
resignation which is unmistakable in those who attempt
to mask their true feelings in order to earn their daily
bread . . .

And when I speak with those who are not involved in

288

politics – the cabmen, the porters, the masons, the waiters, the market vendors – the message is much the same. At first the answers are evasive but soon deep-seated complaints overcome momentary caution, and the sad but suspected truth emerges: slogans without substance, new individuals running the same old corrupt institutions, which the people have endured to suffer in silence . . .

. . . And in the countryside many kilometers from Mérida, one finds the same legacy bestowed by Yucatecan socialism . . . "*Compañero*," an ancient *campesino* confided in me, "Come closer and you will see our humiliation at first hand . . ."

. . . Everywhere in Yucatán I searched for the legacy of Felipe Carrillo and nowhere have I found it.[2]

Only the outer trappings of Don Felipe's socialism had endured in Yucatán. The decade following Carrillo's death in 1924 witnessed a reconsolidation of the power of the peninsular bourgeoisie, the infiltration and weakening of the Socialist Party of the Southeast by that ruling group, and a sharp fall-off in ejidal distributions, especially within the henequen zone. (See Table 10.) However, although some of the governors and political leaders of these years were receptive to the bribes and blandishments of the wealthy – as traditional interpretations hold[3] – this was certainly not true of the entire Socialist Party leadership, nor was it the principal explanation for the political and economic prostration that Yucatán experienced during this decade. For, as we have seen, with the exception of a brief period in the mid-1920s, the price of henequen continued to plummet on the international market and foreign competition reduced Yucatán's former monopoly to a mere third of the market by the mid-1930s. (See Table 6.) Even had the revolutionary drive of the earlier period continued, the short supply of revenues would have made an extension of the costly reform programs of Alvarado and Carrillo virtually impossible. By the mid-1930s, the reassertion of a downward secular trend in the export economy rendered obsolete Carrillo's former plans for the systematic socialization of the henequen plantations. The *campesinos* had no capital and little inclination to assume the management and upkeep of fields that had been abandoned by the planters or remained only marginally productive. Faced once again with conditions of retrenchment, they turned their full attention to eking out subsistence wages in those *henequenales* still under production. Many vehemently protested against the prosposal of an agrarian

Table 10. *Agrarian reform after Carrillo, 1924–1933*

Year	Governor	Provisional deliveries			Definitive deliveries			Deliveries within henequen zone	
		Pueblos benefited	No. of campesinos	Hectares distributed	Pueblos benefited	No. of campesinos	Hectares distributed	Provisional	Definitive
1924	Iturralde	25	4,610	72,357	7	1,174	22,518	11 of 25	5 of 7
1925	Iturralde	19	3,841	79,042	25	4,957	82,158	2 of 19	16 of 25
1926	Torre Díaz	12	2,786	51,088	20	2,467	43,663	0 of 12	3 of 20
1927	Torre Díaz	6	1,039	20,135	10	1,522	44,086	0 of 6	1 of 10
1928	Torre Díaz	9	579	22,921	9	1,539	28,876	0 of 9	3 of 9
1929	Torre Díaz	10	796	28,996	9	1,257	15,818	0 of 10	4 of 9
1930	García Correa	4	758	29,461	4	2,521	26,990	0 of 4	2 of 4
1931	García Correa	No deliveries made							
1932	García Correa	2	593	3,769	1	13	720	0 of 2	0 of 1
1933	García Correa	2	141	8,307	None	None		0 of 2	None

Sources: Tierra, 12 Oct. 1924; Archivo General del Estado de Yucatán, Ramo de Tierras, Ledgerbook, "Comisión Agrarian Mixta, 1938," providing year-by-year account of land distributed, 1919–1933.

reform based upon the "collective *ejido*," the model then gaining ascendancy in the agrarian ministry of the Cárdenas administration in Mexico City. The new model called for the expropriation and breakup of existing estates and their rearrangement into a variety of new ejidal units that would be collectively cultivated. Although they objected to this new central Mexican agrarian formula, occasionally Yucatecan *campesinos* did petition the Agrarian Department for their accustomed access to small *parcelas* (plots) on which they might grow corn and beans to supplement their dwindling *jornales*.[4] However, their main concern was best articulated in a slogan of the time, popularized by a newly organized militant *campesino* organization: "El pueblo se muere de hambre. ¡Antes que tierras, trabajo!" ("The people are dying of hunger. Before land, work!")[5]

When the agrarian revolution did come to Yucatán, it came from without. Given the increasingly centralized nature of federal–state relations throughout the 1920–1940 period, this federal hegemony was inevitable. The opportunities for independent strategy and action that Alvarado had enjoyed in 1915 and Carrillo Puerto, to a lesser extent, in 1922, were nonexistent in

President Lázaro Cárdenas discusses agrarian problems with *campesinos*, 1934. (Reprinted from John W. F. Dulles, *Yesterday in Mexico: A Chronicle of the Revolution, 1919–1936*, Austin, Tex., 1961, p. 587. © 1961 by John W. F. Dulles.)

Epilogue

the late 1920s and early 1930s. By 1934, the once proud and autonomous *Gran Partido Socialista del Sureste* existed only in name; in actual fact, it had become the errand boy of Cárdenas' increasingly omnicompetent PNR. And, whereas the evidence shows that Obregón in 1923 and Calles in the late 1920s and early 1930s were opposed to substantial agrarian reform in the hene-quen zone, Cárdenas, a sincere *agrarista,* chose Yucatán precisely for the purpose of making it, along with the Laguna cotton-pro-ducing region, a showcase for his collective *ejido* program. The spiraling urban and rural unrest in Yucatán, which some regarded to be a bona fide *lucha de clases* (class struggle) but which was itself fanned by *Cardenista* agents and labor organizers, merely provided the federal government with a suitable pretext to attempt a re-structuring of Yucatecan society.[6]

Early in August 1937, President Lázaro Cárdenas arrived in Progreso with a boatload of engineers, surveyors and bureaucrats and, on 7 August, presided over the largest single episode of agrarian reform ever carried out in Mexico. Henceforth, all ha-cienda lands, whether cultivated in henequen or not, would be-come the property of the *campesinos*, with the exception of 150 hectares of *tierra cultivada* and 150 hectares of *monte* that the pro-prietor might retain as his *pequeña propiedad.* Cárdenas further decreed that the administration of the reform would begin im-mediately, with the expropriation of the largest estates first, and no *henequenero* would be exempt. Within only two weeks, Cárdenas's entourage of *técnicos* had superintended the transfer of tenure, consolidating unequal segments of hundreds of planta-tions into 272 collective *ejidos.* Cárdenas had been adamant on the issue of collectivization, maintaining that because henequen pro-duction was a commercial process that demanded the collabora-tion of many *campesinos* in a common enterprise, the new *ejidos* should be managed and cultivated collectively.

Unfortunately, it quickly became apparent that many irregular-ities and contradictions were embedded in the hasty distribution process. Although the planters had been promised their *cascos* – the nuclei of the plantations, which included the major buildings and machinery – in some instances, these were expropriated and distributed piecemeal to neighboring *ejidos.* In fact, despite Cárdenas's guidelines, some *hacendados* suffered total expropriation of their *fincas.* At the other extreme, cases were reported of *hacen-dado* families that managed to preserve much more than the stipu-lated 300 hectares. Typically, several members of a single family

President Cárdenas and officials of the agrarian reform ministry prepare to embark for Yucatán, 1937. (Reprinted from Gustavo Casasola, *Historia gráfica de la Revolución Mexicana*, *1910–1970*, 2d ed., Mexico, 1973, vol. 7, p. 2293. Casasola, INAH.)

would establish legal identity and succeed in retaining a much larger block of land. By the end of 1938, it was clear that a crazy quilt of tenure arrangements had emerged as a result of Cárdenas's reform. Once reasonably productive enterprises, most plantations were now carved up in a manner that suggested the absence of rational criteria in the planning and execution of the reform. Rarely did individual *ejidos* receive the appropriate number of henequen plants at each stage of maturity, which they would require to maintain continuity of production. Some *ejidos* received *henequenales* in full decline with few mature or young plants. Others were top-heavy with young shoots and would not realize an income for years to come. Instances were also reported in which urbanites from Mérida and Progreso had been included on the rolls of nearby *ejidos*, whereas numbers of eligible *campesinos* in the area had been completely excluded.[7]

Perhaps most distressing about the agrarian distribution was its dismemberment, in many cases, of operating agro-industrial units: the separation of *disfibradoras* from their surrounding fields. As their ultimate goal, Cárdenas and his agrarian advisors envisioned the creation of a series of large centralized processing plants (*centrales*) that would rasp the fiber of many surrounding collective *ejidos*. Consequently, it did not particularly matter to the federal *agraristas* if initially some *ejidos* were granted rasping machines whereas others remained with the *hacendado*. Eventually, the system would be rationalized around the strategically placed *centrales*, much as the central Mexican sugar industry was being organized around centrally located mills.

Unfortunately, the *Cardenista* vision of the collective henequen *ejido* was fatally flawed, primarily because it failed to consider the most basic requirements of commercial fiber production. Almost a century before, the industry's pioneers had learned from painful experience that rasping machinery had to be installed on each estate. Failure to do so meant that there was no way to ensure stripping of the fiber within the crucial twenty-four-hour period before the fiber dried out and rendered proper processing of the leaf almost impossible. Thus, the idiosyncracies of regional production had obliged these pioneer planters to combine the agricultural and industrial facets of production on their individual estates. Cárdenas's advisors, in their haste to bring collectivization to Yucatán, never grasped this fact, much to the industry's subsequent detriment.

Moreover, although under the terms of the new reform the *campesinos* had theoretically become the owners of the land they collectively cultivated, in practice the system worked to give them little participation in the management of the *ejidos*. Many felt alienated from the operations of these new units, pointing out that they had exchanged their former *patrón* – who, for all of his drawbacks, was a known quantity – for the impersonal bureaucracy of the federal government's ejidal bank. Although the bank provided technical assistance and doled out credit advances, it virtually excluded the *ejidatarios* from all production and marketing decisions. It is not surprising, therefore, that by 1938 the initial trickle of memorials protesting the agrarian reform had broadened into a torrent, with the petitioners now including groups of *ejidatarios* as well as disgruntled ex-*hacendados*.[8]

The 1934–1940 period, which constitutes the second phase of the Revolution in Yucatán, reveals a monocrop region caught in the throes of severe economic depression, in large part exacerbated by its external dependence upon the United States, and forced to accept solutions dictated by a central government that had convinced a substantial segment of that region's population that it did not understand Yucatán's peculiar problems. During the Cárdenas period, the region's condition of dependency – economic, political, and intellectual – stands out in sharp relief. Whereas local thinkers had a long-established tradition of proposing the ideological alternatives from which policy sprang, the 1930s witnessed a complete reversal in form, with Mexico City now becoming the principal source for ideological solutions to local problems. Whether we consider the militantly collectivist ideology of the federal agrarian socialists, centering on the collective *ejido*, or the futile counterattack in the press, led by Luis Cabrera and other veteran revolutionaries on behalf of the independently owned *pequeña propiedad*, we are forced to conclude that the arguments that fueled the controversies in Yucatán surrounding Cárdenas's ejidal collectivization program were all imported from without.[9]

Today, from every level of Yucatecan society emanates the criticism that the Revolution that came from without in the 1930s was not suited to the region's peculiar conditions and needs and has proven to be something less than a blessing. One is confronted by the stark fact that, within the past half-century, Yucatán fell from being perhaps Mexico's richest state to one of the Republic's most troublesome, depressed areas. One encounters middle-class intellectuals who lament the region's loss of autonomy and cry "internal colonialism";[10] workers who allege corruption and inefficiency in the management of the federal–state condominium (Cordemex) controlling the henequen industry;[11] and members of the former *hacendado* class who complain bitterly that, in breaking up once productive agro-industrial units and failing to substitute a viable and integrated economic system for the old plantation economy, the Revolution effectively scuttled the regional economy without conferring significant improvements upon rural workers.[12]

In leveling these charges, the Revolution's critics give little importance to the secular decline of the henequen industry, attributable, in large part, to the proliferation of international competitors and the invention of synthetic fibers. Nevertheless, the government's own statistics offer a sad commentary on the long-term effects of the Revolutionary regime's henequen strategy. In 1977, the 80,000 *ejidatarios* underemployed in the henequen zone received salaries ranging from $4 to $9 per week, in most cases less than was needed to support their families at the subsistence level. Whenever possible, *ejidatarios* or their family members attempt to supplement these wages with outside jobs, often in Mérida and smaller centers. According to Cordemex's director, the zone can now support only 28,000; consequently, the government must featherbed or subsidize the remaining workers, absorbing staggering losses in the process. During 1975–1976, Cordemex officially publicized its deficit at 333.5 million pesos, and although exact figures have not been revealed for subsequent years, losses are estimated to have been substantially greater.

Production figures are even more depressing. Although the mass of *campesinos* is greater today than at the turn of the century, Yucatán now produces substantially less fiber and the figures continue to decline with each passing year. An average of 140,000 tons were produced annually during the 1964–1970 period. Today the yield is somewhat less than 100,000 tons and, by the early 1980s, it is estimated that production will not even satisfy Mexico's domestic needs, let alone provide fiber for export. Only by comparing these figures with the 202,000 tons that were produced during henequen's *auge* in 1916 can we get a true picture of the magnitude of the current crisis. Ironically, although Yucatán's share of the world market has plummeted to 12.5 percent (1977), Cordemex has been finding it increasingly difficult to meet even this reduced market share. Poor productivity has existed in Yucatán since Cárdenas's ejidal distribution of 1937, when planter interest in the fiber plummeted. In the years that followed, corruption at all levels of the administrative hierarchy and the *ejidatario's* lack of incentive and know-how have also been responsible for underproduction. Recently, a Cordemex official estimated conservatively that it would take a federal government investment of about 1 billion pesos to improve productive capacity and put the regional fiber industry back on its feet.[13]

It is worth noting that the agrarian reform program implemented after the 1959 revolution in the sugar-producing areas of Cuba – like Yucatán, essentially a monocrop region – stands in sharp contrast to the policy carried out by the Cárdenas administration in the peninsula's henequen zone. Mindful, perhaps, of the neighboring Yucatecan model, under which existing plantations were broken up and new economic units were created at the cost of a significant loss in productive capacity, the revolutionary Cuban government, after expropriating the sugar plantations, opted to leave them intact, offering substantial incentives – improved material conditions, worker management, and so on – to the rural proletariat manning them. It has been suggested above that Yucatán's rural workers, an emerging proletariat, probably would have preferred, and benefited from, a similar agrarian reform strategy.[14] Indeed, this was precisely what Carrillo Puerto's projected reform would have done. Moreover, we have seen that even Alvarado's moderate agrarian program, weighted heavily toward wage increases with little emphasis upon the division of existing plantations, would have had a less damaging effect on the Yucatecan economy than Cárdenas's 1937 reform. Unlike Cárdenas, who drew upon ideological models derived from the agrarian experience of central Mexico, both Alvarado and Carrillo geared their reform strategies to the specific characteristics of Yucatán's agrarian structure and to the relations of production that had grown out of it.[15]

Undoubtedly, few states in the Republic have experienced such a disappointing history of agrarian reform as Yucatán. Apologists for the Revolutionary regime have sought – and still seek – to justify Cárdenas's massive 1937 reform, claiming that the strategy was well conceived, only poorly implemented by corrupt officials. Alternatively, government officials have claimed that the Yucatecan agrarian case is a special one, atypical of Mexican rural conditions. In doing so, they have taken great pains to preserve the central myths of the Revolution by writing Yucatán off as an exotic problem incapable of resolution. However, left- and right-wing critics alike have vehemently disagreed. They argue that although Yucatán's agrarian problems are unusual and the regime's failure to provide solutions is extreme, the Yucatecan case provides significant insight into the agrarian process throughout Mexico as a whole.[16]

Ironically, both viewpoints are not only correct, they are complementary. Yucatán's checkered history of agrarian reform and frustration is indeed an idiosyncratic one, yet it brings the entire process of land reform in Mexico sharply into focus. Significantly, the award-winning film *México, la revolución congelada* (*Mexico, the Frozen Revolution*) chose Yucatán as its central case study in dealing with the Revolutionary regime's failure to bring effective agrarian reform to Mexico. It may well be that few Mexican *campesinos* have experienced so many problems or disappointments as the *Yucatecos*. On the other hand, virtually every problem typically encountered throughout the Mexican countryside – and, it should be added, in other Latin American countries that have implemented programs of agrarian reform – is to be found in contemporary Yucatán: overpopulation; ejidal boundary disputes setting group against group and village against village; the illegal rental or sale of plots; *caciquismo*, *liderismo*, and the disenfranchisement of *ejidatarios* in agrarian affairs; chronic political unrest, factional violence, and assassination – to name only the more outstanding ones.[17]

It would be incorrect to minimize the major accomplishments of the Mexican Revolution in Yucatán. It put an end to slave peonage and developed a political and social consciousness among the working classes, created thousands of new schools, and dramatically increased health, sanitation, and other social welfare benefits for the region's population.[18] On the other hand, an appreciation of these reforms should not blind us to the underlying truth about the Yucatecan revolutionary experience: that when we speak of a revolution from within in contrast to a revolution from without, we are not merely engaging in a semantic exercise. During the first phase of the Revolution, from 1915 to 1924, and especially during the Socialist regime of Felipe Carrillo Puerto (1922–1924), forces within the region made a concerted drive for social revolution that was undercut by powerful external constraints compounded by significant internal weaknesses (low mobilization and the reliance upon traditional *cacique* networks). In the process, the revolutionary forces were unable to capitalize on the rich opportunities provided by World War I – most notably soaring henequen prices – opportunities that were not to repeat themselves during the 1934–1940 second phase. The revolution that came during these later years was of the imported variety and, although it has conferred some important benefits upon the region, the social and economic impact registered has never approached the radical restructuring of Yucatecan society envisioned by Felipe Carrillo Puerto and the socialist revolutionaries active during the first phase.

One nagging question remains: Was a genuine revolutionary transformation ever really within the grasp of Yucatán's Socialists? Were Carrillo and the local insurgents defeated primarily because of flaws in their program, or did objective conditions preclude any significant revolutionary change? Yucatán's debilitating monoculture, which subordinated the local economy to a foreign-dominated market, as well as the region's continued marginalization within the national power structure, were conditions under which revolution might well prove futile. Realistically speaking, how could Yucatán's penny-pinching Socialists stand up to their formidable opponents in the board rooms of Chicago and the corridors of power in Washington and Mexico City?

Yet the flat assertion of external control glosses over subtle dimensions of the regional revolutionary process from which useful lessons might emerge. Some final observations regarding the nature of Yucatán's political economy and its implications for the revolutionary process are therefore in order.

At least for the first phase of the Revolution in Yucatán (1915–1924), there is much to suggest the validity of aspects of the "chain of colonialism" idea – put forward by André Gunder Frank and the radical wing of the "dependency" school – which posits foreign dominance of a region through intermediary control of a national metropolis.[19] Quite clearly, Mexico City, reluctant to infuriate powerful North American economic interests, at least prior to legitimization and recognition of the Revolutionary regime by the United States, was instrumental in thwarting revolutionary influences in Yucatán. However, the "concentric circles of dependency" idea has much less validity for the later Cárdenas era. For although Mexico City's control of the region and its henequen industry steadily increased during the 1934–1940 second phase of the Revolution, President Cárdenas did *not* respond to U.S. pressure in the manner of his predecessors. Rather than acquiesce in a middleman role as they did, and impede agrarian reform impulses in the region that proved threatening to North American cordage interests, Cárdenas deliberately selected Yucatán as the proving ground for his ambitious collective *ejido* program, which entailed the comprehensive expropriation of privately owned *henequenales*. Thus, although dependency literature, North American and Mexican alike, has tended to portray Cárdenas conspiratorially as the father of a corporatist state that worked most effectively in the interests of an emerging national bourgeoisie collaborating with a foreign bourgeoisie,[20] it is difficult to fit Cárdenas's policy toward Yucatán into this neat, symmetrical framework. If Frank and other neo-Marxian analysts are correct in their formulation of the intermediary circle of neo-colonialism as consisting of a collaborator bourgeoisie in conjunction with the state, the non-collaborationist politics of Cárdenas would appear to constitute a significant exception.

Rather than overschematize and turn Yucatán into just another regional link in the chain of colonialism, we might view the problem directly from the regional level, examining Yucatán's structural dependency on a foreign-dominated market that remained even after Yucatán succeeded in industrializing its henequen and produced binder twine locally, a process that began in the 1920s and gained momentum in the 1930s and 1940s. As late as 1947, International Harvester alone still consumed almost 60 percent of Yucatán's annual yield of fiber and cordage.[21] Here, then, is a classic case in which industrialization did not break the relationship of dependency and promote economic "take-off," because industrialization issued from a monocrop economy tied to a fluctuating world market, the terms of which still favored the North American buyer over the Yucatecan seller and permitted frequent manipulation of that market in the buyer's interest. Many *Yucatecos* have commented that they regarded the informal control of Harvester and the United States over their region, with its legacy of economic dependence, as more enduring and damaging than the formal domination of the old Spanish empire or the current Mexican Republic, from which they had been able temporarily to secede on two separate occasions in the nineteenth century. Recalling a venerable central Mexican proverb, one local intellectual suggested: "To divorce one's wife is simple, to divorce one's mistress impossible."[22]

There is no question, then, that the cordage trust's long-term domination of the market and its ability to manipulate hard fiber stocks throughout the world cost the *Yucatecos* dearly in export revenues at a time when the terms of trade for fiber producers had not yet gone into terminal decline. On the other hand, Harvester had not yet become a modern multinational corporation, nor was its power unlimited. We should keep in mind that its invisible fiber empire, which would ultimately extend to Yucatán, Cuba, the Philippines, and other primary producing regions, was still being consolidated during the first two and a half decades of the twentieth century.[23] Moreover, as we have seen, at certain periods and in certain areas of this informal empire, such as in Yucatán during the the 1916–1918 wartime period, Harvester and the manufacturers were still surprisingly vulnerable to an aggressive pricing policy mounted by the primary producers. During such historical junctures, exporting regions were in a position to register substantial economic gains, although sustained growth and a stable, long-term path to development were not available to them.

However, the fact that Harvester's informal empire was operated indirectly through local collaborators and reflected modern economic imperialism in its earlier stages should not blind us to the more stark aspects of the unequal relationship that bound Yucatán's monocrop export economy[24] to its North American buyers and their Yucatecan agents. The informal nature of the control relationship absolved Harvester's henequen trust from putting anything back into Yucatán in the form of social investment and obviated the development of all economic infrastructure beyond that needed to get fiber quickly to market.[25] Moreover, the relationship would become progressively more unequal, because the manufacturers realized that time was on their side. For with additional production areas opening up all the time, Yucatán would be forced to come down significantly in price to remain competitive with the higher-quality fiber of its new rivals. And whereas the Mexican region had to sell its fiber to the cordage trust, the trust could become more and more choosy about with whom it did business.

The problem of political mobilization was an internal constraint on the revolutionary process every bit as great as those imposed externally by the international economy and the national power structure. The Yucatecan case stresses the point that spontaneous popular movements cannot be assumed on the basis of conditions of severe oppression alone. Many variables enter into the success or failure of revolutionary mobilization and must be examined carefully from region to region. We have seen how in Yucatán following the Caste War a strong tradition of peasant protest had been eroded, along with the peasant community itself. The war and the henequen export boom that followed revolutionized Yucatán demographically and geographically, uprooting Indian communities and rearranging traditional settlement patterns and labor systems. By the turn of the century, the great majority of free Maya pueblos had lost their land base. Those that continued to survive lacked the stability to resist that characterized the deep-rooted *Zapatista* pueblos of the central plateau or the free villagers of central Veracruz who formed the backbone of Úrsulo Galván's peasant leagues.[26] Lacking the ability to resist the expanding henequen plantations, Yucatán's *campesinos* were first enslaved by the plantations and then restricted to them. In addition to having virtually no contact with their fellows on different estates, Yucatecan rural workers were isolated from potential allies in the urban centers. Unlike Veracruz and the central plateau, where links between the urban and rural working classes developed early and membership in each sector often overlapped,[27] Yucatán's urban and rural workers rarely interacted, let alone made common cause.

The frustration of an urban–rural alliance and the absence of a vital revolutionary tradition through which Yucatán's revolutionaries might identify with the mass of people and upon which they might build – as Ho Chi Minh's Viet Minh did in Vietnam and Fidel Castro's "July 26 Movement" did in Cuba[28] – severely undercut the revolutionary process, scaling down immediate options. Consequently, Felipe Carrillo's elaborate efforts to link his modern social revolution with the symbols of the Maya past may be seen as a bold, although necessarily hurried, attempt to resurrect a historical tradition of protest with which the *campesinos* could proudly identify, one that would hasten the process of political mobilization. Ultimately, in the case of both Alvarado's bourgeois revolution and Carrillo's socialist revolutionary movement, there was no recourse but to wage revolution from the top down and, at least over the short run, to accept the inevitability of limited popular participation. For General Alvarado, who relied upon an extensive army and ordinarily favored a controlled political mobilization that would serve an authority-legitimizing rather than an interest-articulating function, this situation presented few problems. For Carrillo Puerto, a civilian leader and a committed agrarian socialist, Yucatán's low mobilization necessitated significant ideological compromises and pushed him into a series of problematical alliances with local petty bourgeois *caciques* that ultimately proved detrimental to the continued survival of his socialist revolution. In addition, both regimes found themselves compelled to strike bargains with certain members of the planter bourgeoisie who offered them valuable economic and technical expertise.

Thus, although a basic distinction has been drawn in this study between revolution from without (as reflected in the revolutionary drives led by Alvarado and Cárdenas) and revolution from within (represented by Carrillo's socialist revolution), it must be emphasized that, given the almost total lack of mobilization in Yucatán prior to the Revolution and the isolation of the rural masses, even Carrillo's Yucatecan revolution must have been perceived by many *campesinos* as something imposed from without. We sense the alien quality of Carrillo's revolution in the circumstances surrounding the regime's demise. Hunted across the state by his enemies, be-

trayed by leaders of *campesino* communities that were supposedly
Socialist, Carrillo's end – although popularly compared with the
fall of President Salvador Allende of Chile – may, in fact, bear a
much more interesting similarity to the death of Ché Guevara, a
revolutionary who died a virtual stranger in the Bolivian region
he sought to mobilize.[29] Although Allende approximated Carrillo
as an elected civilian leader overthrown by a reactionary bourgeoisie allied with the military, he differed significantly from the Yucatecan in operating within a sophisticated and highly politicized
society with a far more homogeneous ethnic cultural base. And –
to extend the comparative perspective further – when Carrillo's
tragic flight is compared with communist leader Luís Carlos
Prestes's far more successful and roughly contemporary march
across the backlands of Brazil (hardly a highly mobilized revolutionary society when the Prestes Column was active in the
1920s),[30] the absence of political mobilization and popular participation in the Yucatecan revolutionary process is cast in even
sharper relief.

If Carrillo, like Ché, was doomed to end his career as a revolutionary leader stranded without a revolution, it was ultimately the
element of time that played a crucial role in his defeat. It has been
written, "As of marriages, so with revolutions: the best take years
to turn out well."[31] Confronted with a depressed export economy,
limited in his maneuverability vis-à-vis the federal government,
plagued by Yucatán's poor internal and external communications
network, and lacking trained cadres of teachers and propagandists
because he had no money, Carrillo attempted to buy time for long-
term political mobilization by recruiting the support of powerful
caciques – arbitrary, largely apolitical rural bosses. Simultaneously,
he sought, often personally and with the assistance of a small,
dedicated group of veteran revolutionaries, to mobilize groups of
campesinos, even succeeding in infiltrating many of the *acasillado*
communities that had hitherto been under the complete control
of the estate owners. In this sense, Carrillo attempted to do what
other more successful, highly mobilized rural revolutionary movements accomplished: He placed emphasis on the long-term political mobilization of the most oppressed segments of the population. Unlike Lenin and the Russian revolutionaries, he never
waited for the "right moment."[32] He did not know, nor did he
have the luxury of learning, the meaning of the concept. Like the
Chinese, the Vietnamese, and the Cubans, more successful Third

World revolutionaries who followed them, Carrillo and the Yucatecan socialists knew that every moment was the right moment for something. Furthermore, they, too, recognized that a revolutionary struggle is an unremitting struggle, one requiring energy, patience, and hope – even in the face of enormous odds.

APPENDIX

Agrarian reform, 1915–1927

Source: Mexico, Secretaría de Agricultura y Fomento, Comisión Nacional Agraria, *Estadística, 1915–1927*, Appendices, Mexico, 1928.

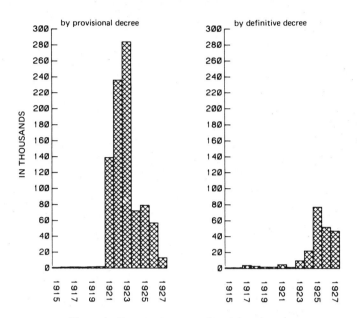

Figure A. Yucatán: hectares of land distributed.

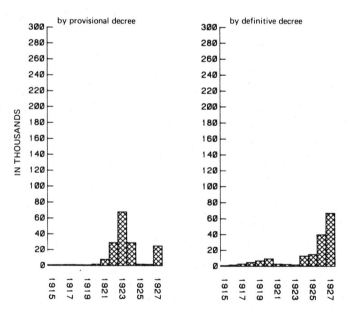

Figure B. Campeche: hectares of land distributed.

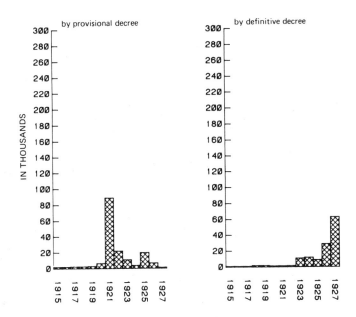

Figure C. Morelos: hectares of land distributed.

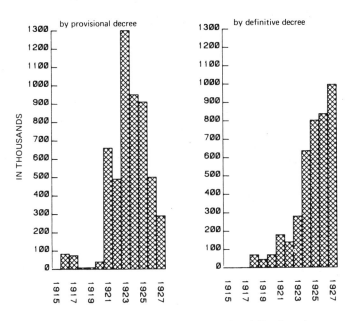

Figure D. Mexican Republic: hectares of land distributed.

Abbreviations used in notes

A	*El Agricultor*
AA	*American Anthropologist*
AC	Archivo de Carranza
AGE	Archivo General del Estado de Yucatán
AGN	Archivo General de la Nación
AHR	*American Historical Review*
Anderson Mss.	Chandler P. Anderson Papers
ANE	Archivo Notarial del Estado de Yucatán
ASA	Archivo de la Secretaría del Arzobispado
BdEL	*Boletín de Estudios Latinoamericanos y del Caribe*
BdLAS	*Boletín de la Liga de Acción Social*
BdU	*Boletín de la Universidad Nacional del Sureste*
C	*El Correo*
CJD	Colección Jorge Denegre V.
CR	*Congressional Record*
CSSH	*Comparative Studies in Society and History*
CTJ	*Cordage Trade Journal*
D	*El Demócrata*
DdY	*Diario de Yucatán*
DdelH	*Diario del Hogar*
DdelS	*Diario del Sureste*
DHRM	Isidro and Josefina Fabela, eds., *Documentos Históricos de la Revolución Mexicana*
DO	*Diario Oficial*
DY	*Diario Yucateco*
E	*Excélsior*
ECM	*Estudios de Cultura Maya*
ED	*El Día*
EHM	*Estudios de Historia Moderna y Contemporánea de México*
EY	*Enciclopedia Yucatanense*
FIN	*Farm Implement News*
Fletcher Mss.	Henry P. Fletcher Papers

FR-NA	*American Universities Field Staff Reports*, North American Series
H	*El Henequén*
HAHR	*Hispanic American Historical Review*
has.	hectares
HM	*Historia Mexicana*
Hughes Mss.	Charles Evans Hughes Papers
IEA	*Inter-American Economic Affairs*
IHCA	International Harvester Company Archives
J	*Juzgue*
JPS	*Journal of Peasant Studies*
LAP	*Latin American Perspectives*
LARR	*Latin American Research Review*
LC	Library of Congress
McC Mss.	Records of the McCormick Harvesting Machine Company
MMB	National Archives, Records of the Modern Military Branch, Military Intelligence and War College Division
N	*El Nacional*
NdY	*Novedades de Yucatán*
NMHR	*New Mexico Historical Review*
NYC	*New York Commercial*
NYT	*New York Times*
O	*Orbe*
P	*El Popular*
PCC	Plymouth Cordage Company Records
PCR	Henry W. Peabody and Company Records
PR	*Proceso*
RdM	*Revista de Mérida*
RdY	*Revista de Yucatán*
RMS	*Revista Mexicana de Sociología*
RUY	*Revista de la Universidad de Yucatán*
SD	National Archives, *Records of the Department of State Relating to the Internal Affairs of Mexico, 1910–1929*
SD-CPR	National Archives, Department of State Consular Post Records
SD-CPR, *Con. Corr.*	*Confidential Correspondence, 1917–1936*
SJA	*Southwestern Journal of Anthropology*
STP	Silvestre Terrazas Papers

T	*Tierra*
TLP	Thomas Lamont Papers
U	*El Universal*
VdR	*La Voz de la Revolución*
Wilson Mss.	Woodrow Wilson Papers
WTBR	National Archives, Records of the War Trade Board

NOTES

Prologue

1. *Huach* is a derogatory term that has been used for some time in Yucatán to designate people from the interior of the Republic, principally military personnel and manual laborers. It is not a Maya word.

2. Friedrich Katz, "Labor Conditions on Haciendas in Porfirian Mexico: Some Trends and Tendencies," *HAHR* 54:1 (Feb. 1974), 22–23, 44–47; Jorge Flores D., "La vida rural en Yucatán en 1914," *HM*, 10:3 (Jan.–Mar. 1961), 471–483; Moisés González Navarro, *Raza y tierra: La guerra de castas y el henequén,* Mexico, 1970, p. 231.

3. For a detailed political history of Yucatán during this period, see Ramón D. Chacón, "Yucatán and the Mexican Revolution: The Preconstitutional Years, 1910–1918," unpublished Ph.D. dissertation, Stanford University, Stanford, Calif., 1981, chaps. 1–3; and David A. Franz, "Bullets and Bolshevists: A History of the Mexican Revolution and Reform in Yucatán, 1910–1924," unpublished Ph.D. dissertation, University of New Mexico, Albuquerque, 1973, chaps. 1–3.

4. John Womack, *Zapata and the Mexican Revolution,* New York, 1968, p. 192.

5. Quoted in Benjamin Keen and Mark Wasserman, *A Short History of Latin America,* Boston, 1980, p. 278.

6. Martín Luis Guzmán, *The Eagle and the Serpent,* tr. Harriet de Onís, Garden City, N.Y., 1965, p. 163.

7. Womack, *Zapata,* p. 191, and see the revolutionary *corridos* (ballads) cited in Merle E. Simmons, *The Mexican Corrido as a Source for Interpretive Study of Modern Mexico (1870–1950),* Bloomington, Ind., 1957, pp. 132–133, 521.

8. Katz, "Labor Conditions," 22–23, 44–47; Ramón Berzunza Pinto, "El Constitucionalismo en Yucatán," *HM* 12:2 (Oct.–Dec. 1962), 278.

9. It has been argued that Ávila changed his mind about the decree after he received "a very fine hacienda" and "a regular sum of money" from the planters. CJD, roll 3, Toribio de los Santos to Carranza, 14 Jan. 1915; cf. Nelson Reed, *The Caste War of Yucatán,* Stanford, Calif., 1964, p. 257; and Franz, "Bullets and Bolshevists," pp. 78–79, 83, 89. Luis Amendolla, "Política regional: Yucatán," *Mañana,* 6 (Feb. 1944), 19–20, goes so far as to suggest that the 8-million-peso forced loan decreed by Ávila in September 1914 was actually a bribe by the *henequeneros* to ensure that emancipation remained a dead letter.

10. CJD, roll 3, de los Santos to Carranza, 14 Jan. 1915; AC, Calixto Maldonado R. to Carranza, 9 Jan. 1915; AC, Carranza to Alvarado, 16 Feb. 1915; Berta Ulloa, *Historia de la Revolución Mexicana,* vol. 5: *La encrucijada de 1915,* Mexico, 1979, pp. 63–67.

11. AC, Carranza to de los Santos, 20 Jan. 1915; SD, 812.00/14561; Franz,

"Bullets and Bolshevists," pp. 91–93; Álvaro Gamboa Ricalde, *Yucatán desde 1910*, Veracruz 1943, vol. 2, p. 331; Reed, *Caste War*, p. 258.

12. SD, 812.00/14554; Gamboa, *Yucatán*, vol. 2, p. 331; Fernando Benítez, *Ki: El drama de un pueblo y de una planta*, 2d ed., Mexico, 1962, p. 95.

13. SD, 812.61326/31; 812.00/14561, 14484; Santiago Pacheco Cruz, *Recuerdos de la propaganda constitucionalista en Yucatán*, Mérida, 1953, p. 52; Roberto Villaseñor, *El separatismo en Yucatán: Novela histórico–política mexicana*, Mexico, 1916.

14. SD, 812.61326/45, 83; SD-CPR, *Correspondence, 1915* (hereafter, *Corr.*), vol. 2, file 800, Young to Secretary of State, 23 Feb.; Florencio Ávila y Castillo, *Diario Revolucionario*, Mérida, 1915, p. 163; Renán Irigoyen, *Salvador Alvarado: Extraordinario estadista de la Revolución*, Mérida, 1973, pp. 20–21; Ulloa, *La encrucijada*, p. 77.

15. Pacheco Cruz, *Recuerdos*, p. 55; Allan Moe Blein (Antonio Mediz Bolio), *Alvarado es el hombre*, 2d ed., Culiacán, 1961, p. 31; Villaseñor, *El separatismo*, pp. 219–223.

16. Pacheco Cruz, *Recuerdos*, pp. 94–95; cf. Ávila y Castillo, *Diario*, pp. 3–4; AGE, Benito Aznar to Archbishop Tritschler y Córdoba, 15 Mar. 1915.

17. *NYT*, 21 Mar. 1915; SD, 812.61326/56; SD, 812.00/14961; SD-CPR, *Corr. 1915*, vol. 2, 800, Young to Secretary of State, 30 Mar., exaggerates the exodus to the point of hyperbole, reporting that one-half of Mérida fled before Alvarado's arrival.

18. AC, Carranza to Alvarado, 16 Feb. 1915.

19. Ávila y Castillo, *Diario*, p. 4; Pacheco Cruz, *Recuerdos*, p. 60; Ricardo Pinelo Río, "El batallón de 'La Plancha,'" *N*, 6 Mar. 1932.

20. Wenceslao Moguel H., *El milagro del Santo de Halachó o historia de un fusilado*, 2d ed., Mérida, 1967; Julio Molina Font, *Halachó, 1915*, Mérida, 1960.

21. Salvador Alvarado, "En legítima defensa," *D*, 4 May 1922; Ávila y Castillo, *Diario*, p. 4.

22. "Prólogo" to Alvarado, *Actuación revolucionaria*, p. 14.

1. Plant and plantation

1. Asael T. Hansen, "The Ecology of a Latin American City," in E. B. Reuter, ed., *Race and Culture Contacts*, New York, 1934, pp. 124–142. *Yucatecos* liked to boast that their state was Mexico's wealthiest, a claim backed up by many contemporary observers. However, Veracruz, with its oil and various other lines of production (sugar, textiles, tobacco) – none of which greatly suffered during the Revolution – might have rivaled Yucatán in wealth.

2. Luis Echeagaray Bablot, *Irrigación, crisis henequenera y condiciones agrícolas y económicas de Yucatán*, Mexico, 1956, p. 44; IHCA, H. L. Boyle Economic Research Files, E. W. Brewster, *Memorandum in re. Fiber and Twine*, 1937, "The Economic Reconstruction of Yucatán."

3. Nelson Reed, *The Caste War of Yucatán*, Stanford, Calif., 1964, p. 232;

Frederick J. T. Frost and Channing Arnold, *The American Egypt*, New York, 1909, pp. 60–61, 67–68.

4. A. J. G. Knox, "Regionalism as a Problem in Mexican National History: Yucatán, a Case Study, 1821–1940," unpublished manuscript, 1973, pp. 17–18, 22; Jan Bazant, *A Concise History of Mexico*, London, 1977, p. 54.

5. Arnold Strickon, "Hacienda and Plantation in Yucatán," *América Indígena* 25:1 (Jan. 1965), 42–57; SD-CPR, *Corr., 1920*, vol. 2, 610, "International Trade Competition," 26 May.

6. Quoted in Roland E. P. Chardon, *Geographic Aspects of Plantation Agriculture in Yucatán*, Washington, D.C., 1961, p. v. For the basic ecology of the Yucatán region, see also Cyrus L. Lundell, "Preliminary Sketch of the Phytogeography of the Yucatán Peninsula," in Carnegie Institution, *Contributions to American Archaeology*, Washington, D.C., 1934, pp. 255–321.

7. SD-CPR, *Corr., 1923*, vol. 3, 815.4, Marsh to Secretary of State, 12 May.

8. Nathaniel C. Raymond, "Land Reform and the Structure of Production in Yucatán," *Ethnology* 7:4 (Oct. 1968), 461–462; SD-CPR, *Corr., 1923*, vol. 4, 861.1, Marsh to Secretary of State, 31 July. Frustrated attempts at intensive irrigation farming in the south of the state are discussed in Echeagaray B., *Irrigación*.

9. SD-CPR, *Corr., 1923*, vol. 4, 861.1, Marsh to Secretary of State, 31 July; Renán Irigoyen, *Los mayas y el henequén*, Mérida, 1950; Howard Cline, "The Henequen Episode in Yucatán," *IEA* 2:2 (Autumn 1948), 30.

10. SD-CPR, *Corr., 1922*, vol. 2, 610, Marsh to Consul General, 26 Apr.

11. George C. Shattuck, *The Peninsula of Yucatán: Medical, Biological, Meteorological and Sociological Studies*, Washington, D.C., 1933, pp. 5–9; Strickon, "Hacienda and Plantation," 40–41.

12. SD-CPR, *Corr., 1922*, II, 610, Marsh to Consul General, 26 Apr.; Donald O. Doehring and Joseph H. Butler, "Hydrogeologic Constraints on Yucatán's Development," *Science* 86:4164 (Nov. 1974), 591–595; interview with Engineer Richard Hedlund, Sr., 1 July 1975.

13. John L. Stephens and Frederick Catherwood, *Incidents of Travel in Central America, Chiapas, and Yucatán*, New York, 1841, vol. 2, 404; Strickon, "Hacienda and Plantation," 41, 45.

14. Ralph L. Roys, *The Indian Background of Colonial Yucatán*, Washington, D.C., 1943, p. 9.

15. Gilbert M. Joseph, "British Loggers and Spanish Governors: The Logwood Trade and Its Settlements in the Yucatán Peninsula," *Caribbean Studies* 14:2 (July 1974), 7–37.

16. Robert Chamberlain, *The Conquest and Colonization of Yucatán, 1517–1550*, Washington, D.C., 1948, pp. 330–331.

17. See Sidney Mintz and Eric Wolf, "Haciendas and Plantations in Middle America and the Antilles," *Social and Economic Studies* 6:3 (1957), 380–412, for the characteristics that mark the large estate's transformation from hacienda to plantation.

18. The following discussion draws upon Strickon, "Hacienda and Plantation," 42–57; Robert Patch, *La formación de estancias y haciendas en Yucatán*

durante la colonia, Mérida, 1976, pp. 37–42; and Allen Wells, "Henequén and Yucatán: An Analysis in Regional Economic Development, 1876–1915," unpublished Ph.D. dissertation, State University of New York at Stony Brook, 1979, chap. 5.

19. Strickon, "Hacienda and Plantation," 48.

20. José M. Regil and Alonso M. Peón, "Estadística de Yucatán," *Boletín de la Sociedad Mexicana de Geografía y Estadística,* 3 (1852), 296, 299–300.

21. The expansion of the sugar plantation, although it did trigger the Caste War, was merely one of many causal factors, a discussion of which is beyond the scope of this chapter. Howard Cline's series of publications on Yucatán, although a quarter-century old, remain most authoritative. E.g., see "Regionalism and Society in Yucatán, 1825–1847: A Study of 'Progressivism' and the Origins of the Caste War," *Microfilm Collection of Manuscripts in Middle American Cultural Anthropology,* no. 32, University of Chicago Library, 1950. A popular survey and a detailed analysis of the military aspects of the war is Reed, *Caste War.* The most recent scholarly account of the war's origins, based on extensive regional archival research, is Robert Patch, "El fin del régimen colonial en Yucatán y los orígenes de la Guerra de Castas: El problema de la tierra, 1812–1846," *RUY,* forthcoming.

22. Sergio Baqueiro, *Ensayo histórico sobre las revoluciones de Yucatán . . .* Mérida, 1878, vol. 2, pp. 233–237, 358; Eligio Ancona, *Historia de Yucatán desde la época más remota hasta nuestros días,* 2d ed., Barcelona, 1889, vol. 1, 16–18.

23. Cline, "Regionalism," pp. 555–556.

24. Gonzalo Cámara Zavala, "Historia de la industria henequenera hasta 1919," in *EY,* Mexico, 1947, vol. 3, pp. 702ff.

25. Chardon, *Geographic Aspects,* p. 25; Juan Francisco Molina Solís, *Historia de Yucatán desde la Independencia de España hasta la época actual,* Mérida, 1921, vol. 1, p. 103.

26. Regil and Peón, "Estadística," 49; Víctor M. Súarez Molina, "La industria cordelera en Yucatán en el siglo XIX," *DdY,* 20 Feb. 1972.

27. Cline, "Regionalism," p. 546; Friedrich Katz, "El sistema de plantación y la esclavitud," *Ciencias Políticas y Sociales* 8:27 (Jan.–Mar. 1962), 104.

28. Rasping or cleaning, the process of stripping the spines of their fibrous filaments.

29. *CTJ* 35:2 (July 1907), 24–26; Frederick Ober, *Travels in Mexico and Life among the Mexicans,* Boston, 1884, p. 83.

30. Katz, "El sistema," 104; *H,* 15 July 1916. Although designed in Yucatán, these machines would be manufactured in the United States.

31. Reed, *Caste War,* pp. 230–231.

32. Chardon, *Geographic Aspects,* p. 35; Cámara Zavala, "Historia," p. 702.

33. Strickon, "Hacienda and Plantation," 53–54; H. T. Edwards, *Production of Henequen Fiber in Yucatán and Campeche,* Washington, D.C., 1924, pp. 7–11.

34. Renán Irigoyen, *¿Fué el auge del henequén producto de la guerra de castas?,* Mérida, 1947; Fidelo Quintal Martín, *Yucatán: Carácter de la guerra campesina de 1847,* Mérida, 1976, p. 37. Recent research suggests, however, that the impact

of the Caste War upon the later henequen boom has been somewhat exaggerated. See Cline, "Henequen Episode," and Patch, *La formación*, pp. 40–42.

35. Frank Tannenbaum, *The Mexican Agrarian Revolution*, Washington, D.C., 1930, p. 33.

36. Katz, "El sistema," 116–118; George M. McBride, *The Land Systems of Mexico*, New York, 1923, p. 154.

37. Víctor M. Suárez Molina, "Veinte años de economía yucateca," *DdY*, 3 Dec. 1975.

38. John K. Turner, *Barbarous Mexico*, Chicago, 1910, p. 15; Katz, "El sistema," 114.

39. Katz, "El sistema," 130.

40. Francisco Benet, "Sociology Uncertain: The Ideology of the Rural–Urban Continuum," *CSSH* 6:1 (Oct. 1963), 1–23; personal communications with Prof. Jorge Montalvo F. (Universidad de Yucatán), 1974–1975.

41. Strickon, "Hacienda and Plantation," 56; cf. Turner, *Barbarous Mexico*, p. 23.

42. Friedrich Katz, "Labor Conditions on Haciendas in Porfirian Mexico: Some Trends and Tendencies," *HAHR* 54:1 (Feb. 1974), 14–23; Alan Knight, "Peasant and Caudillo in Revolutionary Mexico, 1910–1917," in D. A. Brading, ed., *Caudillo and Peasant in the Mexican Revolution*, Cambridge (U.K.), 1980, p. 26. By emphasizing the proletarianizing effect of the Yucatecan hacienda, I mean to imply here the first stage in an extended process whereby Yucatán's traditional peasantry evolved into an agricultural proletariat. Generally speaking, in Yucatán the alienation of the peasant from his traditional land base was not part and parcel of the more celebrated process in Latin American history wherein dispossessed peasants supplied the first ranks of an urban proletariat. As we shall see, the Yucatecan peasant, once shaken free of his land, was not in a position to sell his labor, either in the city or in the countryside. Rather, he fell prey to an extreme form of debt peonage that culminated in his being sold as a commodity on the regional labor market. Following this experience of slavery, which lasted approximately one generation (1880–1915), attempts would be made by national and local revolutionaries to organize the rural worker and to promote in him a sense of class consciousness. By the end of the period that is examined in this study (1940), our original peasant had transcended his status as a *peón* and could, more accurately, be described as a rural proletarian.

43. See Patch's map, following p. 36 *(La formación)*, which delineates this northwestern zone of hacienda dominance, c. 1800, and suggests that it was essentially coincident with the boundaries of the modern henequen zone identified by geographers and agronomists. Other variables would also play a role in setting the limits of the modern henequen zone. An inadequate communications network dramatically increased transportation costs as one moved away from Mérida. Moreover, unfavorable soil conditions also inflated costs and reduced yields because henequen grew best in the drier and rockier soil of the northwest, where there were fewer choking weeds. Strickon, "Hacienda and Plantation," 56ff.; Allen Wells, "Economic Growth and Regional Disparity in

Porfirian Yucatán: The Case of the Southeastern Railway Company," *South Eastern Latin Americanist* 22:2 (Sept. 1978), 3; cf. Patch, *La formación*, p. 41.

44. Cline, "Regionalism," pp. 535; Ober, *Travels in Mexico*, pp. 65–66, 88.

45. Chardon, *Geographic Aspects*, p. 31; cf. Patch, *La formación*, p. 41, and Wells, "Henequén and Yucatán," chaps. 3 and 5.

46. Emiliano Busto, Anexo num. 3 a la "Memoria de Hacienda del año económico de 1877 a 1878," *Estadística de la República Mexicana*, Mexico, 1880, p. 264; Katz, "El sistema," 104; cf. Juan Miguel Castro, *El henequén de Yucatán y el monopolio*, Mérida, 1876.

47. Renán Irigoyen, "Don Us Escalante, precursor de la industria henequenera," *Revista de Estudios Yucatecos* 1:1 (Feb. 1949), 17–32; Katz, "El sistema," 104ff.

48. Súarez Molina, "La industria cordelera"; Cámara Zavala, "Historia," p. 692; Manuel Mesa Andrade and Rogelio Villanueva, *La producción de fibras duras en México*, Mexico, 1948, p. 7.

49. Cline, "Regionalism," p. 380.

50. Quoted in Reed, *Caste War*, p. 232.

51. *Ibid.*; Keith Hartman, "The Henequen Empire in Yucatán, 1870–1910," unpublished master's thesis, Univ. of Iowa, Iowa City, 1966, p. 96.

52. Wells, "Economic Growth and Regional Disparity," 3–5.

53. Testimony of Víctor Rendón, 17 Feb. 1916, in U.S. Senate, Committee on Agriculture and Forestry, *Importation of Sisal and Manila Hemp: Hearings*, Washington, D.C., vol. 1, pp. 55 and *passim*.

54. Hartman, "Henequen Empire," pp. 96–97.

2. The henequen boom

1. John Reed, *The Caste War of Yucatán*, Stanford, Calif., 1964, p. 230.

2. *Ibid.*, p. 231; Emiliano Busto, "Memoria de Hacienda del año económico de 1877 a 1878," *Estadística de la República Mexicana*, Mexico, p. 261; Allen Wells, "Henequén and Yucatán: An Analysis in Regional Economic Development, 1876–1915," unpublished Ph.D. dissertation, State University of New York at Stony Brook, 1979, p. 81. Prior to 1905, the peso was at par with the North American dollar, although in times of recession, Mexican silver depreciated against U.S. gold. After 1905, the peso was fixed at 2:1 with the dollar.

3. Reed, *Caste War*, p. 231.

4. *Ibid.*, pp. 231–232; Frederick J. T. Frost and Channing Arnold, *The American Egypt*, New York, 1909, pp. 3–11.

5. *American Egypt*, p. 322; and see SD-CPR, *Despatches* and *Corr.*, 1897–1915, especially File 610, for evidence of the elite's extravagant lifestyle.

6. Víctor M. Suárez Molina, "Veinte años de economía yucateca, *DdY*, 3 Dec. 1975; Keith Hartman, "The Henequen Empire in Yucatán, 1870–1910," unpublished master's thesis, University of Iowa, Iowa City, 1966, p. 78; cf. John H. Coatsworth, "Railroads, Landholding, and Agrarian Protest in the Early *Porfiriato*," *HAHR* 54:1 (Feb. 1974), 68–69.

7. Elmer Llanes Marín, "La llanura aislada," o 49 (Oct. 1957), 19–35.

8. Frost and Arnold, *American Egypt*, pp. 60–61.

9. Suárez Molina, "Veinte años"; SD-CPR, letterbook, *Despatches to the State Department, Nov. 9, 1897 to Dec. 19, 1904*, pp. 53–54 and *passim;* Mireyra Priego de Arjona, *Orígen y evolución de Progreso*, Mérida, 1973.

10. Roland E. P. Chardon, *Geographic Aspects of Plantation Agriculture in Yucatán*, Washington, D.C., 1961, p. 35; Frank Tannenbaum, *The Mexican Agrarian Revolution*, Washington, D.C., 1930, p. 98. Nathaniel C. Raymond, "The Impact of Land Reform in the Monocrop Region of Yucatán, Mexico," unpublished Ph.D. dissertation, Brandeis University, Waltham, Mass., 1971, pp. 99–100; George M. McBride, *The Land Systems of Mexico*, New York, 1923, p. 37; *The Mexican Year Book, 1912*, London, 1912, p. 108; Frost and Arnold, *American Egypt*, p. 362.

11. Cf. Mark Wasserman, "Oligarquía y intereses extranjeros en Chihuahua durante el Porfiriato," *HM* 22:3 (Jan.–Mar. 1973), 284–285.

12. Frost and Arnold, *American Egypt*, pp. 366–367; Raymond, "Impact," p. 107; Siegfried Askinasy, *El problema agrario de Yucatán*, 2d ed., Mexico, 1936, p. 13; SD, 812.61326/210; Daniel Cosío Villegas, ed., *Historia moderna de México*, Mexico, 1965, vol. 7, part 1, p. 119.

13. Hartman, "Henequen Empire," pp. 84–85 and see graph, p. 221.

14. Wells, "Henequén and Yucatán," pp. 235–240, computing production costs and planter profits during the economic recession of the mid-1890s, still finds that the *hacendado* could expect a 9 percent return on his investment in 1894. "Even when henequen prices dipped as low as three cents a pound planters could be assured a small return on their investments." Cf. *Boletín de Estadística*, 1 and 16 Oct. 1894, for the production costs that Wells uses to calculate the profit; and *Mexican Herald*, 16 June 1908, for planters' statements regarding profitability in the midst of the 1907–1908 crisis.

15. Hartman, "Henequen Empire," pp. 130–131; Chardon, *Geographic Aspects*, p. 35.

16. Wells, "Henequén and Yucatán," pp. 83–84; cf. Antonio Betancourt Pérez, "La verdad sobre el orígen de las escuelas rurales en Yucatán," *RUY* 13:76 (July–Aug. 1971), 41–43; Renán Irigoyen, "Orígen y trayectoria del henequén," *RUY* 15:86 (Mar.–Apr. 1973), 125; and John K. Turner, *Barbarous Mexico*, Chicago, 1910, p. 8, for slightly varying estimates of the size of the Divine Caste.

17. Cf. Wasserman, "Oligarquía," 279–319, for many interesting similarities between the Yucatecan oligarchy and its Chihuahuan counterpart, led by the Terrazas–Creel family. The following discussion of the Molina family draws heavily upon Wells, "Henequén and Yucatán," chap. 3; Francisco A. Casasús, "Ensayo biográfico del Licenciado Olegario Molina Solís," *RUY* 14:81 (May–June 1972), 68–95; and José María Valdés Acosta, *A través de las centurias*, Mérida, 1926, vol. 2, pp. 1–19.

18. Betancourt Pérez, "La verdad," 44.

19. *Ibid.*, 44; Edmundo Bolio, *Yucatán en la dictadura y la Revolución*, Mexico, 1967, pp. 12–121.

20. *H*, 15 Feb. 1916.

21. Henry Baerlein, *Mexico: The Land of Unrest,* Philadelphia, 1914, pp. 18, 167–170.

22. Humberto Lara y Lara, *Sobre la trayectoria de la reforma agraria en Yucatán,* Mérida, 1949, pp. 8–9; Irigoyen, "Orígen," 125.

23. In 1907, for example, Don Porfirio made Molina his minister of development.

24. Cf. Wasserman, "Oligarquía," pp. 279–319, *passim.*

25. Manuel Irabién Rosado, *Historia de los ferrocarriles,* Mérida, 1928, p. 13.

26. Chardon, *Geographic Aspects,* p. 160.

27. Friedrich Katz, "El sistema de plantación y la esclavitud," *Ciencias Políticas y Sociales* 8:27 (Jan.–Mar. 1962), 113n.

28. Wells, "Henequén and Yucatán," chaps. 3 and 5, *passim.*; cf. Robin W. Winks, "On Decolonization and Informal Empire," *AHR* 81:3 (June 1976), 554; SD, 812.61326/236.

29. Winks, "On Decolonization," 552; cf. Ronald Robinson, "Non-European Foundations of European Imperialism: Sketch for a Theory of Collaboration," in Bob Sutcliffe and Roger Owen, eds., *Studies in the Theory of Imperialism,* London, 1972, pp. 117–141.

30. Winks, "On Decolonization," 554.

31. The relations of Harvester and earlier North American buyers with this succession of exporting houses are discussed in Gonzalo Cámara Zavala, "Historia de la industria henequenera hasta 1919," *EY,* Mexico, 1947, vol. 3, pp. 691–708.

32. D. C. M. Platt, "Economic Imperialism and the Businessman: Britain and Latin America before 1914," in Sutcliffe and Owen, *Studies,* pp. 295–297, 303–304.

33. *Ibid.,* pp. 303–304.

34. Katz, "El sistema," 112–113.

35. Henry W. Peabody and Company was an international trading and shipping firm based in Boston, Mass., with a branch office in New York. Peabody entered the fiber trade in the late 1860s, dealing at first almost exclusively in manila. In 1891, the firm selected the British-born merchant, Arturo Pierce, as its agent in Mérida and began to concentrate on the purchase of henequen. The firm also invested in Australian and New Zealand goods and fibers and had secondary interests in real estate and manufacturing. The Plymouth Cordage Company of Plymouth, Mass., was founded in 1837 and, from its inception, specialized exclusively in the manufacture of twines, cords, and ropes. Plymouth's operations were dwarfed by those of the Chicago-based Harvester Company, which, in addition to buying and selling fiber and twine, specialized in a complete line of harvesting machinery. PCC, various files; PCR, memorandum, "J. P. B. to R. W. H. re. Henry W. Peabody and Co.," 19 Nov. 1964, and ledger books of Peabody and Company, vol. AB-1, 1867–1869.

36. The contract was published in *RdY,* 27 Nov. 1921, and has been reproduced in a variety of secondary accounts, e.g., Bernardino Mena Brito, *Reestructuración histórica de Yucatán,* Mexico, 1969, vol. 2, p. 205. An English version and analysis are found in SD, 812.61326/372,375.

37. *Boletín de Estadística,* nos. 10, 11 (1, 16 Oct. 1894); Wells, "Henequén and Yucatán," p. 239.

38. Reed, *Caste War,* p. 261.

39. Winks, "On Decolonization," 552; Robinson, "Non-European Foundations," pp. 120–129 and *passim;* and cf. Yen-p'ing Ho, *The Comprador in Nineteenth-Century China: Bridge between East and West,* Cambridge, Mass., 1970.

40. All subsequent quotations regarding fiber will be in U.S. currency.

41. See note 36; IHCA, doc. file 2395 ("Early Developments of Fiber and Twine Operation"), H. L. Daniels to Cyrus McCormick, 2 Oct. 1906; and memorandum "Re. H. L. D. Sisal Purchase 1909," from "E. A. B.," 19 Dec. 1912.

42. IHCA, 2395, Daniels to Alex Legge, 16 July 1909; and see the testimony of Víctor Rendón, Faustino Escalante, and Fernando Solís Cámara, dated 16 and 17 Feb. 1916, in U.S. Senate, Committee on Agriculture and Forestry, *Importation of Sisal and Manila Hemp: Hearings,* Washington, D.C., 1916.

43. *RdY,* 27 Nov. 1921; SD, 812.61326/375; Yucatán, *Mensajes del Gobernador Constitucional C. Lic. Olegario Molina al Congreso de Yucatán, 1902–1906,* Mérida, 1906, pp. 48–49, 121.

44. Fernando Benítez, *Ki: El drama de un pueblo y de una planta,* 2d ed., Mexico, 1962, p. 74.

45. See Celso Furtado's discussion of the "System of International Division of Labour" in *Economic Development of Latin America,* Cambridge (U.K.), 1976, pp. 42–47.

46. SD-CPR, *Despatches to the Department, Nov. 9, 1897 to Dec. 19, 1904,* Thompson to State Department, 25 Feb. 1899; SD, 812.61326/283; Víctor M. Suárez Molina "La industria cordelera en Yucatán en el siglo XIX," *DdY,* 20 Feb. 1972. Although Yucatecan artisans had produced sacks, bags, and hammocks on a small scale throughout much of the nineteenth century, La Industrial would represent the first attempt to manufacture a significant portion of the region's primary export.

47. AGN, Ramo de Fomento, Industrias Nuevas, legajo 17, *passim.* Olegario Molina led the way with an investment of 83,000 pesos.

48. ANE, José Patrón Zavlegui, oficio 5, vol. 99, 8 May 1901, p. 526.

49. Benítez, *Ki,* pp. 73–74; Wells, "Henequén and Yucatán," pp. 55–56. La Industrial folded in 1903 but was revived during the recession of 1907–1908, when raw fiber prices were again low and Yucatecan planters had an incentive to industrialize. This time, however, Molina did not lend his support to the venture. Heavily encumbered with debt, the plant soon fell into the hands of Molina's son-in-law, Avelino Montes, who foreclosed on the mortgage late in 1908. Under Montes's control, the factory slipped quietly into oblivion and was virtually moribund in 1915, when a fire gutted the premises. See SD-CPR, *Corr., 1915,* vol. 2, 800, Young to Secretary of State, 30 Mar.; Antonio Rodríguez, *El henequén: Una planta calumniada,* Mexico, 1966, pp. 233–234, 305.

50. Winks, "On Decolonization," 552.

51. *Ibid.,* 554.

52. The name of the firm was formally changed from "Olegario Molina y Compañía, Sucesores" to "Avelino Montes, S. en C." on 18 May 1905. ANE, Patricio Sabido, oficio 17, vols. 8, 9, pp. 589–604. Beginning in 1905, Molina kept a lower profile in local affairs; in 1908, he became a member of Díaz's cabinet in Mexico City.

53. PCC, file "Fiber – Mexican Sisal – Monopoly to 1921," folder K, A. B. Loring to Peabody and Co., 27 Apr. 1913; and Harold McCormick to Víctor Rendón, 30 Nov. 1915.

54. Diane Roazen, "The Olegario Molina Family of Yucatán," unpublished manuscript, 1977.

55. Bolio, *Yucatán*, p. 101; Gabriel Ferrer de Mendiolea, "Historia de las comunicaciones," *EY*, Mexico, 1947, vol. 3, pp. 567–626, and *passim;* SD, 812.61326/54, 136.

56. SD, 812.61326/193; U.S. Senate, *Importation of Sisal*, testimony of Fernando Solís Cámara and Henry Wolfer, 17 Feb. and 30 Mar. 1916, respectively; cf. Alberto García Cantón, "Memorias de un ex-hacendado," xeroxed copy, IHCA, *Abstract Summary of the Sisal Investigation Index*, parts I–X.

57. Salvador Alvarado, *Actuación revolucionaria del General Salvador Alvarado en Yucatán*, Mexico, 1965, pp. 70–78; and see PCR, *Yucatán Letters*, file HG-1, 1913–1914, correspondence between Edward Bayley and Arturo Pierce. Don Olegario, on the other hand, would retain his cherished reputation as the "Father of Modern Yucatán" and, upon occasion, his prestigious name would be recruited by the *Alvaradistas* in their campaign against Harvester.

58. ANE, Patricio Sabido, oficio 17, vols. 8, 9, 18 May 1905, pp. 589–604; Wells, "Henequén and Yucatán," p. 21; Roazen, "Molina Family." From 1905 to 1916, Avelino Montes S. en C's capitalization of roughly 1.8 million pesos was evenly divided between Montes and Molina.

59. See IHCA, doc. file 2864 ("Cuban Fiber Operation").

60. For the elaborate proceedings surrounding Molina's funeral in January 1925, see *DdY*. Following Molina's death, one of Mérida's main avenues was named in his honor by the revolutionary government.

61. The agreement (as yet unpublished) may be found in McC Mss., 2x, box 621. I am indebted to Dr. Fred V. Carstensen and Diane Roazen for bringing it to my attention.

62. McC Mss., 2x, boxes 621 and 478.

63. See note 61.

64. E.g., testimony of Edward Bayley in U.S. Senate, *Importation of Sisal*, 12 Apr. 1916.

65. Although a variety of oblique references in correspondence between Bayley and Arturo Pierce, from February 1902 to March 1903, suggest that Bayley did indeed know of the agreement. See PCR, HL-3, Bayley to Pierce, 18 Feb. 1902, 14 Oct. 1902, and 11 Mar. 1903 (in which Bayley promises to tell Pierce all about the settlement "at some [later] time").

66. E.g., testimony of Víctor Rendón in U.S. Senate, *Importation of Sisal*, 17 Feb. 1916.

67. See p. 47 for the specific terms of the contract.

68. SD, 812.61326/193, 200.

69. For a discussion of the boom-and-bust economy's impact on entrepreneurial activity, see Wells, "Henequén and Yucatán," chap. 3.

70. On the face of it, fiber prices appear to have increased slightly throughout the period despite the constant fluctuations. However, Yucatán's henequen industry experienced the effects of the same inflationary spiral that plagued the rest of Mexico during the Porfiriato. Real prices actually declined as labor and other costs of production increased.

71. For example, the "new perspective" of Harvester's participation in the Yucatecan henequen trade, which Thomas Benjamin, "International Harvester and the Henequen Marketing System in Yucatán, 1898–1915: A New Perspective," *IEA* 31:3 (Winter 1977), 3–19, offers, turns on "less visible" macroeconomic variables that "bound [Yucatán] to the thoughtless whims of world trade." Benjamin's revisionist analysis totally ignores the web of power relationships that affected the structure and control of fiber production within Yucatán.

72. U.S. Department of Commerce, Bureau of Corporations, *International Harvester Company,* Washington, 1913, p. 184. Diane Roazen's provisional analysis of Harvester, Plymouth, and Peabody account books reveals that Harvester made good profits during the 1902–1916 period, indeed, returns that were substantially higher than those of its competitors. Profits fell off sharply after 1916, and Harvester began increasingly to invest in the fiber of other regions, such as Cuba. And see *Harvester World* 8:1 (Jan. 1917), 8–9.

73. SD, 812.61326/124, 181.

74. SD, 812.61326/372.

75. *Ibid.*

76. IHCA, 2395, Mary Trieb to Edgar A. Bancroft, n.d. (1912?); Bureau of Corporations, *International Harvester,* p. 184.

77. SD, 812.61326/229.

78. SD, 812.61326/181, 229.

79. *CTJ* 39:6 (Sept. 1909), 1ff; and see the assorted press clippings and correspondence in PCC, file I, drawer 1, section K ("Monopoly to 1921") and file H, drawer 2.

80. PCC, file I, drawer 3, assorted documents illustrating Plymouth's trade in sisal from Africa and Asia; G. F. Holmes, "What Every Farmer Should Know . . . ," file I, drawer 1, section K.

81. IHCA, various documents in the following files: 2395 ("Early Operations in Fiber and Twine"); 2924 ("Philippine Operation in Fiber and Twine"); 2864 ("Cuban Fiber Operation"). Cf. McC Mss., *Letters Received,* 2x, boxes 478–479 (early experimentation in Brazil and Spanish South America, 1898–1902).

82. Regarding the flimsy binder twine made from flax, one Harvester executive lamented: "It's nice food for crickets." See *In the District Court of the United States for the District of Minnesota. United States of America versus International Harvester Company, et al.,* vol. 13, Minneapolis, 1917, pp. 52–56.

83. IHCA, 2395, Daniels to McCormick, 18 Sept. 1906.

84. *Ibid.,* and IHCA, 2395, Daniels to McCormick, 2 Oct. 1906.

85. In Cuba and the Philippines, on the other hand, Harvester found it necessary directly to control the factors of production, purchasing large latifundia and existing import–export houses to marshall exports of sisal and manila fiber. IHCA, 2395, "Report of Fiber Department," 25 Mar. 1905, and various documents in files 2395, 2924, and 2864.

86. McC Mss., *Letters Received, 1901–1902,* 2x, boxes 613 and 621; IHCA, 2395, E. H. Thompson to Daniels, 26 Feb. 1906, Daniels to McCormick, 1 Mar. 1906.

87. McC Mss., *Letters Received, 1901–1902,* 2x, box 621. In the case of Tabí, the Yucatecan seller offered to manage the estate, secure additional workers, and plant the fields.

88. IHCA, 2395, Daniels to McCormick, 1 Mar. 1906.

89. Bureau of Corporations, *International Harvester,* pp. 149–150; Katz, "El sistema," 108–110.

90. Katz, "El sistema," 108.

91. *Ibid.,* 111–112. Data for the following account of McCormick's involvement in La Industrial has also been gathered from McC Mss., *Letters Received,* 2x, boxes 521, 535, 537, 609, 613, 616, and 620–621 (correspondence between La Industrial and McCormick Harvesting Machine Company); *CTJ,* 1899–1900, *passim;* ANE, José Patrón Zavlegui, oficio 5, vol. 99, 8 May 1901, 526; and Wells, "Henequén and Yucatán," pp. 52–56.

92. *CTJ* 15:6 (Sept. 1897), 91; 19:4 (Aug. 1899), 52.

93. Thus, by 1915, the British were establishing sisal plantations in East Africa, India and Nepal, New Zealand and Mauritius; the French in Madagascar; the Germans in East and West Africa and New Guinea; and the Dutch in their East Indian colonies.

94. Katz, "El sistema," 111.

95. Reed, *Caste War,* pp. 260–262; Wells, "Henequén and Yucatán," pp. 239–240; Katz, "El sistema," 114.

96. Reed, *Caste War,* p. 261; *A,* 1908, *passim;* and see Chapter 5 of this text.

97. Turner, *Barbarous Mexico,* pp. 9–66; Evelyn Hu-Dehart, "Pacification of the Yaquis in the Late *Porfiriato:* Development and Implications," *HAHR* 54:1 (Feb. 1974), 72–93; Frederich Katz, "Labor Conditions on Haciendas in Porfirian Mexico: Some Trends and Tendencies," *HAHR* 54:1 (Feb. 1974), 22–23.

98. Roazen, "Molina Family"; Reed, *Caste War,* p. 261.

99. *H,* 15 July 1916; Katz, "El sistema," 113–114.

100. Roazen, "Molina Family," IHCA, H. L. Boyle Files, unsigned letter to Boyle, n.d.; Allen Wells, "Economic Growth and Regional Disparity in Porfirian Yucatán: The Case of the Southeastern Railway Company," *South Eastern Latin Americanist* 22:2 (Sept. 1978), 9.

101. For a colorful description of Díaz's reception in Yucatán by the *Casta,* see Benítez, *Ki,* pp. 77–94.

102. Although briefly vice-president of Mexico under the Liberals, Zavala is best known for his Yucatecan separatism and promotion of the independence of Texas. Sierra served as Díaz's minister of education and gained a national reputation as Mexico's foremost educator. Although *Yucatecos* claim him as their own, he was actually born in Campeche and lived most of his adult life in Mexico City.

103. Roazen, "Molina Family"; cf. Wasserman, "Oligarquía."

104. Hu-Dehart, "Pacification," 72–73, 84–85, 92–93.

105. Wells, "Economic Growth," 12–14; Reed, *Caste War,* pp. 242–243; Hartman, "Henequen Empire," pp. 162–163.

106. Often these *baldíos,* judged vacant by Molina's government, constituted the traditional *ejidos* of local Indian pueblos. Frequently, these pueblos were unable to prove clear title to their properties and were arbitrarily stripped of their lands. Mena Brito, *Reestructuración,* vol. 2, pp. 220–221, 223, 267; *VdR,* 19 Nov. 1915; Raymond, "Impact," p. 107.

107. Roazen, "Molina Family"; Hartman, "Henequen Empire," pp. 96–97; Baerlein, *Mexico,* pp. 168ff.

108. Wells, "Economic Growth," 11–13.

109. Reed, *Caste War,* pp. 257–285; Hartman, "Henequen Empire," pp. 189, 201.

110. See, e.g., Manuel M. Escoffié, *Yucatán en la cruz,* Mérida, 1957.

3. The revolutionary equation within Yucatán

1. See, e.g., Nelson Reed, *The Caste War of Yucatá,* Stanford, Calif., 1964, and *passim;* Moisés González Navarro, *La guerra de castas y el henequén,* Mexico, 1970, pp. 31–42, 76–107; and Ermilo Abreu Gómez's acclaimed fictional epic, *Canek: History and Legend of a Maya Hero,* tr. Mario L. Dávila and Carter Wilson, Berkeley, Calif., 1980 (originally published 1940).

2. Reed, *Caste War,* Part 3. Yucatán's unique ethnic categories are discussed in Richard Thompson, *The Winds of Tomorrow: Social Change in a Maya Town,* Chicago, 1974.

3. The following discussion draws upon John K. Turner's contemporary account (*Barbarous Mexico,* Chicago, 1910, pp. 9–66) and the more recent findings of Friedrich Katz ("El sistema de plantación y la esclavitud," *Ciencias Políticas y Sociales* 8:27 [Jan.–Mar. 1962], 114–131; "Labor Conditions on Haciendas in Porfirian Mexico: Some Trends and Tendencies," *HAHR* 54:1 [Feb. 1974], 14–23, 44–47; *La servidumbre agraria en México en la época porfiriana,* Mexico, 1976, pp. 7–122) and Allen Wells ("Henequén and Yucatán: An Analysis in Regional Economic Development, 1876–1915," unpubblished Ph.D. dissertation, State University of New York at Stony Brook, 1979, pp. 260–315).

4. Wallace Thompson, *The People of Mexico,* New York, 1921, p. 327; cf. Turner, *Barbarous Mexico,* p. 167 and *passim.*

5. Turner, *Barbarous Mexico,* p. 33.

6. *H,* 30 Apr. 1918.

7. Karl Kaerger, quoted in Katz, *La servidumbre,* p. 92.

8. In addition to Turner, contemporary observers Henry Baerlein, Channing

Arnold and F. J. T. Frost, and Karl Kaerger all described the hardening of the slave regime.

9. Wells, "Henequén and Yucatán," pp. 293–296; Colegio de México, *Estadísticas económicas del Porfiriato: Fuerza de trabajo y actividad económica por sectores*, Mexico, 1964, pp. 159, 163, 165.

10. Turner, *Barbarous Mexico*, p. 17; Katz, "El sistema," 125. Each of the contemporary observers cited above (note 8) stresses the insignificance of the real debt.

11. Frank Tannenbaum, *The Mexican Agrarian Revolution*, Washington, D.C., 1930, p. 101; Frederick J. T. Frost and Channing Arnold, *The American Egypt*, New York, 1909, p. 362; AGE, Ramo dee Justicia, "Intestado de José Clotilde Baqueiro," 1899 (planter entrepreneurship and absenteeism).

12. Turner, *Barbarous Mexico*, p. 24.

13. Frost and Arnold, *American Egypt*, p. 324.

14. Malcolm K. Shuman, "The Town Where Luck Fell: The Economics of Life in a Henequen Zone Pueblo," unpublished Ph.D. dissertation, Tulane University, New Orleans 1974, p. 147.

15. *Ibid.*, p. 146; Wells, "Henequén and Yucatán," p. 276.

16. Benítez, *Ki: El drama de un pueblo y de una planta*, 2d ed, Mexico, 1962, pp. 49, 51.

17. Salvador Alvarado, *Actuación revolucionaria del General Salvador Alvarado en Yucatán*, Mexico, 1965, pp. 50, 78, 150.

18. Turner, *Barbarous Mexico*, pp. 18–19; United Kingdom, *Diplomatic and Consular Reports: Trade of Yucatán for the Year 1898*, London, 1899, p. 2.

19. Evelyn Hu-Dehart, "Pacification of the Yaquis in the Late *Porfiriato*: Development and Implications," *HAHR* 54:1 (Feb. 1974), 72–93.

20. Mexico, *Boletín de la Dirección General de Agricultura*, Mexico, 1911, p. 590.

21. Katz, "Labor Conditions," 19. Roland E. P. Chardon's (*Geographic Aspects of Plantation Culture in Yucatán*, Washington, D.C., 1961, pp. 103–116) and Siegfried Askinasy's (*El problema agrario de Yucatán*, 2d ed., Mexico, 1936, pp. 30–31) descriptions of the labor regime of hacienda Sacapúc suggest that the *finca's* proprietor attempted to cling to an older, less harsh form of paternalism.

22. Katz, "Labor Conditions," 14–23, documents similar treatment of workers on tropical plantations in Tabasco, Chiapas, Veracruz, and the Valle Nacional in Oaxaca; cf. evidence in the works by Turner, Baerlein, Arnold and Frost, and Kaerger, cited above.

23. See, for example, Ramón D. Chacón, " Yucatán and the Mexican Revolution: The Pre-constitutional Years, 1910–1918," unpublished Ph.D. dissertation, Stanford University, 1981, *passim*.

24. See, for example, Ernesto Laclau, "Feudalism and Capitalism in Latin America," *New Left Review* 67 (May–June 1971), 19–38; and Jay R. Mandle, "The Plantation Economy: An Essay in Definition," *Science and Society* 36:1 (Spring 1972) 49–62.

25. E.g., see André Gunder Frank, *Capitalism and Underdevelopment in Latin America*, New York, 1967; *Latin American Underdevelopment and Revolution*, New

York, 1969; and Frank, James D. Cockcroft and Dale L. Johnson, eds., *Dependence and Underdevelopment*, Garden City, N.Y., 1972.

26. Cf. the analogous contemporary situation described in Warren Dean's examination of Brazilian coffee, *Rio Claro: A Brazilian Plantation System, 1820–1920*, Stanford, Calif., 1976, p. 196.

27. Mandle, "Plantation Economy," 56–62.

28. This concept is discussed in Fernando Henrique Cardoso, "The Consumption of Dependency Theory in the United States," *LARR* 12:3 (Fall 1977), 13.

29. Félix F. Palavicini, *Mi vida revolucionaria*, Mexico, 1937, p. 36.

30. Raymond Th. J. Buve, "Peasant Movements, Caudillos and Land Reform 75during the Revolution (1910–1917) in Tlaxcala, Mexico," *BdEL* 18 (June 1975), 116.

31. *Ibid.*, 117.

32. Ronald Waterbury, "Non-revolutionary Peasants: Oaxaca Compared to Morelos in the Mexican Revolution," *CSSH* 17:4 (Oct. 1975), 410–442. The "non-revolutionary" potential of the free villagers of Oaxaca (and Chiapas) is further explained by the pivotal role of powerful Indian *caciques*. These bosses served as economic and cultural middlemen between the *comuneros* and *hacendados* and wanted no disruption of the local markets that they controlled. Their clients, the villagers, acquiesced in such an exploitative arrangement because it did not – at least until recently – compromise their communal way of life or threaten their access to land. Henning Siverts, "The 'Cacique' of K'ankujk'," *ECM* 5 (1965), 339–360.

33. Wells, "Henequén and Yucatán," pp. 280–283; *El Peninsular*, 31 Mar. 1905; *El Eco del Comercio*, 11 July 1891.

34. For fifty years following the Caste War, the state government had, at great cost, attempted to root out the remaining pockets of Maya resistance in Quintana Roo because the plantocracy feared that an independent Maya state might encourage outbreaks of violence by Maya workers in the henequen zone. Wells, "Henequén and Yucatán," p. 306, chap. 4, *passim*. The planters' fears were heightened when they learned that small groups of *Morelense* prisoners, deported to labor camps in Quintana Roo following land disputes in their own country, had escaped and were free to make cause with the rebel Maya. John Womack, *Zapata and the Mexican Revolution*, New York, 1968, pp. 39, 51.

35. Buve, "Peasant Movements," 116; Heather Fowler Salamini, *Agrarian Radicalism in Veracruz, 1920–38*, Lincoln, Neb., 1978, chap. 2 and *passim;* Paul Friedrich, *Agrarian Revolt in a Mexican Village*, Englewood Cliffs, N.J., 1970, pp. 58–77; Womack, *Zapata*, pp. 6–7.

36. Elmer Llanes Marín, "La llanura aislada," *O* 49 (Oct. 1957), 19–20.

37. Fowler Salamini, *Agrarian Radicalism*, chaps. 1–2, and "Los orígenes de las organizaciones campesinas en Veracruz: Raíces políticas y sociales," *HM* 22:1 (July–Sept. 1972), 52–76.

38. Adolfo Gilly, *La revolución interrumpida*, Mexico, 1971, pp. 385–399.

39. Cf., e.g., Caio Prado's discussion of the structure of slave society in colonial Brazil. *The Colonial Background of Modern Brazil*, Berkeley, 1969, especially the chapters "Economy," "Large-Scale Agriculture," and "Social Organization."

40. See the annual (pre-1915) economic reports of the U.S. consul in SD-CPR, *Corr.*, file 610, which examine over time the low level of industrialization in Yucatán.

41. David A. Franz, "Bullets and Bolshevists: A History of the Mexican Revolution and Reform in Yucatán, 1910–1924," unpublished Ph.D. dissertation, University of New Mexico, Albuquerque, 1971, pp. 12–13; Fidelio Quintal Martín, "Quince años trascendentales en la historia de Yucatán," *RUY* 16:93–94 (May–Aug. 1974), 130–131. John Johnson's broader understanding of a disparate middle range or sector of society is more appropriate here than the notion of a coherent, self-conscious middle class. *Political Change in Latin America: The Emergence of the Middle Sectors*, Stanford, Calif., 1958.

42. Quintal Martín, "Quince años," 130–131; Keith Hartman, "The Henequen Empire in Yucatán, 1870–1910," unpublished master's thesis, University of Iowa, Iowa City, 1966, pp. 125–126, 182–183; Bernardino Mena Brito, *Reestructuración histórica de Yucatán,* Mexico, 1969, vol. 2, pp. 221–222.

43. Alberto García Cantón, "Memorias de un ex-hacendado," IHCA, *Abstract Summary of the Sisal Investigation Index, Parts I–IX;* Franz, "Bullets and Bolshevists," p. 12; and see Chapters 4, 7, and 9.

44. SD-CPR, *Despatches to the Department, Jan. 1, 1905 to Dec. 20, 1909,* memorandum, "The Commerce and Industries of Yucatán," 7 Aug. 1908; E. H. Thompson to Assistant Secretary of State, 27 Feb. 1909.

45. Franz, "Bullets and Bolshevists," p. 12. For an indication of the numbers of these smaller fiber producers, *rancheros* and *parcelarios,* see the property census commissioned by General Alvarado in *DO,* 1916–1917, *passim.*

46. Franz, "Bullets and Bolshevists," chap. 2.

47. Buve, "Peasant Movements," 117.

48. AGN, Ramo de Madero, paquete 2–16, Faustino Escalante to Madero, 7 Feb. 1912; Álvaro Gamboa Ricalde, *Yucatán desde 1910,* Veracruz, 1943, vol. 1, p. 198. For a detailed account of *Maderismo* and politics in Yucatán from 1910 to 1915, see Chacón, " Yucatán and the Mexican Revolution," chaps 1–3, and Franz, "Bullets and Bolshevists," chaps. 1–3.

49. Although I have stressed the very low level of mobilization that existed among the Yucatecan *campesinado* on the eve of the Revolution, I have not meant to imply that unrest did not exist in the rural sector. Indeed, recent evidence uncovered by Allen Wells suggests that the image of a mass of passive, inert *campesinos,* which is portrayed in the contemporary accounts of Turner, Frost and Arnold, Baerlein, and Alvarado, was clearly exaggerated. The Yucatecan *campesinado* did not meekly accept its fate during the "Age of Slavery." Wells's investigation of the 1880–1915 period has produced a variety of isolated episodes of rural protest, often accompanied by violence but always in response to a specific local cause. Thus, on Avelino Montes's hacienda Oxcúm, near Umán, unrest reflected *campesino* outrage directed at an *encargado* in the wake of excessive punishments for work infractions (1907). The plantation of Olegario Molina's sister-in-law, Luisa, became the scene of violence when the administrator arbi-

trarily cut the wages of several platform drivers (1909). In Maxcanú, a confrontation occurred between villagers and hacienda residents following the loss of the town's *ejidos* (1910). Violence erupted in Valladolid in response to the activities of an especially egregious *jefe político* (1910), whereas on the remote sugar hacienda Catmís, near Peto, an especially brutal labor regime provided the spark for perhaps the most violent episode of *campesino* protest under the Old Regime (1911). In each case, the violence was spontaneous, narrowly circumscribed, and quickly and easily repressed. More importantly, there were no recognizable ideological connections or organizational links between the incidents. The fact that these episodes seemed to increase markedly in 1910 and 1911, Wells notes, was perhaps attributable less to increased unrest and more to increased press coverage. Such isolated episodes recurred throughout the Porfiriato. It was only during the later years, however, that the alienation of Yucatán's middle-sector journalists intensified to the point where, by and large, they became the opponents rather than the supporters of the Old Regime. Wells, "Henequén, and Yucatán," pp. 214, 297, 307–311; cf. *RdM*, 5 Sept. 1907, 20 Sept. 1909, 9 July 1910; *El Imparcial*, 24 Sept. 1909.

4. Salvador Alvarado and bourgeois revolution from without

1. Interview with José Monsreal, 24 Oct. 1975. This recollection, passed on from a father to his son, was one of several I collected. *Huach* is a derogatory Yucatecan term designating people from the interior of the Republic, principally soldiers and laborers.

2. Cf. the stylized descriptions of the invasion in Antonio Betancourt Pérez, "Nuestro viejo abuelo," *RUY* 15:85 (Jan.–Feb. 1973), 64–65, and Dr. Eduardo Urzáiz R., "La entrada de Alvarado," *0*, 41 (April 1955), 85–86; and see Martín Luis Guzmán's description of Alvarado in *The Eagle and the Serpent*, tr. Harriet de Onís, Garden City, N.Y., 1965, pp. 72–73.

3. Alvarado and the Constitutionalist invaders are pictured in Gustavo Casasola, *Historia gráfica de la Revolución Mexicana, 1910–1970*, 2d ed., Mexico, 1973, vol. 3, pp. 833, 914, 994–997. In addition to *norteños*, Alvarado's Army of the Southeast included detachments from Veracruz, Tabasco, and Campeche. Edmundo Bolio O. *Yucatán en la dictadura y en la Revolución*, Mexico, 1967, pp. 78ff.

4. Alan Knight, "Peasant and Caudillo in Revolutionary Mexico, 1910–1917," in D. A. Brading, ed., *Caudillo and Peasant in the Mexican Revolution*, Cambridge (U.K.), 1980, pp. 53–54. Earlier, in December 1914, one of Villa's political advisors, Silvestre Terrazas, had shrewdly recommended a similar strategy for the Conventionists. However, Villa refused to act on his suggestion that a military expedition be sent to Yucatán. STP, box 84, Silvestre Terrazas to Villa, 2 Dec. 1914.

5. Hans Werner Tobler, "Las paradojas del ejército revolucionario: Su papel social en la reforma agraria mexicana," *HM* 21:1 (July–Sept. 1971), 38–79.

6. Enrique Montalvo Ortega, "Caudillismo y estado en la Revolución Mexicana: El gobierno de Alvarado en Yucatán," *Nova Americana* 2 (1979), 16–17.

7. *DO*, 23 Mar. 1915, p. 713; Florencio Ávila y Castillo, *Diario Revolucionario*, Mérida, 1915, pp. 4–5, 8, 14.

8. *DHRM*, 17, 135, Alvarado to Carranza, 26 Sept. 1916; Roberto Villaseñor, *El separatismo in Yucatán: Novela histórico–política Mexicana*, Mexico, 1916, pp. 226–236.

9. Renán Irigoyen, *Salvador Alvarado: Extraordinario estadista de la Revolución,* Mérida, 1973, pp. 43–44.

10. *VdR*, 5 Apr. 1915; *DO*, 7 Apr. 1915, p. 821.

11. Alvarado returned the confiscated properties and businesses to their owners in late 1916 and early 1917. For the career of the Dept. of Attached Properties, see AGE, Alvarado to General Administrator of Attached Properties, 20 Apr. 1915, 20 Feb. 1916, 31 May 1916; AGE, Alvarado to General Francisco Cosío Robledo, 14 May 1915; AGE, Alvarado decree 15, 15 Apr. 1915; Yucatán, *Breves apuntes acerca de la administración del General Salvador Alvarado como Gobernador de Yucatán . . . ,* Mérida, 1916, p. 27. Cf. the similar program of confiscation that was carried out by Alvarado's former colleagues in their native Sonora. Héctor Aguilar Camín, "The Relevant Tradition: Sonoran Leaders in the Revolution," in D. A. Brading, ed. *Caudillo and Peasant*, pp. 112–114.

12. AGE, Alvarado to Carranza, 9 Nov. 1916.

13. *DO*, 19 May 1915, pp. 1323–1324.

14. AGE, Alvarado to Carlos Castro Morales, 25 Dec. 1916; AGE, Alvarado to all comandantes militares, 28 Dec. 1916.

15. *DO*, 8 Apr. 1915, pp. 833–834, 10 May 1915, p. 1195.

16. SD, 812.00/14961; Nelson Reed, *The Caste War of Yucatán*, Stanford, Calif., 1964, p. 259.

17. David A. Franz, "Bullets and Bolshevists: A History of the Mexican Revolution and Reform in Yucatán, 1910–1924," unpublished Ph.D. dissertation, University of New Mexico, Albuquerque, 1973, pp. 110–111.

18. AGE, Calixto Maldonado to Alvarado, Feb. 1916; Luis F. Sotelo Regil, "La Revolución en Yucatán: Salvador Alvarado," *RUY* 2:12 (June–July 1960), 56–57.

19. SD-CPR, *Corr.*, 1917, vol. 4, 877, "Ferrocarriles Unidos de Yucatán," 19 June; SD, 812.61326/54, 136; AGE, Comisión Reguladora del Mercado de Henequén, "Acta número 50," 20 Aug. 1918; Arturo Sales Díaz, *Síntesis y breve análisis de la actuación del General Salvador Alvarado en Yucatán,* Mexico, 1956, pp. 13–18. In some cases, Alvarado forced members of the ruling class to serve in his administration as window dressing. AGE, Jefe del Dpto. del Trabajo to Macedonio Velázquez, 8 Apr. 1916.

20. AGE, memorial from Jacinto Cohuich et al. to Alvarado, 20 Dec. 1916; AGE, Víctor J. Manzanilla and Rafael Matos E. to Alvarado, 30 Aug. 1917; Rosa Castro, "Sobre la ruta de Carrillo Puerto, el Mesías de Motul," *Hoy*, 9 Feb. 1952; Sales Díaz, *Síntesis y breve análisis*, pp. 17–18.

21. Irigoyen, *Salvador Alvarado*, p. 22; cf. *VdR*, 5 May 1916.

22. *VdR*, 12 Feb. 1916; and see the repeated allegations of graft and corruption in Alvarado's bureaucracy among its elite members in the following U.S. State Department documents: SD, 812.61326/136, 220, 230, 254.

23. Salvador Alvarado, *La reconstrucción de México: Un mensaje a los pueblos de América*, Mexico, 1919, vol. 1, p. 11. Cf. the dissatisfaction of the other lower-middle-class Sonoran chiefs under the Díaz regime, in Aguilar Camín, "The Relevant Tradition," in Brading, ed., *Caudillo and Peasant*, pp. 117–119.

24. On Alvarado's early career, see Adolfo de la Huerta, *Memorias de Don Adolfo de la Huerta según su propio dictado*, ed. Roberto Guzmán Esparaza, Mexico, 1957, pp. 70–71, 286; Alberto Morales Jiménez, *Hombres de la Revolución Mexicana: 50 semblanzas biográficas*, Mexico, 1960, pp. 223–225; Daniel Moreno, *Los hombres de la Revolución*, Mexico, 1960, p. 306; Edwin Lieuwen, *Mexican Militarism: The Political Rise and Fall of the Revolutionary Army, 1910–1940*, Albuquerque, N.M., 1968, p. 24. Some sources claim Alvarado was born in Sinoloa.

25. See, for example, SD, 812.61326/254, 259.

26. Salvador Alvarado, *Actuación revolucionaria del General Salvador Alvarado en Yucatán*, Mexico, 1965, p. 40; AGE, Alvarado to Carranza, 20 May 1915; SD, 812.61326/20, 197; *DHRM*, 16, 139–140, 144.

27. The Obregón–Alvarado rivalry is discussed in Héctor Aguilar Camín, *La frontera nómada: Sonora y la Revolución Mexicana*, México, 1977, pp. 349–354, 401, and *passim*.

28. Alvarado's perception of himself, which he cast in these very terms in a 1915 speech, is cited in Villaseñor, *El separatismo*, p. 219.

29. Frank Tannenbaum, *Peace by Revolution: Mexico after 1910*, New York, 1933, p. 117; cf. the less flattering evaluation of Alvarado's contribution as a revolutionary ideologue in Guzmán, *The Eagle and the Serpent*, pp. 72–74.

30. Albert Bacon Fall Papers: 1850–1927, University of New Mexico Library, Special Collections, box 5, file 2, "Summary of Mexican Intelligence," Headquarters, 8th Corps Area, 1920. Some modern writers have also portrayed him as a socialist. See Diego Valadés, "Ideas políticas y sociales de Salvador Alvarado," *EHM* 5 (1976), 109–118.

31. Alvarado, *La reconstrucción*, vol. 1, pp. 113–130, 162–164, 186ff.; Víctor Manuel Villaseñor, "Salvador Alvarado," *RUY* 6:34 (July–Aug. 1964), 125; SD, 812.00/18110; Jesús Silva Herzog, *Trayectoria ideológica de la Revolución Mexicana, 1910–1917*, Mexico, 1963, pp. 106–107.

32. Alvarado, *Actuación revolucionaria*, p. 15; James D. Cockcroft, *Intellectual Precursors of the Mexican Revolution, 1900–1913*, Austin, Tex., 1968, p. 124.

33. The ideological and political tradition of the Sonoran chiefs is brilliantly fleshed out in the work of Aguilar Camín. See *La frontera nómada*, pp. 411–446, and "The Relevant Tradition," in Brading, ed., *Caudillo and Peasant*, pp. 92–123.

34. Alvarado, *Actuación revolucionaria*, p. 36.

35. See, for example, Antonio Bustillos Carrillo, *Yucatán al servicio de la Patria y la Revolución*, Mexico, 1959; and Fidelio Quintal Martín, "Quince años

trascendentales en la historia de Yucatán," *RUY* 16:93–94 (May–Aug. 1974), 99–131.

36. See, for example, *VdR*, 4 May 1915, and the file of correspondence in the AGE between Alvarado's *Departamento de Información y Propaganda Revolucionaria* and the governments of the states of Sonora, Coahuila, Oaxaca, San Luis Potosí, Michoacán, Puebla, Querétaro, and Chiapas: e.g., Governor, Oaxaca, to Salvador Alvarado, 12 Dec. 1916 (soliciting a 300,000-pesos loan).

37. Tannenbaum, *Peace by Revolution*, p. 117.

38. Cf. Antonio Rodríguez, *El henequén: Una planta calumniada*, Mexico, 1966, p. 221, who estimates the number freed at 70,000.

39. *DO*, 4 Oct. 1915, p. 3657; *VdR*, 24 Oct. 1916; Álvaro Torre Díaz, "La labor del Constitucionalismo en Yucatán," *El Paso del Norte*, 23 May 1917. The Sonoran Yaquis and political prisoners from elsewhere in Mexico who had been forcibly transported to Yucatán during the Porfiriato now left Yucatán for good, bound for their former homelands.

40. Pedro Castro Aguilar, *Colonizar es poblar*, Mérida, 1948, p. 2; Alvarado, *Actuación revolucionaria*, pp. 90–91; AC, report, Mexican Consul in Galveston, Tex., to Carranza, 23 Mar. 1916; *VdR*, 24 Oct. 1916; *DO*, 13 Dec. 1916, p. 4259; SD, 812.55/23.

41. Alvarado, decreto num. 20, 24 Apr. 1915, cited in Álvaro Gamboa Ricalde, *Yucatán desde 1910*, Veracruz, 1943, vol. 2, pp. 370, 374.

42. Gamboa Ricalde, *Yucatán*, vol. 2, pp. 385–386; Reed, *Caste War*, p. 260.

43. Salvador Alvarado, *La reconstrucción*, vol. 2, pp. 305–306; *VdR*, 16 Feb. 1916; Congreso Feminista de Yucatán, *Anales de esa memorable asamblea*, Mérida, 1916; Anna Macías, "Felipe Carrillo Puerto and Women's Liberation in Mexico," in Asunción Lavrin, ed., *Latin American Women: Historical Perspectives*, Westport, Conn., 1978, pp. 287–288, and "The Mexican Revolution Was No Revolution for Women," in Lewis Hanke, ed., *History of Latin American Civilization: Sources and Interpretations*, 2d ed., Boston, 1973, vol. 2, pp. 463–465.

44. *DO*, 4 Oct. 1916, p. 3272; Bolio O., *Yucatán*, pp. 117, 143–148; Osvaldo Baqueiro Anduze, *Los mayas y el problema de la cultura indígena*, Mérida, 1937, p. 73. Alvarado's moral regime is almost identical to the one promulgated the same year for Sonora by Governor Plutarco Elías Calles. Aguilar Camín, *La frontera nómada*, pp. 421–422.

45. AGE, typescript, "Informe que el Gral. Salvador Alvarado . . . rinde al Primer Jefe . . . Venustiano Carranza . . . ," 28 Feb. 1917, pp. 22, 27–28; *DHRM*, 17, 326, Alvarado to Carranza, 26 Sept. 1916.

46. Gamboa Ricalde, *Yucatán*, vol. 2, pp. 566–569; U.S. Senate, *Investigation of Mexican Affairs: Preliminary Report and Hearings of the Committee on Foreign Relations . . . ,* Washington, D.C., 1920, vol. 1, p. 881; *DO*, 4 Oct. 1916, p. 3272.

47. Francisco Cantón Rosado, *Historia de la Iglesia en Yucatán desde 1887*, Mérida, 1943, pp. 98–129; CJD, roll 3, Archbishop Martín Tritschler y Córdoba to Carranza, 6 Dec. 1915; SD, 812.00/16442, 18110, 18114; *DHRM*, 16, 177, Alvarado to petitioners, 21 June 1915. The best secondary

treatment of Alvarado's conflict with the Church is Ramón D. Chacón, "Yucatán and the Mexican Revolution: The Pre-constitutional Years, 1910–1918," unpublished Ph.D. dissertation, Stanford University, Stanford, Calif., 1981, pp. 194–202.

48. Aguilar Camín, "The Relevant Tradition," pp. 117, 280.

49. ASA, Pedro Rubio Mendoza to Archbishop Tritschler y Córdoba, 11 May 1917; ASA, Manuel Casares Escudero to Tritschler y Córdoba, 11 Nov. 1918. The more publicized anticlerical displays are discussed in Ernest Gruening, *Mexico and Its Heritage,* New York, 1928, p. 214, and Carlos Loveira, *El obrerismo yucateco y la Revolución Mexicana,* New York, 1917, pp. 41–42.

50. Gruening, *Mexico,* p. 214. Cf. similar statements in AGE, Alvarado to Joaquín Peón et al., 21 June 1915, and *Actuación revolucionaria,* p. 56.

51. ASA, Rafael Peón to Archbishop Tritschler y Córdoba, 23 Oct. 1915; Cantón Rosado, *Historia de la Iglesia,* pp. 128–129.

52. ASA, Abilo Sabido to Archbishop Tritschler y Córdoba, 12 Mar. 1916; cf. SD, 812.00/442, Young to Secretary of State, 27 Sept. 1915.

53. AGE, Alvarado to vecinos of Acanceh, 20 Jan. 1917; AGE, Alvarado to all comandantes militares, 13 Feb. 1917; ASA, Pedro M. de Regil to Tritschler y Córdoba, 25 Oct. 1917, 20 Dec. 1917; *VdR,* 21 Feb. 1918.

54. For example, see *VdR,* 4 Sept. 1915; SD, 812.61326/220; and p. 108.

55. Alvarado, "Informe," *DO,* 4 Jan. 1918, p. 60; William Gates, "Yucatán – an Experiment in Syndicalism," *World's Work* 38 (May 1919), 61.

56. George Miner, "Opiniones sobre la labor del Gral. Salvador Alvarado," *D,* 6 Nov. 1916.

57. Gamboa Ricalde, *Yucatán,* vol. 2, pp. 415, 421–431, 440–448; *VdR,* 22 Mar. 1916; *Municipio Libre,* 30 May 1917, pp. 275–277 (for Alvarado's well-publicized, though short-lived *Ciudad Escolar de los Mayas*).

58. Santiago Burgos Brito, "Las actividades culturales de Alvarado," *RUY* 7:38 (Mar.–Apr. 1965), 33; Alvarado, "Informe," *DO,* 4 Jan. 1918, p. 62.

59. Alvarado, *La reconstrucción,* vol. 1, p. 22. Although Alvarado's great books program smacked of a bourgeois mentality absent in José Vasconcelos's later campaign as Obregón's minister of education in the early 1920s to disseminate the classics throughout the Mexican countryside, there is a similarity in the idealistic (and unrealistic) vision and ultimate futility of the two programs.

60. Manuel Correa Delgado, *Breve relación histórica de la Liga de Acción Social: Sus principales trabajos durante los 50 años de su existencia,* Mérida, 1959, pp. 19–67; Hernán Morales Medina, "Don Gonzalo Cámara Zavala: Pionero de la educación rural," *RUY* 4:22–23 (July–Oct. 1962), 71–72.

61. J. D. Ramírez Garrido, "La instrucción en Yucatán," *Acción Mundial,* 4 Mar. 1916; Antonio Betancourt Pérez, "La verdad," 34–56; Luis Álvarez Barret, "Orígenes y evolución de las escuelas rurales en Yucatán," *RUY* 13:78 (Nov.–Dec., 1971), 26–51.

62. Betancourt Pérez, "La verdad," 53–54; Álvarez Barret, "Orígenes," 51.

63. Santiago Pacheco Cruz, *Recuerdos de la propaganda constitucionalista en Yucatán,* Mérida, 1953, p. 302; Betancourt Pérez, "La verdad," 53–54.

64. Moisés González Navarro, *Raza y tierra: La guerra de castas y el henequén,* Mexico, 1970, p. 236.

65. Antonio Betancourt Pérez, *La escuela de la Revolución Mexicana,* Mérida, 1965, pp. 25–26; Álvarez Barret, "Orígenes," 51; cf. James Cockcroft, "El maestro de primaria en la Revolución Mexicana," *HM* 16:4 (Apr.–June 1967), 565–588; AGE, Gregorio Torres Quintero, Jefe del Dpto. de Educación Pública, to Alvarado, 6 June 1916.

66. In his decrees and circulars, Alvarado alternately referred to the *maestros* as "los portavoces de la Revolución," "pregonadores de derechos," and "heraldos del progreso," e.g., *DO,* 21 Sept. 1915, p. 3448.

67. AGE, memorandum, Gobierno del Estado, Dirección General de Enseñanza Rural, 25 Oct. 1915; AGE, Torres Quintero to Alvarado, 6 June 1916; *VdR* 30 Oct. 1915; *DO,* 20 July 1915, pp. 2391–93.

68. *DO,* 22 Mar. 1916, pp. 1189–1190; *VdR,* 18 Mar. 1916 and throughout March and April 1916.

69. AGE, Franco Fernández to Alvarado, 1 Dec. 1915; *DO,* 10 July 1915, p. 2245; *VdR,* 30 Jan. 1916, 23 Mar. 1916, 9 May 1916; and Chacón, "Yucatán and the Mexican Revolution," chap. 6. For an eyewitness account of retroactive revolution in action by one of Alvarado's *agentes de propaganda* in the eastern part of the state, see Pacheco Cruz, *Recuerdos,* pp. 123–255; cf. the day-by-day account (*Diario Revolucionario*) compiled by the director of Alvarado's Labor Department, Ávila y Castillo.

70. AGE, Agentes de Propaganda, Tomás Alpuche S. and Aurelio Briceño, to Carlos Loveira, Jefe del Dpto. del Trabajo, 27 Mar. 1916; *VdR,* 30 Jan. 1916. Loveira, *El obrerismo,* pp. 45–46.

71. *VdR,* 15 Jan. 1916, 20 Jan. 1916; *Ariete,* 21p9.5 Oct. 1915; Esteban Durán Rosado, *La primera huelga ferrocarrilera en Yucatán,* Mérida, 1944; SD-CPR, *Corr., 1913,* vol. 3, 800, Gracey to Secretary of State, 4 Jan.

72. Montalvo, "Caudillismo y estado," 21–22; Bolio O., *Yucatán,* p. 151.

73. *DO,* 7 July 1915, pp. 2188–2189, 5 Aug. 1915, pp. 2685–2686, 27 Oct. 1915, p. 4098; *Quienes son en Yucatán los enemigos de la Revolución . . . ,* Mérida, 1916, p. 9; Bustillos Carrillo, *Yucatán,* pp. 119, 125–126; Montalvo, "Caudillismo y estado," 23.

74. Francisco J. Paoli and Enrique Montalvo, *El socialismo olvidado de Yucatán,* Mexico, 1977, pp. 50–52; Ramón Espadas, *Fundación del Partido Socialista Obrero,* Mérida, 1972.

75. Ramón Mendoza Medina, "Influencia de Salvador Alvarado en la Constitución de 1917," *DdelS,* 28 Mar. 1965, Cultural Supplement.

76. *DO,* 17 May 1915, pp. 1291–1292, 4 May 1916, pp. 1798–1799; Mario de la Cueva, *Derecho mexicano del trabajo,* Mexico, 1943, vol. 1, pp. 105–112.

77. Montalvo, "Caudillismo y estado," 21–22.

78. Marjorie R. Clark, *Organized Labor in Mexico,* Chapel Hill, N.C., 1934, pp. 209, 213; Gruening, *Mexico,* pp. 340–341; SD, 812.61326/396.

79. AGE, Loveira to Alvarado, 29 Nov. 1916; SD, 812.00/18110; Gruening, *Mexico,* p. 338.

80. SD, 812.00/18110; AGE, Loveira to Alvarado, 29 Nov. 1916; Loveira, *El obrerismo*, pp. 35–37.

81. AGE, Loveira to Alvarado, 29 Nov. 1916, Alvarado to Loveira, 15 Dec. 1916; *VdR*, 12 Jan. 1916, 13 Jan. 1916, 14 Jan. 1916, 26 Feb. 1916; Loveira, *El obrerismo*, pp. 35–37, 52–53. Again, cf. the similar contemporary policy of the Sonoran revolutionary governors, Calles and de la Huerta. Aguilar Camín, *La frontera nómada*, pp. 436–440.

82. Clark, *Organized Labor*, p. 201. Cf. Alvarado's own comment late in 1916: "Recently, events . . . have demonstrated the danger that would develop if the government fell into hands less energetic and capable than mine." *VdR*, 14 Dec. 1916.

83. Chacón, "Yucatán and the Mexican Revolution," pp. 188–189.

84. AGE, Alvarado to all comandantes militares, 20 Apr. 1916; *DO*, 2 Dec. 1915, *passim*.

85. *DO*, 25 May 1915, p. 1425, 20 July 1915, p. 2279; *VdR*, 23 Feb. 1916.

86. *DO*, 14 May 1915, pp. 1261–1262; cf. *DO*, 10 July 1915, pp. 2244–2245, 3 Sept. 1915, pp. 3186–3187.

87. AGE, Tomás Villa González to Alvarado, 21 Jan. 1917; AGE, Inspector of the Treasury Department to Alvarado, 23 Mar. 1916; *DO*, 15 Nov. 1915, pp. 4413–4414; *VdR*, 12 Mar. 1916.

88. Chacón, " Yucatán and the Mexican Revolution," pp. 189–191.

89. AGE, Jefe del Dpto. del Trabajo to Prof. Villalbazo, n.d., 1916; AGE, Jefe del Dpto. del Trabajo to Prof. Vázquez, 3 Apr. 1916; AGE, Salvador Alvarado to Presidentes Municipales, 3 May 1917.

90. Montalvo, "Caudillismo y estado," 30.

91. Ironically, although the members of the Yucatecan delegation at the Querétaro Constitutional Convention played an influential role in the drafting of several key articles and effectively defended Alvarado's regional program of social reforms, they were not persuasive on the relatively minor issue of a lenient residency requirement, thereby nullifying Alvarado's chances of succession. See Chacón, "Yucatán and the Mexican Revolution," pp. 217–222.

92. For Carranza's reassignment of Alvarado and the Yucatecan succession issue, see Franz, "Bullets and Bolshevists," pp. 160–162, and Chacón, "Yucatán and the Mexican Revolution," pp. 213–214.

93. *VdR*, 19 May 1917; Franz, "Bullets and Bolshevists," pp. 177–181.

94. AGE, Comandante Militar of Izamal to Alvarado, 11 Oct. 1915; *DO*, 5 June 1915, pp. 1620–1621; *VdR*, 28 Aug. 1916, 9 Sept. 1916; AGE, anonymous report to Alvarado, 17 Feb. 1917; Mena Brito, *Reestructuración*, vol. 3, p. 176.

95. AGE, anonymous report to Alvarado, 17 Feb. 1917; Mena Brito, *Bolshevismo y democracia en México*, 2d ed., Mexico, 1933, p. 17.

96. AGE, Torre Díaz to Carranza, 6 Sept. 1917, 22 Sept. 1917.

97. Mena Brito, *Reestructuración*, vol. 3, pp. 213–214; Paoli and Montalvo, *El socialismo olvidado*, pp. 58–59.

98. AGE, Mena Brito to Carranza, 20 Aug. 1917.

99. AGE, Tránsito Medina to Alvarado, 29 May 1917.

100. A *cacicazgo* is the power domain of a *cacique*, a local boss, strong man, or chief. According to the foremost student of *caciquismo*, the *cacique* is "a strong and autocratic leader in local and regional politics whose characteristically informal, personalistic, and often arbitrary rule is buttressed by a core of relatives, 'fighters,' and dependents, and is marked by the diagnostic threat and practice of violence." Paul Friedrich, "The Legitimacy of a Cacique," in M. J. Swartz, ed., *Local-Level Politics*, Chicago, 1968, p. 247. The caudillo is a *cacique* writ large, one who has mobilized his supporters for the purpose of extending his local base of power.

101. Chacón, " Yucatán and the Mexican Revolution," pp. 207–213; José Castillo Torre, *A la luz del relámpago: Ensayo de biografía subjetiva de Felipe Carrillo Puerto*, Mexico, 1934, pp. 88–89.

102. For González and his henchmen, see Mena Brito, *Bolshevismo*, p. 76; *D*, 26 Aug. 1917; AGE, petition from Partido Liberal Yucateco to Carranza, 9 Apr. 1917; AGE, Pedro Sánchez Cuevas, Partido Liberal, to Alvarado, 5 Feb. 1917; AGE, Felipe Alonzo, Partido Liberal, Committee of Opichén, to Mena Brito, 30 Apr. 1917; AGE, Carlos González and vecinos of Opichén to Alvarado, 4 June 1917.

103. *D*, 26 Aug. 1917.

104. AGE, Carlos González et al. to Alvarado, 4 June 1917.

105. AGE, Eraclio Carrillo Puerto to Alvarado, 11 Apr. 1918.

106. AGE, Dr. Roberto Reyes B. to Alvarado, 15 Feb. 1918.

107. AGE, Francisco Díaz et al. to Alvarado, 14 Apr. 1918.

108. AGE, Gordiano Ortiz to Alvarado, 3 Aug. 1917.

109. AGE, Carranza to Torre Díaz, 22 Aug. 1917, Torre Díaz to Carranza, 6 Sept. 1917.

5. The theory and practice of bourgeois reform

1. Mexico, Congreso, *Diario de los debates de la Cámara de Diputados . . . 1912*, Mexico, 1922, *passim*.; Jesús Silva Herzog, ed., *La cuestión de la tierra: Colección de folletos para la historia de la Revolución Mexicana*, vol. 1:1910–1911, Mexico, 1960; vol. 2:1911–1913 (1961); Félix Palavicini, *Los diputados: Lo que se ve y lo que no se ve de la Cámara*, Mexico, n.d., pp. 559–570.

2. For a biographical sketch of Cabrera, see Vicente Fernández Bravo, *El ideario de la Revolución Mexicana*, Mexico, 1973, pp. 159–160. An effective treatment of Cabrera's thought is Eugenia Meyer, *Luis Cabrera: Teoría y crítica de la Revolución Mexicana*, Mexico, 1972. For Molina Enríquez's influence, see Moisés González Navarro, "La ideología de la Revolución Mexicana," *HM* 10:4 (Apr.–June 1961), 631.

3. Cabrera's most famous *Cámara* speech on the agrarian question is printed and discussed in a variety of sources, most notably: *Diario de los debates*, 3 Dec. 1912; *El pensamiento de Luis Cabrera*, ed. Eduardo Luquín, Mexico, 1960, pp. 179–210; Jesús Silva Herzog, *El agrarismo y la reforma agraria*, Mexico, 1959, pp. 199–208.

4. Stanley R. Ross, *Francisco I. Madero: Apostle of Mexican Democracy*, New

York, 1955, pp. 219ff; Eyler N. Simpson, *The Ejido: Mexico's Way Out,* Chapel Hill, N.C., 1937, pp. 49–50.

5. Clarence Senior, *Land Reform and Democracy,* Gainesville, Fla., 1958, p. 25; Silva Herzog, *La cuestión,* vol. 1, pp. 165–175; vol. 3, pp. 357–393; Pastor Rouaix, *Génesis de los artículos 27 y 123 de la Constitución política de 1917,* Mexico, 1959, pp. 277–284.

6. Héctor Aguilar Camín, "The Relevant Tradition: Sonoran Leaders in the Revolution," in D. A. Brading, ed., *Caudillo and Peasant in the Mexican Revolution,* Cambridge (U.K.), 1980, pp. 94–102; *La frontera nómada: Sonora y la Revolución Mexicana,* Mexico, 1977, pp. 376, 420–421, 431–436, 440–444.

7. Cabrera had been a resident schoolmaster on an estate in Tlaxcala (1895), an experience that apparently was critical in shaping his negative opinion of the hacienda. Molina Enríquez served for many years as a local justice of the peace in rural Mexico State.

8. Quite clearly this was the vision that was subtly injected into Cabrera's 3 Dec. 1912 *Cámara* speech. Cf. Andrés Molina Enríquez, *Los grandes problemas nacionales,* Mexico, 1909, pp. 68–76.

9. Silva Herzog, *El agrarismo,* p. 233.

10. Rouaix, *Génesis,* pp. 261–274.

11. Silva Herzog, *El agrarismo,* p. 233.

12. Simpson, *The Ejido,* pp. 59–62; cf. Paul Friedrich, *Agrarian Revolt in a Mexican Village,* Englewood Cliffs, N.J , 1937, pp. 95–96.

13. See the following explicit references to the *pequeña propiedad* in Salvador Alvarado, *La reconstrucción de México: Un mensaje a los pueblos de America,* Mexico, 1919, vol. 1, pp. 112–116, 127–130; vol. 2, p. 56.

14. Moisés González Navarro, *Raza y tierra: La guerra de castas y el henequén,* Mexico, 1970, p. 243.

15. *VdR,* 5 May 1916.

16. Alvarado, *La reconstrucción,* vol. 2, pp. 273–275.

17. Salvador Alvarado, *Actuación revolucionaria del General Salvador Alvarado en Yucatán,* Mexico, 1965, pp. 69–73; *La reconstrucción,* vol. 2, pp. 5–7, 56, 272–275; González Navarro, *Raza,* pp. 245–246.

18. Salvador Alvarado, "Reglamento de la Ley Agraria de 6 enero de 1915" in Álvaro Gamboa Ricalde, *Yucatán desde 1910,* Veracruz, 1943, vol. 2, p. 513; cf. Molina Enríquez, *Los grandes problemas,* pp. 68–76. Elsewhere, Alvarado regards the *pequeña propiedad* as the cornerstone and chief legacy of the Revolution in Yucatán. *DO,* 8 Apr. 1915, pp. 833–834, 11 June 1915, p. 1710, 30 Dec. 1915, pp. 5230–5232.

19. AGE, "Proyecto de reglamento para los trabajos agrarios," 5 Apr. 1915; *VdR,* 5 June 1916, 7 Aug. 1916, 21 Aug. 1916.

20. Gamboa, *Yucatán,* vol. 2, p. 513; Salvador Alvarado, *Carta al pueblo de Yucatán,* Mérida, 1916; González Navarro, *Raza,* pp. 241–242.

21. *VdR,* 16 Jan. 1916.

22. AGE, Comisario Municipal, Euán, to Carlos Baz, President, Comisión Local Agraria, 4 Sept. 1917; *VdR,* 22 Oct. 1915.

23. Alvarado, *La reconstrucción*, vol. 2, pp. 5–7; González Navarro, *Raza*, p. 244.

24. Alvarado, *La reconstrucción*, vol. 1, pp. 113–114, 128. During their administrations in the 1920s, Obregón and Calles would continue to grant special exemptions to henequen and other cash crops under the provisions of the agrarian reform.

25. *Ibid.*, pp. 113–119; *DO*, 9 July 1915, p. 2225 (uncultivated lands of Montes and the Peón family affected for *ejido* distribution); AGE, "Relación de solares abandonados en el pueblo de Telchaquillo . . . repartidos . . . a los vecinos de dicho pueblo," 11 Aug. 1917.

26. Alvarado, *La reconstrucción*, vol. 1, p. 116; cf. vol. 1, p. 38.

27. *DO*, 27 Sept. 1915, p. 3544, 5 June 1915, pp. 1621–1622; *VdR*, 15 Oct. 1915, 27 July 1916; AGE, Comisario Municipal, San José Dzal, to Alvarado, 5 Dec. 1917; AGE, Presidente Municipal, Dzununcán, to Alvarado, 13 Dec. 1917.

28. AGE, Circular num. 16, President, Comisión Nacional Agraria, Eduardo Hay, to Alvarado, 1 Feb. 1917.

29. *DO*, 5 Jan. 1918, pp. 80–81; Mexico, Dpto. de la Estadística Nacional, *Anuario estadístico, 1930*, Tacubaya, 1932, pp. 375–376; Mexico, Sría. de Agricultura y Fomento, Comisión Nacional Agraria, *Estadística, 1915–1927*, Mexico, 1928, pp. 49–51, 83–85, 125–127, 168, 214–215.

30. *DO*, 1 July 1915, pp. 2096–2097, 19 June 1915, p. 1875; AGE, Lic. Patricio Sabido to Ramón García Núñez, 29 July 1915; AGE, Ramón García Núñez to Alvarado, 26 Aug. 1915; *VdR*, 13 Jan. 1916, 14 Mar. 1916.

31. Alvarado, *La reconstrucción*, vol. 2, p. 56; vol. 1, pp. 128, 155; González Navarro, *Raza*, pp. 245, 250. No doubt, Alvarado's bitter experiences in his home state battling the Yaquis – the only sector of Sonoran society to demand ejidal restitutions and distributions – reinforced his anti-*ejido* position. Aguilar Camín, "The Relevant Tradition," pp. 94–100, 113.

32. Alvarado, *La reconstrucción*, vol. 2, p. 56; cf. Aguilar Camín, *La frontera nómada*, pp. 427–428, 431–436.

33. E. g., see AGE, Consejo Directivo, Comisión Reguladora del Mercado de Henequén, to Alvarado, 23 Jan. 1917; and *DO*, 8 Dec. 1915, pp. 4799–4802.

34. Salvador Alvarado, *Mi sueño*, Mérida, 1965 (originally published in 1917); *La reconstrucción*, vol. 2, pp. 272–275; vol. 1, pp. 112–130, 138, 144.

35. Eric Wolf, *Peasant Wars of the Twentieth Century*, New York, 1969, p. 42; Ramón Berzunza Pinto, "El Constitucionalismo en Yucatán," HM 12:2 (Oct.–Dec. 1962), 281, 295.

36. Aguilar Camín, "The Relevant Tradition," p. 99; Humberto Lara y Lara, *Sobre la trayectoria de la reforma agraria en Yucatán*, Mérida, 1949, p. 23.

37. *DO*, 15 Feb. 1916, pp. 717–718, 5 Jan. 1918, pp. 80–81, 24 May 1917, p. 1; AGE, Comandante Militar, Izamal, to Alvarado, 18 Feb. 1916; Simpson, *The Ejido*, p. 78.

38. Alvarado, *Carta*, p. 197; AGE, Alvarado to Pastor Rouaix, 3 Aug. 1916; AC, Alvarado to Carranza, 29 Mar. 1916; SD, 812.61326/213.

39. AGE, Carlos Baz to Alvarado, 11 Sept. 1917; AGE, vecinos of Citilcúm, Izamal, to Alvarado, 15 Dec. 1916; AGE, "Relación de solares abandonados en el pueblo de Telchaquillo," 11 Aug. 1917; *DO*, 16 May 1917, p. 2337. These documents suggest that in some cramped areas of the henequen zone, Alvarado acted as much to provide the *campesinos* with housing as he did to grant access to *milpa* land.

40. AGE, Jacinto Cohuich et al. to Alvarado, 20 Dec. 1916; AGE, Alvarado to Comandantes Militares del Estado, 25 Dec. 1916.

41. That Carranza's opposition was that "force beyond his control" is also demonstrated by a comparison of the texts of Alvarado's *Informes* (official reports) of 1917 and 1918. In the 1917 report, sent to Carranza, Alvarado virtually omits any reference to land reform. By contrast, his 1918 report before the State Congress is honeycombed with references to his inability to bring agrarian reform to fruition. AGE, typescript, "Informe que el Gral. Salvador Alvarado . . . rinde al Primer Jefe . . . Venustiano Carranza . . .," 28 Feb. 1917; "Informe que . . . rinde ante el H. Congreso del Estado . . . Gral. Salvador Alvarado," *DO*, 3 Jan. 1918, p. 35, 5 Jan. 1918, pp. 79–84.

42. U.S. responsibility is charged by Francisco Bulnes, *The Whole Truth about Mexico: President Wilson's Responsibility*, tr. Dora Scott, New York, 1916, pp. 355–356, and Antonio Betancourt Pérez, *Revoluciones y crisis en la economía de Yucatán*, Mérida, 1953, p. 67.

43. Lara y Lara, *Sobre la trayectoria*, p. 19.

44. Fidelio Quintal Martín, "Quince años trascendentales en la historia de Yucatán," *RUY* 16:93–94 (May–Aug. 1974), 104–105.

45. SD, 812.61326/197, 202, 236; SD-CPR, *Corr.*, *1919*, vol. 5, 800/861.3, Marsh to Secretary of State, 6 Jan.

46. E.g., David A. Franz, "Bullets and Bolshevists: A History of the Mexican Revolution and Reform in Yucatán, 1910–1924," unpublished Ph.D. dissertation, University of New Mexico, Albuquerque, 1973, pp. 140–141; cf. SD, 812.00/17995. This argument would seem to carry more weight in two other areas – the free municipality and labor reform – where Alvarado successfully implemented his programs around, or in the face of, Carranza's disapproval. That he was able to do so suggests that the First Chief was not opposed to the reforms but merely sought to delay their introduction until they could be legitimized by the power of a new Mexican constitution.

47. Wolf, *Peasant Wars*, pp. 37–43; Robert Quirk, "Liberales y radicales en la Revolución Mexicana," *HM* 2:4 (Apr.–June 1953), 509–511.

48. AC, Frank Pendas to "Muy estimada señora y amiga," 8 Jan. 1917, citing the purloined letter from Rolland to Alvarado.

49. Alvarado, *Actuación revolucionaria*, p. 85.

50. Alvarado, *La reconstrucción*, vol. 1, p. 11; Eduardo W. Villa, *Compendio de historia del Estado de Sonora*, Mexico, 1937, p. 466; SD, 812.00/14693; cf. Aguilar Camín, "The Relevant Tradition," pp. 122–123.

51. Alvarado, *Actuación revolucionaria*, pp. 71–72; SD, 812.61326/194; U.S. Senate, Committee on Foreign Relations, *Investigation of Mexican Affairs: Pre-*

liminary Report and Hearings of the Committee on Foreign Relations, pursuant to S. Res. 106, Washington, D.C., 1920, vol. 2, pp. 1590–1591.

52. Antonio Rodríguez, *El henequén: Una planta calumniada,* Mexico, 1966, p. 224; Leopoldo Peniche Vallado, "La obra del Gral. Salvador Alvarado en Yucatán," *DdelS,* 28 Mar. 1965, Cultural Supplement.

53. Alvarado, *Actuación revolucionaria,* pp. 71–72.

54. Humberto Lara y Lara, "Proyección social de la obra en Yucatán del Gral. Salvador Alvarado," *DdelS,* 28 Mar. 1965, Cultural Supplement.

55. Alvarado, *Actuación revolucionaria,* pp. 69–73. *Agente de Propaganda* Pacheco Cruz, *Recuerdos de la propaganda constitucionalista en Yucatán,* Mérida, 1953, pp. 147, 178, 186, 199, reported that treatment of *peones* on the financially strained smaller *fincas* was consistently worse than on the larger plantations.

56. SD-CPR, *Despatches to the Department, Jan. 1, 1905 to Dec. 20, 1909,* Thompson to Secretary of State, 7 Aug. 1908, Thompson to Assistant Secretary of State, 27 Feb. 1909.

57. *VdR,* 5 May 1916. This is acknowledged in a series of reports by U.S. State Department personnel, e.g., SD, 812.61326/174, 197, 229, 236.

58. E.g., Alvarado, *Actuación revolucionaria,* pp. 69–75 and *passim.*

59. Alvarado, *Actuación revolucionaria,* p. 70; cf. SD, 812.61326/236.

60. SD, 812.61326/189, 135; cf. Thomas H. Holloway, *The Brazilian Coffee Valorization of 1906: Regional Politics and Economic Dependence,* Madison, Wis., 1975.

61. *RdM,* 12 Nov. 1910; *DY,* 12 Sept. 1911; SD-CPR, *Despatches to the Department, Jan. 1, 1905 to Dec. 20, 1909,* Thompson to Secretary of State, 7 Aug. 1908; SD, 812.00/1084.

62. *DO,* 10 Jan. 1912, pp. 168–170; Gabriel Ferrer de Mendiolea, "Leyes precursores de la Carta de 1917," *N,* 21 July 1957.

63. AGN, Ramo de Madero, paquete 2–16, Faustino Escalante to Madero, 7 Feb. 1912; Gamboa Ricalde, *Yucatán,* vol. 1, p. 198.

64. Nelson Reed, *The Caste War of Yucatán,* Stanford, Calif., 1964, pp. 261–262; Lara y Lara, *Sobre la trayectoria,* p. 17.

65. Gamboa Ricalde, *Yucatán,* vol. 1, p. 197; Franz, "Bullets and Bolshevists," pp. 52–53.

66. Reed, *Caste War,* p. 262; Yucatán, Comisión especial . . . para investigar, examinar y depurar los manejos de la Comisión Reguladora del Mercado de Henequén, *Informe acerca de los operaciones . . . en el período 1 mayo 1912–10 septiembre 1914,* Mérida, 1919.

67. Manuel Zapata Casares, *Vía-Crucis del henequén: Colección de escritos sobre el gran problema de Yucatán,* Mérida, 1961, pp. 22–23.

68. *La reconstrucción,* vol. 1, pp. 194–195, 162–163.

69. Víctor A. Rendón, *Notas breves,* New York, 1917, p. 9; Yucatán, Comisión Reguladora del Mercado de Henequén, *La cuestión palpitante en Yucatán: Fructífera gestión de la Comisión Reguladora . . . en 18 meses de labor activa, inteligente y honrada,* Mérida, 1916.

70. SD, 812.61326/193, 236.
71. SD, 812.61326/194.
72. SD, 812.61326/118, 136.
73. SD, 812.61326/194.
74. Evidence of the small and medium planters' support for Alvarado is found in SD, 812.61326/194, 229, 236.
75. SD, 812.61326/194; SD, 812.00/18110; Alvarado, "En legítima defensa," *D,* 4 May 1922.
76. U.S. Senate, Committee on Agriculture and Forestry, *Importation of Sisal and Manila Hemp: Hearing before the Sub-committee of the Committee on Agriculture and Forestry, pursuant to S. Res. 94,* Washington, D.C., 1916, vol. 2, p. 1218.
77. *Ibid.,* SD, 812.61326/214; SD, 8.1200/19828.
78. U.S. Senate, *Importation of Sisal,* vol. 2, p. 1218; Franz, "Bullets and Bolshevists," p. 121.
79. SD, 812.61326/124.
80. SD, 812.61326/194.
81. Franz, "Bullets and Bolshevists," p. 124.
82. For the origins and actual terms of the credit agreement, see SD, 812.61326/194, 220, 229, 236.
83. Nathaniel C. Raymond, "The Impact of Land Reform in the Monocrop Region of Yucatán, Mexico," unpublished Ph.D. dissertation, Brandeis University, Waltham, Mass., 1971, p. 55; Fernando Benítez, *Ki: El drama de un pueblo y de una planta,* 2d ed., Mexico, 1962, p. 107.
84. Gamboa Ricalde, *Yucatán,* vol. 2, p. 552; Rodríguez, *El henequén,* p. 241.
85. SD-CPR, *Corr., 1918,* vol. 8, 861.3, Marsh to Secretary of State, 21 Feb.; SD, 812.61326/210.
86. Alvarado, quoted in Fernando Benítez, *Ki,* p. 110.
87. *VdR,* 24 Mar. 1917.
88. *DO,* 8 Dec. 1915, pp. 4799–4802, 28 Dec. 1916, pp. 4511–4512; Rodríguez, *El henequén,* pp. 236–237.
89. AGE, Consejo Directivo, Comisión Reguladora del Mercado de Henequén, to Alvarado, 23 Jan. 1917.
90. See, e.g., AGE, Manuel R. Castellanos to Director del Catastro, n.d. (1918), only one of many such petitions from *hacendados.* Perhaps the greatest beneficiary of Alvarado's land tax has been the historian. In 1915, in preparation for his real estate law, the general conducted a painstaking property census throughout the state and published the results in *DO,* 1916–1917. The census constitutes an invaluable document, providing a comprehensive rundown by *partido* of Yucatán's proprietors, their properties, and the values at which they were appraised.
91. Yucatán, *Breves apuntes acerca de la administración del Gral. Salvador Alvarado, como Gobernador de Yucatán, con simple expresión de hechos y sus consecuencias,* Mérida, 1916, pp. 27ff.
92. Throughout his tenure in Yucatán, Alvarado preferred to pay for his new projects by collecting revenues directly from the henequen export sector and

funneling them through the *Reguladora*. Infrequently, he engaged in the more common revolutionary practice of imposing forced loans on *hacendados* and merchants. Unlike most revolutionary caudillos, Alvarado made a point of paying back the loans.

93. SD-CPR, *Correspondence, Jan. 3, 1912 to July 31, 1912,* W. P. Young to Secretary of State, pp. 0232; *Corr., 1923,* vol. 2, 610, "Trade Promotion Work at Progreso," 26 July; "The Grocery Trade of Yucatán," 10 Sept.

94. SD-CPR, *Corr., 1918,* vol. 5, 711.3, Robert Haberman to Marsh, 6 May; *DO,* 10 May 1915, p. 1197.

95. AGE, Petition by "200 vecinos and obreros of Mérida," to Alvarado, June 1915; *VdR,* 2 Apr. 1915.

96. *DO,* 8 May 1915, pp. 1176–1177, 1 July 1915, pp. 2096–2097; Yucatán, *Breves apuntes,* p. 27.

97. AGE, Ing. Ramón Guevara Jiménez to Alvarado, 14 June 1915.

98. AGE, "Relación de los sres. hacendados que contribuyen para el aumento del capital de la Comisión Reguladora de Comercio," Aug. 1915; *DO,* 6 Sept. 1915, pp. 3223–3224, 7 Sept. 1915, p. 3241.

99. *DO,* 8 May 1915, pp. 1176–1177; SD-CPR, *Corr., 1919,* vol. 4, 690, Marsh to Secretary of State, 15 May.

100. SD, 812.61326/254; *VdR,* 12 Feb. 1916.

101. AGE, "Copias de las notas de los asuntos resueltos en este Dpto. del Trabajo durante el transcurso del mes de febrero del presente año (1918) . . . ," Feb. 1918; *VdR,* 20 Mar. 1918.

102. *VdR,* 12 Feb. 1916, 23 Feb. 1916; AGE, Felipe Solís, President, Comisión Reguladora de Comercio, Motul, to Alvarado, 24 Sept. 1915.

103. SD-CPR, *Con. Corr.,* 800, Marsh to Secretary of State, 11 Oct. 1918.

104. *Ibid.* The politics of food during wartime will be taken up in greater detail with Carrillo Puerto's cooperative movement in Chapter 7.

105. Rodríguez, *El henequén,* p. 233; Renán Irigoyen, "El impulso a la economía de Yucatán durante el gobierno de Alvarado," *RUY* 7:38 (Mar.–Apr. 1965), 14–25.

106. Anastasio Manzanilla D., *El bolchevismo criminal de Yucatán.* Mérida, 1921, p. 13; AGE, Comisión Reguladora del Mercado de Henequén, "Acta num. 50 . . . ," 25 Aug. 1918.

107. AGE, "Acta num. 50"; AGE, Letters from A. Ailloud, Gerente, La Industrial, to Comisión Reguladora, 11 and 13 Aug. 1917; Franz, "Bullets and Bolshevists," p. 133. Alvarado did make a bold but unsuccessful attempt to manufacture binder twine in Argentina. See Chapter 6.

108. Martín Luis Guzmán, *The Eagle and the Serpent,* tr. Harriet de Onís, Garden City, N.Y., 1965, p. 73.

109. Cf., e.g., the view in Irigoyen, "El impulso," 14–25, with that in SD, 812.61326/254.

110. *DO,* 3 May 1916, p. 1778.

111. *Ibid.;* Irigoyen, "El impulso," 14–25.

112. *DO,* 3 June 1916, pp. 2181–2184.

113. *DO,* 5 Jan. 1918, p. 84.

114. Irigoyen, "El impulso," 24–25.

115. John Womack will discuss these themes in his forthcoming work on labor and the Mexican Revolution in Veracruz.

116. Irigoyen, "El impulso" 25.

117. See Chapter 8; cf. Joan L. Bak, "Some Antecedents of Corporatism: State Economic Intervention and Rural Organization in Brazil. The Case of Rio Grande do Sul, 1890–1937," unpublished Ph.D. dissertation, Yale University, New Haven, Conn., 1977.

6. The breakdown of bourgeois revolution, 1918–1920

1. Salvador Alvarado, *Actuación revolucionaria del General Salvador Alvarado en Yucatán*, Mexico, 1965, p. 124.

2. SD, 812.61326/232.

3. SD, 812.61326/89, 26.

4. Eliot Jones, *The Trust Problem in the United States*, New York, 1921, pp. 243–247.

5. SD, 812.61326/224–225, 229; *United States v. Pan-American Commission et al.*, 261 Fed. 229 (S.D.N.Y. 1918); Fernando Benítez, *Ki: El drama de un pueblo y de una planta*, 2d ed., Mexico, 1962, p. 107.

6. U.S. Senate, comments of Senator McCumber on the sisal situation, 64th Cong., 1st Sess., 6 Jan. 1916, *CR*, vol. 52, part 1, pp. 587–588; SD, 812.61326/299; U.S. Senate, speech by Senator Ransdell, 64th Cong., 2nd Sess., 12 Jan. 1917, *CR*, vol, 54, part 2, p. 1246.

7. SD, 812.61326/162, 262, 273.

8. Robert Freeman Smith, *The United States and Revolutionary Nationalism in Mexico, 1913–1932*, Chicago, 1972, p. 42; SD, 812.61326/109.

9. SD, 812.61326/12–13, 24–25; Álvaro Gamboa Ricalde, *Yucatán desde 1910*, Veracruz, 1943, vol. 2, pp. 338–339.

10. SD, Bryan–Wilson Correspondence, Wilson to Bryan, 21 Mar. 1915; U.S. Department of State, *Papers Relating to the Foreign Relations of the United States (1915–1924)*, Washington, D.C., 1924, p. 824. Juan Barragán R., *Historia del ejército de la Revolución Constitucionalista*, Mexico, 1946, vol. 2, pp. 251–252.

11. LC, Wilson Mss, Series 2, Bryan to Wilson, 13 Mar. 1915. Bryan was referring to the celebrated occupation of Mexico's chief port by the U.S. marines, which had taken place from April to November 1914. Justifying the occupation of Veracruz on a rather flimsy pretext, President Wilson had sought to save the Mexicans from a larger evil, the dictatorial rule of Victoriano Huerta.

12. SD, 812.61326/15 (Whitlock Cordage to Bryan); cf. SD, 812.61326/29a, 42a.

13. See, e.g., the correspondence in SD, 812.61326/12–159, *passim*.

14. E.g., SD, 812.61326/24, 35, 56a, 90; PCR, letterbook, *Yucatán Letters*, HG-1, p. 52, Peabody and Co. to Arturo Pierce, 31 Mar. 1915; PCR, letterbook, *Fibres and Domestic Letters*, no. 37, HE-2, p. 711, Peabody to Secretary of Commerce, 17 May 1917; pp. 738–739, Peabody to Hooven and Allison Co.,

Peabody to Peoria Cordage Co., both 24 May 1917; p. 970, Peabody to B. W. Long, 12 Aug. 1915.

15. SD, 812.00/15281. Significantly, Harvester continued throughout the summer of 1915 to clamor for visits by "an American warboat . . . at least until provision has been made to protect the supply of binder twine for the coming harvest . . . [W]ithout the moral influence of an American naval vessel," the company argued, "the situation of American interests is unsafe." SD, 812.61326/98, 141. Josephus Daniels, then secretary of the navy, disagreed, maintaining that the boats of the Atlantic Fleet's Cruiser Squadron were needed more at other Mexican ports. SD, 812.61326/102. In later years, Harvester would continue to press for armed intervention on behalf of the sisal trade. LC, Anderson Mss, Chandler P. Anderson Diary, 12, 18, 24 March 1923 (Anderson represented Harvester); and see Chapter 9.

16. SD, 812.61326/49, Bryan to manufacturers, dealers, congressmen, etc., discounting rumors regarding the burning of fields; Nathaniel C. Raymond, "The Impact of Land Reform in the Monocrop Region of Yucatán, Mexico," unpublished Ph.D. dissertation, Brandeis University, Waltham, Mass., 1971, pp. 60–61; SD, 812.00/14693.

17. SD, 812.61326/84.

18. SD, 812.61326/84.

19. SD, 812.61326/120.

20. SD, 812.61326/159.

21. SD, 812.61326/296, 298–299, 305.

22. SD, 812.61326/174.

23. Joseph S. Tulchin, *The Aftermath of War: World War I and U.S. Policy toward Latin America,* New York, 1971, pp. 13–16; SD, 812.50/61.

24. SD, 812.61326/229, 207, regarding testimony of *hacendado* Domingo Evia to Senate sub-committee; SD-CPR, *Con. Corr.,* no file designation, "Extract of Testimony Taken in the Hearings Before the Senate Sub-Committee on Agriculture and Forestry . . . ," Feb. 1916, testimony of planters Solís, Cámara, and Cantón.

25. SD, 812.61326/188.

26. SD, 812.61326/135, 181–183, 194–195, 200; AC, M. C. Rolland to Carranza, 10 Jan. 1917; CJD, roll 3, E. Robleda M. to Carranza, 10 June 1917. Representative of the work churned out by Alvarado's propagandists is: M. C. Rolland, "A Trial of Socialism in Mexico: What the Mexicans Are Fighting For," *Forum* 56 (July 1916), 79–90; and Carlo de Fornaro, "Yucatán and the International Harvester Company," *Forum,* 54 (Sept. 1915), 337–344.

27. W. C. Mullendore, *History of the United States Food Administration, 1917–1919,* introduction by Herbert Hoover, Stanford, Calif., 1941, pp. 3, 312–313.

28. PCC, file I, drawer 3, "Agreement with the U.S. Food Administration," 1 Nov. 1917; Mullendore, *History of the Food Administration,* pp. v, 312–315; Louis Crossette, *Sisal Production, Prices and Marketing,* U.S. Department of Commerce, Supplement to *Commerce Reports,* Trade Information Bulletin No. 200, Washington, D.C., 1924, p. 4.

29. Mullendore, *History of the Food Administration*, p. 313.

30. LC, Henry P. Fletcher Mss, memorandum, 6 Feb. 1918; WTBR, Entry 192, box 26, Bureau of Research and Statistics–Mexico, Herman Oliphant to Hoover, 27 Nov. 1917; SD, 812.50/61; Tulchin, *Aftermath of War*, pp. 15–16.

31. SD, 812.61326/235, 240.

32. SD, 812.61326/240.

33. Mullendore, *History of the Food Administration*, p. 313.

34. SD-CPR, *Corr., 1924*, vol. 7, 861.3, A. V. Dye to American Ambassador, 18 Nov.; IHCA, doc. file 9409, *Fibre Costs, 1914 to 1933*, cf. entries for "Manila" and "Mexican Sisal"; SD, 812.61326/259; Crossette, *Sisal Production*, pp. 2–3; typescript of article by Harold M. Pitt, "Manila Hemp and the Export Duty," dated 14 Nov. 1912, in IHCA, doc. file 2395.

35. SD, 812.61326/229.

36. Alvarado's case justifying a greatly increased price, based on inflationary trends and greatly increased production and transportation costs, is set out in SD-CPR, *Conn. Corr.*, no file designation, "Outline Showing the Cost of a Pound of Henequen Fibre . . . ," 22 Oct. 1917. Cf. the North American indictment found in Mullendore's official *History of the Food Administration*, pp. 312–313.

37. SD, 812.61326/228.

38. SD-CPR, *Con. Corr.*, 861.3, "Stenographic Report of a Meeting between Representatives of the Food Administration and the Comisión Reguladora . . . in . . . Washington, D.C. . . . March 5, 1918"; SD, 812.61326/252.

39. SD-CPR, *Corr., 1918*, vol. 8, 861.3, C. W. Merrill, Food Administration, to Comisión Reguladora, 5 and 12 Apr.

40. SD-CPR, *Corr., 1919*, vol. 5, 861.3, Marsh to Secretary of State, 4 Apr. 1919, citing 4 Apr. 1919 letter from Food Administration to W. B. Parish.

41. SD, 812.61326/252.

42. Mullendore, *History of the Food Administration*, p. 314.

43. SD, 812.61326/302–303.

44. SD, 812.61326/287.

45. Alvarado, "En legítima defensa," *D*, 4 May 1922.

46. Benítez, *Ki*, p. 114. For a month-by-month coverage of sales and price trends, see SD-CPR, *Corr., 1919*, vol. 2, 610, "Monthly Economic Reports," Marsh to Secretary of State.

47. SD, 812.61326/254, 259, 283, 294; and see SD-CPR, *Corr., 1917*, vol. 3, 851.6, Marsh to Secretary of State, 4 June.

48. SD, 812.61326/254.

49. SD, 812.00/21951; SD-CPR, *Corr., 1918*, vol. 8, 861.3, "Copia simple de la escritura de constitución de la Asociación de Hacendados Henequeneros," n.d.

50. These *folletos* or briefs presented before the federal authorities may be found in SD, 812.61326/254–259.

51. SD, 812.61326/254; Humberto Lara y Lara, *Sobre la trayectoria de la reforma agraria en Yucatán*, Mérida, 1949, pp. 20–21.

52. *RdY*, 15 Nov. 1918; SD, 813.61326/283.

53. Alvarado, "En legítima defensa"; AC, Alvarado to Luis Cabrera, 9 Jan. 1919.

54. SD, 812.00/22315.

55. LC, Anderson Mss, Diary of Chandler P. Anderson, 23 Apr. 1915. This estimate was made to Anderson, then assistant to Secretary of State Lansing, by former Mexican Ambassador Calero.

56. Thomas W. F. Gann, *In an Unknown Land*, London, 1924, p. 233.

57. U.S. Senate, Committee on Foreign Relations, *Investigation of Mexican Affairs: Preliminary Report and Hearings of the Committee on Foreign Relations, pursuant to S. Res 106*, Washington, D.C., 1920, vol. 1, p. 887; SD, 812.61326/315.

58. SD, 812.61326/331, 343.

59. SD-CPR, *Con. Corr.*, no file designation, Daniels to Frank L. Polk, Counsel, Department of State, 29 Mar. 1918.

60. Manuel A. Torre, *La ruina y el hambre o una guerra intestina amenazan a Yucatán*, Mérida, 1918, pp. 22–23; Jorge I. Rubio Mañé, *El separatismo de Yucatán*, Mérida, 1935, p. 61.

61. AGN, Papeles Presidenciales, Ramo Obregón–Calles, 424-H-2, "Cuadro que demuestra la decadencia de la industria henequenera de Yucatán," 9 July 1924.

62. AC, Carranza to Alvarado, 25 Mar. 1915.

63. SD, 812.61326/156; Carleton Beals, *Mexico: An Interpretation*, New York, 1923, p. 55.

64. SD, 812.61326/260.

65. PCR, *Fibres and Domestic Letters*, no. 37, HE-2, p. 840, Edward Bayley to Secretary of Commerce, 25 June 1915; cf. McC Mss., McCormick Collection, "I. H. Brief," Conference 335, 4; and Edward Bell, "Yucatán Sisal Big Carranza Asset," *FIN*, 16 Nov. 1915.

66. SD, 812.61326/298–299.

67. SD-CPR, *Con. Corr.*, 800, Marsh to Secretary of State, 21 Jan. 1919.

68. José Castillo Torre, *A la luz del relámpago: Ensayo de biografía sujetiva de Felipe Carrillo Puerto*, Mexico, 1934, pp. 88–89; SD, 812.61326/254; SD, 812.00/22315, 22887.

69. Álvaro Gamboa Ricalde, *Yucatán desde 1910*, Mexico, 1955, vol. 3, p. 89.

70. Enrique Montalvo, "Caudillismo y estado en la Revolución Mexicana: El gobierno de Alvarado en Yucatán," *Nova Americana* 2 (1979), 31; Francisco J. Paoli and Enrique Montalvo, *El socialismo olvidado*, Mexico, 1977, pp. 18–31, 61–71.

71. SD-CPR, *Con. Corr.*, 800, Marsh to Secretary of State, 21 Jan. 1919; *VdR*, 15 Dec. 1918; AGE, Presidente Municipal, Valladolid, to Castro Morales, 18 Jan. 1919; AGE, Presidente, Liga de Resistencia de Sanahcat, to Castro Morales, 13 May 1919.

72. AC, Hernández to Carranza, 16 May 1919; CJD, roll 3, Castro Morales to Carranza, 29 Aug. 1919.

73. Gamboa Ricalde, *Yucatán*, vol. 3, p. 134; CJD, roll 3, Castro Morales to Carranza, 29 Aug. 1919.
74. Bernardino Mena Brito, *Reestructuración histórica de Yucatán*. Mexico, 1969, vol. 3, p. 267.
75. Beals, *Mexico*, pp. 63–64.
76. *RdY*, 11 Feb. 1919, 13 May 1919, 15 May 1919; SD-CPR, *Con. Corr.*, 800, Marsh to Secretary of State, 21 Jan. 1919; 855, Marsh to Secretary of State, 21 Feb. 1919; SD, 812.52/503.
77. AC, Hernández to Carranza, 16 May 1919.
78. *RdY*, 23 Nov. 1919, 19 Dec. 1919; AGE, Presidente Municipal, Dzitzantún, to Castro Morales, n.d.; Juan Rico, *Yucatán: La huelga de junio*, Mérida, 1922, vol. 1, p. 104.
79. *RdY*, 29 May 1919, 25 Nov. 1919, 27 Mar. 1920.
80. AGE, Hernández to Castro Morales, 2 Oct. 1919; David A. Franz, "Bullets and Bolshevists: A History of the Mexican Revolution and Reform in Yucatán, 1910–1924," unpublished Ph.D. dissertation, University of New Mexico, Albuquerque, p. 185.
81. Ernest Gruening, "Felipe Carrillo Puerto," *The Nation* 117 (Jan. 1924), 61; Gruening, *Un viaje al Estado de Yucatán: Felipe Carrillo Puerto, su obra socialista*, Guanajuato, 1924, pp. 9–10; *RdY*, 21 Dec. 1919.
82. SD, 812.61326/299, 369; AGE, Alvarado to Castro Morales, 13 Feb. 1919, Alvarado to Luis Cabrera, 13 Feb. 1919.
83. SD-CPR, *Con. Corr.*, 800, Marsh to Secretary of State, 11 Oct. 1919.
84. Benítez, *Ki*, pp. 106–109.
85. *Ibid.*
86. Cf. *ibid.* and SD, 812.61326/254, 259, 294.
87. Lara y Lara, *Sobre la trayectoria*, pp. 20–21; Benítez, *Ki*, pp. 115–116.
88. Again, see SD-CPR, *Corr., 1919*, vol. 2, 610, "Monthly Economic Reports," especially those for January, February, May, and June; AC, Hernández to Carranza, 16 May 1919.
89. SD, 812.61326/358–359; SD-CPR, *Corr., 1919*, vol. 2, 610, "Monthly Economic Report: January," 6 Feb.; *ibid.*, vol. 5, 861.3, A. P. Rice to Marsh, 8 Dec.
90. SD-CPR, *Corr., 1919*, vol. 2, 610, "Monthly Economic Report: September," 1 Oct.; SD, 812.61326/312, 319.
91. PCR, *Yucatán Letters*, HG-2, p. 21, Peabody to Rice, 21 Apr. 1920; HG-1, p. 451, Peabody to Rice, 23 Dec. 1919.
92. SD, 812.61326/325, 283; SD-CPR, *Corr., 1919*, vol. 5, 800, 861.3, various reports filed by Marsh in October and November, describing the events leading up to and following the liquidation of the *Reguladora*.
93. SD, 812.61326/325–326; SD-CPR, *Corr., 1919*, vol. 5, 861.3, Marsh to Secretary of State, 8 Oct.; *DO*, 30 Oct. 1919, pp. 4819–4823.
94. The original financing scheme forming the Pan-American Commission Corporation is described and analyzed in SD, 812.61326/194, 220, 229, 236.
95. Copies of the contracts between the Yucatecan government and the ERIC

Corporation appear in SD, 812.61326/335, 349. The effects of the new financing arrangement are analyzed from the diverse perspectives of producers, manufacturers, consumers, and bankers in SD, 812.61326/327–328, 331–332, 338, 388; SD-CPR, *Corr., 1920,* vol. 1, 123; cf. *RdY,* 23 Feb. 1920.

96. PCR, *Yucatán Letters,* HG-2, p. 146, Peabody to Rice, 17 Dec. 1920.

97. SD, 812.61326/336, 343.

98. SD, 812.61326/338.

99. SD, 812.61326/343.

100. SD, 812.61326/359.

101. SD, 812.61326/364.

102. Revised edition, Boston, 1916.

103. William Z. Ripley, *Trusts, Pools and Corporations,* rev. ed., Boston, 1916, p. 337; SD, 812.61326/364.

104. SD, 812.61326/364; Ripley, *Trusts,* p. 343; Jones, *The Trust Problem,* pp. 237–238, 251.

105. SD, 812.61326/372. For example, Sharp discovered that Daniels had been eager to contract with fiber speculators at 26.4 cents per kilogram in an effort to break the *Reguladora* at a time when the Food Administration was committed to the *Reguladora* at 41.8 cents per kilogram. Both Hoover and the State Department vetoed Daniels's proposal, however. SD, 812.61326/364.

106. SD, 812.61326/364.

107. SD, 812.61326/370.

108. SD, 812.61326/365.

109. SD, 812.61326/366.

110. Benítez, *Ki,* p. 115.

111. SD-CPR, *Corr., 1918,* vol. 8, 861.3, Marsh to Secretary of State, 18 Dec., reports that the Yucatecan government was considering issuing a production-restriction decree. The first restriction would take place under Carrillo Puerto in the early 1920s.

112. Antonio Betancourt Pérez, *¿Necesita Yucatán una nueva revolución técnica en su industria henequenera?,* Mérida, 1953; Crossett, *Sisal Production,* p. 1.

113. Torre Díaz, quoted in Benítez, *Ki,* p. 118 (emphasis mine).

114. Quoted in *ibid.*

115. *RdY* (soon to become *DdY*), 19 Mar. 1920; Benítez, *Ki,* pp. 118–119.

116. See, e.g., the articles by regional historians commemorating Alvarado's achievements in Yucatán that appeared in the official party's newspaper on the fiftieth anniversary of Alvarado's arrival. *DdelS,* 28 Mar. 1965, Cultural Supplement.

117. Antonio Rodríguez, *El henequén: Una planta calumniada,* Mexico, 1966, p. 242.

118. E.g., Enrique Aznar Mendoza, "Historia de la industria henequenera desde 1919 hasta nuestros días," *EY,* Mexico, 1947, vol. 3, p. 728.

119. E.g., SD, 812.61326/184, 201, 206, 248; Renán Irigoyen, "El comercio del henequén a través del tiempo," *RUY* 7:41–42 (Sept.–Dec. 1965), 67–69. IHCA, doc. files 441, 2395, 2919, and 2924 contain correspondence

and documents relating to Harvester's fiber interests in the Philippines, 1905–1931, and the scheme for developing sisal plantations in Ecuador, 1913; see also Chapter 2, note 81.

120. Rodríguez, *El henequén*, pp. 242–243. U.S. Consul Henry Perrine has incorrectly been held by many Mexicans and Yucatecans to be singularly responsible for the onset of foreign competition. In the late nineteenth century, Perrine allegedly stole a number of shoots and sent them to the United States, where they were propagated and disseminated abroad.

121. Leopoldo Peniche Vallado, "La obra del Gral. Salvador Alvarado en Yucatán," *DdelS*, 28 Mar. 1965, Cultural Supplement; Rodríguez, *El henequén*, pp. 242–243.

122. SD, 812.61326/375.

123. SD, 812.61326/182.

7. Felipe Carrillo Puerto and the rise of Yucatecan socialism

1. AGE, 1916, Felipe Carrillo Puerto to Rafael Gamboa, 7 June 1916; cf. *VdR*, 5 June 1916.

2. Acrelio Carrillo Puerto, *La familia Carrillo Puerto de Motul*, Mérida, 1959, pp. 11–12, 23–32; interview with Angelina Carrillo Puerto de Triay Esperón, 7 Nov. 1975; Francisco J. Paoli and Enrique Montalvo, *El socialismo olvidado de Yucatán*, Mexico, 1977, pp. 75–76; Alberto Morales Jiménez, *Hombres de la Revolución Mexicana: 50 semblanzas biográficas*, Mexico, 1960, p. 230; Frank Tannenbaum, *Peace by Revolution: Mexico after 1910*, New York, 1933, p. 159.

3. Paoli and Montalvo, *El socialismo olvidado*, p. 77; Morales Jiménez, *Hombres de la Revolución*, p. 230.

4. Renán Irigoyen, *Felipe Carrillo Puerto: Primer gobernante socialista en México*, Mérida, 1974, pp. 8–9.

5. Paoli and Montalvo, *El socialismo olvidado*, p. 78.

6. Irigoyen, *Felipe Carrillo*, p. 10; *RdM*, 12 Aug. 1911.

7. Acrelio Carrillo Puerto, *Lo que no se olvida, Felipe Carrillo Puerto*, Mérida, 1964, pp. 45–47; Roberto Blanco Moheno, *Zapata*, Mexico, 1970, p. 262; Marte R. Gómez, "Carrillo Puerto visto por Marte," *Hoy*, 1 Mar. 1952.

8. Marte R. Gómez, *Las comisiones agrarias del sur*, Mexico, 1957, p. 48.

9. The letter is reproduced in Acrelio Carrillo Puerto, *Felipe Carrillo Puerto: Redentor de los mayas*, Mérida, 1972, pp. 169–171.

10. Irigoyen, *Felipe Carrillo*, p. 6; cf. Julio Cuadros Caldas, *México–Soviet*, Puebla, 1926, p. 510.

11. Carrillo Puerto, *La familia*, pp. 31–32; Luis Amendolla, *La Revolución comienza a los cuarenta*, Mexico, 1948, pp. 200–201; cf. John Womack, *Zapata and the Mexican Revolution*, New York, 1968, pp. 3–9.

12. Paoli and Montalvo, *El socialismo olvidado*, pp, 85–87; Gabriel Ferrer de Mendiolea, *Historia del Congreso Constituyente de 1916–1917*, Mexico, 1957, p. 172.

13. AGE, Jacinto Cohuich et al. to Alvarado, 20 Dec. 1916.

14. SD-CPR, *Corr., 1918,* vol. 4, 690, miscellaneous documents, e.g., Carrillo Puerto to Gaylord Marsh, 11 July; Ekin Birch to Marsh, 1 Sept.; Marsh to H. P. Fletcher, 12 July; Marsh to Secretary of State, 15 May; vol. 6, 800, Haberman to Robert Murray, 18 Aug.

15. SD-CPR, *Con. Corr.,* 800, Marsh to Secretary of State, 11 Oct. 1918.

16. The name of the party had been changed, early in 1921, to *Partido Socialista del Sureste.*

17. Álvaro Gamboa Ricalde, *Yucatán desde 1910,* Mexico, 1955, vol. 3, p. 273; J. W. F. Dulles, *Yesterday in Mexico: A Chronicle of the Revolution, 1919–1936,* Austin, Tex., 1961, pp. 141–144; SD, 81200/25654; *RdY,* 9 Dec. 1921.

18. *Sucúm:* Yucatec Maya for "Our Big Brother," a term of great respect and affection, which Carrillo's status as Yucatán's regional caudillo warranted and which he openly encouraged. AGE, Felipe Ayala M. to Carrillo Puerto, 21 Mar. 1922; cf. *RdY,* 5 July 1920.

19. E.g., *RdY,* 23 July 1921; Irigoyen, *Felipe Carrillo,* pp. 6, 18–19, 39; Roque A. Sosa Ferreyro, *El crimen del miedo: Cómo y por qué fue asesinado Felipe Carrillo Puerto,* Mexico, 1969, pp. 25–29. Because he had sent Lenin's embattled Soviet regime shipments of food and medical supplies in 1920, a street in Moscow was named after Yucatán's revolutionary governor. Cf. Carrillo's correspondence with Argentine Socialist Alfredo Palacios, *P,* 27 Mar. 1923.

20. The tenor of the traditional literature, suggesting a widespread mobilization of the Yucatecan countryside almost because of the sheer force of Carrillo's ideals and personality, is captured in the imagery of Yucatán's revolutionary poet, Elmer Llanes Marín, whose verse has been chosen as an introductory epigraph for this chapter. "Poemas de Elmer Llanes Marín," *O,* 44 (Dec. 1955), 98.

21. Certainly superior numerically to the large peasant forces assembled by Adalberto Tejeda and Úrsulo Galván in Veracruz or Primo Tapia in Michoacán. Cf. Heather Fowler Salamini, *Agrarian Radicalism in Veracruz, 1920–38,* Lincoln, Neb., 1977, p. 45; and Paul Friedrich, *Agrarian Revolt in a Mexican Village,* Englewood Cliffs, N.J., 1970, pp. 78–90. Luis Monroy Durán, *El último caudillo,* Mexico, 1924, pp. 53, 236–292, 331–349; and *E,* 9 and 10 January, confirm that Yucatán's *ligas* were also numerically stronger than the peasant militias of Morelos, Guerrero, Puebla, Hidalgo, Mexico State, San Luis Potosí, Durango, Zacatecas, Chihuahua, Nuevo León, Coahuila, and Jalisco.

22. E.g., Jaime Orosa Díaz, "Carrillo Puerto en la historia y en la literatura," *O,* 31 (Aug. 1951), 75–77; Carlton Beals, *Mexican Maze,* Philadelphia, 1931, pp. 11–12; and see the June 1974 issue of "Riuz's" satirical comic book, *Los Agachados,* entitled "Felipe Carrillo Puerto: El Salvador Allende Mexicano."

23. E.g., the award-winning play by Jaime Orosa Díaz, *Se vende un hombre,* Mérida, 1974, and Antonio Magaña Esquivel, *La tierra enrojecida,* Mexico, 1951.

24. In addition to the political positions that have already been discussed,

Carrillo served as deputy and president of the state legislature from 1917 to 1919, as interim governor and head of the *Comisión Reguladora* for several months late in 1918, and as federal deputy for Yucatán in 1920–1921.

25. Irigoyen, *Felipe Carrillo*, p. 7.

26. Paoli and31Montalvo, *El socialismo olvidado*, pp. 77–78, 80.

27. *Ibid.*, pp. 81–82; Tannenbaum, *Peace by Revolution*, p. 159.

28. Marjorie Ruth Clark, *Organized Labor in Mexico*, Chapel Hill, N.C., 1934, p. 202.

29. AGE, typescript, Partido Socialista de Yucatán, *Memorias del Congreso Obrero Socialista de Motul*, Mérida, 1918; Paoli and Montalvo, *El socialismo olvidado*, pp. 62–65.

30. Francisco Paoli B., "Carrillo Puerto y el PSS," *RUY* 16:91 (Jan.–Feb. 1974), 89–91; Sosa Ferreyro, *El crimen*, pp. 26–29.

31. Carrillo Puerto, quoted in Paoli and Montalvo, *El socialismo olvidado*, p. 90.

32. Carrillo Puerto, quoted in Paoli and Montalvo, *El socialismo olvidado*, p. 184; AGE, typescript, Partido Socialista del Sureste, *Congreso Obrero de Izamal*, Meérida, 1922.

33. AGE, *Congreso Obrero de Izamal*; Paoli and Montalvo, *El socialismo ollvidado*, pp. 150–151; *P*, 30 Jan. 1922.

34. Rosendo Salazar and J. G. Escobedo, *Las pugnas de la gleba*, Mexico, 1923, vol. 2, p. 84.

35. Quoted in *P*, 1 Feb. 1922, and Juan Rico, *Yucatán: La huelga de junio*, Mérida, 1922, vol. 1, pp. 55–56.

36. Rico, *La huelga*, vol. I, pp. 105–131; Gamboa Ricalde, *Yucatán*, vol. 3, pp. 229–232.

37. MMB, 10058–0–3 (140), "Political, Radical and Labor Activities," translation of anonymous report, 21 Dec. 1920.

38. Paul Friedrich, "The Legitimacy of a Cacique," in M. J. Swartz, ed., *Local-Level Politics*, p. 247; Gilbert M. Joseph, "Caciquismo and the Revolution: Carrillo Puerto in Yucatán," in D. A. Brading, ed., *Caudillo and Peasant*, pp. 196–202; and see Chapter 4, note 100, for definitions of *cacique* and "caudillo."

39. E.g., Eduardo Urzáiz, "El simbolismo de la Resurrección," *BdU*, Época 2, 4:1 (June 1924), 6–8; Renán Irigoyen, "Carrillo Puerto, Mártir de la cultura," *RUY* 1:1 (Jan.–Feb. 1959), 20–21.

40. AGE, Jacinto Cohuich, Nicolás Sánchez et al., to Alvarado, 20 Dec. 1916; Carrillo, *La familia*, pp. 28–31.

41. Sosa Ferreyro, *El crimen*, pp. 31ff.; Paoli and Montalvo, *El socialismo olvidado*, pp. 136–138.

42. E.g., Gamboa Ricalde, *Yucatán*, vol 3, p. 271–273.

43. Mexico, Congreso, *Diario de los debates del Congreso de la Unión*, 10 July 1919.

44. Cf. the similar process by which Primo Tapia constructed a local power base in Michoacán, in Friedrich, *Agrarian Revolt*, pp. 58–130.

45. AGN, 307–C–9, report by José Domingo Chávez, n.d.

46. Carrillo, *La familia*, pp. 15–116; cf. Raymond Th. Buve, "Peasant Movements, Caudillos, and Land Reform during the Revolution (1910–1917) in Tlaxcala, Mexico," *BdEL* 18 (June 1975), 132, for a similar use of family members in the revolutionary regime of Tlaxcala.

47. AGE, telegram, Carlos Castro Morales to Pres. Carranza, 13 Apr. 1920; *RdY*, 15 Apr. 1920.

48. Alfonso Taracena, *La verdadera Revolución Mexicana*, Mexico, 1961, vol. 7, p. 70; Dulles, *Yesterday*, pp. 57, 77–78, 121, 136–137; SD, 812.00/25608.

49. José Vasconcelos, *El desastre: Tercera parte de Ulisés Criollo*, Mexico, 1968, p. 86.

50. AGE, typescript, "Que el Gobierno de Yucatán fomenta el bolchevismo en México y en Cuba," n.d. (1924); *RdY*, 28 July 1924. Also, see the warm cable correspondence between Calles and Carrillo in the AGE's special "Telegramas" files for 1922 and 1923.

51. SD, 812/25188; SD-CPR, *Con. Corr.*, 800, Marsh to Secretary of State, 29 Sept. 1921; AGN, 424–H–2, Ma. del Pilar Pech to Manuel Carpio, 8 Jan. 1921; *RdY*, 21 Feb. 1921; Paoli and Montalvo, *El socialismo olvidado*, pp. 152–154.

52. *P*, 8 Mar. 1923; Paoli, "Carrillo Puerto," 87–91; Ernest Gruening, *Mexico and Its Heritage*, New York, 1928, pp. 404–405; Clark, *Organized Labor*, p. 208.

53. *P*, 31 Oct. 1921; Paoli and Montalvo, *El socialismo olvidado*, p. 157.

54. AGE, Rafael Gamboa to Carrillo, 3 Mar. 1923; *RdY*, 28 July 1924; Paoli, "Carrillo Puerto," 89.

55. Nelson Reed, *The Caste War of Yucatán*, Stanford, Calif., 1964, pp. 258ff. and *passim*.

56. AGE, "Relación de los departamentos administrativos del Estado . . . ," 23 Sept. 1924 (see especially the category entitled "localidades deshabitadas"); cf. ASA, *Visitas Parroquiales, 1913–1931*, "Informes Parroquiales, 1920–1923," for extensive evidence of *haciendas despobladas* and violence in the *partidos* of Tekax, Temax, Espita, and Peto. The pueblo of Libre Unión was among those completely depopulated during the period.

57. SD, 812.00/25068; SD-CPR, *Corr.*, 1924, vol. 3, 350, "Declaration of Manuel López," n.d. (1921); AGE, Berzunza to Procurador General de Justicia, 27 June 1921; *RdY*, 7 Nov. 1920, 21 Dec. 1920, 10 June 1922; Anastasio Manzanilla D., *El bolchevismo criminal de Yucatán*, Mérida, 1921, p. 162; and see Chapter 4.

58. Cf. Luisa Paré, "Caciquismo y estructura de poder en la Sierra Norte de Puebla," in Roger Bartra, ed., *Caciquismo y poder político en el México rural*, Mexico, 1975, p. 39.

59. Friedrich Katz, "Labor Conditions on Haciendas in Porfirian Mexico: Some Trends and Tendencies: *HAHR* 54:1 (Feb. 1974), 44–45; Moisés González Navarro, *Raza y tierra: La guerra de castas y el henequén*, Mexico, 1970, p. 231; for a general discussion of the "social bandit" phenomenon, see E. J. Hobsbawm, *Primitive Rebels*, New York, 1959, pp. 3–6, 13–56.

60. The table summarizes disparate data uncovered during the course of systematic year-by-year archival (e.g., AGE, AGN, SD, SD-CPR, ASA) and press research (*RdY, DdY, P, C, VdR*) for the 1915–1940 period. Documentary evidence was corroborated, in several cases, by interviewing at the local level.

61. SD-CPR, *Corr., 1921,* vol. 4, 800, news clipping of editorial from *RdY,* 24 June; *RdY,* 10 June 1922; AGE, memoriall from vecinos of Yaxcabá to Carrillo, 25 Aug. 1920; AGE, Bartolomé García Correa to Gov. Iturralde, 2 Oct. 1925.

62. *U,* 8 Nov. 1920.

63. AGE, Municipal Presidents, Sotuta and Dzán, to Carrillo, 10 Oct. 1920 and 3 Oct. 1922, respectively; *RdY,* 12 Nov. 1920, 11 Aug. 1921; *P,* 21 Mar. 1923.

64. *RdY,* 19 Apr. 1922; AGN, 408–Y–1, José B. Garma to Obregón, 9 Mar. 1922; AGN, 492–Y–3, Carmela Aragón to Obregón, 26 July 1922; SD, 812.00/25608, 25654; AGE, "Circular num. 27 a los Presidentes y Comisarios Municipales . . . ," 11 Aug. 1924; *P,* 27 Mar. 1923, 4 Apr. 1923. Also see *DO* for 1922–1923, where the frequent replacement of municipal governments by order of the governor, in conjunction with other evidence, suggests that Carrillo often strengthened an opposing faction at the expense of the incumbent *cacicazgo.*

65. *RdY,* 27 Mar. 1920, 6 May 1921, 31 Oct. 1922; *DO,* 3 Jan. 1922, p. 3.

66. *C,* 21 Apr. 1923, 13 Oct. 1923, 1 Dec. 1923; *RdY,* 13 July 1920, 19 Nov. 1923; Manzanilla, *El bolchevismo,* p. 162.

67. AGE, Municipal President, Tahmek, to Liga Central, 11 June 1919; AGE, Miguel Cantón to Carrillo, 21 Dec. 1920, 28 Mar. 1921; AGE, vecinos of Dzilnup to Carrillo, 11 Dec. 1922; AGE, Gonzalo Lewis to Carrillo, March and April 1923; *RdY,* 13 Mar. 1919; *C,* 15 Nov. 1923; Victor Goldkind, "Class Conflict and Cacique," *SJA* 22:4 (Winter 1966), 333–334.

68. AGE, decree by Carrillo amending *El Estado Seco,* 14 June 1923; AGE, Regidor, Ayuntamiento de Umán, to Carrillo, 29 June 1922.

69. AGE, Felipe Carrillo, authorization of García Correa's concession, 28 Mar. 1923; AGE, El Oficial Mayor Segundo, Sría. de Fomento, Dpto. de Colonización, to Carrillo, 75 Nov. 1922; AGE, Miguel Cantón to Braulio Euán, 26 Aug. 1921; *RdY,* 18 Aug. 1921.

70. AGE, circular, Benjamín Carrillo Puerto, to "compañeros," n.d. (1923); *C,* 23 Nov. 1923; *T,* 27 May 1923; *P,* 10 July 1922, 12 July 1922; *RdY,* 12 Sept. 1921.

71. AGN, 408–Y–1, José B. Garma to Obregón, 9 Mar. 1922; SD, 812.61326/254, 812.00/22315, 22887; Manuel M. Escoffié, *Yucatán en la cruz,* Mérida, 1957, pp. 197–203, and see the frequent accounts of violence, *bandolerismo,* and *caciquismo* in *C* and *RdY* during the 1918–1923 period.

72. AGN, 424–H–1, Cámara Agrícola de Yucatán to Obregón, 3 Jan. 1923; AGN, 424–H–3, Manuel de Irabién Rosado to Obregón, 28 June 1923; Claudio Osalde Medina, "El problema ejidal de Yucatán," *N,* June 1936; SD, 812.61326/408; *NYT,* 16 Sept. 1923; *RdY,* 9 Apr. 1922.

73. AGE, "Relación de las Ligas de Resistencia . . . ," 1 Sept. 1922; Felipe Carrillo Puerto, "The New Yucatán," *Survey*, 52 (May 1924), 141. Cf. J. W. F. Dulles, *Yesterday*, p. 137, and Carleton Beals, *Latin America: World in Revolution*, London, 1968, p. 69, who estimate the membership of the *ligas* to be as high as 90,000 and 100,000, respectively.

74. SD, 812.00/985, 1260; *P*, 17 Apr. 1923; *DO*, 10 July 1915, p. 2245; Henry Baerlein, *Mexico: The Land of Unrest*, Philadelphia, 1914, pp. 51, 150, 183.

75. *P*, 17 Apr. 1923.

76. *Ibid.*

77. E.g., AGE, Municipal President, Tepakán, to Carrillo, 21 Feb. 1922; cf. AGE, Municipal President, Tecoh, to Gov. Francisco Vega y Loyo, 23 Feb. 1920.

78. Siegfried Askinasy, *El problema agrario de Yucatán*, 2d ed., Mexico, 1936, p. 145. Also, see the spate of *campesino* protests against *hacendado* labor abuses that recur throughout the *legajos* of AGE, 1924–1925.

79. E.g., *RdY*, 7 Jan. 1920; cf. Thomas W. F. Gann, *Ancient Cities and Modern Tribes*, London, 1926, p. 77, and Gann, *In an Unknown Land*, London, 1924, p. 175.

80. Partido Socialista del Sureste, *Tierra y libertad: Bases que discutieron y aprobaron el Primer Congreso Obrero Socialista* . . . , Mérida, 1919; AGE, Director, Liga de Estudiantes de la Escuela Granja, to Carrillo, 13 Aug. 1923; Mary Kay Vaughan, "Education and Class in the Mexican Revolution," *LAP* 2:2 (Summer 1975), 29–31.

81. José de la Luz Mena y Alcocer, *La escuela socialista, su desorientción y fracaso, el verdadero derrotero*, Mexico, 1941, pp. 197–198.

82. SD-CPR, *Corr.*, *1922*, vol. 4, 842, "Ley de Institución de la Escuela Racionalista" (6 Feb. 1922); AGE, "Reglamento de la preparación social para los maestros," 18 Mar. 1922; *P*, 9 Mar. 1922; *BdU*, Época 1, 1:1 (March 1922), 8–12, 37–42, 70–74, 98–106; Fernando Gamboa Berzunza, "Visión pedagógica de Felipe Carrillo Puerto," *RUY* 3:13 (Jan.–Feb. 1961), 35–41.

83. *RdY*, 14 Mar. 1921, 9 Mar. 1922, 6 May 1922; Gonzalo Cámara Zavala, "Paralelo entre las escuelas racionalistas de Barcelona y Mérida," *BdLAS* 2:17 (May 1922), 66–69.

84. Gamboa Berzunza, "Visión pedagógica," 40; AGE, Dpto. de Educación Pública, "Relación de las escuelas públicas del Estado," n.d. (1924).

85. Gamboa Berzunza, "Visión pedagógica," 36; cf. Luis Rosado Vega, "El proletariado profesional," *BdU* 2:2 (Oct. 1922), 61–70; Betancourt, "Nuestro viejo abuelo" *RUY* 15:85 (Jan.–Feb. 1973), 67–68.

86. Gamboa Berzunza, "Visión pedagógica," 40; *BdU* 1:5 (July 1922), 333–348; AGE, A. Pérez Toro, Director, Escuela Granja, to Carrillo, 3 May 1923, 14 Nov. 1923; AGE, Carrillo to Municipal Presidents, 16 Jan. 1923; *P*, 22 Jan. 1923. In its basic philosophical approach, Carrillo's rural literacy program prefigured Brazilian educator Paulo Freire's more recent method of *concientización*. See Freire's *Pedagogy of the Oppressed*, New York, 1970.

87. *P*, 11 Mar. 1922; *DO*, 13 Mar. 1922, p. 1; AGN, 243–Y–1–I–1, Carrillo to Obregón, 13 Mar. 1922; cf. *BdLAS* 2:15 (March 1922), 45–47 (editorial against birth control).

88. *P*, Feb. 1922, 5 Sept. 1922.

89. Gann, *Ancient Cities*, pp. 72–73; Sosa Ferreyro, *El crimen*, p. 25.

90. *RdY*, 9 Nov. 1922; AGE, "Relación de las Ligas," 1 Sept. 1922; AGE, Benjamín Carrillo Puerto to Felipe Carrillo, 22 May 1923; Anna Macías, "Felipe Carrillo Puerto and Women's Liberation in Mexico," in Asunción Lavrin, ed., *Latin American Women: Historical Perspectives*, Westport, Conn., p. 291; Rosemary L. Lee, "Who Owns Boardwalk?: The Structure of Control in the Tourist Industry of Yucatán," paper presented at the seventy-third meeting of the American Anthropological Association, Mexico City, November 1974.

91. The following biographical information and assessment of Elvia Carrillo draws heavily upon Acrelio Carrillo's *La familia*, pp. 82–92, and is corroborated by documents from the AGE (cited below).

92. *RdY*, 30 Sept. 1923, 2 Oct. 1923; Acrelio Carrillo, *La familia*, p. 88, recalls Felipe Carrillo reassuring his sister in a moment of self-doubt: "Don't be afraid, sister, you can depend on me; you work with the women, I'll organize the men, and together we'll go forward."

93. AGE, "Relación de las Ligas . . . ," 1 Sept. 1922; AGE, Benjamín Carrillo to Felipe Carrillo, 22 May 1923; Clark, *Organized Labor*, p. 208.

94. AGE, Elvia Carrillo to Felipe Carrillo, 28 June 1923.

95. *Ibid.*; AGE, Felipe Carrillo to Elvia Carrillo, 2 July 1923; Ernest Gruening, "A Maya Idyl: A Study of Felipe Carrillo Puerto, Late Governor of Yucatán," *The Century Magazine* 107 (April 1924), 834.

96. AGE, "Relación de las Ligas . . . ," 1 Sept. 1922; Rico, *La huelga*, vol. 1, pp. 19–27.

97. AGE, President, Liga Máximo Gorki, to Carrillo, and Carrillo's reply, both 8 Dec. 1923; William Gates, " Yucatán – an Experiment in Syndicalism," *World's Work* 38 (May 1919), 66.

98. *VdR*, 8 May 1918; Rico, *La huelga*, vol. 1, pp. 19–27. Gann, *Unknown Land*, p. 178, expressed surprise that *béisbol* had become so popular among the Maya *campesinos* by 1924. This was largely due to Carillo's promotion of the sport among the workers. To this day, baseball continues to be the game most preferred by Yucatán's humble country people, whereas *fútbol* (soccer), traditionally Mexico's most "popular" sport, is regarded as a game for well-to-do city folk.

99. José Castillo Torre, "La muerte del Mártir," *BdU* 4:1 (June 1924), 12–13; Rico, *La huelga*, vol. 1, pp. 19–27.

100. Paoli and Montalvo, *El socialismo olvidado*, p. 150.

101. *Ibid.*, p. 165.

102. Carrillo Puerto, "New Yucatán," 140–141.

103. *DO*, 13 Mar. 1922; *RdY*, 23 Mar. 1922; Vasconcelos, *El desastre*, p. 69; SD-CPR, *Con. Corr.*, 840.5, March to Secretary of State, 26 Mar. 1923. The party also encouraged Socialists to wear red sashes and instructed presidents of the *ligas* to conduct all official correspondence in red ink.

104. Ernest Gruening, *Un viaje al Estado de Yucatán: Felipe Carrillo Puerto, su obra socialista.* Guanajuato, 1924, p. 14.

105. *P,* 7 Feb. 1977.

106. Carrillo, "New Yucatán," 141; "Conditions in Yucatán," *NYC,* 5 May 1923, Section 2. Also, see ASA, *Correspondencia, 1919–1928,* "Cartas, 1923," Pedro M. Regil to Tritschler y Córdoba, 7 Nov. 1923, regarding the increasing disdain of the *campesinos* of hacienda Tekik for church ritual; cf. ASA, *Colección de Papeles de Tritschler y Córdoba,* "Diversos Documentos, 1899–1939," Archbishop of Mexico to Tritschler, 21 Mar. 1922.

107. E.g., see AGE, President, Liga de Oxkutzcab, to Carrillo, 24 Oct. 1922; Paoli and Montalvo, *El socialismo olvidado,* p. 172.

108. *Ibid.,* p. 173.

109. Rosa Castro, "Sobre la ruta de Carrillo Puerto, el Mesías de Motul," *Hoy,* 15 Mar. 1952; *P,* 9 Mar. 1923; Gann, *Ancient Cities,* pp. 76, 79.

110. Robert L. Brunhouse, *Sylvanus G. Morley and the World of the Ancient Mayas,* Norman, Okla., 1971, p. 176; Ernest Gruening, "The Assassination of Mexico's Ablest Statesman," *Current History* 19:5 (Feb. 1924), 737.

111. Clark, *Organized Labor,* p. 213. We have seen that Yucatán's urban workers were in most cases recruited from Mérida, Progreso, and the larger regional centers. Thus, even those of predominantly Maya descent quickly became assimilated in the capital and port.

112. Fowler Salamini, *Agrarian Radicalism,* p. 27; Rico, *La huelga, passim.*

113. Rocío Guadarrama, "La CROM en la época del caudillismo en México," *Cuadernos Políticos* 20 (Apr.–June 1979), 52–63; Fowler Salamini, *Agrarian Radicalism,* pp. 28–29. Carrillo's overthrow in 1924 was a severe setback to the CROM's organizing efforts in the peninsula.

114. Gann, *Ancient Cities,* p. 70, *Unknown Land,* p. 172; Yucatán's *hacendados* lamented to President Obregón that it cost more to move goods from a ship in the port to Mérida than it did to bring them all the way from New York to Progreso. SD, 812.61326/369, 403. Similar charges were leveled against the stevedores working in the port of Veracruz.

115. *P,* 14 Mar. 1922; SD-CPR, *Corr., 1920,* vol. 4, 861.3, Marsh to U.S. Consul General, 13 Jan. 1920; *Corr., 1923,* vol. 5, 377, "The United Railroads of Yucatán," n.d.

116. AGE, Diego Rendón to Carrillo, 27 July 1920; AGE, Carrillo to Jefe de la Guarnación, 5 June 1922; *P,* 18 Mar. 1922.

117. SD, 812.00/25654.

118. Rico, *La huelga, passim;* Paoli and Montalvo, *El socialismo olvidado,* p. 174.

119. Dulles, *Yesterday,* p. 143; Rico, *La huelga,* vol. 2, pp. 104–105 and *passim.;* Gruening, *Mexico,* pp. 340–341; Clark, *Organized Labor,* pp. 209–210.

120. See Bo Anderson and James Cockcroft, "Control and Co-optation in Mexican Politics," in Irving L. Horowitz et al., eds., *Latin American Radicalism,* New York, 1969, pp. 366–389.

121. E.g., AGE, President, Liga Obrera de Tranviarios de Mérida, to Carrillo, 4 Apr. 1923; González Navarro, *Raza,* p. 246.

8. The ideology and praxis of a socialist revolution

1. Cf. the similar dilemma faced by Ho Chi Minh's Marxist revolution in Vietnam, which is analyzed in Frances Fitzgerald's *The Fire in the Lake: The Vietnamese and the Americans in Vietnam*, New York, 1973, pp. 284–304.

2. *P*, 20 Jan. 1922.

3. SD, 812.61326/410; AGE, Pedro Arjona Moguel to Governor Berzunza, 7 Mar. 1921; SD-CPR, *Corr., 1921*, vol. 2, 610, "World Trade Directory: Retired Business File."

4. AGE, President, Liga de Resistencia de Oxkutzcab, to Carrillo, 26 Oct. 1922; AGE, Manuel de Arrigunaga to Carrillo, 21 June 1922; AGE, State Treasurer to Carrillo, 26 July 1922.

5. E.g., AGE, Carrillo to Treasurer, Asilo Ayala, 20 Mar. 1922; AGE, Col. Francisco Irabién to Carrillo, 27 Dec. 1922; AGE, Carrillo to State Treasurer, 11 Mar. 1922.

6. AGE, memorial from Profs. Severiano and Roberto Echeverría to Carrillo, 28 June 1922.

7. *RdY*, 5 July 1921, 11 Aug. 1921, 10 June 1922.

8. E.g., AGE, Carrillo to Procurador General de Justicia, 27 June, 10 Aug., and 6 Nov. 1921; AGE, Municipal President, Maxcanú, to Carrillo, 9 Aug. 1921.

9. *RdY*, 10 Mar. 1921.

10. *RdY*, 18 Oct. 1921.

11. *P*, 20 Jan. 1922.

12. Carrillo told the reporters: "Because of the lack of economic resources, my government may not be able to fulfill all of these lofty socialist goals, but it will begin immediately to carry them out in those social areas and in those communities where they are most needed." *P*, 28 Jan. 1922.

13. SD-CPR, *Corr., 1918*, vol. 4, 690, Marsh to Prof. W. M. Adriance, 1 Mar.

14. *P*, 28 Jan. 1922, reprinting interview given to *El Heraldo de México* (Mexico City).

15. *RdY*, 27 June 1922; cf. Alvarado's search for oil, described in Chapter 5.

16. *P*, 28 Jan. 1922.

17. Frank Tannenbaum, *The Mexican Agrarian Revolution*, Washington, D.C., 1930, pp. 489–499. But see Appendix, Figures A and C, which suggest otherwise, at least in terms of has. officially distributed (many of Zapata's earlier distributions may have gone unrecorded in the government's figures). Of course, Morelos is a much smaller state than Yucatán and the agrarian reform there may have been proportionately more extensive. Note, too, the effect that Carrillo's regime had on neighboring Campeche's agrarian program (Figure B) and how favorably Yucatán's land distribution compared with the national agrarian reform during the Carrillo Puerto period (Figure D).

18. Even the most basic questions about what happened and why, which might clarify the magnitude of and motivation behind Don Felipe's agrarian reform, have been ignored or answered so unconvincingly that the explanations

raise more questions than they answer. There are several reasons for the interpretive muddle and the significant lacunae in the historical literature. Carrillo wrote surprisingly little, and what he said in his speeches was frequently tailored to meet immediate propaganda needs and often quoted out of context. This historiographical problem is compounded by the fact that Carrillo's regime and life were snuffed out – hardly a coincidence – just at the moment he seemed to be revealing a new direction in his agrarian policy and clarifying certain ambiguities in his earlier posture. Finally, the official party's resurrection of Carrillo as the embodiment or quasi-deity of a regional myth, coupled with a failure by many writers to engage in archival research, has served to discourage a rigorous interpretation of his *actuación revolucionaria*, especially in the crucial areas of land and henequen.

19. E.g., Conrado Menéndez Díaz, "La mística del trabajo campesino en Yucatán," *O* 3 (Dec. 1946), 35–39; Moisés González Navarro, *Raza y tierra: La guerra de castas y el henequén*, Mexico, 1970, p. 248; cf. the attitude toward Carrillo in *NYT* ("Slow Death for the Henequen Industry of Yucatán"), cited in *RdY*, 19 Sept. 1923.

20. Thus, Carrillo is likened to Gandhi, another ideological opponent of modernization, who advocated a return to the sturdy cottage textile industry that the Indian peasantry had developed prior to the British Raj. Traditional characterizations of Carrillo as the gentle, pacifist people's leader, content to sacrifice himself for Yucatán's pariah class, support this comparison with the Indian nationalist in other respects.

21. Carrillo Puerto, quoted in Siegfried Askinasy, *El problema agrario de Yucatán*, 2d ed., Mexico, 1936, p. 13.

22. Menéndez Díaz, "La mística," 35–36.

23. E.g., David A. Franz, "Bullets and Bolshevists: A History of the Mexican Revolution and Reform in Yucatán," unpublished Ph.D. dissertation, University of New Mexico, Albuquerque, 1973, pp. 243–245.

24. *Ibid.*, p. 243, quoting a phrase from Carrillo, "The New Yucatán," *Survey* 52 (May 1924), 139.

25. E.g., Humberto Lara y Lara, *Sobre la trayectoria de la reforma agraria en Yucatán*, Mérida, 1949, pp. 24–25; Miguel Ángel Menéndez, *La industria de la esclavitud*, Mexico, 1947, pp. 51–52.

26. The view that equates Carrillo's agrarian thinking with Zapata's, in addition to misreading the logic of Carrillo's program, misinterprets the agrarian strategy of *Zapatismo* as well. John Womack, *Zapata and the Mexican Revolution*, New York, 1968, pp. 373–374, has shown that Zapata never attempted, in anarchist style, to do away with Morelos's sugar plantations and usher in an exclusive system of peasant autarky. Rather, he attempted, although unsuccessfully, to encourage the *campesinos* to manage collectively a number of the plantations in addition to cultivating their own small plots, thereby preserving productive capacity and providing valuable earnings for the movement. Similarly, we will see that Felipe Carrillo never discounted (and indeed, actively promoted) the prospect that one day the Maya *campesinos* would possess and collectively operate Yucatán's henequen plantations.

27. It will be noted that I have dispensed with Landsberger's all-inclusive understanding of "peasant" as any "rural cultivator of low political and economic status" for the more specific differentiation of "peasants" from "rural workers" that is derived from an examination of a particular agrarian structure and the relations of production or systems of labor that are generated by it. Cf. Henry Landsberger, "The Role of Peasant Movements and Revolts in Development," in Landsberger, ed., *Latin American Peasants,* Ithaca, N.Y., 1969, pp. 3–5, with the approach found in Sidney W. Mintz, "The Rural Proletariat and the Problem of Rural Proletarian Class Consciousness," *JPS* 1:3 (April 1973), 291–325.

28. Askinasy, *El problema,* pp. 113–114.

29. E.g., see AGE, Juez Supernumerario de Distrito to Carrillo, 27 Dec. 1922, regarding Berzunza's *afectaciones* of henequen land on several of Felipe G. Solís's *fincas* and on Mercedes Castellanos viuda de Zapata's *finca* Tecat; or see the *amparo* files in AGE, 1923–1924, which document Carrillo's attempts to distribute *henequenales* from the haciendas of, among others, Felipe G. Cantón, Lorenzo and Hernando Ancona Pérez, the Molina and Montes family, the Bolios, Peóns, Manzanillas, Cerveras, and Palomeques – in short, from most of the interrelated families that made up the old *Casta Divina.*

30. George M. McBride, *The Land Systems of Mexico,* New York, 1923, pp. 165–166; J. W. F. Dulles, *Yesterday in Mexico: A Chronicle of the Revolution, 1919–1936,* Austin, Tex., 1961, p. 40. A comprehensive record of all agrarian actions taken during the Berzunza governorship may be found in AGE, Ramo de Tierras, legajo 1 (1917–1929), handwritten "Relación de la reforma agraria," providing dates of *solicitudes,* provisional and definitive decrees, the size of ejidal grants, and the number of *campesinos* benefited. Cf. ledgerbooks in AGE, Tierras, legajos 4 and 14, "Comisión Agraria Mixta," which also provide summaries of the agrarian reform in Yucatán through the present and contain a record of all ejidal *ampliaciones* (additional supplementary grants) following the initial *dotaciones.*

31. González Navarro, *Raza,* pp. 247–248; *P,* 2 Jan. 1923; SD, 812.52/ 1110. Also see AGE, Tierras, legajo 1, "Relación de la reforma agraria."

32. AGN, 818-Ch-4, Carrillo to Obregón, 7 Feb. 1922; Renán Irigoyen, *Felipe Carrillo Puerto: Primer gobernante socialista en México,* Mérida, 1974, pp. 19–20; Rosa Castro, "Sobre la ruta de Carrillo Puerto, el Mesías de Motul," *Hoy,* 15 Mar. 1952.

33. *DO,* 30 Dec. 1922, decretos nums. 275–285, "Vuelven a asumir la categoría de pueblos, las ciudades y villas siguientes: Motul, Valladolid, Ticul, Tekax, Temax, Tizimín, . . . etc.," 28 Dec. 1922, pp. 1–4.

34. Robert Redfield and Alonso Villa Rojas, *Chan Kom: A Maya Village,* Chicago, 1962, pp. 27–28. Carrillo made no attempt, however, to include hacienda communities in this decree; but see the discussion below regarding his strategy for the large estate.

35. *P,* 2 Jan. 1923; AGE, Tierras, legajo 1, "Relación de la reforma agraria"; AGE, amparo file, memorial from Narciso Campos S. et al. to Juez Supernumerario de Distrito, 23 Dec. 1921, Berzunza to Juez Supernumerario, 28 Dec.

1921, Sentencia de Juez Supernumerario, 19 May 1922. This file is representative of numerous other *amparo* cases in AGE, 1922, all of which contain *hacendado* protests of Berzunza's ejidal distributions.

36. AGE, Tierras, legajo 1, "Relación de la reforma agraria"; SD, 812.52/1110; *P*, 2 Jan. 1923. More importantly, see AGE, *legajo* marked "Correspondencia de Gobernación, Exps. 66, 1923" (hereafter "Correspondencia"), which contains more than 30 amparo files, many of which document *solicitudes* by pueblos that had been made in the middle to late 1910s but were not acted upon until the early days of Carrillo's administration: e.g., "Ejidos de Ixil" (*solicitud*, 1917), "Ejidos de Dzilám González" (*solicitud*, 1917).

37. See the amparo files in AGE, "Correspondencia," e.g., the "agrarian timetable" listed in the file "Ejidos de Mama," which is representative of the time sequences reported in many of the other files in the *legajo:*

12 Aug. 1922: Mama *vecinos* make *solicitud*

18 Dec. 1922 (only 4 mos. later): C.L.A. calls *solicitud* "justa," awards 6,624 has. as *dotación*

18 Dec. 1922 (same day): Carrillo issues provisional decree, remanding the file over to the C.L.A. and instructing it to notify Mama's *Comité Particular Ejecutivo* that provisonal delivery will be made as soon as it can be scheduled on the calendar of *jueves agrarios*.

38. Rodolfo Stavenhagen, "Collective Agriculture and Capitalism in Mexico: A Way Out or a Dead End?" LAP 2:2 (Summer 1975), 146–147. Stavenhagen's survey of files in the Agrarian Reform Ministry reveals that, on the average, the entire process from *solicitud* to definitive decree and conferral of title took thirteen years. Approximately 75,000 cases are still clogged in the agrarian bureaucracy.

39. AGE, Municipal President, Kantunil, to Carrillo, 1 Sept. 1922; AGE, Buenaventura Sabido et al. to Carrillo, 25 Sept. 1922; AGE, Joaquín Peón to Carrillo, 10 Oct. 1922.

40. E.g., AGE, Municipal President, Tekantó, to Carrillo, 19 Aug. 1922; AGE, Lorenzo Matos Pérez to Carrillo, 28 Aug. 1922.

41. E.g., AGE, "Correspondencia," Srio. Gral. del Gobierno to Juez Supernumerario, 14 Aug. 1923 ("Ejidos de Hocabá"), Manuel Casellas Rivas to Juez Numerario, 18 Sept. 1923 ("Ejidos de Dzityá"); and AGE, Juez Supernumerario to Iturralde, 9 July 1924 ("Ejidos de Dzilám González").

42. E.g., AGE, "Correspondencia," file "Ejidos de Telchaquillo" includes brief of *amparo* submitted by Señora Martina Gutiérrez viuda de Cano, 27 Feb. 1923, and Carrillo to Juez Numerario, 3 Mar. 1923, regarding Supreme Court's decision. Obregón praised Carrillo's "discreción and efficiency" in distributing *tierras incultas*, although in most cases he was slow in legitimizing Carrillo's provisional deliveries with definitive decrees. *DO*, 29 June 1923, p. 1; Irigoyen, *Felipe Carrillo*, p. 21.

43. E.g., AGE, "Correspondencia," file "Ejidos de Caucel," Juez Numerario de Distrito to Carrillo, 30 May 1923, transcribing Supreme Court's opinion of 20 Jan. 1923; AGE, "Ejidos de Cacalchén," Juez Supernumerario to Carrillo, 27 Dec. 1922.

44. Ramón Mendoza Medina, ed., *La cuestión henequenera y otras cuestiones de Yucatán,* Mérida, 1946, pp. 14–15. Yucatán's largest *hacendados* were already in the process of adapting themselves to the provisions of Obregón's April 1922 decree, and other planters would soon follow their lead. It was common knowledge in May 1922, for example, that the Molina, Montes, and Peón families had distributed their properties in 500 has. parcels to assorted sons, daughters, and close relatives. *RdY,* 25 May 1922.

45. E.g., *RdY,* 11 Nov. 1922; AGE, "Correspondencia," Juez Supernumerario to Carrillo, 27 and 29 Mar. 1923 ("Ejidos de Chuburná"); Juez de Distrito to Carrillo, 21 May 1923 ("Ejidos de Muxupip"); Juez Supernumerario to Carrillo, 6 Apr. 1923 ("Ejidos de Kanasín").

46. AGN, 243-Y1-I-1, Carrillo to Obregón, 18 Apr. 1922; González Navarro, *Raza,* pp. 248–249.

47. González Navarro, *Raza,* pp. 248–249; *P,* 5 Feb. 1923.

48. *P,* 2 Jan. 1923, 5 Feb. 1923; Felipe Carrillo Puerto, *Informe . . . ante la . . . Legislatura del Estado,* el 1º de enero de *1923,* Mérida, 1923, p. 104.

49. Carrillo had promised, for example, to provide milling facilities and to guarantee buyers for the sugar cooperatives planting a minimum of 20 has. in cane. AGN, 243-Y1-I-1, Carrillo to Obregón, 18 Apr. 1922.

50. SD, 812.61326/425; *RdY,* 12 Nov. 1922, 15 Nov. 1922; *DO,* 29 June 1923, p. 4, 24 July 1923, p. 3.

51. AGN, 243-Y-1-I-1, Carrillo to Obregón, 18 Apr. 1922; Jaime Orosa Díaz, ed., *Legislación henequenera en Yucatán,* Mérida, 1961, vol. 4, pp. 54–56.

52. *DO,* 18 Sept. 1923, p. 1.

53. *P,* 22 Aug. 1922, 2 Apr. 1923; *RdY,* 1 July 1923.

54. AGE, José M. Castro S. en C. to Carrillo, 15 Dec. 1922; AGE, Presidente, Liga de Resistencia "Evolución Social" to Carlos Escalante, Gerente, Cordelería Mayapán, 21 Mar. 1923; *RdY,* 6 Nov. 1921, 17 Nov. 1922; SD-CPR, *Corr., 1922,* vol. 2, 610, Marsh's business reports of 2 Jan. and 4 Aug.

55. *RdY,* 4 Aug. 1921.

56. SD, 812.61326/388, 390; Bernardino Mena Brito, *Bolshevismo y democracia en México,* 2d ed., Mexico, 1933, pp. 334–335; *P,* 6 Apr. 1922; SD-CPR, *Corr., 1924,* vol. 4, 600, "Annual Report on Commerce and Industry, 1923." The search for new markets is discussed in some detail in the 861.3 file of SD-CPR, *Corr., 1923* and *1924.*

57. SD, 812.61326/379, 380; *DO,* 15 Dec. 1921, p. 10327; Orosa Díaz, *Legislación,* vol. 4, pp. 33–35.

58. *NYC,* 5 May 1923; *NYT,* 16 Sept. 1923; cf. *A* 10:10 (Dec. 1923), articles written by members of the *Liga de Pequeños y Medianos Productores.*

59. Orosa Díaz, *Legislación,* vol. 4, *passim.*

60. SD, 812.61326/368, 382, 384; Acrelio Carrillo Puerto, *La familia Carrillo Puerto de Motul,* Mérida, 1959, pp. 33–34.

61. SD, 812.61326/272; SD-CPR, *Corr., 1914,* vol. 2, 800, Gracey to Secretary of State, 21 Mar.; Lara y Lara, *Sobre la trayectoria,* pp. 16–17, 25–26; *DdelH,* 24 Jan. 1912; Irigoyen, "Orígen y trayectoria del henequén," *RUY* 15:86 (Mar.–Apr. 1973), 125–126.

62. *RdY,* 9 Nov. 1922; *P,* 26 Feb. 1923.

63. Carrillo, *La familia,* p. 32.

64. *Ibid.,* pp. 33–34; *RdY,* 4 Dec. 1921; *P,* 14 Aug. 1922; cf. *RdY,* 29, 30, 31 Dec. 1922 for a more negative view of Castellanos Acevedo.

65. SD-CPR, *Corr., 1920,* vol. 2, 610, "Monthly Economic Report: December," 1 Jan. 1921.

66. SD-CPR, *Corr., 1924,* vol. 7, 861.3, Alexander V. Dye, Commercial Attaché, to American Ambassador, 18 Nov. Statistical data taken from files of the commercial attaché.

67. SD-CPR, *Corr., 1924,* vol. 4, 600, "Annual Report on Commerce and Industry, 1923."

68. SD-CPR, *Corr., 1924,* vol. 7, 861.3, Lyster H. Dewey to Dr. O. C. Stone, U.S. Dept. of Agriculture, 29 May.

69. AGE, 8, 11 Mar. 1922, Carrillo to State Treasurer; AGE, 28 June 1922, Profs. Severiano and Roberto Echeverría to Carrillo.

70. E.g., Humberto Peniche Vallado, *La incorporación del indio a la civilización es la obra complementaria del reparto ejidal,* Mérida, 1938. The development of this notion is examined in Conrado Menéndez Díaz, "Psicología de la explotación de nuestros indios," *O* 1 (Apr.–June 1937), 33–38.

71. Elmer Llanes Marín, "La llanura *aislada, O* 49 (Oct. 57), 29; also see references to Carrillo's *escuelas granjas* in Chapter 7. Cf. Marilyn Gates, "Peasants Speak: Alfredo Pech, A Modern Maya," *JPS* 3:4 (July 1976), 465–471.

72. González Navarro, *Raza,* p. 248; Irigoyen, *Felipe Carrillo,* pp. 27–31.

73. *P,* 22 Mar. 1922; Nelson Reed, *The Caste War of Yucatán,* Stanford, Calif., 1964, pp. 229–280 and *passim.*

74. *P,* 22 Mar. 1922. "General" Pancho May's violent exploits and those of other *rebelde* chiefs appeared frequently in the Mérida press during the 1910s and 1920s. Following Carrillo's death, the *rebeldes* stepped up their depredations. E.g., see SD-CPR, *Miscellaneous Record Book,* p. 164 (destruction of chicle camps by General May in October 1925).

75. *P,* 27 Jan. 1922, 28 Jan. 1922, 30 Jan. 1922.

76. *RdY,* 6 Nov. 1921.

77. SD, 812.61326/403, 376.

78. AGE, Carrillo to Municipal President, Tepakán, 21 Feb. 1922; AGE, Alcalde Municipal, Tecoh, to Carrillo, 23 Feb. 1920; *DO,* 27 Mar. 1922, p. 1; Edward A. Ross, *The Social Revolution in Mexico,* New York, 1923, p. 109. Marte R. Gómez, visiting Yucatán as a delegate of the *Comisión Nacional Agraria,* reported that members of the *Casta Divina* offered him 50,000 pesos if he would oppose the delivery of an *ejido.* "Resistí ese cañonazo," reported Don Marte in his *Historia de la Comisión Nacional Agraria,* Mexico, 1975, p. 264.

79. AGE, Municipal President, Izamal, to Carrillo, 23 Mar. 1922; *A,* 10:19 (Dec. 1923), *passim.* and *A* 11:1 (Sept. 1924), 1; cf. AGE, El Juez Tercero de lo Civil to Director Público de la Propiedad, 8 Nov. 1923 (Montes's foreclosure on smaller *hacendados*).

80. SD, 812.61326/369.

81. PCR, *Yucatán Letters,* HG-2, p. 402, Peabody to Rice, 21 Feb. 1922.

82. SD, 812.61326/414; PCC, file I, drawers 2 and 3, F. C. Holmes, Plymouth Cordage, to "The Farmers of Yucatán," 10 Feb. 1923.

83. Louis Crossette, *Sisal Production, Prices and Marketing*, U.S. Department of Commerce, Supplement to *Commerce Reports*, Trade Information Bulletin No. 200, Washington, D.C., 1924, p. 1.

84. SD-CPR. *Corr.*, *1924*, vol. 7, 861.3, Dewey to Stone, 29 May.

85. *P*, 14 Aug. 1922.

86. Tomás Castellanos Acevedo, *Informe presentado ante el H. Consejo Directivo de la Comisión Exportadora de Yucatán*, Mérida, 1922, p. 5; also appearing in AGN, 424-H-1.

87. SD-CPR, *Corr.*, *1924*, vol. 7, 861.3, Dewey to Stone, 29 May.

88. Crossette, *Sisal Production*, pp. 4–5, 7. The Agriculture Department report admitted that, during the 19229–1923 period, the *Exportadora* had kept the price of henequen slightly below its value in relation to competing fibers. The Commerce Department investigation revealed that, under Alvarado, although the price had soared to 41.8 cents per kilogram, the planter had at best received 15.4 cents per kilogram. Under Carrillo Puerto's *Exportadora*, the price had been kept relatively stable at between 13.2 and 14.3 cents per kilogram and the producer had averaged between 6.6 and 9.9 cents per kilogram.

89. PCC, file H, drawer 2, contains a series of letters and press clippings, dated late in 1921 and throughout much of 1922, recording Plymouth's apprehensions regarding the "new trust," which it likened to Alvarado's *Reguladora*. There was one rather ironic, novel twist to the new partnership arrangements. The New York fiber brokerage house of Hanson and Orth, perhaps the most vehement critic of Alvarado's *Reguladora*, whose representatives had conspired openly with a variety of planters to undermine the Socialist Party in 1918, now agreed to represent the Socialists as the *Exportadora's* New York agent. Formerly, Hanson and Orth had excoriated the bankers as traitors to the American economic system; now they signed on as accomplices. Upon hearing the news, the U.S. consul, appalled and bewildered, asked: "Who shall defend the capitalist from his worst enemy, himself?" SD, 812.61326/384; PCC, file H, drawer 2, Charles Orth to Plymouth Cordage, 2 Jan. 1922.

90. SD, 812.61326/388.

91. Carrillo, *La familia*, pp. 32–34.

92. SD, 812.61326/389, 390. Similar fears of German domination had surfaced more plausibly during World War I. See SD-CPR, *Corr.*, *1915–1918*, especially files 600, 800, and 861.3; and PCC, file I, drawer 3 ("World War I–U.S. Food Administration"); *FIN*, 31 Jan. 1918.

93. SD, 812.61326/391.

94. SD, 812.61326/400, 404, 406, 415, 474. Peabody was occasionally joined in its protests by Plymouth Cordage, for which it regularly bought fiber, and several of the larger midwestern prisons (most notably the Minnesota State Prison), which also produced large amounts of cordage and binder twine. Plymouth and the prisons suspected that Harvester was being given special treatment by the Yucatecan monopoly in terms of the price and quality of the fiber it received. E.g., see PCC, file I, drawers 2 and 3, Plymouth Cordage to Sen. Henry Cabot Lodge, 21, 28 Feb. 1924.

95. *DO,* 29 June 1923, p. 1; Irigoyen, *Felipe Carrillo,* pp. 26–27.

96. Orosa Díaz, *Legislación,* vol. 4, pp. 59–63; Irigoyen, *Felipe Carrillo,* pp. 27–29; SD-CPR, *Corr., 1923,* vol. 4, 861.3/852, Marsh to Secretary of State, 12 Dec., appending text of the decree.

97. SD-CPR, *Corr., 1922,* vol. 4, 861, enclosing decreto num. 127, signed 27 Dec. 1920.

98. The justificatory preamble of a decree.

99. Orosa Díaz, *Legislación,* vol. 4, pp. 62–63; Irigoyen, *Felipe Carrillo,* pp. 29–32.

100. *P,* 2 Jan. 1923.

9. The failure of revolution from within, 1923–1924

1. E.g., see the recent debate between Antonio Betancourt Pérez, *El asesinato de Carrillo Puerto,* Mérida, 1974, and Roque Armando Sosa Ferreyro, *El crimen del miedo: Cómo y por qué fue asesinado Felipe Carrillo Puerto,* Mexico, 1969; see also Chapter 7, note 23.

2. E.g., Betancourt, *El asesinato;* Renán Irigoyen, *Felipe Carrillo: Primer gobernante socialista en México,* Mérida, 1974, p. 41; *Los Agachados,* "Felipe Carrillo Puerto: El Allende Mexicano," p. 20.

3. Betancourt, *El asesinato,* pp. 17–28; Alma Reed, "Felipe Carrillo Puerto," *BdU,* Época 2, 4:1 (June 1924), 20–21; J. W. F. Dulles, *Yesterday in Mexico: A Chronicle of the Revolution, 1919–1936,* Austtin, Tex., 1961, p. 231.

4. Sosa Ferreyro, *El crimen,* pp. 42, 114ff; Rosa Castro, "Sobre la ruta de Carrillo Puerto, el Mesías de Motul," *Hoy,* 15 Mar. 1952.

5. E.g., Antonio Betancourt Pérez, "¿Ángel, o demonio?: Carrillo Puerto y 'Peregrina,'" *J* 2:2 (May 1973), 19.

6. Irigoyen, *Felipe Carrillo,* p. 31; Moisés González Navarro, *Raza y tierra: La guerra de castas y el henequén,* Mexico, 1970, p. 248.

7. *RdY,* 7 Dec. 1923; Rafael Trujillo, *Adolfo de la Huerta y los tratados de Bucareli,* 2d ed., Mexico, 1966, pp. 139–148; Adolfo de la Huerta, *Memorias de Don Adolfo de la Huerta según su propio dictado,* ed. Roberto Guzmán Esparza, Mexico, 1957, pp. 219, 263–264; cf. Aarón Sáenz, *La política internacional de la Revolución,* Mexico, 1961, pp. 50–72; and TLP, File 1973, "Scheider, Franz, Jr., 1926–1929," press release by Arturo Elías, 15 June 1926.

8. *T,* 9 Dec. 1923; *RdY,* 8 Dec. 1923.

9. *RdY,* 12 Dec. 1923: Álvaro Gamboa Ricalde, *Yucatán desde 1910,* Mexico, 1953, vol. 3, p. 345.

10. See the increasingly vitriolic attack on Carrillo's government that was mounted in the conservative paper *El Correo* (*C*) as the power of the rebels grew throughout December.

11. González Navarro, *Raza,* p. 249; *La Confederación Nacional Campesina, un grupo de presión en la Revolución Mexicana,* Mexico, 1968, pp. 81–83. In the case

of Alvarado, personal animosity seems to have played as much if not more of a role than ideological persuasion in distancing him from Obregón. We have seen that, early on, Alvarado had regarded Obregón as a bar to his own national political ambitions. Like his former ally, Carrillo Puerto, Alvarado did not survive the rebellion. He was killed by *Obregonistas* at *rancho* La Hormiga in Chiapas, on 9 June 1924.

12. Irigoyen, *Felipe Carrillo,* p. 32.

13. SD, 812.00/26624; Gamboa Ricalde, *Yucatán,* vol. 3, p. 345.

14. *RdY,* 12 Dec. 1923; AGE, "Relación de los destacamentos existentes en los pueblos del Estado . . . ," 30 Jan. 1923; AGE, Felipe Ayala M. to Carrillo, 21 Mar. 1922; and see AGE, 1920, for the scores of petitions from various pueblos and *campesino* groups asking the return of their shotguns.

15. *RdY,* 13 Dec. 1923; AGN, 101-R2-E-3, memorandum by Miguel J. López,3 11 7 Mar. 1924.

16. In addition to the secondary sources already cited, the following brief narrative also draws upon these contemporary accounts: Edmundo Bolio O., *De la cuna al paredón,* Mérida, 1921; José M. ("Chato") Duarte, *¿Fatalismo . . . ?,* Mérida, 1924; Manuel Cirerol S., *La salida del Gobernador,* Mérida, 1924; Cirerol, "*Yo no asesino a Felipe Carrillo,*" Mérida, 1938; and Joaquín de Arrigunaga Peón, "Felipe Carrillo Puerto y la revolución delahuertista: Declaraciones de los señores . . . ," *NdY,* 21, 28 July 1968.

17. Betancourt, *El asesinato,* p. 46.

18. The evidence to support such an interpretation is drawn from the testimony of former participants and eyewitnesses, who had access to the principals during the negotiations within the prison; from judgments found in the memoirs of Adolfo de la Huerta himself; and from a variety of circumstantial facts and clues that seem to provide an inference of guilt when viewed against the established motives of the planters. E.g., Betancourt, *El asesinato,* pp. 38–51; Bernardino Mena Brito, *Reestructuración histórica de Yucatán,* Mexico, 1969, vol. 3, pp. 336–337; de la Huerta, *Memorias,* pp. 262–263; but cf. Sosa Ferreyro, *El crimen,* pp. 92–94, 135, and David A. Franz, "Bullets and Bolshevists: A History of the Mexican Revolution and Reform in Yucatán," unpublished Ph.D. dissertation, University of New Mexico, Albuquerque, 1973, pp. 300–303.

19. Betancourt, *El asesinato,* p. 46.

20. González Navarro, *Raza,* pp. 249–250; Roberto Blanco Moheno, *Tata Lázaro: Vida, obra y muerte de Cárdenas, Múgica y Carrillo Puerto,* Mexico, 1972, p. 213; Dulles, *Yesterday,* p. 232.

21. Dulles, *Yesterday,* p. 232; Bolio, *De la cuna,* p. 83.

22. Betancourt, *El asesinato,* pp. 35–37, 41; Sosa Ferreyro, *El crimen,* p. 57 and *passim.*

23. Blanco Moheno, *Tata Lázaro,* p. 213; and cf. Robert L. Brunhouse, *Sylvanus G. Morley and the World of the Ancient Mayas,* Norman, Okla., 1971, pp. 205–206.

24. Betancourt, *El asesinato,* pp. 41–42; cf. Manuel M. Escoffié, *Ya,* Mérida, n.d.

25. To cite but one example, the G. Cantóns were allied by marriage with the Campos.

26. The following are important illustrations: (a) *Felipe G. Cantón:* AGE, Felipe Valencia López to Carrillo, 21 May 1923, regarding expropriation of 198 has. henequen land from hacienda Kancabchén for "Ejidos de Yaxkukul." AGE, legajo "Juzgados, 1924," references to *embargo precautorio* on San Juan Koop, Cantón's henequen hacienda in Motul. The entire hacienda was confiscated for a temporary period by the Socialists in 1924. (b) *Felipe G. Solís:* AGE, Juez Supernumerario de Distrito to Carrillo, 27 Dec. 1922, regarding *afectaciones* of *tierras cultivadas* from several of Solís's henequen *fincas* (Ruinas de Aké, Dzoyolá, and San Antonio) for "Ejidos de Cacalchén." (c) *Lorenzo Manzanilla M.:* AGE, Manzanilla to Carrillo, 20 Nov. 1922, protesting the "unfair and discriminatory" ejidal grant to the pueblo of Muna, which took 3,000 has. of *monte* and henequen land from his hacienda Uxmal. Many more such examples could be cited from the extensive *amparo* files found in AGE, Ramo de Gobierno, 1923 and 1924.

27. Betancourt Pérez, *El asesinato,* pp. 43–44.

28. *Ibid.,* pp. 45–46; cf. e.g., Antonio Bustillos Carrillo, *Los mayas ante la cultura y la Revolución,* Mexico, 1956, pp. 197–203; Mena Brito, *Reestructuración,* vol. 3, pp. 334–350.

29. SD-CPR, *Con. Corr.,* 800, Marsh to Secretary of State, 27 Feb. 1924; Betancourt, *El asesinato,* p. 44; and see Hans Werner Tobler's insightful study of the Revolutionary army, "Las paradojas del ejército revolucionario: Su papel social en la reforma agraria mexicana, 1920–1935," *HM* 21:1 (July–Sept. 1971), 38–79, which examines on a national scale the consistency with which high-ranking officers allied with regional elites against the masses.

30. *C,* 15 Dec. 1923; cf. Sosa Ferreyro, *El crimen,* pp. 107–110.

31. *RdY,* 17 Dec. 1923.

32. *Ibid.;* AGE, President, Liga de Opichén, to Gov. Iturralde, 17 Feb. 1925; ASA, *Visitas Parroquiales, 1913–1931,* "Informes Parroquiales, 1923–1924," P. José Y. Góngora, 10 Jan. 1924.

33. *RdY,* 17 Dec. 1923. Baak would later claim that he took his 140 men over to the *Delahuertistas* because a rival Socialist boss in Santa Elena had murdered his son late in 1923. *RdY,* 24 Apr. 1924.

34. Mena Brito, *Reestructuración,* vol. 3, p. 336; cf. Betancourt, *El asesinato,* p. 50.

35. E. J. Hobsbawm's insights regarding the problem of effectively incorporating social bandits into revolutionary movements seem apropos here. The truth is that few of Don Felipe's *cacique* allies were ideologically motivated or organizationally prepared to transcend their condition as "primitive rebels" and become dedicated and disciplined socialist revolutionaries. According to Hobsbawm, the lack of ideological commitment and a coherent organizational structure are the two major limitations that social bandits pose for modern social movements. *Primitive Rebels,* New York, 1959, pp. 26–28.

36. *RdY,* 13 Dec. 1923, 18 Dec. 1923; Luis Monroy Durán, *El último caudillo,* Mexico, 1924, pp. 466–468. A reading of the AGE, "Gobierno" documents for 1924 and 1925, clearly reveals a decline in the vitality and organiza-

tion of the *ligas* following the defeat of *Delahuertismo* and the reinstatement of Socialist Party rule. Cf. Victor Goldkind, "Social Stratification in the Peasant Community: Chan Kom Revisited," *AA*, 67:4 (Aug. 1965), 879–880, for the decadent condition of the *ligas* in the early 1930s.

37. *RdY*, 7 Dec. 1923, 8 Dec. 1923, 11 Dec. 1923; AGE, Cuerpo de Policía, "Legajo de listas de revista de administración . . . 3 de mayo de 1923"; AGE, "Ejército Revolucionario [i.e., *Delahuertista*]. Documentos de entrega de la Comandancia Militar," April 1924; Betancourt, *El asesinato*, pp. 31–32. Strangely, historians have minimized the element of surprise that the rebels used effectively against the Socialist regime.

38. "Militarización de las Ligas de Resistencia será desconocida la que no presente una sección cuando menos bien organizada," *RdY*, 12 Dec. 1923.

39. *RdY*, 17 Aug. 1923; Loló de la Torriente, *Memoria y razón de Diego Rivera*, Mexico, 1959, vol. 2, pp. 225–228.

40. *RdY*, 17 Aug. 1923.

41. *Ibid.*

42. AGE, Felipe Ayala M. to Carrillo, 21 Mar. 1922. As early as 1920, the Socialist Party had resolved to implement "a general instruction for the defense of the state" centered on workers' militias. There is no evidence, however, that the resolution was ever seriously implemented. *RdY*, 5 July 1920.

43. SD-CPR, *Con. Corr.*, 800, Marsh to Secretary of State, 11 Dec. 1923; Gamboa Ricalde, *Yucatán*, vol. 3, p. 345; Monroy Durán, *El último caudillo*, p. 465.

44. Betancourt, *El asesinato*, pp. 20–22; Irigoyen, *Felipe Carrillo*, pp. 36–37.

45. See, e.g., Jan Bazant, *A Concise History of Mexico*, London, 1977, pp. 157–158.

46. Fidelio Quintal Martín, "Quince años trascendentales en la historia de Yucatán, *RUY* 16:93 (May–Aug. 1974), 130–131; AGN, 428-Y-5, Federico Carlos León, Elvia Carrillo Puerto, and Pedro Lugo et al., to Obregón, dated 28 Apr., 2 Sept., and 3 Sept. 1924, respectively; AGN, 101-R2-4, José de la Luz Mena to Obregón, 13 May 1924.

47. Enrique Montalvo Ortega, "Caudillismo y estado en la Revolución Mexicana: El gobierno de Alvarado en Yucatán," *Nova Americana* 2 (1979), 30, 34; Randall G. Hansis, "Álvaro Obregón, the Mexican Revolution and the Politics of Consolidation, 1920–1924," unpublished Ph.D. dissertation, University of New Mexico, Albuquerque, 1971; D. A. Brading, ed., *Caudillo and Peasant in the Mexican Revolution*, Cambridge (U.K.), 1980, *passim*.

48. Cf. Heather Fowler Salamini, "Revolutionary Caudillos in the 1920s: Francisco Mújica and Adalberto Tejeda," in D. A. Brading, ed., *Caudillo and Peasant in the Mexican Revolution*, Cambridge (U.K.), 1980, pp. 169–192; Paul Friedrich, *Agrarian Revolt in a Mexican Village*, Englewood Cliffs, N.J., 1970, pp. 124–130; Francisco J. Paoli and Enrique Montalvo, *El socialismo olvidado de Yucatán*, Mexico, 1977, pp. 176–186.

49. Dudley Ankerson, "Saturnino Cedillo: A Traditional Caudillo in San Luis Potosí" and Ian Jacobs, "Rancheros of Guerrero: The Figueroa Brothers and the

Revolution," in Brading, ed., *Caudillo and Peasant*, pp. 140–168 and 76–91, respectively. The Figueroas subsequently returned to power in Guerrero, yet today operate within the institutionalized confines of the official party.

50. SD-CPR, *Corr.*, *1922*, vol. 3, 800, Marsh to Secretary of State, 22 June; SD, 812.00/25730, 26454. North American bureaucrats and businessmen made much of Carrillo's public statement, *DO*, 2 Feb. 1922, p. 1, that "the era of politics has ended; now we enter a period of administration." Some, in fact, likened it to Don Porfirio's more famous directive that there be "menos política y más administración" ("less politics and more administration"). Harvester's closest rival, Plymouth, although grumbling about the importance of fair and equal treatment for all manufacturers, generally seemed content to abide by the existing arrangements. See PCC, file H, drawer 2 and file I, drawers 2 and 3 (1921–1923).

51. SD, 812.61326/442, 445; Robert Freeman Smith, *The United States and Revolutionary Nationalism in Mexico, 1913–1932*, Chicago, 1972, p. 224.

52. SD, 812.61326/437–490; Franz, "Bullets and Bolshevists," p. 270.

53. SD, 812.61326/449.

54. SD, 812.61326/442, 445.

55. SD, 812.61326/445, 464.

56. SD, 812.61326/457.

57. SD, 812.61326/466.

58. SD, 812.61326/466, 476.

59. SD, 812.61326/474.

60. SD, 812.61326/459, 479.

61. SD, 812.61326/468, 478; AGN, 424-H-2, memorandum from Cámara de Senadores to Obregón, 10 Sept. 1924.

62. LC, Anderson Mss., Chandler P. Anderson Diary, 12, 18, 24 Mar. 1923; SD, 812.61326/455.

63. SD, 812.61326/480; Monroy Durán, *El último caudillo*, p. 482.

64. SD, 812.61326/486.

65. SD, 812.61326/482, 488.

66. SD, 812.61326/490.

67. LC, Hughes Mss., Lamont to Hughes, 15 Jan. 1924; Joseph S. Tulchin, *The Aftermath of War: World War I and U.S. Policy toward Latin America*, New York, 1971, *passim*; Smith, *Mexican Revolutionary Nationalism*, pp. 223–227; Sáenz, *La política internacional*, pp. 50–72.

68. Dwight W. Morrow, "Who Buys Foreign Bonds?," *Foreign Affairs* 5:2 (Jan. 1927), 231.

69. *Ibid.*

70. Lamont quoted in Smith, *Mexican Revolutionary Nationalism*, p. 246. Also, see Donald L. Wyman, "Trust and Trade: Dwight Morrow and Mexico," unpublished manuscript, 1972.

71. Of course, although the United States henceforth sought to adhere to such business diplomacy based on partnerships with trusted foreign collaborators, it was not adverse to carrying out some form of intervention when the collaborator mechanism irreparably broke down, e.g., in Central America and

the Caribbean (1920s and 1930s), Guatemala (1954), the Dominican Republic (1965), and Chile (1970–1973).

72. Irigoyen, *Felipe Carrillo,* p. 35.

73. Duarte, *Fatalismo,* p. 31; Dulles, *Yesterday,* p. 231.

74. Bolio, *De la cuna,* p. 84.

75. Renán Irigoyen, "Carrillo Puerto, Mártir de la cultura," *RUY* 1:1 (Jan.–Feb. 1959), 20–21; but cf. Gamboa Ricalde, *Yucatán,* vol. 3, p. 360 ("Don Benjamín Carrillo asked that they shoot him cleanly in the heart, but Don Felipe Carrillo Puerto did not utter a single word").

76. Eduardo Urzáiz R., "El simbolismo de la Resurrección," *BdU,* Época 2, 4:1 (June 1924), 6–8.

77. Reed, "Felipe Carrillo," 20–21.

78. *BdU,* Época 2, 4:1 (June 1924), *passim.*

79. Although I originally reached this conclusion on the basis of conversations with *Meridanos* and a careful reading of the local press, it was graphically verified for me after I attended several celebrations in small Yucatecan pueblos, each of which marked a major regional Revolutionary holiday (e.g., Carrillo's birthday, the anniversary of his death, "El Día de la Revolución"). These celebrations featured reenactments of events from Yucatán's Revolutionary past, which were organized by government teachers and acted out by the children of the pueblo. In virtually every case, Carrillo was cast in a passive martyr's role.

80. Antonio Pérez Betancourt, "Nuestro viejo abuelo," *RUY* 15:85 (Jan.–Feb. 1973), 60–61.

81. Irigoyen, "Mártir de la cultura," 20–21.

82. *NdY,* 31 Aug. 1973, 1 Sept. 1973; Roldán Peniche Barrera, "Tres nuevos murales," *J* 4:3 (Sept. 1975), 44–45; "Avances del programa de ciudades industriales," *El Mercado de Valores* 36:24 (June 1976), 437–39; *DdelS,* 24 Oct. 1974; *DdY,* 7 Nov. 1974, 8 Nov. 1974. It is significant that in Yucatán support for the PAN (*Partido de Acción Nacional*), chief among the token political opposition that the PRI tolerates, has reached levels unmatched elsewhere in the Republic. *Panistas* have elected Mérida's mayor and would likely carry the governorship if the PRI honored election results for that office.

83. This hypothesis is based on eighteen months of personal observation (1974–1975) and interviews with regional intellectuals, students, and some henequen workers.

84. My account is taken from "La estatua de Felipe Carrillo señorea ya la metrópoli," *NdY,* 31 Aug. 1973.

85. Because of substantial press censorship surrounding this sensitive incident, the following analysis leans heavily upon interviews with local intellectuals, in most cases affiliated with the regime in some capacity, and radical students who oppose it. In every case, anonymity was either requested by my sources or made a precondition for granting the interview. Also, see the retrospective editorial appearing in the "independent" newspaper *Avance,* 26 Jan. 1975, and the more recent exposé in *El Día* (*ED*), 2 July 1977.

86. See, for example, Margaret A. Goodman's case study of the political

career of Víctor Cervera Pacheco, who in the 1950s was a radical student leader and is today a respectable PRI politician and a leading candidate for the state governorship. "The Effectiveness of the Mexican Revolution as an Agent of Change in the State of Yucatán, Mexico," unpublished Ph.D. dissertation, Columbia University, New York, 1970, pp. 128–171.

87. Hearings before a state court in Quintana Roo implicated several members of Mérida's police force in the crime and suggested the possibility that not only the chief of police but also Yucatán's former governor may have been involved. The government of Quintana Roo publicly stated that the judicial process would continue "until all guilty parties have been brought to justice." *ED*, 2 July 1977.

88. *DdelS*, 4 Jan. 1975; *DdY*, 4 Jan. 1975; interviews with student leaders.

Epilogue

1. The central god of the ancient Yucatecan Maya.

2. Coverage of Lombardo's visit and his controversial observations on Yucatecan society are found in *DdY*, 16 Mar. 1934; also see the later collection of essays, *El llanto del sureste*, Mexico, 1934.

3. The existing literature provides little insight into the demise of revolution in Yucatán following the assassination of Carrillo Puerto because it concentrates almost exclusively on personalities and political groups rather than on underlying social and economic relationships. The 1925–1934 decade has been analyzed largely on an *ad hominem* basis: Hard-core hagiography of Carrillo Puerto gives way to invectives against the political leaders who succeeded him, bartering his social ideals for the gold of the *hacendado* elite. Having proclaimed Carrillo a martyr, local historians have regarded the next decade as an empty interval, a time when the region slumbered – or drifted back into old repressive patterns – and waited for its next redeemer, Lázaro Cárdenas. E.g., see the works of Benítez and Bustillos Carrillo listed in the Bibliography.

4. See the flow of correspondence and petitions by *campesino* groups that appears in *DdY* – and less frequently in *DdelS* – during the early to mid-1930s.

5. Moisés González Navarro, *Raza y tierra: La guerra de castas y el henequén,* Mexico, 1970, pp. 254–255; cf. AGE, B. García, Presidente, Liga Central de Resistencia, "Tarifa gradual para el pago de jornales en las fincas henequeneras del Estado," 12 Aug. 1933; and Siegfried Askinasy, *El problema agrario de Yucatán,* 2d ed., Mexico, 1936, pp. 113–114.

6. E.g., see *DdY,* for July 1936; Fernando López Cárdenas, *Revolucionarios contra la Revolución,* Mexico, 1938; Nelson Reed, *The Caste War of Yucatán,* Stanford, Calif., 1964, p. 266.

7. Nathaniel C. Raymond, "The Impact of Land Reform in the Monocrop Region of Yucatán, Mexico," unpublished Ph.D. dissertation, Brandeis University, Waltham, Mass., 1971, p. 139; Manuel A. Mesa and Rogelio Villanueva, *La producción de fibras duras en México,* Mexico, 1948, p. 30.

8. Thomas G. Sanders, "Henequen: The Structure of Agrarian Frustration,"

FR-NA, 5:3 (July 1977), 2–7; Rodney C. Kirk, "San Antonio, Yucatán: From Henequen Hacienda to Plantation Ejido," unpublished Ph.D. dissertation, Michigan State University, East Lansing, Mich., 1975; and see notes 4, 5, 9, 11, and 17, this chapter.

9. Luis Cabrera (alias Lic. Blas Urrea), "La conquista de Yucatán," *DdY,* 10 July 1936, and *Un ensayo comunista en México,* Mexico, 1937; cf. *DdY,* 26 Jan. 1936; *U,* 29, 30 July 1936; and *DdY,* 7 Dec. 1936 for rebuttals against Cabrera by leading federal *agraristas.*

10. E.g., Manuel M. Escoffié, *Yucatán en la cruz,* Mérida, 1957; Bernardino Mena Brito, *Reestructuración histórica de Yucatán,* Mexico, 1969, vol. 3, *passim.*

11. *DdY,* 6 Nov. 1975; *NdY,* 11 Nov. 1975; *E,* 22 July 1977; *U,* 5 July 1977.

12. E.g., Gustavo Molina Font, *La tragedia de Yucatán,* Mexico, 1941, which contains a prologue by Luis Cabrera; Manuel Zapata Casares, *Vía-Crucis del henequén: Colección de escritos sobre el gran problema de Yucatán,* Mérida, 1961.

13. *E,* 22 July 1977; *PR,* 9 May 1977, p. 34; *DdelS,* 13 Mar. 1976; Cordemex, *Informe Anual,* March 1974 and March 1975; Manuel Pasos Peniche, *Historia de la industria henequenera desde 1945,* Mérida, 1974, pp. 15–16; Malcolm H. Shuman, "The Town Where Luck Fell: The Economics of Life in a Henequen Zone Pueblo," unpublished Ph.D. dissertation, Tulane University, New Orleans, 1974, pp. 43–44; Sanders, "Henequen," 4–12.

14. Michel Gutelman, "The Socialization of the Means of Production in Cuba" in Rodolfo Stavenhagen, ed., *Agrarian Problems and Peasant Movements in Latin America,* New York 1970, pp. 347–368.

15. Cf. Thomas Sanders's recent judgment ("Henequen," 13) of Cárdenas's agrarian reform in Yucatán:

The case of henequen demonstrates that a strong concern for improving the condition of rural workers and the institution of radical structural changes do not necessarily create a better life for them. The point needs to be made because many idealistic but poorly informed people view agrarian reform (usually unspecified as to type and implications) as a panacea for rural Latin America. Undoubtedly, agrarian reform would be a useful experiment in some settings, and it has already proved its worth in others. Nevertheless, structural changes are only one factor in bettering rural life, along with others such as favorable market conditions, effective administration, genuine participation and involvement of peasants in meaningful enterprise. . . . Poor government involvement may be worse than none.

16. Cf., e.g., *E,* 22 July 1977 (an official defense of the agrarian reform), and Juan José Hinojosa, "Henequén: Fracaso, espina, remordimiento," *PR,* 9 May 1977.

17. A partial bibliography of negative evaluations of Yucatán's agrarian reform appears in Gilbert M. Joseph, "Apuntes hacia una nueva historia regional: Yucatán y la Revolución Mexicana, 1915–1940," *RUY* 19:109 (Jan.–Feb. 1977), 21–22. Cf. the problems experienced by *campesinos* in other collective *ejido* regimes, described by David Ronfeldt, *Atencingo: The Politics of Agrarian*

Struggle in a Mexican Ejido, Stanford, Calif., 1973 (Puebla: sugar); Clarence Senior, *Land Reform and Democracy,* Gainesville, Fla., 1958 (La Laguna: cotton); and Rodolfo Stavenhagen, "Collective Agriculture and Capitalism in Mexico: A Way Out or a Dead End?" *LAP* 2:2 (Summer 1975), 146–163 (various regions, various crops).

18. However, one of the serious failings of the region's program of social security (*seguro social*) is the provision that only henequen workers are entitled to receive welfare benefits.

19. See Chapter 3, note 25; cf. Fernando Henrique Cardoso, "The Consumption of Dependency Theory in the United States," *LARR* 12:3 (Fall 1977), 7–24.

20. This literature is reviewed in James D. Cockcroft's chapter on Mexico in Ronald H. Chilcote and Joel C. Edelstein, eds., *Latin America, The Struggle with Dependency and Beyond,* New York, 1974, pp. 259–285.

21. IHCA, H. L. Boyle Files, "History of the International Harvester Company," n.d. (1947).

22. The proverb has been cited in Robin W. Winks, "On Decolonization and Informal Empire," *AHR* 81:3 (June 1976), 540–556.

23. IHCA, doc. files 441, 2395, 2919, 2924, various documents pertaining to IHC's fiber interests in the Philippines, Cuba, and elsewhere prior to 1924.

24. For a discussion of export economies and the social structures that they articulate, see Fernando Henrique Cardoso and Enzo Faletto, *Dependencia y desarrollo en América Latina,* Lima, 1967; and see Celso Furtado's typology of such economies exporting raw materials in *Economic Development of Latin America,* Cambridge (U.K.), 1976, pp. 47–50.

25. Cf. Peter Winn, *El imperio informal británico en el Uruguay en el siglo XIX,* Montevideo, 1975, and see Winks's discussion of the differences between "formal" and "informal" empires in "On Decolonization," 543.

26. John Womack, *Zapata and the Mexican Revolution,* New York, 1970, especially pp. 3–9; Heather Fowler Salamini, *Agrarian Radicalism in Veracruz, 1920–38,* Lincoln, Neb., 1977, *passim.*

27. Raymond Th. Buve, "Peasant Movements, Caudillos and Land Reform during the Revolution (1910–1917) in Tlaxcala, Mexico," *BdEL* 18 (June 1975), 114–118 and *passim,* and "State Governors and Political Mobilization of Peasants: Tlaxcala," in D. A. Brading, ed., *Caudillo and Peasant in the Mexican Revolution,* Cambridge, (U.K.), 1980, pp. 222–244; Fowler Salamini, *Agrarian Radicalism,* chap. 2, and "Los orígenes de las organizaciones campesinas en Veracruz: Raíces políticas y sociales," *HM* 22:1 (July–Sept. 1972), 52–76; Henry A. Landsberger, "The Role of Peasant Movements and Revolts in Development," in Landsberger, ed., *Latin American Peasants,* Ithaca, N.Y., 1969, pp. 19–22.

28. Frances Fitzgerald, *The Fire in the Lake: The Vietnamese and the Americans in Vietnam,* New York, 1973, pp. 284–304; Gérard Chaliand, *Revolution in the Third World: Myths and Prospects,* New York, 1977. pp. 133–146 ("The Case of

North Vietnam"); Cole Blasier, "Studies of Social Revolution: Origins in Mexico, Bolivia, and Cuba," *LARR* 2 (Summer 1967), 28–64.

29. The Bolivian *campesino's* perception of Ché as a foreigner is discussed in Richard L. Harris, *Death of a Revolutionary*, New York, 1970, pp. 140ff.

30. Neill Macaulay, *The Prestes Column: Revolution in Brazil*, New York, 1974.

31. Womack, *Zapata*, p. 67.

32. Cf. Immanuel Wallerstein, foreward to Chaliand, *Revolution*, pp. xi–xii.

Select bibliography

Archives

United States

Baker Library, Harvard School of Business Administration, Cambridge, Massachusetts. Manuscript Collections.
 Thomas Lamont Papers
 Henry W. Peabody and Company Records
 Plymouth Cordage and Company Records
Albert Bacon Fall Papers, 1850–1927. University of New Mexico Library, Special Collections, Albuquerque, New Mexico.
International Harvester Company Archives, Chicago, Illinois.
Library of Congress, Washington, D.C. Manuscript Collections.
 Chandler P. Anderson Papers
 Henry P. Fletcher Papers
 Charles Evans Hughes Papers
 Woodrow Wilson Papers
Records of the McCormick Harvesting Machine Company. The McCormick Collection, Manuscript Library, State Historical Society, Madison, Wisconsin.
National Archives, Washington, D.C.
 Modern Military Branch, Military Intelligence Division and War College Division
 Record Group 59, Records of the Department of State Relating to the Internal Affairs of Mexico, 1910–1929. Microfilm publication 274, 1959.
 Record Group 84, U.S. Department of State Consular Post Records: Progreso.
 Record Group 182, Records of the War Trade Board.
Silvestre Terrazas Papers. University of California, Bancroft Library, Berkeley, California.

Mexico City

Centro de Estudios de Historia de México, Condumex. Manuscript Collections.
 Archivo de Venustiano Carranza
 Manuscritos de Manuel González
Archivo General de la Nación.
 Papeles Presidenciales

Ramo de Madero
Ramo de Obregón-Calles
Archivo de la Secretaría de Relaciones Exteriores.
Ramo de la Revolución Mexicana, 1910–1920
Colección Jorge Denegre V. Instituto Nacional de Antropología e Historia.
Microfilm.

Mérida

Archivo General del Estado de Yucatán.
  Ramo de Congreso
  Ramo de Gobierno
  Ramo de Justicia
  Ramo de Tierras
Archivo Notarial del Estado de Yucatán.
Archivo Público de la Propriedad.
Archivo de la Secretaría del Arzobispado.

Motul

Correspondencia de Felipe Carrillo Puerto. Museo Felipe Carrillo Puerto.

Campeche

Archivo del Estado de Campeche.

Periodicals

Government Serials – United States
  Congressional Record
Government Serials – Mexico
  Diario de los debates del Congreso de la Unión (Mexico City)
  Boletín de Estadística (Mérida)
  Diario Oficial (Mérida)
Journals and Newspapers – United States
  Cordage Trade Journal
  El Paso del Norte
  Farm Implement News
  Harvester World
  New York Commercial
  New York Times
  Textile Trade Journal
  Tractor and Truck Review
  Wall Street Journal
Journals and Newspapers – Mexico City
  Acción Mundial
  Ariete

El Demócrata
El Día
El Diario del Hogar
Excélsior
Hoy
El Imparcial
El Mercado de Valores
Mañana
Mexican Herald
El Nacional
Proceso
El Universal
Journals and Newspapers – Mérida
El Agricultor
Avance
Boletín de la Liga de Acción Social
Boletín de la Universidad Nacional del Sureste
El Comercio
Cooperación
El Correo
Diario del Sureste
Diario de Yucatán
Diario Yucateco
El Eco del Comercio
El Henequén
Juzgue
Municipio Libre
Novedades de Yucatán
Orbe
El Peninsular
El Popular
Revista de Estudios Yucatecos
Revista de Industria y Comercio
Revista de Mérida
Revista de la Universidad de Yucatán
Revista de Yucatán
Siempre Adelante
El Sisal Mexicano
Tierra
La Voz de la Revolución
Yucatán: Historia y economía

Books

Abreu Gómez, Ermilo. *Canek: History and Legend of a Maya Hero,* tr. Mario Dávila and Carter Wilson. Berkeley, Calif., 1980.

Aguilar Camín, Héctor. *La frontera nómada: Sonora y la Revolución Mexicana.* Mexico, 1977.

Alvarado, Salvador. *Carta al pueblo de Yucatán.* Mérida, 1916.

La reconstrucción de México: Un mensaje a los pueblos de América, 3 vols. Mexico, 1919.

Actuación revolucionaria del General Salvador Alvarado en Yucatán. Mexico, 1965 (originally published 1920).

Mi sueño. Mérida, 1965 (originally published 1917).

Amendolla, Luis. *La Revolución comienza a los cuarenta.* Mexico, 1948.

Ancona, Eligio. *Historia de Yucatán desde la época más remota hasta nuestros días,* 2d ed., 5 vols. Mérida and Barcelona, 1889–1905.

Askinasy, Siegfried. *El problema agrario de Yucatán,* 2d ed. Mexico, 1936.

Ávila y Castillo, Florencio. *Diario Revolucionario.* Mérida, 1915.

Baerlein, Henry. *Mexico: The Land of Unrest.* Philadelphia, 1914.

Bailey, David C. *¡Viva Cristo Rey! The Cristero Rebellion and the Church–State Conflict in Mexico.* Austin, Tex., 1974.

Bailey, T. A. *The Policy of the United States toward the Neutrals, 1917–1918.* Baltimore, 1942.

Baqueiro, Sergio. *Ensayo histórico sobre las revoluciones de Yucatán . . . ,* 2 vols. Mérida, 1878.

Baqueiro Anduze, Osvaldo. *Los mayas y el problema de la cultura indígena.* Mérida, 1937.

Barragán R., Juan. *Historia del ejército de la Revolución Constitucionalista,* 2 vols. Mexico, 1946.

Bartra, Roger, ed. *Caciquismo y poder político en el México rural.* Mexico, 1975.

Bataillon, Claude. *Les régions géographiques au Mexique.* Paris, 1967.

Beals, Carleton. *Mexico: An Interpretation.* New York, 1923.

Mexican Maze. Philadelphia, 1931.

Beezley, William H. *Insurgent Governor: Abrahám González and the Mexican Revolution in Chihuahua.* Lincoln, Neb., 1973.

Benítez, Fernando. *Ki: El drama de un pueblo y de una planta,* 2d ed. Mexico, 1962.

Betancourt Pérez, Antonio. *¿Necesita Yucatán una nueva revolución técnica en su industria henequenera?* Mérida, 1953.

Revoluciones y crisis en la economía de Yucatán. Mérida, 1953.

La escuela de la Revolución Mexicana. Mérida, 1965.

El asesinato de Carrillo Puerto. Mérida, 1974.

Blanco Moheno, Roberto. *Tata Lázaro: Vida, obra y muerte de Cárdenas, Múgica y Carrillo Puerto.* Mexico, 1972.

Blein, Allan Moe (Antonio Mediz Bolio). *Alvarado es el hombre,* 2d ed. Culiacán, 1961.

Bolio, José A. *Manual práctico del henequén, su cultura y explotación.* Mérida, 1914.

Bolio O., Edmundo. *De la cuna al paredón.* Mérida, 1921.

Yucatán en la dictadura y en la Revolución. Mexico, 1967.

Brading, D. A., ed. *Caudillo and Peasant in the Mexican Revolution.* Cambridge (U.K.), 1980.

Brunhouse, Robert L. *Sylvanus G. Morley and the World of the Ancient Mayas.* Norman, Okla., 1971.

Bulnes, Francisco. *The Whole Truth about Mexico: President Wilson's Responsibility,* tr. Dora Scott. New York, 1916.

Bustillos Carrillo, Antonio. *Los mayas ante la cultura y la Revolución.* Mexico, 1956.

Yucatán al servicio de la Patria y la Revolución. Mexico, 1959.

Cabrera, Luis (alias Lic. Blas Urrea). *Un ensayo comunista en México.* Mexico, 1937.

Cámara Nacional de Comercio de Mérida. *Reseña histórica de la . . . , 1906–1956.* Mérida, 1956.

Canto López, Antonio. *La guerra de castas en Yucatán.* Mérida, 1976.

Cantón Rosado, Francisco. *Historia de la Iglesia en Yucatán desde 1887.* Mérida, 1943.

Carr, Barry. *El movimiento obrero y la política en México, 1910–1929,* 2 vols. Mexico, 1976.

Carrillo Puerto, Acrelio. *La familia Carrillo Puerto de Motul.* Mérida, 1959.

Lo que no se olvida, Felipe Carrillo. Mérida, 1964.

Felipe Carrillo Puerto: Redentor de los mayas. Mérida, 1972.

Carrillo Puerto, Felipe. *Informe . . . ante la . . . Legislatura del Estado, el 1º de enero de 1923.* Mérida, 1923.

Casasola, Gustavo. *Historia gráfica de la Revolución Mexicana, 1910–1970,* 2d ed., 10 vols. Mexico, 1973.

Castellanos Acevedo, Tomás. *Informe presentado ante el H. Consejo Directivo de la Comisión Exportadora de Yucatán.* Mérida, 1922.

Castillo Torre, José. *A la luz del relámpago: Ensayo de biografía sujetiva de Felipe Carrillo Puerto.* Mexico, 1934.

Castro, Juan Miguel. *El henequén de Yucatán y el monopolio.* Mérida, 1876.

Castro Aguilar, Pedro. *Colonizar es poblar.* Mérida, 1948.

Chamberlain, Robert. *The Conquest and Colonization of Yucatán, 1517–1550.* Washington, D.C., 1948.

Chardon, Roland E. P. *Geographic Aspects of Plantation Agriculture in Yucatán.* Washington, D.C., 1961.

Cirerol S., Manuel. *La salida del Gobernador.* Mérida, 1924.

"Yo no asesino a Felipe Carrillo." Mérida, 1938.

Clark, Marjorie Ruth. *Organized Labor in Mexico.* Chapel Hill, N.C., 1934.

Cockcroft, James D. *Intellectual Precursors of the Mexican Revolution, 1900–1913.* Austin, Tex., 1968.

Colegio de México. *Estadísticas económicas del Porfiriato: Fuerza de trabajo y actividad económica por sectores.* Mexico, 1964.

Congreso Feminista de Yucatán. *Anales de esa memorable asamblea.* Mérida, 1916.

Correa Delgado, Manuel. *Breve relación histórica de la Liga de Acción Social: Sus principales trabajos durante los 50 años de su existencia.* Mérida, 1959.

Cosío Villegas, Daniel, ed. *Historia moderna de México*, 9 vols. Mexico, 1955–1972.

Crossette, Louis. *Sisal Production, Prices and Marketing*. U.S. Department of Commerce, Supplement to *Commerce Reports*, Trade Information Bulletin No. 200. Washington, D.C., 1924.

Cumberland, Charles C. *Mexican Revolution: Genesis under Madero*. Austin, Tex., 1952.

Mexican Revolution: The Constitutionalist Years. Austin, Tex., 1972.

Cuadros, Caldas, Julio. *México–Soviet*. Puebla, 1926.

De la Cueva, Mario. *Derecho mexicano del trabajo*, 2 vols. Mexico, 1943.

De la Huerta, Adolfo. *Memorias de Don Adolfo de la Huerta según su propio dictado*, ed. Roberto Guzmán Esparza. Mexico, 1957.

Dewing, Arthur S. *A History of the National Cordage Company*. Cambridge, Mass., 1913.

Díaz de Cossío, Martín. *Yucatán's Henequen*. Barcelona, 1928.

Duarte, José M. ("Chato"). *¿Fatalismo . . . ?* Mérida, 1924.

Dulles, J. W. F. *Yesterday in Mexico: A Chronicle of the Revolution, 1919–1936*. Austin, Tex., 1961.

Durán Rosado, Esteban. *La primera huelga ferrocarrilera en Yucatán*. Mérida, 1944.

Echeagaray Bablot, Luis. *Irrigación, crisis henequenera y condiciones agrícolas y económicas de Yucatán*. Mexico, 1956.

Edwards, H. T. *Production of Henequen Fiber in Yucatán and Campeche*. Washington, D.C., 1924.

Escoffié, Manuel M. *Yucatán en la cruz*. Mérida, 1957.

Ya. Mérida, n.d.

Espadas, Ramón. *Fundación del Partido Socialista Obrero*. Mérida, 1972.

Fabela, Isidro, and Fabela, Josefina, eds. *Documentos Históricos de la Revolución Mexicana*, 24 vols. Mexico, 1960–

Falcón, Romana. *El agrarismo en Veracruz: La etapa radical (1928–1935)*. Mexico, 1977.

Ferrer, Adolfo. *El archivo de Felipe Carrillo: El callismo. La corrupción del régimen obregonista*. New York, 1924.

Ferrer de Mendiolea, Gabriel. *Historia del Congreso Constituyente de 1916–1917*. Mexico, 1957.

Fowler Salamini, Heather. *Agrarian Radicalism in Veracruz, 1920–38*. Lincoln, Neb., 1977.

Frank, André Gunder. *Capitalism and Underdevelopment in Latin America*. New York, 1967.

Friedrich, Paul. *Agrarian Revolt in a Mexican Village*. Englewood Cliffs, N.J., 1970.

Frost, Frederick J. T., and Arnold, Channing. *The American Egypt*. New York, 1909.

Gamboa Ricalde, Álvaro. *Yucatán desde 1910*, 3 vols. Veracruz and Mexico, 1943–1955.

Gann, Thomas W. F. *In an Unknown Land*. London, 1924.

Ancient Cities and Modern Tribes. London, 1926.

Gilly, Adolfo. *La revolución interrumpida*. Mexico, 1971.

Gilly, Adolfo, et al. *Interpretaciones de la Revolución Mexicana*. Mexico, 1979.

Gómez, Marte. *Las comisiones agrarias del sur*. Mexico, 1961.

Historia de la Comisión Nacional Agraria. Mexico, 1975.

González, Luis. *Pueblo en vilo*. Mexico, 1968.

Invitación a la microhistoria. Mexico, 1973.

González Navarro, Moisés. *La Confederación Nacional Campesina, un grupo de presión en la Revolución Mexicana*. Mexico, 1968.

Raza y tierra: La guerra de castas y el henequén. Mexico, 1970.

Gruening, Ernest. *Un viaje al Estado de Yucatán: Felipe Carrillo Puerto, su obra socialista*. Guanajuato, 1924.

Mexico and Its Heritage. New York, 1928.

Guzmán, Martín Luis. *The Eagle and the Serpent*, tr. Harriet de Onís. Garden City, N.Y., 1965.

Irabién Rosado, Manuel. *Historia de los ferrocarriles*. Mérida, 1928.

Irigoyen, Renán. *¿Fué el auge del henequén producto de la guerra de castas?* Mérida, 1947.

Los mayas y el henequén. Mérida, 1950.

Salvador Alvarado: Extraordinario estadista de la Revolución. Mérida, 1973.

Felipe Carrillo Puerto: Primer gobernante socialista en Mexico. Mérida, 1974.

Jones, Eliot. *The Trust Problem in the United States*. New York, 1921.

Katz, Friedrich, ed. *La servidumbre agraria en México en la época porfiriana*. Mexico, 1976.

Lara y Lara, Humberto. *Sobre la trayectoria de la reforma agraria en Yucatán*. Mérida, 1949.

Lieuwen, Edwin. *Mexican Militarism: The Political Rise and Fall of the Revolutionary Army, 1910–1940*. Albuquerque, N.M., 1968.

Lombardo Toledano, Vicente. *El llanto del Sureste*. Mexico, 1934.

López Cárdenas, Fernando. *Revolucionarios contra la Revolución*. Mexico, 1938.

Loveira, Carlos. *El obrerismo yucateco y la Revolución Mexicana*. New York, 1917.

El socialismo en Yucatán. Havana, 1923.

Luz Mena y Alcocer, José de la. *La escuela socialista, su desorientación y fracaso, el verdadero derrotero*. Mexico, 1941.

Magaña Esquivel, Antonio. *La tierra enrojecida*. Mexico, 1951.

Manero, Enrique. *La anarquía henequenera de Yucatán*. Mexico, 1966.

Manzanilla D., Anastasio. *El bolchevismo criminal de Yucatán*. Mérida, 1921.

McBride, George M. *The Land Systems of Mexico*. New York, 1923.

Mena Brito, Bernardino. *Bolshevismo y democracia en México*, 2d ed. Mexico, 1933.

Reestructuración histórica de Yucatán, 3 vols. Mexico, 1969.

Mendoza Medina, Ramón, ed. *La cuestión henequenera y otras cuestiones de Yucatán*. Mérida, 1946.

Menéndez, Miguel Ángel. *La industria de la esclavitud*. Mexico, 1947.

Menéndez, Rodolfo. *Rita Cetina Gutiérrez*. Mérida, 1909.

Menéndez Rodríguez, Mario. *Yucatán o el genocidio*. Mexico, 1964.

Mesa Andrade, Manuel, and Villanueva, Rogelio. *La producción de fibras duras en México*. Mexico, 1948.

The Mexican Year Book: A Financial and Commercial Handbook. London, 1912.

Mexico. *Boletín de la Dirección General de Agricultura*. Mexico, 1911.

Mexico. Comisión Nacional Agraria. *Boletín Mensual*. Mexico, 1920.

Mexico. Congreso. *Diario de los debates de la Cámara de Diputados . . . 1912*. Mexico, 1922.

Mexico. Departamento de la Estadística Nacional. *Anuario estadístico, 1930*. Tacubaya, 1932.

Mexico. Departamento de la Estadística Nacional. *Censo general de habitantes: 30 noviembre de 1921: Estado de Yucatán*. Mexico, 1928.

Mexico. Secretaría de Agricultura y Fomento. *Tercer censo de población de los Estados Unidos Mexicanos. Verificado el 27 de octubre de 1910*, 2 vols. Mexico, 1918.

Mexico. Secretaría de Agricultura y Fomento. Comisión Nacional Agraria. *Estadística, 1915–1927*. Mexico, 1928.

Meyer, Eugenia. *Luis Cabrera: Teoría y crítica de la Revolución Mexicana*. Mexico, 1972.

Meyer, Jean. *La Revolución Mejicana*. Barcelona, 1973.

   The Cristero Rebellion: The Mexican People between Church and State, 1926–1929, tr. Richard Southern. Cambridge (U.K.), 1976.

Meyer, Jean, Krauze, Enrique, and Reyes, Cayetano. *Historia de la Revolución Mexicana*, vol. 11: *Estado y sociedad con Calles*. Mexico, 1977.

Meyer, Michael C. *Pascual Orozco: Mexican Rebel*. Lincoln, Neb., 1967.

Moguel H., Wenceslao. *El milagro del Santo de Halachó o historia de un fusilado*, 2d ed. Mérida, 1967.

Molina Enríquez, Andrés. *Los grandes problemas nacionales*. Mexico, 1909.

Molina Font, Gustavo. *La tragedia de Yucatán*, prologue by Luis Cabrera. Mexico, 1941.

Molina Font, Julio. *Halachó, 1915*. Mérida, 1960.

Molina Solís, Juan Francisco. *Historia de Yucatán desde la Independencia de España hasta la época actual*, 2 vols. Mérida, 1921–1927.

Monroy Durán, Luis. *El último caudillo*. Mexico, 1924.

Morales Jiménez, Alberto. *Hombres de la Revolución Mexicana: 50 semblanzas biográficas*. Mexico, 1960.

Moreno, Daniel. *Los hombres de la Revolución*. Mexico, 1960.

Moseley, Edward H., and Terry, Edward D., eds. *Yucatán: A World Apart*. University, Ala., 1980.

Mullendore, William C. *History of the United States Food Administration, 1917–1919*, introduction by Herbert Hoover. Stanford, Calif., 1941.

Ober, Frederick. *Travels in Mexico and Life among the Mexicans*. Boston, 1884.

Orosa Díaz, Jaime. *Se vende un hombre*. Mérida, 1974 (originally published 1959).

   ed. *Legislación henequenera en Yucatán*, 4 vols. Mérida, 1936–1961.

Pacheco Cruz, Santiago. *Recuerdos de la propaganda constitucionalista en Yucatán*. Mérida, 1953.

Pani, Alberto J. *Las Conferencias de Bucareli*. Mexico, 1953.

Paoli, Francisco, J., and Montalvo, Enrique. *El socialismo olvidado de Yucatán.* Mexico, 1977.

Partido Socialista de Yucatán. *Tierra y libertad: Bases que discutieron y aprobaron el Primer Congreso Obrero Socialista celebrado en . . . Motul . . . para todas las Ligas de Resistencia . . .* Mérida, 1919.

Partido Socialista del Sureste. *Memorias del Congreso Obrero de Izamal.* Mérida, 1922.

Pasos Peniche, Manuel. *Historia de la industria henequenera desde 1945.* Mérida, 1974.

Patch, Robert. *La formación de estancias y haciendas en Yucatán durante la colonia.* Mérida, 1976.

Peniche Vallado, Humberto. *La incorporación del indio a la civilización es la obra complementaria del reparto ejidal.* Mérida, 1938.

Piña Soria, Antolín. *El caso de Yucatán ante la ley.* México, 1937.

Priego de Arjona, Mireyra. *Orígen y evolución de Progreso.* Mérida, 1973.

Quienes son en Yucatán los enemigos de la Revolución . . . Mérida, 1916.

Quintal Martín, Fidelio. *Yucatán: Carácter de la guerra campesina de 1847.* Mérida, 1976.

Quirk, Robert E. *The Mexican Revolution, 1914–1915: The Convention of Aguascalientes.* Bloomington, Ind., 1960.

Redfield, Robert, and Villa Rojas, Alonso. *Chan Kom: A Maya Village.* Chicago, 1962.

Reed, Nelson. *The Caste War of Yucatán.* Stanford, Calif., 1964.

Rendón, Víctor A. *Notas breves.* New York, 1917.

Rico, Juan. *Yucatán: La huelga de junio,* 2 vols. Mérida, 1922.

Ripley, William Z. *Trusts, Pools and Corporations,* rev. ed. Boston, 1916.

Rodríguez, Antonio. *El henequén: Una planta calumniada.* Mexico, 1966.

Ronfeldt, David. *Atencingo: The Politics of Agrarian Struggle in a Mexican Ejido.* Stanford, Calif., 1973.

Rosado Vega, Luis. *El desastre: Asuntos yucatecos. La obra revolucionaria del General Alvarado.* Havana, 1919.

Ross, Edward A. *The Social Revolution in Mexico.* New York, 1923.

Ross, Stanley R. *Francisco I. Madero: Apostle of Mexican Democracy.* New York, 1955.

Rouaix, Pastor. *Génesis de los artículos 27 y 123 de la Constitución política de 1917.* Mexico, 1959.

Roys, Ralph L. *The Indian Background of Colonial Yucatán.* Washington, D.C., 1943.

Rubio Mañé, Jorge Ignacio. *El separatismo de Yucatán.* Mérida, 1935.

Sáenz, Aarón. *La política internacional de la Revolución.* Mexico, 1961.

Salazar, Rosendo, and Escobedo, J. G. *Las pugnas de la gleba,* 2 vols. Mexico, 1923.

Sales Díaz, Arturo. *Síntesis y breve análisis de la actuación del General Salvador Alvarado en Yucatán.* Mexico, 1956.

Schryer, Frans J. *The Rancheros of Pisaflores: The History of a Peasant Bourgeoisie in Twentieth-Century Mexico.* Toronto, 1980.

Senior, Clarence. *Land Reform and Democracy.* Gainesville, Fla., 1958.

Shattuck, George C. *The Peninsula of Yucatán: Medical, Biological, Meteorological and Sociological Studies*. Washington, D.C., 1933.

Silva Herzog, Jesús. *El agrarismo y la reforma agraria*. Mexico, 1959.

Trayectoria ideológica de la Revolución Mexicana, 1910–1917. Mexico, 1963.

ed. *La cuestión de la tierra: Colección de folletos para la historia de la Revolución Mexicana*, 4 vols. Mexico, 1960–1962.

Simmons, Merle E. *The Mexican Corrido as a Source for Interpretive Study of Modern Mexico (1870–1950)*. Bloomington, Ind., 1957.

Simpson, Eyler N. *The Ejido: Mexico's Way Out*. Chapel Hill, N.C., 1937.

Smith, Robert Freeman. *The United States and Revolutionary Nationalism in Mexico, 1913–1932*. Chicago, 1972.

Sosa Ferreyro, Roque Armando. *El crimen del miedo: Cómo y por qué fue asesinado Felipe Carrillo Puerto*. Mexico, 1969.

Southworth, J. R. *Yucatán Illustrated: The State of Yucatán, Its Description, Government, History, Commerce and Industries*. Liverpool, 1905.

Stephens, John L., and Catherwood, Frederick. *Incidents of Travel in Central America, Chiapas, and Yucatán*, 2 vols. New York, 1841.

Tannenbaum, Frank. *The Mexican Agrarian Revolution*. Washington, D.C., 1930.

Peace by Revolution: Mexico after 1910. New York, 1933.

Taracena, Alfonso. *La verdadera Revolución Mexicana*, 18 vols. Mexico, 1960–1965.

Thompson, Richard. *The Winds of Tomorrow: Social Change in a Maya Town*. Chicago, 1974.

Thompson, Wallace. *The People of Mexico*. New York, 1921.

Torre, Manuel A. *La ruina y el hambre o una guerra intestina amenazan a Yucatán*. Mérida, 1918.

Torriente, Loló de la. *Memoria y razón de Diego Rivera*, 2 vols. Mexico, 1959.

Trujillo, Rafael. *Adolfo de la Huerta y los tratados de Bucareli*, 2d ed. Mexico, 1966.

Tulchin, Joseph S. *The Aftermath of War: World War I and U.S. Policy toward Latin America*. New York, 1971.

Turner, John K. *Barbarous Mexico*. Chicago, 1910.

Ulloa, Berta. *Historia de la Revolución Mexicana*, vol. 5: *La encrucijada de 1915*. Mexico, 1979.

United Kingdom. *Diplomatic and Consular Reports: Trade of Yucatán for the Year 1898*. London, 1899.

United States. Department of Commerce, Bureau of Corporations. *International Harvester Company*. Washington, D.C., 1913.

United States. Senate, Committee on Agriculture and Forestry. *Importation of Sisal and Manila Hemp: Hearing before the Sub-committee of the Committee on Agriculture and Forestry, pursuant to S. Res. 94*, 2 vols. Washington, D.C., 1916.

United States. Senate, Committee on Foreign Relations. *Investigation of Mexican Affairs: Preliminary Report and Hearings of the Committee on Foreign Relations, pursuant to S. Res. 106*, 2 vols. Washington, D.C., 1920.

United States. Department of State. *Papers Relating to the Foreign Relations of the United States* (1915–1924). Washington, D.C., 1924–1933.

Valadés, José C. *Historia general de la Revolución Mexicana,* 10 vols. Mexico, 1963–1967.

Valdés Acosta, José María. *A través de las centurias,* 3 vols. Mérida, 1923–1931.

Valenzuela, Clodoveo, and Chaverri Matamoros, Amado. *Sonora y Carranza.* Mexico, 1921.

Villa, Eduardo W. *Compendio de historia del Estado de Sonora.* Mexico, 1937.

Villaseñor, Roberto. *El separatismo en Yucatán: Novela histórico–política mexicana.* Mexico, 1916.

Weyl, Sylvia, and Weyl, Nathaniel. *The Reconquest of Mexico: The Years of Lázaro Cárdenas.* New York, 1939.

Wilkie, James W. *The Mexican Revolution: Federal Expenditure and Social Change since 1910.* Berkeley, Calif., 1967.

Wolf, Eric. *Peasant Wars of the Twentieth Century.* New York, 1969.

Wolfskill, George, and Richmond, Douglas W., eds. *Essays on the Mexican Revolution: Revisionist Views of the Leaders.* Austin, Tex., 1979.

Womack, John. *Zapata and the Mexican Revolution.* New York, 1968.

Yucatán. *Breves apuntes acerca de la administración del Gral. Salvador Alvarado, como Gobernador de Yucatán, con simple expresión de hechos y sus consecuencias.* Mérida, 1916.

Yucatán. Comisión especial . . . para investigar, examinar y depurar los manejos de la Comisión Reguladora del Mercado de Henequén. *Informe acerca de los operaciones . . . en el período 1 mayo 1912–10 septiembre 1914.* Mérida, 1919.

Yucatán. *Enciclopedia Yucatanense,* 8 vols. Mexico, 1944–1947.

Yucatán. Comisión Reguladora del Mercado de Henequén. *La cuestión palpitante en Yucatán: Fructífera gestión de la Comisión Reguladora . . . en 18 meses de labor activa, inteligente y honrada.* Mérida, 1916.

Yucatán. *Mensajes del Gobernador Constitucional C. Lic. Olegario Molina al Congreso de Yucatán, 1902–1906.* Mérida, 1906.

Zapata Casares, Manuel. *Vía-Crucis del henequén: Colección de escritos sobre el gran problema de Yucatán.* Mérida, 1961.

Articles

Aguilar Camín, Héctor. "The Relevant Tradition: Sonoran Leaders in the Revolution." In *Caudillo and Peasant in the Mexican Revolution,* edited by D. A. Brading, pp. 92–123. Cambridge (U.K.), 1980.

Alvarado, Salvador. "Mi actuación revolucionaria." *El Universal,* 28 December 1918.

———. "En légitima defensa." *El Demócrata,* 4 May 1922.

Álvarez Barret, Luis. "Orígenes y evolución de las escuelas rurales en Yucatán." *Revista de la Universidad de Yucatán* 13:78 (Nov.–Dec. 1971), 26–51.

Amendolla, Luis. "Política regional: Yucatán." *Mañana* 6 (Feb. 1944), 19–21.

Anderson, Bo, and Cockcroft, James D. "Control and Co-optation in Mexican

Politics." In *Latin American Radicalism,* edited by Irving Louis Horowitz, pp. 366–389. New York, 1969.

Ankerson, Dudley. "Saturnino Cedillo: A Traditional Caudillo in San Luis Potosí, 1890–1938." In *Caudillo and Peasant in the Mexican Revolution,* edited by D. A. Brading, pp. 140–168. Cambridge (U.K.), 1980.

Arrigunaga Peón, Joaquín de. "Felipe Carrillo Puerto y la revolución delahuertista: Declaraciones de los señores . . ." *Novedades de Yucatán,* 21 and 28 July 1968.

Aznar Mendoza, Enrique. "Historia de la industria henequenera desde 1919 hasta nuestros días." In *Enciclopedia Yucatanense,* vol. 3, pp. 727–87. Mexico, 1947.

Bailey, David C. "Revisionism and the Present Historiography of the Mexican Revolution." *Hispanic American Historical Review* 58:1 (Feb. 1978), 62–79.

Benet, Francisco. "Sociology Uncertain: The Ideology of the Rural–Urban Continuum." *Comparative Studies in Society and History* 6:1 (Oct. 1963), 1–23.

Benjamin, Thomas. "International Harvester and the Henequen Marketing System in Yucatán, 1898–1915: A New Perspective." *Inter-American Economic Affairs* 31:3 (Winter 1977), 3–19.

Berzunza Pinto, Ramón. "Las vísperas yucatecas de la Revolución." *Historia Mexicana* 6:1 (July–Sept. 1956), 75–88.

"El Constitucionalismo en Yucatán." *Historia Mexicana* 12:2 (Oct.–Dec. 1962), 274–295.

Betancourt Pérez, Antonio. "La verdad sobre el orígen de las escuelas rurales en Yucatán." *Revista de la Universidad de Yucatán* 13:76 (July–Aug. 1971), 34–56.

"Nuestro viejo abuelo." *Revista de la Universidad de Yucatán* 15:85 (Jan.–Feb. 1973), 64–69.

"¿Ángel, o demonio?: Carrillo Puerto y 'Peregrina.'" *Juzgue* 2:2 (May 1973), 19.

Burgos Brito, Santiago. "Las actividades culturales de Alvarado." *Revista de la Universidad de Yucatán* 7:38 (Mar.–Apr. 1965), 32–40.

Busto, Emiliano. "Memoria de Hacienda del año económico de 1877 a 1878." *Estadística de la República Mexicana.* Mexico, 1880.

Buve, Raymond Th. "Patronaje en las zonas rurales de México." *Boletín de Estudios Latinoamericanos y del Caribe* 16 (June 1974), 3–15.

"Peasant Movements, Caudillos and Land Reform during the Revolution (1910–1917) in Tlaxcala, Mexico." *Boletín de Estudios Latinoamericanos y del Caribe* 18 (June 1975), 112–52.

"State Governors and Peasant Mobilization in Tlaxcala." In *Caudillo and Peasant in the Mexican Revolution,* edited by D. A. Brading, pp. 222–244. Cambridge (U.K.), 1980.

Cabrera, Luis (alias Lic. Blas Urrea). "La conquista de Yucatán." *Diario de Yucatán,* 10 July 1936.

Cámara Patrón, Alberto, and Ayora Sarlat, Vicente. "Vida y obra de Felipe Carrillo Puerto." In *Memoria de los actos realizados en el quincuagésimo aniversario de la Universidad de Yucatán,* pp. 97–127. Mérida, 1973.

Cámara Zavala, Gonzalo. "Paralelo entre las escuelas racionalistas de Barcelona y Mérida." *Boletín de la Liga de Acción Social* 2:17 (May 1922), 66–69.

"Historia de la industria henequenera hasta 1919." In *Enciclopedia Yucatanense,* vol. 3, pp. 657–725. Mexico, 1947.

Canto López, Antonio. "Historia de la imprenta y del periodismo." *Enciclopedia Yucatanense,* vol. 5, pp. 5–107. Mexico, 1946.

Cardoso, Fernando Henrique. "The Consumption of Dependency Theory in the United States." *Latin American Research Review* 12:3 (Fall 1977), 7–24.

Carr, Barry. "Las peculiaridades del norte mexicano, 1880–1927: Ensayo de interpretación." *Historia Mexicana* 22:3 (Jan.–Mar. 1973), 320–346.

"Recent Regional Studies of the Mexican Revolution." *Latin American Research Review* 15:1 (Spring 1980), 3–14.

Carrillo Puerto, Felipe. "The New Yucatán." *Survey* 52 (May 1924), 138–142.

Casasús, Francisco A. "Ensayo biográfico del Licenciado Olegario Molina Solís." *Revista de la Universidad de Yucatán* 14:81 (May–June 1972), 68–95.

Castillo Torre, José. "La muerte del Mártir." *Boletín de la Universidad Nacional del Sureste* 4:1 (June 1924), 12–13.

Castro, Rosa. "Sobre la ruta de Carrillo Puerto, el Mesías de Motul." *Hoy,* 5, 12, 19, 26 Jan.; 2, 9, 16, 23 Feb.; 15, 29 Mar.; 12 Apr. 1952.

Cline, Howard. "The Henequen Episode in Yucatán." *Inter-American Economic Affairs* 2:2 (Autumn 1948), 30–51.

Coatsworth, John H. "Railroads, Landholding, and Agrarian Protest in the Early *Porfiriato.*" *Hispanic American Historical Review* 54:1 (Feb. 1974), 48–71.

Cockcroft, James. "El maestro de primaria en la Revolución Mexicana." *Historia Mexicana* 16:4 (Apr.–June 1967), 565–588.

Doehring, Donald O., and Butler, Joseph H. "Hydrogeologic Constraints on Yucatán's Development." *Science* 86:4164 (Nov. 1974), 591–595.

Ferrer de Mendiolea, Gabriel. "Historia de las comunicaciones." In *Enciclopedia Yucatanense,* vol. 3, pp. 507–626. Mexico, 1947.

"Leyes precursores de la Carta de 1917." *El Nacional,* 21 July 1957.

Flores D., Jorge. "La vida rural en Yucatán en 1914." *Historia Mexicana* 10:3 (Jan.–Mar. 1961), 471–483.

Fornaro, Carlo de. "Yucatán and the International Harvester Company." *Forum* 54 (Sept. 1915), 337–344.

Fowler Salamini, Heather. "Los orígenes de las organizaciones campesinas en Veracruz: Raíces políticas y sociales." *Historia Mexicana* 22:1 (July–Sept. 1972), 52–76.

"Revolutionary Caudillos in the 1920s: Francisco Múgica and Adalberto Tejeda." In *Caudillo and Peasant in the Mexican Revolution,* edited by D. A. Brading, pp. 169–192. Cambridge (U.K.), 1980.

Friedrich, Paul. "A Mexican Cacicazgo." *Ethnology* 4:2 (Apr. 1965), 190–209.

"The Legitimacy of a Cacique." In *Local-Level Politics,* edited by M. J. Swartz, pp. 243–269. Chicago, 1968.

Gamboa Berzunza, Fernando. "Visión pedagógica de Felipe Carrillo Puerto." *Revista de la Universidad de Yucatán* 3:13 (Jan.–Feb. 1961), 35–41.

Gates, Marilyn. "Peasants Speak: Alfredo Pech, A Modern Maya." *Journal of Peasant Studies* 3:4 (July 1976), 465–471.

Gates, William. "Yucatán – an Experiment in Syndicalism." *World's Work* 38 (May 1919), 58–68.

Goldkind, Victor. "Social Stratification in the Peasant Community: Chan Kom Revisited." *American Anthropologist* 67:4 (Aug. 1965), 863–884.

"Class Conflict and Cacique." *Southwestern Journal of Anthropology* 22:4 (Winter 1966), 325–345.

Gómez, Marte R. "Carrillo Puerto visto por Marte." *Hoy,* 1 March 1952.

González Navarro, Moisés. "La ideología de la Revolución Mexicana." *Historia Mexicana* 10:4 (Apr.–June 1961), 628–636.

Gruening, Ernest. "Felipe Carrillo Puerto." *The Nation* 117 (Jan. 1924), 61–62.

"The Assassination of Mexico's Ablest Statesman." *Current History* 19:5 (Feb. 1924), 736–740.

"A Maya Idyl: A Study of Felipe Carrillo Puerto, Late Governor of Yucatán." *The Century Magazine* 107 (Apr. 1924), 832–836.

Guadarrama, Rocío. "La CROM en la época del caudillismo en México." *Cuadernos Políticos* 20 (Apr.–June 1979), 52–63.

Hall, Linda B. "Álvaro Obregón and the Agrarian Movement, 1912–1920." In *Caudillo and Peasant in the Mexican Revolution,* edited by D. A. Brading, pp. 124–139. Cambridge (U.K.), 1980.

Hansen, Asael T. "The Ecology of a Latin American City." In *Race and Culture Contacts,* edited by E. B. Reuter, pp. 124–142. New York, 1934.

Hinojosa, Juan José. "Henequén: Fracaso, espina, remordimiento." *Proceso,* 9 May 1977.

Hu-Dehart, Evelyn. "Pacification of the Yaquis in the Late *Porfiriato*: Development and Implications." *Hispanic American Historical Review* 54:1 (Feb. 1974), 72–93.

Irigoyen, Renán. "Don Us Escalante, precursor de la industria henequenera." *Revista de Estudios Yucatecos* 1:1 (Feb. 1949), 17–32.

"Carrillo Puerto, Mártir de la cultura." *Revista de la Universidad de Yucatán* 1:1 (Jan.–Feb. 1959), 20–23.

"El impulso a la economía de Yucatán durante el gobierno de Alvarado." *Revista de la Universidad de Yucatán* 7:38 (Mar.–Apr. 1965), 14–25.

"El comercio del henequén a través del tiempo." *Revista de la Universidad de Yucatán* 7:41–42 (Sept.–Dec. 1965), 45–71.

"Orígen y trayectoria del henequén." *Revista de la Universidad de Yucatán* 15:86 (Mar.–Apr. 1973), 114–128.

Jacobs, Ian. "Rancheros of Guerrero: The Figueroa Brothers and the Revolution." In *Caudillo and Peasant in the Mexican Revolution,* edited by D. A. Brading, pp. 76–91. Cambridge (U.K.), 1980.

Joseph, Gilbert M. "British Loggers and Spanish Governors: The Logwood Trade and Its Settlements in the Yucatán Peninsula." *Caribbean Studies* 14:2 (July 1974), 7–37.

"Apuntes hacia una nueva historia regional: Yucatán y la Revolución Mexicana, 1915–1940." *Revista de la Universidad de Yucatán* 19:109 (Jan.–Feb. 1977), 12–35.

"Mexico's 'Popular Revolution': Mobilization and Myth in Yucatán, 1910–1940." *Latin American Perspectives* 6:3 (Summer 1979), 46–65.

"Caciquismo and the Revolution: Carrillo Puerto in Yucatán." In *Caudillo and Peasant in the Mexican Revolution*, edited by D. A. Brading, pp. 193–221. Cambridge (U.K.), 1980.

Katz, Friedrich. El sistema de plantación y la esclavitud." *Ciencias Políticas y Sociales* 8:27 (Jan.–Mar. 1962), 103–135.

"Labor Conditions on Haciendas in Porfirian Mexico: Some Trends and Tendencies." *Hispanic American Historical Review* 54:1 (Feb. 1974), 1–47.

"Villa: Reform Governor of Chihuahua." In *Essays on the Mexican Revolution: Revisionist Views of the Leaders*, edited by George Wolfskill and Douglas W. Richmond, pp. 25–45. Austin, Tex., 1979.

"Pancho Villa, Peasant Movements and Agrarian Reform in Northern Mexico." In *Caudillo and Peasant in the Mexican Revoluion*, edited by D. A. Brading, pp. 59–75. Cambridge (U.K.), 1980.

Knight, Alan. "Peasant and Caudillo in Revolutionary Mexico, 1910–1917." In *Caudillo and Peasant in the Mexican Revolution*, edited by D. A. Brading, pp. 17–58. Cambridge (U.K.), 1980.

Knox, A. J. Graham. "Henequén Haciendas, Maya Peones, and the Mexican Revolutionary Promises of 1910: Reform and Reaction in Yucatán, 1910–1940." *Caribbean Studies* 17:1–2 (Apr.–July 1977), 55–82.

Laclau, Ernesto. "Feudalism and Capitalism in Latin America." *New Left Review* 67 (May–June 1971), 19–38.

Lara y Lara, Humberto. "Proyección social de la obra en Yucatán del Gral. Salvador Alvarado." *Diario del Sureste*, 28 March 1965, Cultural Supplement.

Llanes, Marín Elmer. "Poemas de Elmer Llanes Marín." *Orbe* 44 (Dec. 1955), 95–102.

"La llanura aislada." *Orbe* 49 (Oct. 1957), 19–35.

Love, Joseph L. "An Approach to Regionalism." In *New Approaches to Latin American History*, edited by Richard Graham and Peter H. Smith, pp. 137–155. Austin, Tex., 1974.

Lundell, Cyrus L. "Preliminary Sketch of the Phytogeography of the Yucatán Peninsula." In *Contributions to American Archaeology*, edited by the Carnegie Institution, pp. 255–321. Washington, D.C., 1934.

Macías, Anna. "Felipe Carrillo Puerto and Women's Liberation in Mexico." In *Latin American Women: Historical Perspectives*, edited by Asunción Lavrin, pp. 286–301. Westport, Conn., 1978.

Mandle, Jay R. "The Plantation Economy: An Essay in Definition." *Science and Society* 36:1 (Spring 1972), 49–62.

Menéndez Díaz, Conrado. "Psicología de la explotación de nuestros indios." *Orbe* 1 (Apr.–June 1937), 33–38.

"La mística del trabajo campesino en Yucatán." *Orbe* 3 (Dec. 1946), 35–39.

Mendoza Medina, Ramón. "Influencia de Salvador Alvarado en la Constitución de 1917." *Diario del Sureste*, 28 March 1965, Cultural Supplement.

Meyer, Jean. "Les ouvriers dans la Révolution Mexicaine: Les bataillons rouges." *Annales,* 25:1 (Jan.–Feb. 1970), 30–55.

"Periodización e ideología." In *Contemporary Mexico,* edited by James Wilkie, Michael C. Meyer, and Edna Monzón de Wilkie, pp. 711–718. Berkeley, Calif., 1976.

Meyer, Lorenzo. "Cambio político y dependencia: México en el siglo XX." *Foro Internacional* 13:2 (Oct.–Dec. 1972), 101–138.

Meyer, Michael C. "Perspectives in Mexican Revolutionary Historiography." *New Mexico Historical Review* 44 (Apr. 1969), 167–180.

Miner, George. "Opiniones sobre la labor del Gral. Salvador Alvarado." *El Demócrata,* 6 November 1916.

Mintz, Sidney W. "The Rural Proletariat and the Problem of Rural Proletarian Class Consciousness." *Journal of Peasant Studies* 1:3 (Apr. 1973), 291–325.

Mintz, Sidney W., and Wolf, Eric. "Haciendas and Plantations in Middle America and the Antilles." *Social and Economic Studies* 6:3 (1957), 380–412.

Morales Medina, Hernán. "Don Gonzalo Cámara Zavala: Pionero de la educación rural." *Revista de la Universidad de Yucatán* 4:22–23 (July–Oct. 1962), 71–72.

Montalvo Ortega, Enrique. "Caudillismo y estado en la Revolución Mexicana: El gobierno de Alvarado en Yucatán." *Nova Americana* 2 (1979), 13–36.

Morrow, Dwight W. "Who Buys Foreign Bonds?" *Foreign Affairs* 5:2 (Jan. 1927), 219–232.

Orosa Díaz, Jaime. "Carrillo Puerto en la historia y en la literatura, *Orbe* 31 (Aug. 1951), 75–77.

"Síntesis biográfica del Gral. Salvador Alvarado." *Diario del Sureste,* 28 March 1965, Cultural Supplement.

Osalde Medina, Claudio. "El problema ejidal de Yucatán." *El Nacional,* 12 June 1936, 2d sect.

Paoli B., Francisco. "Carrillo Puerto y el PSS." *Revista de la Universidad de Yucatán* 16:91 (Jan.–Feb. 1974), 75–91.

Peniche Barrera, Roldán. "Tres nuevos murales." *Juzgue* 4:3 (Sept. 1975), 44–45.

Peniche Vallado, Leopoldo. "La obra del Gral. Salvador Alvarado en Yucatán." *Diario del Sureste,* 28 March 1965, Cultural Supplement.

Pinelo Río, Ricardo. "El batallón de 'La Plancha.'" *El Nacional,* 6 March 1932.

Platt, D. C. M. "Economic Imperialism and the Businessman: Britain and Latin America before 1914." In *Studies in the Theory of Imperialism,* edited by Bob Sutcliffe and Roger Owen, pp. 295–311. London, 1972.

Quintal Martín, Fidelio. "Análisis de la pobreza y la educación en una hacienda henequenera." *Revista de la Universidad de Yucatán* 6:33 (May–June 1964), 37–41.

"Apuntes para la historia de la educación secundaria en Yucatán." *Revista de la Universidad de Yucatán* 15:86 (Mar.–Apr. 1973), 97–106.

"Quince años trascendentales en la historia de Yucatán." *Revista de la Universidad de Yucatán* 16:93–94 (May–Aug. 1974), 99–131.

Quirk, Robert. "Liberales y radicales en la Revolución Mexicana." *Historia Mexicana* 2:4 (Apr.–June 1953), 503–528.

Ramírez Garrido, J. D. "La instrucción en Yucatán." *Acción Mundial,* 4 March 1916.

Raymond, Nathaniel C. "Land Reform and the Structure of Production in Yucatán." *Ethnology* 7:4 (Oct. 1968), 461–470.

Reed, Alma. "Felipe Carrillo Puerto." *Boletín de la Universidad Nacional del Sureste,* Época 2, 4:1 (June 1924), 20–21.

Regil, José M., and Peón, Alonso M. "Estadística de Yucatán." *Boletín de la Sociedad Mexicana de Geografía y Estadística* 3 (1852), 296–300.

Repetto Milán, Francisco. "La vida fecunda y generosa de Gonzalo Cámara Zavala." *Revista de la Universidad de Yucatán* 6:22–23 (July–Oct. 1962), 69–70.

(Rius). "Felipe Carrillo Puerto: El Salvador Allende Mexicano." *Los Agachados* 5:156 (June 1974).

Robinson, Ronald. "Non-European Foundations of European Imperialism: Sketch for a Theory of Collaboration." In *Studies in the Theory of Imperialism,* edited by Bob Sutcliffe and Roger Owen, pp. 117–141. London, 1972.

Rolland, Modesto C. "A Trial of Socialism in Mexico: What the Mexicans Are Fighting For." *Forum* 56 (July 1916), 79–90.

Rosado Vega, Luis. "El proletariado profesional." *Boletín de la Universidad Nacional del Sureste* 2:2 (Oct. 1922), 61–70.

Rosales, Salatiel. "En tierras de Yucatán." *El Demócrata,* 8 January 1924.

Sanders, Thomas G. "Henequen: The Structure of Agrarian Frustration." *American University Field Staff Reports,* North American Series, 5:3 (July 1977).

Siverts, Henning. "The 'Cacique' of K'ankujk.'" *Estudios de Cultura Maya* 5 (1965), 339–360.

Sotelo Regil, Luis F. "La Revolución en Yucatán: Salvador Alvarado," *Revista de la Universidad de Yucatán* 2:12 (June–July 1960), 47–58.

Stavenhagen, Rodolfo. "Collective Agriculture and Capitalism in Mexico: A Way Out or a Dead End?" *Latin American Perspectives* 2:2 (Summer 1975), 146–163.

Strickon, Arnold. "Hacienda and Plantation in Yucatán." *América Indígena* 25:1 (Jan. 1965), 42–57.

Suárez Molina, Víctor M. "La industria cordelera en Yucatán en el siglo XIX." *Diario de Yucatán,* 20 Feb. 1972.

"Veinte años de economía yucateca." *Diario de Yucatán,* 3 Dec. 1975.

Tobler, Hans Werner. "Las paradojas del ejército revolucionario: Su papel social en la reforma agraria mexicana, 1920–1935." *Historia Mexicana* 21:1 (July–Sept. 1971), 38–79.

Torre Díaz, Álvaro. "La labor del Constitucionalismo en Yucatán." *El Paso del Norte,* 23 May 1917.

Urzáiz R., Eduardo. "La entrada de Alvarado." *Orbe* 41 (April 1955), 85–86.

"Historia de la educación pública y privada desde 1911." In *Enciclopedia Yucatanense,* vol. 4, pp. 197–259. Mexico, 1944.

Urzáiz R., Eduardo. "El simbolismo de la Resurrección." *Boletín de la Universi-*

dad Nacional del Sureste, Época 2, 4:1 (June 1924), 6–8.

Valadés, Diego. "Ideas políticas y sociales de Salvador Alvarado." *Estudios de Historia Moderna y Contemporánea de México* 5 (1976), 109–118.

Vaughan, Mary Kay. "Education and Class in the Mexican Revolution." *Latin American Perspectives* 2:2 (Summer 1975), 17–33.

Villaseñor, Víctor Manuel. "Salvador Alvarado." *Revista de la Universidad de Yucatán* 6:34 (July–Aug. 1964), 117–126.

Wasserman, Mark. "Oligarquía y intereses extrajeros en Chihuahua durante el Porfiriato." *Historia Mexicana* 22:3 (Jan.–Mar. 1973), 279–319.

Waterbury, Ronald. "Non-revolutionary Peasants: Oaxaca Compared to More-los in the Mexican Revolution." *Comparative Studies in Society and History* 17:4 (Oct. 1975), 410–442.

Wells, Allen. "Economic Growth and Regional Disparity in Porfirian Yucatán: The Case of the Southeastern Railway Company." *South Eastern Latin Americanist* 22:2 (Sept. 1978), 1–16.

Winks, Robin W. "On Decolonization and Informal Empire." *American Historical Review* 81:3 (June 1976), 540–556.

Womack, John. "The Mexican Economy During the Revolution, 1910–1920: Historiography and Analysis." *Marxist Perspectives* 4 (Winter 1978), 80–123.

Theses, dissertations, and unpublished works

Barber, Gerald. "Horizon of Thorns: Yucatán at the Turn of the Century." Master's thesis, University of the Americas, Cholula, Mexico, 1974.

Chacón, Ramón D. "Yucatán and the Mexican Revolution: The Pre-constitutional Years, 1910–1918." Ph.D. dissertation, Stanford University, Stanford, Calif., 1981.

Cline, Howard. "Regionalism and Society in Yucatán, 1925–1847: A Study of 'Progressivism' and the Origins of the Caste War." Ph.D. dissertation, *Microfilm Collection of Manuscripts in Middle American Cultural Anthropology,* No. 32. University of Chicago Library, Chicago, 1950.

Espejo-Ponce de Hunt, Marta. "Colonial Yucatán: Town and Region in the Seventeenth Century." Ph.D. dissertation, University of California at Los Angeles, 1974.

Fitchen, Edward D. "Official Policy and the Exigencies of Practice: Indio and Ladino in Yucatán." Paper presented at the seventh meeting of the Latin American Studies Association, Houston, November 1977.

Fowler Salamini, Heather. "The Agrarian Revolution in the State of Veracruz, 1920–1940: The Role of Peasant Organizations." Ph.D. dissertation, American University, Washington, D.C., 1970.

Franz, David A. "Bullets and Bolshevists: A History of the Mexican Revolution and Reform in Yucatán, 1910–1924." Ph.D. dissertation, University of New Mexico, Albuquerque, 1973.

García Cantón, Alberto. "Memorias de un ex-hacendado." International Harvester Company Archives, *Abstract Summary of the Sisal Investigation Index*, parts I–IX. Xeroxed copy.

Goodman, Margaret A. "The Effectiveness of the Mexican Revolution as an Agent of Change in the State of Yucatán, Mexico." Ph.D. dissertation, Columbia University, New York, 1970.

Hansis, Randall G. "Álvaro Obregón, the Mexican Revolution and the Politics of Consolidation, 1920–1924." Ph.D. dissertation, University of New Mexico, Albuquerque, 1971.

Hartman, Keith. "The Henequen Empire in Yucatán, 1870–1910." Master's thesis, University of Iowa, Iowa City, 1966.

Kirk, Rodney C. "San Antonio, Yucatán: From Henequen Hacienda to Plantation Ejido." Ph.D. dissertation, Michigan State University, East Lansing, Mich. 1975.

Knox, A. J. G. "Regionalism as a Problem in Mexican National History: Yucatán, a Case Study, 1821–1940." Manuscript, 1973.

Lee, Rosemary L. "Who Owns Boardwalk?: The Structure of Control in the Tourist Industry of Yucatán." Paper presented at the seventy-third meeting of the American Anthropological Association, Mexico City, November 1974.

Patch, Robert W. "A Colonial Regime: Maya and Spaniard in Yucatán." Ph.D. dissertation, Princeton University, Princeton, N.J., 1979.

"El fin del régimen colonial en Yucatán y los orígenes de la guerra de castas: El problema de la tierra, 1812–1846." Manuscript, 1980.

Raymond, Nathaniel C. "The Impact of Land Reform in the Monocrop Region of Yucatán, Mexico." Ph.D. dissertation, Brandeis University, Waltham, Mass., 1971.

Roazen, Diane. "The Olegario Molina Family of Yucatán." Manuscript, 1977.

"American Enterprise, American Government, and the Sisal Industry of Yucatán, Mexico, 1876–1924." Paper presented at the ninety-third meeting of the American Historical Association, San Francisco, December 1978.

Rodríguez Losa, Salvador. "El henequén: Hoy, ayer y mañana." Manuscript, 1975.

Shuman, Malcom K. "The Town Where Luck Fell: The Economics of Life in a Henequen Zone Pueblo." Ph.D. dissertation, Tulane University, New Orleans, 1974.

Wells, Allen. "Henequén and Yucatán: An Analysis in Regional Economic Development, 1876–1915." Ph.D. dissertation, State University of New York at Stony Brook, 1979.

Whiting, Van R. "The Collective Ejido and the State in Mexico." Paper presented at the seventh meeting of the Latin American Studies Association, Houston, November 1977.

Wyman, Donald L. "Trust and Trade: Dwight Morrow and Mexico." Manuscript, 1972.

Index

acasillados, see peones acasillados
agentes de propaganda: Alvarado's
  use of, 98, 108, 113, 114,
  117, 197; Carrillo Puerto as,
  98, 185–7, 193, 197; Carrillo
  Puerto's use of, 206
agrarian reform, 297–8; see also
  ejidos; henequen plantations;
  pequeña propiedad
Agriculture, Department of (U.S.),
  153, 257
Aguascalientes Convention, 4, 5;
  see also Conventionists
Aguilar, Cándido, 100
Aguirre Colorado, Rafael, 97
Alayola Barrera, César, 98
Allende, Salvador, 303
Alvarado, Salvador, 116, 150,
  180, 231, 257, 268; and
  agrarian reform, 125–31,
  133, 234, 247, 297, 337 n31;
  birth and early career of, 99;
  as bourgeois revolutionary,
  101–2, 107, 111, 127–8,
  129–30, 133, 149, 220, 232–
  3, 234, 247; caciques and,
  118–19, 208; Carranza and,
  8, 114–15, 133, 168, 338
  n46; Carrillo Puerto and, 98,
  166, 187, 192–3, 206; Casta
  Divina and, 37, 53, 56–7,
  96–7, 132, 134–43; Catholic
  Church and, 106; Comisión
  Reguladora and, 58, 133–4,
  137–45, 160; death of, 363–
  4 n11; de la Huerta and, 266,
  269, 363–4 n11; directs revolution from above, 111–12,
  302; educational program of,
  107–8, 214, 216; enters
  Mérida, 8–10, 93, 95–6; es-

tablishes Compañía de Fomento
  del Sureste, 146–8; feminism
  and, 105; formation and
  breakdown of revolutionary
  coalition of, 98–9, 112–14,
  121, 163–5; forms "Study
  Committee for the Reor-
  ganization of the State,"
  165–6; hacendados and, 98–9,
  132, 163–5, 168, 340–1
  n92; International Harvester
  and, 56–7, 66, 134–6, 137–
  43, 154–5, 158, 159–60,
  180; La Industrial and, 98,
  146; makes Yucatán a laboratory of revolution, 102–5;
  Mexican and Yucatecan advisors of, 97–8; moral reforms
  of, 105–6; Obregón and,
  100, 206; problem of revolutionary mobilization and, 70,
  108–11, 187, 193, 229–30,
  302; and responsibility for
  Yucatán's economic woes,
  179–82; as revolutionary
  ideologue, 100–2; urban
  workers and, 109–11,
  224
American Sugar Refining Company, 45
anarcho-syndicalism, 192, 200,
  224, 225, 234
Ancona Cirerol, Mario, 268
Anderson, Chandler P., 277,
  279
Arredondo, Eliseo, 155–6
Asociación de Hacendados Henequeneros, 165, 173, 248
Ávila, Eleuterio: appointment as
  governor, 6; Carrillo Puerto
  and, 98, 191, 192; corruption